T0101282

Voices

— of the —

Faithful

Voices
— of the —
Faithful

WITH

BETH MOORE

AND FRIENDS WHO PUT THEIR LIVES ON THE LINE FOR GOD

KIM P. DAVIS

COMPILING EDITOR

THOMAS NELSON
Since 1798

NASHVILLE   DALLAS   MEXICO CITY   RIO DE JANEIRO

© 2005 International Mission Board of the Southern Baptist Convention and Elizabeth Moore

All rights reserved. No portion of this book may be reproduced, stored in a retrieval system, or transmitted in any form or by any means—electronic, mechanical, photocopy, recording, scanning, or any other—except for brief quotations in printed reviews, without the prior written permission of the publisher.

Published in Nashville, Tennessee, by Thomas Nelson. Thomas Nelson is a registered trademark of Thomas Nelson, Inc.

Thomas Nelson, Inc., titles may be purchased in bulk for educational, business, fund-raising, or sales promotional use. For information, please e-mail SpecialMarkets@ThomasNelson.com.

Published in association with Yates and Yates, LLP, www.yates2.com

Scripture quotations are taken from the following sources:

The New American Standard Bible® (NASB®). © 1960, 1962, 1963, 1968, 1971, 1972, 1973, 1975, 1977, 1995 by The Lockman Foundation. Used by permission. The New King James Version® (NKJV®). © 1982 by Thomas Nelson, Inc. Used by permission. All rights reserved. The New Century Version® (NCV®). © 1987, 1988, 1991 by Thomas Nelson, Inc. Used by permission. All rights reserved. The Holy Bible, New International Version® (NIV®). © 1973, 1978, 1984 by International Bible Society. Used by permission of Zondervan. All rights reserved. The King James Version (KJV). Public domain. The Living Bible (TLB or LB). © 1971 by Tyndale House Publishers, Inc. Used by permission. All rights reserved. The New Revised Standard Version® (NRSV®). © 1989, 1995 by the Division of Christian Education of the National Council of the Churches of Christ in the United States of America. Used by permission. All rights reserved. The Message (MSG) by Eugene H. Peterson. © 1993, 1994, 1995, 1996, 2000, 2001, 2002. Used by permission of NavPress Publishing Group. All rights reserved. The Good News Bible® (GNB®). © 1976 by American Bible Society. Used by permission. The Holy Bible, New Living Translation® (NLT®). © 1996. Used by permission of Tyndale House Publishers, Inc., Wheaton, Illinois 60189. All rights reserved. The Amplified Bible (AMP), New Testament. © 1954, 1958, 1962, 1964, 1965, 1987 by The Lockman Foundation. Used by permission. All rights reserved. The Amplified Bible (AMP), Old Testament. © 1965, 1987 by the Zondervan Corporation. Used by permission. All rights reserved. The Holman Christian Standard Bible® (HCSB). © 1999, 2000, 2002, 2003 by Holman Bible Publishers. Used by permission. The Holy Bible: Revised Standard Version (RSV). © 1946, 1952, 1973 by National Council of Churches of Christ. All rights reserved. The Holy Bible, English Standard Version (ESV). © 2001 by Crossway Bibles, a division of Good News Publishers. Used by permission. All rights reserved.

ISBN 978-0-8499-4624-0 (trade paper)

LIBRARY OF CONGRESS CATALOGING-IN-PUBLICATION DATA
Moore, Beth, 1957–
    Voices of the faithful / by Beth Moore.
        p. cm.
    Includes index.
    ISBN 978-1-59145-364-2 (hardcover)
    1. Devotional calendars—Baptists. I. Title.
BV4810.M619 2005
242'.2—dc22
                                                                        2005008310
_____

Printed in the United States of America
HB 08.14.2017

To every servant of Jesus Christ
on the international field—
I am so honored to be your servant.

To Mary King—for lighting the fire.
You didn't know we were listening,
did you?

Contents

ACKNOWLEDGMENTS

If ever you've held a book that was a group effort, this is it. A large group effort, at that. Not only am I grateful for the nearly 300 missionaries who wrote the daily devotionals, I am deeply thankful for the more than 5,000 missionaries who serve Christ through the International Mission Board (IMB) of the Southern Baptist Convention, based in Richmond, Virginia. You continually inspire me, as you live more life in one year than I could write about in 100 years. Hang in there, and don't get discouraged. Nothing matters more than what you're doing. I just as highly esteem the equally devoted missionaries on the international field from countless other agencies and Christ-centered denominations. My prayer is that this book will draw just as much attention to your efforts, igniting the hearts of many to partner with you through prayer, giving and going.

The fact that I have the privilege of knowing so many IMB missionaries provokes my deepest gratitude to IMB president Jerry Rankin and his incredible wife, Bobbye, who advised the entire project and wrote many of the prayers. The two of you have allowed me—and even invited me—to feel like a constant part of everything the IMB is doing. Will you ever know what this partnership has meant to me? I am so honored to call the two of you friends.

This book would absolutely not exist without the tireless efforts of a pint-sized fireball and missionary named Kim Davis. Keith and I will never forget the peculiar shopping spree in South Africa with Kim and another missionary that led to this book. Between Keith's terrible backseat driving (forgive him, Angie; you really weren't *that* bad!), the mind-boggling stories and some hard belly laughs, God once again showed that His will still triumphs over our complete silliness. God birthed this vision out of a several-minute conversation. Kim requested, compiled and edited every single devotional and spearheaded all the work a book like this demands. At best, I'm big on ideas and small on how to accomplish them. Kim, you are the reason this book exists. And if you take that line out of these acknowledgments, I'll have to beat you up. I'm pretty sure I could take you.

Much gratitude also goes to Elaine Meador for helping in the selection process, Sue Sprenkle for editing assistance, 11 faithful prayer warriors who took the project continually before God's throne and Dan Allen for overseeing all the business details. Larry Cox, Van Payne, Bill Bangham, Vickie Bleick, IMB technical support and others at the IMB, we thank you as well for your gracious willingness to help.

I'd also like to thank the missionaries in various world regions who have allowed Keith and me to serve them. You stole our hearts and vastly increased our passion to support your efforts. We are nuts about you. As long as we live, we'll never forget you. If we never get to worship with you in some of your regions again, we'll see you around the throne ... surrounded by all your people groups. What a day of rejoicing that will be!

I owe a huge debt of gratitude to Mary King, who still serves faithfully at First Baptist Church in Arkadelphia, Arkansas, where I was raised. The flame you lit in my heart for missions every Wednesday night in GAs and Acteens has never gone out. I also have had the joy of serving in a church in Houston for 20 years with the largest Texas-sized heart for missions I've ever witnessed. Harvey and William, you have been used of God to make missions one of the most dominant efforts we have at HFBC. I'm honored to call you brothers.

To Sealy Yates and Integrity Publishers, thank you, thank you, thank you for your investment in the nations, that all people may know Him.

Lastly and very importantly, I'd like to thank our readers. You supported the intentional spread of the gospel of Jesus Christ the moment you purchased this book. Every cent of the authors' profit will go straight to the Lottie Moon Christmas Offering® for International Missions for the effort abroad. You have my word that it will be well spent. My deep prayer is that your support will not end with the purchase, but will greatly expand in numerous ways as you spend the next year with individual missionaries through these pages. They are your brothers and sisters in Christ. Your partners in this generation. You're going to like them so much.

—*Beth Moore*

Lottie Moon Christmas Offering® is a registered trademark of Woman's Missionary Union.

FOREWORD

I am grateful for the encouragement and support from Beth Moore and her husband, Keith, for missionaries around the world, especially those serving with the International Mission Board of the Southern Baptist Convention. Whether through stateside ministries or leading conferences overseas, Beth has been used to strengthen these God-called servants in their walk with the Lord. These relationships have given her an awareness of the awesome way God is working in the lives of missionaries.

Their testimonies are as diverse as their backgrounds and personalities as well as the places they serve. Yet these international missionaries all have one thing in common: a deep, abiding love for our Lord Jesus Christ that compels them to share the good news with a lost world, no matter the sacrifice.

We pray that you will be blessed and encouraged by these missionaries' testimonies of God's grace in personal trials and cross-cultural challenges. May your faith be strengthened as you see through these devotions how God is moving in providence and power to impact a lost world through the faithfulness of these missionaries and the power of the gospel.

—*Jerry Rankin, President*
International Mission Board, SBC

Introduction

I thought the Wassons were the most exotic, exciting people in the whole wide world. They'd laugh to hear me say such a thing, and, to be honest, I did think from time to time that it was a shame they looked so normal. I recall their visits back to my hometown as clearly as any childhood memory I have. Our town was the place they called home, but they rarely lived there. After all, that's what made them exotic. Except for brief seasons on furlough in the United States, the Wassons lived in Nigeria. Nigeria! Can you even imagine?

Oh, but I did imagine. The Wassons gave me permission to imagine. They had children exactly my age growing up in a culture so far removed from mine that they may as well have lived on Mars. They visited our Sunday School classes and missions organizations on every return and mesmerized us with true stories. Sometimes they even cooked and served us African foods. "Native foods," they called them. Meals that real, live Africans ate! Despite countless taste-testings, I never acquired an adventurous palate. How anyone could survive without a bag of Fritos and bean dip was beyond me. I didn't think much of their cuisine, but I was spellbound by their stories.

My mother and Mrs. Wasson were friends. When I was a little girl, she gave my mother a wooden bird carved by a Nigerian, and it sat prominently on a shelf of every home my parents occupied. My mother was a simple woman with simple tastes. I honestly can't recall her treasuring any tangible gift more.

Thanks to the Wassons, I never recall hearing the word "missionary" for the first time. Missionaries were a part of my world before I'd toddled a step beyond my parents' home and my parents' church. Before I understood the first inkling about teachers, doctors or dentists, I knew there were missionaries. In my mind, they were the most adventurous people in the entire world. I didn't understand the deeper things about them, but this my young mind could reason: they were willing to leave behind a life of banana-seat bikes and Superman lunchboxes.

And why? One word: Jesus. Before I clearly knew who He was, I knew there were people willing to go anywhere and do anything to tell people about Him. Jesus must be something, I mused. And that He was.

My church did missions well. I'm not just biased. I don't claim my church did everything well. The thrust of evangelism so overshot discipleship that I grew up without adequately understanding how to apply Scripture. But missions indoctrination was a different story. Every Wednesday night, my church held classes for anyone from preschool to adulthood to study missions and to pray for missionaries. I never recall missing a single meeting, and not necessarily because I wanted to go. Baptists were expected to go. And, for crying out loud, if I was anything, I was a Baptist. I felt pretty good about it because I thought John the Baptist was one, and Jesus liked him. My world grew in adulthood, and God shaped a huge love for interdenominationalism in my heart. Still, the familiar surroundings of a world I've known best—quirks and all—offer this wanderer a rich heritage. While I've added to it through the years, I've never traded it off. Mrs. King was one good reason.

She was my missions organization teacher for at least 100 years. Or that's what it seemed. I think we were so poorly behaved that she thought someone else wouldn't love us enough to keep from killing us ... so she just kept moving up with us at promotion time. Talk about a woman who loved missions!

She made it the most exciting experience we ever had at church. I probably still have Elmer's Glue embedded under my fingernails from endless arts and crafts. I've cut out every continent on earth in construction paper multiple times. Mrs. King took about 10 of us all the way from blunt-end scissors to the sharp kind. No telling how many times she was tempted to put one to her wrist over us. We had our redeeming moments, however, like when we actually thought about what we were praying. We cut out the names and nations of missionaries and glued them to Popsicle sticks so we could take them home with us and remember to pray. Sometimes I remembered, and sometimes I didn't. But if I didn't, I at least felt guilty about it. There's something to be said for good, old-fashioned guilt. Somehow I really was convinced my prayers made a difference. Still am.

Not only did we pray for missionaries on their birthdays, but we also prepared Christmas gifts for missionary children living in other nations. We also got special offering envelopes with red globes on them during the holiday season that allowed us to give straight to world missions. Are you getting the picture? Here's the real picture I need you to get: had I never known the Wassons, missionaries around the world would have been to me what I fear they are to so many other Christians—faceless, far-removed folks who have nothing to do with me.

Oh, but they do. And that's the reason for this book. These daily devotions are written by real, live flesh-and-blood people just like you and me. They love the comforts of home and extended family just like we do. They love their children and desire their safety and health just like we do. They love American soil and American food just like we do. They have fears just like we do. They feel inadequate and ineffective most of the time just like we do. They feel fairly unspiritual sometimes just like we do. They even want to quit sometimes ... just like we do.

My husband, Keith, watched me love missions for two decades. For a number of years, I've had the privilege of partnering with the International Mission Board by going into various regions and retreating with missionaries in worship and Bible study. Keith was sweet about it, but frankly, international missions just didn't ring his bell. He'd shake his head, tell me I was crazy, kiss me goodbye and stick me on a plane to who knows where. Then I was invited to Johannesburg to lead the Southern Africa regional women's missionary retreat. Keith suddenly felt the call. Not to missions, mind you, but to *safari*. The trip was a success. While he wouldn't mind me telling you that four out of five of his trophies made the record books, that wasn't the success. God stole his heart for missions. He's been hooked ever since.

Keith couldn't shut up about how "normal" the missionaries were. He'd repeatedly say things like, "They are as different from one another as they can be. All ages, shapes and sizes. Singles, married. Widowed. Old.

Young. Parents of preschoolers. Grandparents. No, they don't all sing. Nor do they all preach or teach. Some of them farm. Others of them dig wells or do plumbing. They don't have a single talent or skill entirely in common. All they have in common is a willingness to go."

For love of Jesus, they chose obedience over convenience, answering a call from God as old as the Book of Genesis: "*Leave your country, your people and your father's household and go to the land I will show you ... [that] all peoples on earth will be blessed through you*" (12:1, 3, NIV). This side of the cross, that blessing has a name: Jesus.

My earnest prayer is that once you feel like you know a handful of missionaries personally, your motivation to remember them, pray for them and support them in any of many ways will explode into a full-fledged partnership. You see, believers in Christ are supposed to be completely connected, not in spite of our varied locations and vocations, but because of them. We are a family, but fragmented; we're a dysfunctional one. The divine idea for full-throttle function was that God's people would operate as one entity—or one *body*—in each generation. We're meant to be like multicolored Christmas lights attached to one electrical cord called the Holy Spirit and strung strategically all over the earth. Yep, millions of lights on one cord, with the guts to shine more brightly because we know the others are there.

Isaiah 43:10 uses some very interesting words that lend a little Old Testament support to the New Testament concept of one functional entity per generation: "'*You are my witnesses,' declares the* LORD, '*and my servant whom I have chosen, so that you may know and believe me*'" (NIV).

Check out every major translation of the Bible and you will find that "witnesses" is always plural and "servant" is always singular. In Isaiah 44:1, we learn that Israel, God's chosen nation, was this "servant." You see, the entire people were as one servant in God's eyes. And so are we. We are each witnesses (plural) in a host of ways, but God's entire people on earth at any given time constitute His servant (singular).

My point? *You* are also called to the world in partnership with missionaries. Likewise, they are called to local missions in partnership with you. This is our *"partnership in the gospel"* (Phil. 1:5, NIV). It all begins with awareness that each of us is there, appreciating and praying for the other.

The first thing I ever learned about God was that He "so loved the world, that He gave His only begotten Son" (John 3:16, NASB). Did you hear that? God loves the world. Ah, maybe that means it's not so God-forsaken after all. And the more He overtakes our hearts, the more we will love the world.

You may be like Keith. You may have to admit that you're simply not interested in world missions and that the thought of spreading the good news of Jesus Christ to the nations is too remote for your daily thinking. But *what if? What if* you got to know a few of them—their stories, their challenges, their adventures, their fears—like Keith? *What if* they took on real identities, and the wide gulf between your worlds began to shrink? *What if,* having never had an iota of interest before, you fell head over heels in love with them ... like Keith?

Make no mistake: this love is not without consequence. Loving the world has radical effects. It caused God to give up His one and only Son. It caused the Wassons to leave the relative ease of our small Arkansas town and move to Nigeria, for heaven's sake. What radical effect will it have upon you and me? Would you be willing to find out? Would you be willing to let God shake awake that atrophied adventurer wrapped in the cocoon of your crisp, starched shirt? Admit it. Aren't you just a tad bored by your neatly compartmentalized, comfort-fit Christianity? I'll warn you. This could be hazardous. You might start with names and nations on Popsicle sticks and end up catching a flight to the other side of the world to meet them face to face. To tell them you're wild about them. To lighten their load.

What follows is a 366-day call to missions. Not for somebody else. For *you*. While I was humbled to write the introductions to each month's devotions, each of the daily entries has been written by a different missionary serving on the international field. By the time you finish the book, you will have traveled the entire world with them. I dare you not to fall in love. Whether we're called to pray, to give, to go on short-term mission trips or two-year mission stints, or to surrender entirely to career missions, we're all called to the nations. *For God so loved the world.*

Your tenure on this earth will be incomplete without engaging with God across the globe. Find out what on the earth God is doing in your generation ... and join Him.

—*Beth Moore*

God's Character

I love new starts. I used to think I was so fond of them because detours to the pit made them a life necessity. I believed new beginnings were primarily for those drawn to cycles of self-destruction like me. Those who had been humiliated by sin *again*. After all, why would people living in any semblance of victory need a new start?

To the glory of God alone and His relentless grace, I haven't cycled back to that pit in years. But you could have knocked me over with a feather when I came to the startling realization that not all hardship is caused by sin. Sometimes difficulty comes to us smack-dab in the center of God's will. Anyone who lives life plugged into the human race, still bothering to give a rip, nearly loses heart for need of a new start. I've never gotten over the necessity of a fresh beginning. I'm guessing you haven't, either.

God knew we wouldn't. In fact, He created us that way. He fashioned the soul of man in its every intricacy and complexity before He ever breathed it into the ashen new body of Adam. We don't have a single soul-need God didn't deliberately initiate for His own purposes. Our souls crave new beginnings. Fresh starts. Calculate with me just how willing our compassionate God was to accommodate.

God Himself came up with the concept of an annual New Year's Day when He ordered creation and gave the sun and moon their instructions (Gen. 1:14). Though some cultures operate on a lunar schedule and others on a solar schedule, we share the original concept of a calendar year that begins with a specified day. Think how much you and I view segments of time in years. Just the other day, a friend and I discussed what kind of year we'd had. As you open this book and prepare for your January 1 devotional, I wonder what kind of year you've had. Are you glad to see it go? Do you bid it good riddance? Or was it a year of dreams come true and intangible prosperity? Do you conclude it defeated? Or simply exhausted? One way or the other, aren't you glad you have a new start? Brilliant, isn't He?

God didn't think an annual new start was nearly enough. He who created the human psyche also compartmentalized those hundreds of days into 12 months. Every month we get another first. But 12 new starts were not enough, either. The very first verses of Scripture unfold a seven-day period of time we call a week. Think how we look forward to a "week*end*" and a subsequent new beginning on Sunday. Fifty-two new beginnings a year sounds like plenty, doesn't it? Ah, but not to God. He who configured our needy souls ordained the sun to rise every single morning and set every single evening. A curtain of darkness falls systematically on the scene of every single day, calling it history.

Ever had such a bad day that it seemed beyond redeeming? I had a really rough day last week. The problem wasn't just one thing. It was *every*thing. *Every* phone call. *Every* e-mail. *Every* demand. Yes, even the elevator got huffy with me. I dragged my usually buoyant mood behind me to the parking garage like a deflated balloon on a tattered string. And then I accidentally shut the car door on it. My husband, Keith, asked me early that evening if the day had gotten any better. I laughed and responded, "Nope. I think this one's just going to have to end, and let me start a new one tomorrow morning."

Sure enough, night fell and so did I ... right in the middle of my Sealy Posturepedic. I pulled the covers over my head and slept off the exhaustion of the day. The next morning, the sun rose just as God promised it would, and I felt renewed and ready to go at life once again. I don't think I could have waited seven days for another new start. I needed one that would come in only hours. I bet you know what I mean.

The Bible says that God gives us new mercies every morning (Lam. 3:23). The first of those mercies is the new morning itself. Here we are, you and I, making a new start together. A new year. Twelve new months. Fifty-two new weeks. And 365 glorious new days. What might make this one a little different from the others? I'm hoping a deliberately Christ-centered worldview. This new start is designed to take us all over the globe in prayer and partnership, freeing us from the misery of self-absorption. A world exists far beyond our front yard. Ours are not the only problems or the only praises. Let's see what happens when we share them.

Once again ... and not a moment too soon, the old has passed away. Behold, new things have come.

—*Beth Moore*

Devotional time = spirit repair

"I ask him to strengthen you by his Spirit—not a brute strength but a glorious inner strength—that Christ will live in you as you open the door and invite him in." Ephesians 3:16-17a (MSG)

Most workers for our organization must learn a foreign language. For me, it's Mandarin Chinese. While studying, I was intrigued by the phrase *ling xiu* (leeng SHE-oo), which refers to a Christian's daily devotional time.

Although this was new vocabulary, I already had learned both of the characters in different contexts. *Ling* means "spirit" or "soul." *Xiu* means "to repair." I had learned *xiu* with the washing-machine repairman who was coming weekly to keep our ancient model running!

In my notes, I wrote "devotional = spirit repair." What a fitting way to describe our devotional time: repairing the soul by reading God's Word and communing with Him. Like that dilapidated washing machine, my spirit needs the ultimate Repairman. Although I complained about the washer, it was stronger than my own inner man. It needed weekly repair, while I need it daily!

At one point, the repairman explained that the washer was used too often. I laughed inwardly at his solution—if I could just stop dirty laundry from accumulating, all would be well! What a parallel to how the stresses of life wear away our spiritual vitality just like the never-ending laundry wears out the washer's parts.

We can't stop the stresses of life any more than my family can stop producing dirty clothes. So I keep calling the Repairman to patch up my soul. Our daily "spirit repair" time is what keeps me sharing the gospel even with slow results and using my poor Mandarin when I look foolish. It provides compassion for my city so I can fulfill God's call in my life.

—A WORKER IN CHINA

Heavenly Father, I PRAY THAT YOU WILL USE THIS DEVOTIONAL TIME TO REPAIR MY SOUL, PURIFY ME AND DRAW ME CLOSER TO YOU. *Amen.*

King of the jungle

"But I, when I am lifted up from the earth, will draw all men to myself."
John 12:32 (NIV)

Our family went to Lake Nakuru (nah-KOO-roo) National Park, where wildlife was bountiful. We marveled over the massive rhinos and Cape buffaloes. The impressive waterbuck, graceful giraffe and the tiny steenbok antelope all gave evidence to our Father's creativity. Awestruck, we watched the sea of pink flamingoes, thousands upon thousands in flocks flowing together, moving like currents. What gifts of beauty the Father provides to delight His children!

As we drove, we scrutinized the savanna for a rare creature. The barking call of a baboon was heard as we spotted a group of animals, alert and intent upon whatever the baboon was announcing. They weren't the least bit distracted by us. Their attention was fixed on something more important. With curiosity, we inched toward the hailing sentinel who directed all creatures in one direction. What could command such esteem?

Suddenly, in a bushy tree nearby, I noticed a huge, male lion in his secret hideaway. *That* explained it all! The focus was on the "king of the jungle"!

The humans in a white truck didn't distract the animals. Their focus was on the king, and *nothing* would change that. Their focus even drew us to him.

The Lion of Judah commands and deserves the same kind of focus from us. We must stay so intently focused on the King of kings that when distractions come, we are not moved! For when our eyes are fixed on Him, we exalt Him, and others will be drawn to Him ... just as the animals of Nakuru drew us to the king of the jungle.

—JUDI, CENTRAL, EASTERN AND SOUTHERN AFRICA

King of kings and Lord of lords, I FOCUS MY EYES UPON YOU TODAY. KEEP DISTRACTIONS FAR FROM ME. MAY I FOLLOW YOU WHOLEHEARTEDLY. *Amen.*

An amazing discovery

"Many, O LORD *my God, are the wonders you have done. The things you planned for us no one can recount to you; were I to speak and tell of them, they would be too many to declare." Psalm 40:5 (NIV)*

Rain is depended upon in the jungle. Without it, wells will dry up, crops will die and the temperature will continue to rise.

I have become good at predicting the weather in the jungle. If it looks like rain, it won't rain. If it doesn't look like rain, it will rain. When it does rain, if it lasts more than five minutes, it will rain for the rest of the day. If it stops before five minutes are over, it won't rain again until tomorrow.

One Sunday as I sat under the tree where we had church, my thoughts turned to the rain, or more correctly, to the absence of rain. I then realized that in the 14 months that I had lived in the jungle, no church service had ever been canceled for rain. I felt God saying to me, *Of course not. You meet under a tree. You can't have church if it's raining. I've got that detail under control.*

What an amazing realization! It had never occurred to me that we had good weather for church, but God had been taking care of it. I never bothered to pray about having good weather for church. Yet God already had it under control.

When I think about what that means in the rest of my life, I am almost overwhelmed. God proves daily that He is ordering my steps and planning my days. If He takes the time to plan good weather for believers in the jungle who meet under a tree, won't He be planning my life and your life as well?

—KRISTEE, SOUTH AMERICA

Heavenly Father, SOVEREIGN RULER OF THE UNIVERSE, YOU HAVE EVERYTHING UNDER CONTROL. THANK YOU THAT I DO NOT NEED TO FEEL OVERWHELMED WITH WHAT IS GOING ON AROUND ME. *Amen.*

Worthless sacrifice

"But King David said to Ornan, 'No, but I will surely buy it for the full price; for I will not take what is yours for the LORD, *or offer a burnt offering which costs me nothing.'"* 1 Chronicles 21:24 (NASB)

Our weekly Bible study meets in a *paillote* (PIE-yote), which is an open, round, thatched hut in the center of the village. After the study, we sing and give an offering, placing it on an open Bible. In Africa, we "give" our offerings. In America, the expression is to "take" the offering, and it is often a quiet event.

Common practice in Africa is to make change from the offering plate. At the close of one meeting, some asked me if I could make change for them for market the next day. As I counted out coins, one lady said, "I don't want this one. It is too worn; they won't accept it in the market." Silence fell as the realization hit. Someone had offered this useless money to God. We saw more coins worn smooth until the markings were no longer visible. I said, "Someone gave these worthless coins to God. What does the Bible say about that?"

In I Chronicles 21:24, David said he could not offer to a holy God a sacrifice that cost him nothing. We cannot fool God by going through the motions of giving. What value do we place on the gifts we lay before the Lord? What did our gift cost us? I have to admit I was beginning to feel a little "preachy" until the Lord convicted me that I, too, was guilty. I hadn't given worn coins, but I had given less than my best. I am sometimes content to give the leftovers of my time or energy. May I never again offer to God any worthless sacrifice.

—GAYE, WEST AFRICA

Father, MAY I, TOO, NEVER AGAIN OFFER TO YOU ANY WORTHLESS SACRIFICE. FORGIVE ME WHEN I DIDN'T GIVE TO YOU THE BEST. *Amen.*

Prescription for hope

"Now faith is the assurance of things hoped for, the conviction of things not seen."
Hebrews 11:1 (RSV)

A girl around 7 years old came to a medical clinic we sponsored with the help of a volunteer team from Spartanburg, South Carolina. We found out that her father was an alcoholic who mistreated her mother and her siblings. Most of the time, this little girl was left alone in the house to do all the chores and take care of her brothers and sisters. After she had shared these things, she asked, "Do you have any pills that would give me hope?"

So many people run short of hope and wonder how they can continue. It would be marvelous if there were a quick fix for hopeless lives. We were able to tell the little girl that Someone could give her hope. Jesus Christ could share the heavy burdens that she carried. Cheeks were wet with tears as we lovingly put her in touch with the One who truly does offer hope when our way is too hard and our load is too great.

We as Christians should be a people of hope. We often encounter desperate people, and sometimes we despair. In the dark times, we need to embrace faith in our Lord in order to restore hope in our road-weary souls. Faith really is "the assurance of things hoped for." And what do we hope for? Love, forgiveness, relationship and God's sustaining grace can see us through, no matter how hard the road is before us.

Running a little short of hope today? Celebrate your faith and embrace hope! Not only that—give some away to others.

—LILY, MIDDLE AMERICA AND THE CARIBBEAN

Gracious Father, YOU ARE THE GOD OF HOPE. THANK YOU THAT NO MATTER WHAT MY CIRCUMSTANCES ARE, YOU GIVE HOPE IN HOPELESS SITUATIONS. HELP ME TO SHARE HOPE WITH OTHERS. GIVE MISSIONARIES OPPORTUNITIES TODAY TO SHARE HOPE WITH THE LOST. *Amen.*

God, the forgiver

"Where can I go from your Spirit? Where can I flee from your presence? If I go up to the heavens, you are there; if I make my bed in the depths, you are there." Psalm 139:7–8 (NIV)

"Beth" became a believer when she was a teenager. Her strict Wahhabite Muslim family was distressed, but they thought she would eventually return to Islam. But Beth had no intention of forsaking Christianity.

She met a young man at church and became engaged. Beth's mother was unhappy that the groom was a Christian, but her desire for Beth to be married was greater than her fear of the family's disapproval. Tragically, one of Beth's uncles committed suicide the day before the wedding, causing the marriage to be postponed. As the family gathered for the funeral, they discussed the reason for the man's suicide. They decided that Allah was angry about Beth's conversion; thus, a curse was on the family. Beth was told to recant her faith so that no one else would die for her disobedience. Beth refused. She was forced to the floor but still refused to deny Jesus. Finally, her uncles threatened to kill her if she didn't. Terrified, Beth recanted.

Shaken and ashamed, Beth ran from the house and for hours wandered the streets. She wanted to go to her fiancé and church for comfort. But it wasn't their forgiveness she needed; it was Jesus'. But how could He forgive her for denying Him? Tearfully, she cried out to Jesus.

That night, Beth had a dream that she was in a bathtub filled with snow. Then Jesus Himself came and washed her clean. Suddenly, she had a covering of snowy white. When she woke, Beth was filled with peace and God's forgiveness.

Beth's story reminds us that even if we go down to "the depths," Jesus is there.

—S.H., CENTRAL ASIA

Father, FORGIVE ME WHEN I DENY YOU BY DISOBEDIENCE. JUST AS YOU FORGAVE PETER, SOMEONE I CAN IDENTIFY WITH, FORGIVE ME FOR _____. GIVE COURAGE TO BELIEVERS WHO ARE PERSECUTED FOR THEIR FAITH TODAY. HELP THEM TO STAND FAST. *Amen.*

He calls me by name

"But you are a chosen people ... that you may declare the praises of him who called you out of darkness into his wonderful light." 1 Peter 2:9 (NIV)

God is not just interested in the world as a whole, but He knows and loves each individual. One of the Aukaners (au-CAN-ers) God loves is "Don." Don is a soft-spoken, middle-aged man of much influence in his Aukan village. As we developed a relationship with him, God began revealing Himself to Don.

When people, like Don, best benefit from hearing Bible stories instead of reading them, IMB missionaries use a method called chronological Bible storying. So Don listened to tapes in which an Aukaner told the foundational Bible stories from the creation to the ascension of Christ; it was his first exposure to God's Word. After repeated hearings, he asked, "Do you believe that God can speak to you in a dream?" Knowing of examples in the Bible, we said yes. He then began to tell us of his recurring dream since listening to the Bible stories.

"In my dream, I'm in the front of my canoe and my wife is in the back as we paddle down the river. All of a sudden, I look into the clouds and can see Jesus standing. He calls me by name and says, 'Come.' So I paddle over to the shore and follow the path leading to Jesus. I turn around, and my wife, children and much of my village are following as well. What do you think that means?"

With joy we told Don that God was calling him to a relationship with Jesus Christ, and when he chose to follow Christ, he was going to lead much of his family and others to follow Him as well.

What a God we serve! He finds an unlikely man in a remote village and calls him by name!

—VICKI, MIDDLE AMERICA AND THE CARIBBEAN

Thank You, God, THAT YOU CALL ME BY NAME AND THAT YOU ARE A PERSONAL GOD. THANK YOU THAT YOU ARE CALLING THOSE AMONG THE AUKANERS. USE THE CHRONOLOGICAL BIBLE STORYING METHOD TO BRING MANY PEOPLE GROUPS TO A SAVING KNOWLEDGE OF CHRIST. *Amen.*

The God of details

"Sing His praise from the end of the earth ... You islands ... Give glory to the Lord and declare His praise in the coastlands." Isaiah 42:10b, 12 (NASB)

Does God remember me personally? I hate to admit it, but I have had this thought. Recently, my life was in transition and doubt as I found myself in a new culture.

Complicating my transition, I had the responsibility of ministering to colleagues who had been in various crises, including a kidnapping, armed robbery and assault, death of a missionary child, multiple medical evacuations and emergency surgery. I learned that taking breaks were essential to my mental and spiritual health. So, on my birthday, I went with friends to the beach. I went not to swim, but for a chance to see dolphins. In more than three years, neither my friends nor I had seen one.

As we lounged on the beach, my friend tried to encourage me about my impending stateside assignment and how I would be able to share how Jesus was working in Benin (beh-NIN). She reminded me that today, my birthday, people were praying for me specifically. As we watched the waves, I reflected on her words.

Suddenly, about 100 yards offshore, a dolphin appeared! I saw his nose, fin and tail as he arched through the air. I shouted, "Hallelujah; thank You, Jesus!" During the next hour, we watched about a dozen dolphins with their young. What a birthday present! I received presents and many cards, but only the Lord could arrange such a display of His splendor to me so personally. *Happy birthday, Judy! I love you.*

Our God remembers us personally and loves to remind us that He is indeed our caring Father.

—JUDY, WEST AFRICA

You, Father, HAVE LOVED ME WITH AN EVERLASTING LOVE. THANK YOU THAT YOU HAVE NOT FORGOTTEN ME, THAT I AM PRECIOUS IN YOUR SIGHT. HELP MISSIONARIES WHO ARE BY THEMSELVES IN MINISTRY TO KNOW THAT THEY ARE NOT FORGOTTEN BY YOU OR THOSE OF US AT HOME. *Amen.*

My soul thirsts for You

"As the deer pants for the water brooks, so my soul pants for You, O God. My soul thirsts for God, for the living God." Psalm 42:1–2a (NASB)

It was another hot, dry day in a city located on the edge of a desert in South Asia. Internally, I was struggling and grieving. What was I doing here? I thought that I knew what God wanted for me, but now I felt tattered, torn and broken.

Miraculously, God keeps hope alive and truth deep within, even when I don't feel that both really exist. I began to remember His past faithfulness, that He is wholly holy and that His love is supreme. Knowing He knows the best for me, my question still remained: "Why make me a missionary here?" Yet the answer is simple—because He is God, it is so.

I walked to my language class singing Psalm 63, the Jami Smith version: "O God You are my God. Earnestly I seek You. My soul thirsts for You. ... In a dry and weary land where there is no water. You extend Your hand and give life to me."

As I was crossing a major intersection, I sang, "You extend Your hand and give life to me." From out of nowhere, an Asian woman lunged at me, extending her hand toward me. This gesture was uncommon and certainly unexpected. I almost fell to my knees right there, but instead I wept for joy as God tenderly poured His mercy upon me. He revived my soul as He reached toward me through this unknown woman.

My hope was restored, causing me to remember I am His and He is mine.

—G., SOUTH ASIA

Almighty Father, WHEN I AM IN DESPAIR, THEN I REMEMBER TO HOPE IN YOU AND PRAISE YOU. FOR NEW WORKERS IN LANGUAGE SCHOOL WHO ARE STRUGGLING WITH THEIR CALL, I PRAY THAT THEY WILL TRUST YOU AND PERSEVERE. *Amen.*

God is the ruler yet!

"I am the Alpha and the Omega, the Beginning and the End, the First and the Last." Revelation 22:13 (NKJV)

Deep inside this 50-year-old body is the voice of a skinny 14-year-old who told God she was willing to go to India as a missionary doctor and to right the injustices of the world.

Every missionary harbors those same ideals, but then challenges arise. Language school was a challenge as a new missionary at age 30. At 50, studying my second Asian language, I was acutely aware of my inadequacies, reminded daily by a teacher who thought shaming me would goad me to excellence.

Trudging home through the local university campus, I was troubled by many things: my lack of progress, the barriers between those I wanted to share with and myself, the appalling poverty of refugees, the sheer multitudes of Japanese whose god is materialism, the Buddhist Koreans who pray so fervently to gods of stone and brass and the Filipinos who look to Mary, Mohammed or to capricious spirits for aid.

Discouraged, I was praying about all of this when I heard singing. A group of Korean women were gathered around a park table worshiping God. I couldn't understand their words, but I knew the hymn: "This is my Father's world, and to my listening ears all nature sings and 'round me rings the music of the spheres." The next line that came to mind was: "And though the wrong seems oft so strong, God is the ruler yet!"

Encouraged, that idealistic teenager deep inside of me sang those lyrics all the way home.

—JANET, PACIFIC RIM

Sovereign Father, THIS IS YOUR WORLD, AND YOU ARE THE RULER! EVEN WHEN WRONG SEEMS SO STRONG, YOU ARE STILL IN CONTROL. THANK YOU FOR THIS REMINDER TODAY. HELP MISSIONARIES TO CONTINUE TO FOLLOW THEIR CALL EVEN WHEN THEY ARE DISCOURAGED. *Amen.*

God's power

"And whatever you ask in My name, that I will do, that the Father may be glorified in the Son." John 14:13 (NKJV)

The grass withered in the hot sun. Water holes and riverbeds were dry and cracked. Animals were dying from starvation and thirst. People would be next. In desperation, villagers were digging deep holes in the riverbeds in search of water. Everyone knew that rain was needed, but it was not the rainy season.

It was decided that villagers from all over should conduct a "rain dance" to plead with the "rain god" and the ancestors to send rain. One new believer in Jesus consulted the missionary who lived in their village. "Pastor, what should we do?" she asked. "Some people want to pray to the 'rain god.'"

"Let's review some of the characteristics of God," the missionary suggested. "The true God controls all things. God is all-powerful and omniscient. He knows we need rain. I believe God is waiting for us to ask Him. Let's put our faith in God and pray to Him. Let's ask God for rain."

That night, the small group of believers prayed earnestly for rain. Before the witch doctors could arrange a proper "rain dance," the rains came out of season. It rained for a week! The young woman later testified, "I told my father that the pastor led us in prayer for rain. When it rained, my father said that he could see that Jesus had great power. I explained to him that God is the most powerful of all!"

Many people need to know the omnipotent God, who can bring them out of darkness and fear to a life filled with the living Water.

—FAYE, CENTRAL, EASTERN AND SOUTHERN AFRICA

Omnipotent Father, YOUR POWER IS EVIDENT AMONG ALL THE NATIONS. THANK YOU FOR ANSWERED PRAYER AND MIRACLES, WHICH DISPLAY YOUR CHARACTER. *Amen.*

This is my Father's world

"He is like the light of morning at sunrise on a cloudless morning, like the brightness after rain that brings the grass from the earth." 2 Samuel 23:4 (NIV)

Living in the jungle is a learning experience. I've learned how to hot-wire a solar panel, that approaching army ants signify coming rain and that pigs will eat anything you leave in the yard.

But one of my most treasured lessons from my jungle time concerns the beauty of God's creation. Without daylight savings time, the sunrise is early. When I go for a walk at 5:30 a.m., the sun begins to peek out, full of color. Every morning I feel like God has created the sunrise for my pleasure. I feel like He says to me, *I thought of you when I made this today. I couldn't wait to see your face when you saw it.*

I found this same joy in creation in other areas of my walk. When I see a spider web, wet and glistening with dew, I feel like God put it there for me. When I see a leaf-cutter ant hauling his giant leaf home, I know it was there to make me smile. The parrots, the toucans and even the wild pigs are all brought by God into my path on these walks.

God's creation is all around us. He manifests Himself in every sunrise, in the flowers that open, in the insects busy at work and in the multitude of stars at night. Have you noticed? Have you given God a chance to share more of Himself with you in His created world? Are you looking? He makes the world new every day for you to see.

—KRISTEE, SOUTH AMERICA

Creator, THANK YOU FOR THE BEAUTY OF THE WORLD. MAY PEOPLE GROUPS SEE YOUR CREATION AND KNOW THAT THERE IS SOMETHING MORE TO LIFE THAN THEMSELVES. *Amen.*

Shine the light!

"You are the light of the world. A city on a hill cannot be hidden."
Matthew 5:14 (NIV)

We are the "new kids on the block" as new missionaries in Uruguay (oo-roo-GWI). It's been our privilege to visit and learn from wiser missionaries. Church services are held at convenient times for members, so we've been going to church at unusual times on many of these visits.

We were on our way home from church on a Saturday night. One missionary said, "If you look out that way, you can see a glow on the horizon. That's the city of Buenos Aires (BUAY-nos AH-des)! And over there is Montevideo (mon-tay-vay-DAY-oh)!" It was amazing that on a semideserted stretch of highway in San José de Mayo (san ho-SAY day MY-oh), Uruguay, you can see the lights of two major cities in two different countries!

Even more amazing, when I looked straight up into the night sky, there was another glow put there by the Creator. Again the missionary commented, "We can see more of the Milky Way from the Southern Hemisphere." Surrounded by the darkness of night, the city lights were bright, but the Milky Way was radiant!

I suddenly felt small and insignificant. Yet God reminded me that He led us to reflect His light and love to a dark world. I want to shine in our dark world like those lights, like those stars. I want to shine before men so that they might praise my Father in heaven, the Creator of the universe. Even a small light can penetrate the darkness.

—K.C., SOUTH AMERICA

Creator Father, LET YOUR LIGHT SHINE THROUGH MISSIONARIES IN SOUTH AMERICA. TO-DAY LET YOUR LIGHT SHINE THROUGH ME AS WELL AS IN EVERYTHING THAT I DO. *Amen.*

Plans for a future and a hope

"As you know, we consider blessed those who have persevered."
James 5:11a (NIV)

Drought conditions in the state of Orissa (or-RISS-sah), India, caused many deaths one year. People looked to the village priest to perform rituals to appease the spirits, but even the priest suffered as he helplessly watched his malnourished wife die after birthing her fifth child. Fearing his dignity would be tarnished for not saving his wife, he decided a greater sacrifice must be made. He chose to offer his baby daughter as a human sacrifice.

As the father prepared to cremate his wife, he commanded his sister to throw the baby onto the burning pyre. But the aunt had sympathy for the child and tossed a bundle of rags instead. For 15 days, she drugged the infant to prevent her from crying. But the angry father found out and torched his sister's hut for deceiving him.

The aunt escaped with the child and ran miles through the jungle to a mission hospital, where she abandoned the baby. Later, she returned and identified the child. After three months, a Canadian Baptist missionary was given custody of the infant, who was named Lakki (LAH-kee) Joy.

Lakki thrived under the missionary's care. Through her guidance, Lakki came to know Christ as her personal Lord and Savior.

Lakki shares the gospel with her people group, the Soura (SUE-rah), at every opportunity. This once unwanted baby has become a testimony of God's love and is truly a joy to others.

—SUE, SOUTH ASIA

Preserver of life, YOU SAY YOU KNOW THE PLANS THAT YOU HAVE FOR ME, PLANS THAT WILL BRING ME A FUTURE AND A HOPE. THANK YOU THAT YOU HAD A PLAN FOR LAKKI, THAT YOU SPARED HER LIFE. USE HER TO BE A VOICE TO HER PEOPLE GROUP ABOUT JESUS. *Amen.*

The sanctity of life

"From birth I have relied on you; you brought me forth from my mother's womb. I will ever praise you." Psalm 71:6 (NIV)

Richard has cerebral palsy. Few people with his condition live to be adults in the remote Miskito (mees-KEY-toh) villages of Honduras and Nicaragua.

His mother realized that there was something wrong with Richard not long after his birth. A child who couldn't work would be a burden to her, so she gave him to a missionary family.

The family raised Richard and taught him to walk, to speak and to try everything. Richard learned to love the Lord and to be thankful for the gift of life. He began to sing at church. He learned to read his Bible. As a young man, he began to preach.

I first met Richard when we traveled to the small village of Auka (AWE-kah). As we were leaving the village, I almost panicked as I watched Richard walk the 200 feet out on the narrow dock to the boat. Richard's wide, swinging gait almost threw him into the water. But Richard didn't stop. I was nervous to jump from the dock into the dugout canoe, and I wondered how Richard would maneuver it. But quickly, one of the men lifted Richard and set him in the canoe.

Richard's life is a challenge. It takes him longer to do things. His speech is difficult to understand. Yet he has a joyful life that makes him unforgettable. Today, Richard is a loved pastor of a Miskito congregation.

Richard's birth mother judged him as worthless, yet in God's hands, Richard has proven that all things are possible.

—VIOLA, MIDDLE AMERICA AND THE CARIBBEAN

Giver of life, YOU FORMED MY INWARD PARTS. YOU WOVE ME IN MY MOTHER'S WOMB. I WILL GIVE THANKS TO YOU FOR I AM FEARFULLY AND WONDERFULLY MADE. THANK YOU THAT I AM SPECIAL AND THAT YOU LOVE ME. THANK YOU THAT YOU ARE USING RICHARD AND OTHERS LIKE HIM. I PRAISE YOU THAT YOU GIVE VALUE TO LIFE. *Amen.*

He's all I need

"Do not fear, for I am with you; do not anxiously look about you, for I am your God. I will strengthen you, surely I will help you. Surely I will uphold you with My righteous right hand." Isaiah 41:10 (NASB)

The cancer was very advanced, and we had no warning. We were told that my husband had only six months to live. In shock, we tried to process this news. God had so clearly called us as missionaries, and we had willingly given up all to obey Him. We had been on the field a few short months, but now we were stateside again to face an uncertain future. It was hard to understand.

Precious friends took us to a secluded mountain cabin to allow us time alone with each other and the Lord. As we wept and cried out to the Lord, our only comfort came from the Word. I pleaded with God to give me a verse that would assure me that my husband would live. God did not do that. Instead, He gave me Isaiah 41:10. His promise was that He would be with me to strengthen and help me, no matter what came. His promise saw us through four bouts with cancer in the years that followed and helped us take one day at a time.

God, in His grace and mercy, healed my husband. Today, 18 years later, we are still on the field joyfully serving in the harvest!

Though I hate cancer, I am thankful for this trial, which positively changed my family. I have seen God's faithfulness in ways that would not have been possible without suffering and learning to depend totally on Him. It's hard to know that God is all you need until He's all you've got.

—MARGIE, MIDDLE AMERICA AND THE CARIBBEAN

Merciful Father, YOU ARE ALL I NEED. THANK YOU THAT YOU ARE WITH ME THROUGH TRIALS AND SUFFERING. THANK YOU THAT YOU ARE WITH MISSIONARIES WHO EXPERIENCE HEALTH ISSUES OR WATCH A SPOUSE SUFFER. BE CLOSE TO THEM TODAY. *Amen.*

Turning trial into triumph

"What other nation is so great as to have their gods near them the way the LORD our God is near us whenever we pray to him?" Deuteronomy 4:7 (NIV)

My Hakka (HAH-kah) Chinese friends in Taiwan worship countless gods, each seen as having different abilities and power. My friends cannot comprehend my God, who hears me wherever I am and has the power to act, no matter what the request. I've prayed continually for their understanding.

One morning, God answered my request. I was bicycling when I came around a curve, not knowing I was going too fast until I started sliding. On impulse, I put down my left foot, and I heard my leg splinter as I spun and came to a complete stop. I sank to the ground and cried, "Jesus, I'm in the middle of the road between two blind corners." I slid toward the edge of the road, but my injured leg didn't respond. "Oh, Jesus. I need help."

My eyes scanned the area. I saw no one. I called out in Hakka, "Please, someone give me help!" No answer. Then I cried, "Jesus, please send someone to help me!" I raised my head at the sound of a car. A young woman stopped. She'd seen me on the ground in the mirrors posted at the curves.

After the ordeal, every lost friend of mine came to ask about my leg. Each one heard how Jesus answered when I called. Every time my response was, "No matter where you are, Jesus can hear and help you! He is good!" They finally understood the strength of my God. Their idols cannot compete.

Can you fathom the greatness of our God?

—D.T., EAST ASIA

You are the one, TRUE AND OMNIPOTENT GOD! GREAT AND GOOD ARE YOU, LORD, AND THERE IS NO OTHER GOD LIKE YOU! THANK YOU THAT YOU TURN TRAGEDY INTO VICTORY. PROTECT OUR CHRISTIAN WORKERS TODAY, AND USE THEIR TRIALS TO BRING GLORY TO JESUS. *Amen.*

No rush jobs with God

"O LORD, you are my God; I will exalt you and praise your name, for in perfect faithfulness you have done marvelous things, things planned long ago."
Isaiah 25:1 (NIV)

I envision great things, but often life gets in the way. As a mom of young children, I run frantically from one "uh-oh" to the next. "Uh-oh, the juice spilled on the couch." "Uh-oh, the dog ate my sandwich." "Uh-oh, my sock fell in the toilet." And suddenly my day is gone.

Then my week is gone. Then my month. It becomes, "Uh-oh, the birthday party is tomorrow." This is when the perfectionist in me collides with the dreamer.

Oh, the plans I had made! The party would have been fabulous. Should I still shoot for the magnificent array I had planned but accept the fact that the details won't be perfect? Do I give up my creative ideas and aim for a few things done to perfection?

Either way is a compromise. Neither way will be what I had originally hoped.

What a contrast I am to my heavenly Father. *"In perfect faithfulness [He has] done marvelous things, things planned long ago"* (Isa. 25:1, NIV). He doesn't get sidetracked by our everyday emergencies, though He is always there to tend to our needs with tenderness and love. He doesn't run out of time. He doesn't cancel plans at the last minute and settle for less than He had hoped.

I know that my creativity, harried though I may be at times, is a gift from my Creator. But He's not finished with me. It's good to know that *"he who began a good work in [me] will carry it on to completion"* (Phil. 1:6, NIV).

And it won't be a rush job.

—A WORKER IN CENTRAL AND EASTERN EUROPE

Heavenly Father, THANK YOU THAT YOU ARE NOT IN A RUSH TO GUIDE ME, TO MOLD ME AND TO CONFORM ME TO THE IMAGE OF YOUR SON. MAY I REST IN YOU INSTEAD OF RUSH; MAY I TRUST YOU INSTEAD OF MY OWN ABILITIES. *Amen.*

Depending on God when homesick

"I have taken you from the ends of the earth and called you from its most distant places. I said to you, 'You are my servant. I've chosen you; I haven't rejected you. Don't be afraid, because I am with you. Don't be intimidated; I am your God. I will strengthen you. I will help you. I will support you with my victorious right hand. ... Don't be afraid; I will help you.'" Isaiah 41:9–10, 13b (NIV)

During my appointment process and training before heading overseas, I had doubts about God calling me to international missions.

I had experienced homesickness while at a boarding school for the deaf while living in another state as a short-term missionary. I did not want to experience these feelings overseas. Also, I feared I would experience loneliness on the field, since I use sign language to communicate. I was anxious about the future.

I came to God's Word searching for His promises. He led me to Isaiah 41:9–10, 13, and I was humbled by His promise that He would help me at all times. I am learning to trust Him and to allow Him to help, strengthen and support me.

I have been on the field for more than two years and am amazed at how faithful God is. He brought me in contact with deaf people for fellowship, worship and ministry. I have peace, knowing that He desires me to share His love with the deaf.

Yes, I still experience homesickness, but the Lord sustains me through these times. Now I have shared these verses with deaf believers so they may know that God will provide His help for them like He does for me.

—Sheri, Central, Eastern and Southern Africa

Father, strengthen Your servants who are homesick, and meet all their emotional needs. Thank You that You will never leave us. I ask You also to bring Your Word and messengers to the hearing impaired of the world so that they might know You. *Amen.*

Oops, wrong kiss!

"Give each other a kiss of Christian love when you meet." 1 Peter 5:14 (NCV)

Isn't it wonderful to serve a God of love, who is not afraid of affection! Jesus probably hugged the disciples, especially when they were discouraged or weary. People in His culture greeted one another with a kiss.

Europeans give three alternating kisses on the cheeks of close friends and family and only one kiss to acquaintances. Since we mainly work with immigrants, we deal with many cultures and had to learn several different greetings. Our Russian friends give "bear hugs" and two kisses, the Africans give three kisses starting on the left and our Middle Eastern friends only give kisses to same gender, but three times starting on the right!

At one of the refugee centers, A. would make sure that all the other refugees came to welcome us. One day, we started to greet our friends with their appropriate kisses. By the time I got to A., I was so confused that I forgot to begin my kisses on the left and not the right. I ended up kissing him full on the mouth! His face lit up like fireworks, and he grinned. I thought, *Oh no, he thinks we are engaged!*

A. laughed and said, "My sister and mother used to kiss me all of the time. You are like my sister, and it makes me think of my family." Who knew an accidental kiss would allow us to talk about the love of Christ?

However, I try not to make that same mistake again, except with my husband!

—JODY, WESTERN EUROPE

God of love, I PRAISE YOU FOR LOVING US UNCONDITIONALLY. MAY I SHOW CHRISTIAN LOVE TOWARD OTHERS SO THAT THEY WILL KNOW YOUR LOVE. HELP ME TO BE ATTENTIVE TO VISITORS AT MY CHURCH, NEW NEIGHBORS, NEW SCHOOLMATES OR NEW WORK COLLEAGUES. LET YOUR LOVE BE EVIDENT IN THE LIVES OF MISSIONARIES IN WESTERN EUROPE. *Amen.*

Merciful and full of love

"And a little child will lead them all." Isaiah 11:6b (NLT)

The day I first met Naaman (nah-A-mahn), he pounded his fist on the table as he replayed the wrongs his people had suffered at the hands of "Christians." For decades, his people had been mistreated by land grabbers who had prevented development in their communities.

I suggested that we could help, and it was decided to open a preschool. Although there was no teacher, I told Naaman I would ask God to provide one. That's when "Teacher" was called to a place that her people feared.

The first day of class, she was greeted coldly, since she was a Christian. However, because of her mercy, the children soon began fighting over whose house she would visit after school. She had won them over with love.

At the first graduation, Naaman began his speech, but he became emotional. Typically stoic parents and others also began to cry. Naaman shared that no one had ever shown love to their children before, yet this Christian woman had.

At the next year's graduation, Naaman stood to give the opening prayer. He began with the written prayer forms of his religion and then said in a local language, "God, teach us the way of truth and peace that these other people know." A few months later, Naaman put his faith in Christ.

The Lord is full of compassion. By extending mercy and love toward others, it shows the mercy of the Lord. Just as this teacher did, each Christian can choose to demonstrate that God is gracious, compassionate and rich in love.

—A WORKER IN THE PACIFIC RIM

God of mercy, FULL OF LOVE, MAY I BE A PICTURE OF YOUR MERCY TODAY. I PRAY THAT MISSIONARIES TODAY WILL EXTEND THE HAND OF MERCY TO THOSE AROUND THEM. MAY PEOPLE ON THIS ISLAND IN THE PACIFIC RIM BE DRAWN TO YOU THROUGH THE EXAMPLES OF CHRISTIANS. *Amen.*

Mourning together

"But we do not want you to be uninformed, brethren, about those who are asleep,
so that you will not grieve as do the rest who have no hope."
1 Thessalonians 4:13 (NASB)

In an automobile accident, a friend lost his young wife, the mother of their two small children. He and other family members are without hope as they grieve. They are part of "the rest who have no hope" referred to in this verse.

I went to sit with this man and other men from the Middle Eastern community. Many supported him in his grief, but he did not know fellowship with the Spirit. Male friends and relatives sat with him in silence, according to their tradition. Many friends greeted and gave him kisses on his cheeks. Yet, without knowing and feeling the presence of Jesus, this widower was without hope.

Several years ago, we lost our first baby. She was full-term and healthy until the day she was to be born. It was a difficult time, but we cried out to God, knowing that He heard us and was with us. As we grieved, we had hope that we would be reunited for eternity bowing down to worship our King together.

Even after that pain, we can easily forget how much people are hurting. We tend to be preoccupied with our own concerns, or we prefer laughing or not feeling at all. We don't take time to weep with others.

We need help from the Lord to embrace others' pain and to introduce them to our Comforter and Healer. We can lead them to know God by mourning with them. As God comforts us, let us comfort others—especially those who are yet to believe in Jesus.

—G.M., NORTHERN AFRICA AND THE MIDDLE EAST

God of all comfort, I PRAISE YOU THAT YOU BRING HOPE IN THE MIDST OF TRIALS. THANK YOU FOR THE MANY TIMES THAT YOU HAVE COMFORTED ME. MAY YOUR SPIRIT COMFORT OTHERS THROUGH ME THIS WEEK. MAY I NEVER TURN MY HEAD TO THOSE WHO SUFFER AND GRIEVE, BUT USE ME INSTEAD TO BE A FRIEND. *Amen.*

His presence through pain

"When I am weak, then I am strong." 2 Corinthians 12:10b (NASB)

Midnight approached as I waited beside the hospital bed of my 17-year-old daughter. As Hilary lay motionless, images appeared of an overturned motor scooter, her unconscious body, a missionary friend searching for a pulse amid pools of blood.

Fortunately, Hilary couldn't remember the accident as she lay immobilized in cervical spine traction. The night before, she'd slept soundly from the exhaustion of the four-hour ambulance ride. Tonight, however, she remained awake from the excruciating pain.

Waiting for the pain medication, I stroked her hair and stared at the contraption immobilizing her upper body. Aptly named Gardner-Wells tongs, it was fixed against her skull by two metal pins inserted through her clean-shaven temples. The pins connected to a horseshoe-shaped bar arching over the top of her head. A 15-pound weight hung from the crown of the device, pulling against her skull and straightening her vertebrae.

"I can't do this, Mom," she whispered weakly. "Please take it off." We cried together, but I knew that removing the traction would not bring lasting relief. What she needed was strength to endure.

As we prayed, God did not bring Hilary immediate freedom from pain. Instead, the pain became the path by which He drew near. Our faith was enlarged, knowing that His presence is available each day. His power transforms us, resulting in a greater change than merely removing unpleasant circumstances. Faith grows as we draw near to Him. Sometimes only tears can cleanse our eyes enough for us to notice.

—K.P., EAST ASIA

Father, SOMETIMES I DON'T UNDERSTAND WHY YOU ALLOW PAIN IN THE LIVES OF YOUR CHILDREN, BUT I TRUST YOU TO ENLARGE MY FAITH AND TO TRANSFORM ME WITH YOUR POWER AND COMFORT. GIVE ME THE STRENGTH TO NOTICE YOUR PURPOSE IN UNPLEASANT CIRCUMSTANCES. *Amen.*

When confusion abounds

> "Therefore, since through God's mercy, we have this ministry, we do not lose heart. ... We are hard pressed on every side, but not crushed; perplexed, but not in despair. ... Therefore we do not lose heart. Though outwardly we are wasting away, yet inwardly we are being renewed day by day."
> 2 Corinthians 4:1, 8, 16 (NIV)

I like the word "perplexed." It sounds so much better than "confused." Before I became a missionary, I often noticed a quiet depth of many missionaries. This characteristic intrigued and impressed me. However, after I became a missionary, I began to question my initial observation. After our first two years on the field, we returned to the United States for vacation. As I stood in a store overwhelmed by the many choices, I realized that what I had thought was quiet depth actually may have been confusion!

I am often confused. Sometimes I am confused by language, sometimes by culture, sometimes by tradition, and sometimes I am just plain old confused. In any given situation, there are many right answers and approaches, and there are just as many wrong ones. When the chaos reaches maximum proportions, I am tempted to quit.

So why stay? The answer is simple. God has given us a glimpse of His vision clearly stated in Revelation 7:9: "*After this I looked and there before me was a great multitude that no one could count, from every nation, tribe, people and language, standing before the throne and in front of the Lamb. They were wearing white robes and holding palm branches in their hands*" (NIV).

It is God's vision that no one should perish, but that everyone should come to repentance (2 Peter 3:9). And it is the power of God's vision and His grace that sustains us, renews us and keeps us focused on our calling. So, in spite of the chaos and confusion, don't give up!

—ANN, PACIFIC RIM

Lord, WITHOUT A GOD-SIZED VISION, WE WOULD SETTLE FOR MEDIOCRITY. I PRAY THAT WE, ALONG WITH MISSIONARIES, WILL EMBRACE ANEW TODAY YOUR GLOBAL VISION, THAT ONE DAY THE REDEEMED FROM EVERY PEOPLE GROUP WILL BE GATHERED AROUND YOUR THRONE, WORSHIPING THE LAMB OF GLORY. *Amen.*

He gets the glory

"Wherever I cause my name to be honored, I will come to you and bless you."
Exodus 20:24b (NIV)

We have so many plans for ministering among our people group. Often, however, plans fail, never happen or are altered in ways that make our original thoughts completely unrecognizable.

We spent a lot of time, money, energy and prayers in one village. It began to look like a black hole with no results. Then one Sunday, a man from the village told the church he had had a dream in which a man told him to read the Bible! He read through the Gospels in a couple of weeks, seeking the truth.

God has been teaching me that we can plan and strategize, but He causes His name to be honored. How great is that! We aren't responsible for people coming to Christ. When we see God causing His name to be honored, as with this man being drawn to Him solely through the Holy Spirit, we feel His presence and are blessed to witness His glory.

I found a verse that addresses how to build an altar and worship the Lord. God emphasizes that there are to be no "dressed stones" or steps leading up to the altar (Ex. 20:25, NIV). God wants the complete focus of our worship, not the work of our hands. God causes His name to be honored, not us, and if we try to take the credit for His work, our weakness and faults will be exposed.

When we see God moving, we are brought to our knees in worship. We are encouraged that our witnessing is not in vain.

—JULIE, CENTRAL AND EASTERN EUROPE

Father, THANK YOU THAT YOU ARE RESPONSIBLE FOR CALLING PEOPLE TO YOURSELF. USE ME IN THAT PROCESS, AND HELP ME NOT TO BE DISCOURAGED WHEN I DON'T SEE IMMEDIATE RESULTS. ENCOURAGE MISSIONARIES TODAY WHO ARE IN PLACES WHERE THE WORK IS SLOW. *Amen.*

Tutus and touchdowns

> *"For in the gospel a righteousness from God is revealed, a righteousness that is by faith from first to last, just as it is written: 'The righteous will live by faith.'"*
> Romans 1:17 (NIV)

Tutus, tap shoes, free throws and touchdowns. What do these things have in common? More than you think.

During the past months, Jen, a missionary, has donned her tutu and tap shoes, and she has spent more than nine hours a week with more than 150 students ranging from ages 4 to 16. Her husband, Seth, has been plunged into a world of free throws and touchdowns, as he has been asked to teach basketball and American football in a local school.

Are these the things these missionaries envisioned doing when they signed up to plant churches? Not really. Do they *feel* like missionaries as Jen is twirling around the dance floor or when Seth is showing special-needs students how to dribble a basketball? Not necessarily. But isn't that the point? Aren't we, as Christians, told to live not by our feelings, but by our faith, choosing to believe that our dreams are happening even when we can't see it?

God has opened doors to show the people of this country His love through everyday activities. It doesn't feel like work. It doesn't feel like "evangelism." Yet somehow, people are asking questions; somehow, people want to know why we do things differently. God is good, holy and just; but God is also *creative*.

What unsuspecting hobby does God want to use in your life to show His love and truth to others? For more than a year, these missionaries prayed that God would show them how to be involved in the community. He answered in a most unusual way!

—S.E.D. AND J.V.D., WESTERN EUROPE

Lord, THANK YOU FOR HEARING THE PRAYERS OF YOUR SERVANTS AND FOR CREATIVELY OPENING DOORS FOR THE GOSPEL IN A CONTEXT READILY UNDERSTOOD. LORD, I PRAY THAT MANY TODAY WILL BECOME AWARE OF ABILITIES, APTITUDES AND SPIRITUAL GIFTS THAT HAVE BEEN DIVINELY PLACED IN THEIR LIVES FOR A PURPOSE. *Amen.*

The Great Physician

"How beautiful on the mountains are the feet of those who bring good news, who proclaim peace, who bring good tidings, who proclaim salvation, who say to Zion, 'Your God reigns!'" Isaiah 52:7 (NIV)

The lines of tired, undernourished people grew as they waited to see one of three nurses. Many of the women had babies at their breasts and several small children clinging to their skirts. Some people walked miles to get the first medical care they had ever received. Some waited all day without having any food or water. In this faraway valley, food and water were scarce commodities.

As these quiet and humble people sat in front of me, flies dotted their faces. I recognized their obvious need for medical attention, but I saw a much deeper need. The darkness in which they lived needed to be penetrated by our Great Physician. After I prescribed pills, creams or syrups to meet their physical needs, I prayed with them, knowing that the Holy Spirit would meet their spiritual needs if they would let Him.

After my silent prayer, a very old lady approached the table. She had lived 80-plus years in darkness and oppression. I handed her some pills, and I prayed for her.

I asked if she had ever heard of Jesus. She said no. I shared with her the wonderful plan of salvation He offered her if she only believed. Excitedly, she said she wanted to know this Jesus!

As we prayed together, a new child of God was created. When I opened my eyes, the beauty in her face looked almost youthful. She had a new peace that circumstances could never take away. The Great Physician had healed this lady for all eternity.

—NANCY, CENTRAL, EASTERN AND SOUTHERN AFRICA

Father God, YOU TRULY ARE THE ONE WHO MENDS BROKEN LIVES. THANK YOU FOR BEING THE BALM OF GILEAD FOR ALL WHO NEED A TOUCH FROM YOU. USE MEDICAL MISSIONARIES TODAY TO BRING YOUR PHYSICAL AND SPIRITUAL HEALING TO THE NEEDY. *Amen.*

God is trustworthy

"The LORD *lives, and blessed be my rock; and exalted be the God of my salvation. ... He delivers me from my enemies. ... You rescue me from the violent man. Therefore I will give thanks to You among the nations, O* LORD*, and I will sing praises to Your name." Psalm 18:46, 48a, 48c, 49 (NASB)*

My eyes were wide open in the dark. I heard something. I checked the time—2:20 a.m.—and something didn't seem right. Then someone whispered, "Turn around." Suddenly, I was face to face with a flashlight and two armed men.

I stared into eyes of evil intent, and a gun was brought into clear view. To my horror, unthinkable threats flowed from their mouths. I shrieked, and they forced my face into the mattress. As two hours unfolded, I was stripped and bound with computer cords, praying for my life and my purity. I could not understand why this was happening but began quietly praying, "Lord, is this Your determined end for me? Father, may Your sovereign will be done."

My heart immediately filled with peace, and I knew He was with me. I began to softly sing, *"Takwaba uwaba nga Yesu"* (tock-WAH-bah oo-WAH-bah gah YEH-sue). "There's no one like Jesus."

One man's face distorted into confusion, and he began to tie me tighter. "Should we kill her?" he asked. "No," the other responded, grabbing more items to steal. "Let's go."

Despite the bruises and trauma, my life was spared and my purity was left intact. God had saved me. There is *no one* like Jesus! I can't explain why my enemies didn't finish me off. Was it my Lord's convicting presence or His great faithfulness? He has stirred within me an even deeper trust in Him. Even if I had not been delivered, He is still trustworthy and faithful.

—A WORKER IN CENTRAL, EASTERN AND SOUTHERN AFRICA

Father, THANK YOU THAT YOU ARE TRUSTWORTHY AND FAITHFUL. THANK YOU THAT YOU SPARED THIS SINGLE WOMAN FROM FURTHER VIOLATION AND DEATH. PROTECT WOMEN MISSIONARIES ON THE FIELD, AND MAY THEY TRUST AND PRAISE YOU WHENEVER EVIL IS INTENDED TOWARD THEM. I TRUST YOU TODAY WITH MY LIFE. *Amen.*

Never alone

"And I will ask the Father, and he will give you another Counselor to be with you forever. ... I will not leave you as orphans; I will come to you."
John 14:16, 18 (NIV)

It began as an Evangelism Explosion project in Quetzaltenango (keht-sahl-teh-NAHN-go), a city in western Guatemala. A family accepted the Lord and opened their home for a neighborhood Bible study. Slowly the group grew. Land was found for a church building, and the little congregation decided to do much of the work themselves to lower costs.

Since many people have vacation days the week before Easter, they decided that those days could be dedicated to digging the foundation. The first workday was scheduled for 9 a.m. on a Saturday. My husband and children had prior obligations. By the time I dropped them off and got some cookies and juice together, it was nearly 10 a.m.

I drove up to the work site and climbed out with my hoe and shovel. At first, it seemed that no one was there. Then over to one side, I saw the pastor working alone. *He must be discouraged,* I thought, as I poured him a cup of juice and walked over.

"Hello, Brother Celso. Are you out here working all alone?"

"Oh no," he replied with a laugh. "The Lord is here with me."

"Well, now there are three of us," I responded. "Let's get to work!" Before the day was over, others had joined us and a good start was made.

Now when I start to feel like I am all alone in some project or ministry, I remember Brother Celso and say, "Oh no, I'm not alone. The Lord is here with me."

—HELEN, MIDDLE AMERICA AND THE CARIBBEAN

Father, THANK YOU THAT YOU WILL NEVER LEAVE ME, THAT I AM NEVER ALONE. WHEN I FEEL OVERWHELMED WITH WHAT IS BEFORE ME, I KNOW THAT YOU ARE WITH ME. MAY YOUR PRESENCE BE FELT TODAY BY MISSIONARIES IN MIDDLE AMERICA AND THE CARIBBEAN. *Amen.*

A close call

"'Because he loves me,' says the LORD, 'I will rescue him; I will protect him, for he acknowledges my name. He will call upon me, and I will answer him; I will be with him in trouble, I will deliver him and honor him.'" Psalm 91:14–15 (NIV)

A motorcyclist cut in front of us, causing Dave to swerve to the left and sideswipe the cyclist. The car plunged into a wooded ravine. "Jesus, help us!" was Dave's prayer as we left the road. Miraculously, we were unharmed!

A large crowd surrounded our car. In this country, if one seriously hurts someone in an auto wreck, the villagers might injure the driver in retaliation. Fortunately, the motorcyclist was not badly injured, and he left the scene. When Dave heard the news that the motorcyclist was unhurt, he agreed to get out of the car.

The villagers then removed the punctured front tire. In order to get to the spare, we had to open the back, which had boxes containing 100 Bibles in the local language. They either did not notice the Bibles or chose not to mention them. Having Bibles could have put us in more danger.

Since the spare was also punctured, another motorist loaned us his spare tire, which they installed on the car while another took our flat to the shop to be repaired. The villagers then cut down some small trees that had blocked the car and attached a rope to the front of the vehicle. With Dave revving the engine and villagers pulling and pushing, the car was brought out of the 20-feet-deep ravine and onto the road!

Praise God for His protection and the provision of the helpful villagers with whom we have come to share Christ. He hears us when we cry out to Him and answers us in times of trouble.

—A WORKER IN THE PACIFIC RIM

Gracious Father, MY PROTECTOR, I PRAISE AND THANK YOU FOR THE INNUMERABLE, OFTEN UNNOTICED, TIMES THAT YOU PLACE YOUR HEDGE OF PROTECTION AROUND YOUR SERVANTS TO DELIVER THEM FROM HARM. MAY MISSIONARIES, AS WELL AS THE PEOPLE WITH WHOM THEY WORK, RECOGNIZE YOUR SOVEREIGN HAND AND ACKNOWLEDGE YOUR AUTHORITY OVER ALL THINGS. *Amen.*

Under His wings

"He will shield you with his wings. He will shelter you with his feathers. His faithful promises are your armor and protection." Psalm 91:4 (NLT)

Being fearful for the lives of loved ones caught me prepared this time.

It was November 20 in Central Asia. At 11:05 a.m., our lives and the country we lived in would change. *Kaboom!* The sound rang through the city, shaking the house and ground. I waited. Ten minutes later, another *kaboom!* I paused again. What could be so loud? Then silence. Panic rose up in me. Five days earlier, two Jewish synagogues had been bombed. Turning on the television, I looked with horror at torn-apart buildings, destruction and death in our city. My mind turned to my children at school and my husband returning from out of town. Were they safe? One of the two bombings had occurred only one mile from our home.

My response normally in situations like this would be fear, helplessness and despair. But the Lord had prepared me for this moment and gave me peace. This was not the first time I had reason to fear for my family and friends. Anti-American protests about the war in Iraq and bomb threats at our church had brought anxiety.

During those times, I had memorized Psalm 91. Meditating on His Word would sustain me during this trial, too. I continued to recite this chapter out loud. Calm settled over me, instead of fear.

My husband safely arrived home later, and our children returned home early from school. The city we lived in mourned its fallen people.

God's Word gives hope, comfort and peace. Life can be uncertain, but He always remains our refuge.

—GINA, CENTRAL ASIA

Father, MY REFUGE AND STRENGTH, A VERY PRESENT HELP IN TIME OF TROUBLE, THANK YOU THAT YOU COVER YOUR CHILDREN WITH YOUR WINGS. MAY YOUR WILL BE DONE IN THE LIVES OF CHRISTIAN WORKERS SERVING IN DANGEROUS PLACES. I CHOOSE TO REST IN YOU TODAY INSTEAD OF LIVING IN FEAR ABOUT_____. *Amen.*

FEBRUARY V

God's Word

Whether stateside or on foreign soil, believers have the same text in common and the same inability to live well without it. I don't care who we are and how long some of us have been in church or ministry. None of us can make it victoriously without a steady diet of Scripture. And why would we want to? Hebrews 4:12 tells us that God's Word is "living and active" (NIV). Let me say that again a little louder: *living and active!* That means it isn't just an ancient sacred text still making a few relevant applications. The Greek verb tense for "living" in Hebrews 4:12 indicates the Word is presently and continually teeming with life. If we believe the Word is alive and *"all Scripture is Godbreathed"* (2 Tim. 3:16, NIV), we might say that every breath comes to us still warm from the mouth of God. As if He just said it.

Eternal in nature, the Word is ageless. It can't get old; therefore, if something about it seems to be getting old, the more likely culprit is our approach. In Jeremiah 23:29, God asked the rhetorical question, *"Is not my word like fire?"* (NIV). His Word is still like fire, all right; but soggy wood is hard to light. How can we keep a fresh approach to an ageless Word? A few suggestions:

Ask God openly and often for what you feel you lack. If you wish you were more passionate about Him and His Word, don't just sit back and feel guilty. Ask Him for it! Then start thanking Him with full confidence and expectancy before you sense the first hint of it. First John 5:14–15 says, *"This is the confidence we have in approaching God: that if we ask anything according to his will, he hears us. And if we know that he hears us—whatever we ask—we know that we have what we ask of him"* (NIV). What could God want more than our passion for Him? Daily say aloud something like this to Him: "I thank You, Father, for even now igniting a fiery love in my heart for You and Your Word. Continue to make it my soul's deepest desire."

Approach God's Word like the divine, supernatural, power-packed text it is.

Satan knows that the only offensive weapon we have to raise against him is the sword of the Spirit, the Word of God. He can't keep it from being powerful, but if he can tempt us to think little of it, he knows it will never be powerful in us.

Satan has a frightening scheme under operation in Western Christian culture that I fear is devastatingly effective. I call it "intellectual unbelief": numbers of scholarly, highly credentialed people in the world of Christian academics who, in an attempt to explain much of what is unexplainable, theologically drain the Bible of its wonder, its divine inspiration, and snobbishly regard anyone who takes God at His Word as uneducated and gullible. Satan knows that each of us secretly fears proving stupid. I'll keep repeating this as long as God gives me volume: If in our pursuit of higher knowledge God seems to get smaller, we are being deceived. I believe in loving God with our minds as well as our hearts. I am committed to growing in biblical scholarship, but if I reduce the Bible to only the facts that demand no faith, I've depreciated it to the level of any other religious text. Never let anyone—no matter how smart or impressive—talk you out of thinking huge things about God and His Word!

Actively dialogue with God as you read His Word. God is talking to you through His Word, so start talking back! My attentiveness to what God is saying is greatly increased when I read a portion aloud. In my daily reading, I find that I absorb more when I read less but really attempt to meditate on the smaller portion. I try reading it and emphasizing different phrases, then I respond aloud to Him. I might ask Him what a portion means then look for Him to give me insight in coming days or weeks through various sources. I might also comment on what I feel like He's saying to me personally, or I'll use the portion as a guide for intercession as I pray for others. I am dreadfully far from having all the answers, but these practices help me keep a lively attitude toward my time with God in His Word.

If you have some approaches that work, share them with others!

I find that multitudes of believers know *what* they are supposed to be doing, but they are at a loss to know *how* to do them effectively and fervently.

Never forget that all Scripture is God-breathed. When God exhales, beloved, inhale!

—*Beth Moore*

"I have a verse for you"

"The law of the LORD is perfect, restoring the soul. The testimony of the LORD is sure, making wise the simple." Psalm 19:7 (NASB)

We were sitting on the dirt floor of a grass-roofed hut visiting with a 70-year-old chief. In the midst of our laughing and joking he said, "I have a verse from the Koran for you." I had never heard a Muslim say this before.

He read the words carefully in Arabic. Then, with great pride, he told how he had studied the Koran for most of his life and could now read it. Commending him on his reading, I asked, "What does the verse mean?" He replied, "I only read it; I cannot translate it."

I was shocked. How could he give me a verse that he did not understand and that I could not possibly understand? What would be the benefit of reading something without understanding it? I read Scripture to understand God and His will for my life. How could someone work that hard to learn Arabic without understanding it?

After this encounter, God led me to handwrite Genesis 3 in Pular (poo-LAR), but using the Arabic alphabet. I gave it to the chief. He insisted that we read it then. As we read, I had to stop him frequently to talk about the meaning and to be sure he was not just pronouncing the words.

Later, I went back with the express intent to give him the rest of Genesis. I did not have to offer, for he said, "What you left was not enough; it was only part of the story." I was glad to give him more of God's Word.

Am I as hungry for the Word as this man?

—ROBERT AND RHONDA, WEST AFRICA

Father, YOUR VERY WORDS HAVE BEEN GIVEN TO ME THAT I MIGHT KNOW YOU AND YOUR WILL FOR MY LIFE. LET ME NEVER READ YOUR WORD AS ROUTINE AND WITHOUT UNDERSTANDING, BUT ALLOW IT TO PENETRATE MY HEART AND CHANGE ME. *Amen.*

Ancient story still speaks

"Yet faith comes from listening to this message of good news—the Good News about Christ." Romans 10:17 (NLT)

It started out as a friendly conversation in the central plaza of Santa Cruz (SAHN-tah cruise). The man selling the weavings was tired from carrying the bundle of goods all day. With relief, he set down the heavy bundle. Surprise was on his face when I greeted him in Quechua (KET-chew-ah), an ancient language spoken by 3 million Bolivians but by few foreigners. That meeting led to a relationship, not just between a Quechua man and a missionary family, but between the Quechua man and Jesus.

We met when he would come to the city to sell weavings made by his wife and sisters. On each visit, I gave him cassettes of the stories from God's Word, spoken in Quechua. He learned that God is in control. He learned of God's mercy and love. Our friend would then take the tapes to his village far up in the Andes (AN-dees) Mountains. "We've never heard this in Quechua," he told us. Although the name of Jesus arrived in Bolivia hundreds of years ago with the conquistadors, the message did not arrive in the heart language of the people.

One day, he told me that he and his family wanted to believe and be baptized. We had not yet shared the New Testament tapes, so I offered to show him the *JESUS* film in Quechua. After watching the video, he said, "Now, I understand the whole story. I want to follow Jesus."

No matter who we are, where we live or what language we speak God's Word is relevant to our lives.

—DANETTE, SOUTH AMERICA

Your Word is powerful, Father. I PRAY THAT THIS MAN WILL NOT JUST BE A BEARER OF BUNDLES OF WEAVINGS, BUT A BEARER OF THE GOOD NEWS TO THE QUECHUA PEOPLE GROUP. MAY MANY COME TO KNOW THE LORD IN THESE REMOTE PLACES IN THE ANDES MOUNTAINS. *Amen.*

God's stories bring light

"We did not follow cleverly invented stories when we told you about the power and coming of our Lord Jesus Christ, but we were eyewitnesses of his majesty."
2 Peter 1:16 (NIV)

What have you done with the stories of Jesus that you learned as a child? In a South Asian country, a group of young, aspiring pastors and students gathered to learn Bible stories and how to use them to witness.

For five days the group listened to the stories being told chronologically. After the first two days, the trainees had to select one of the stories to tell before the group. Some of the more literate ones "preached" their stories. With difficulty, others told theirs.

In the group was a young woman who was obviously illiterate. She had no Bible to refer to, and she made no notes, only listened intently all week. Her telling of an Old Testament story by memory was one of the best done in the group.

After the stories of Jesus were taught, the young lady did an excellent job again. As the training session drew to a close, the trainees were challenged to be good stewards of the Word. They made promises regarding what they would do with the learned Bible stories. The young lady said, "I am going to return to my village and tell the people all that I have heard this week."

How many times do we tell the simple stories of the Bible or share what we learn from a sermon with others? Have the stories become so routine that we forget the excitement of hearing for the first time? May we never take the Word of God for granted.

—A RETIRED BIBLE STORYTELLER, PACIFIC RIM

Father, YOUR WORD IS A LAMP UNTO MY FEET AND A LIGHT UNTO MY PATH. MAY I NEVER TAKE IT FOR GRANTED. MAY MANY HEAR YOUR WORD BY THE BIBLE STORYING METHOD. *Amen.*

Bible verses

"For the word of God is full of living power. It is sharper than the sharpest knife, cutting swift and deep into our innermost thoughts and desires. It exposes us for what we really are." Hebrews 4:12 (NLT)

He was a teacher, a Christian teacher. One of his Hindu students had a sister who was sick. The teacher asked his student if he could visit his sister in the hospital. He told him yes. The teacher visited her and prayed for her, and she got well.

The short visit began a relationship with this high-caste Brahmin family. The teacher began to regularly visit in the home. The father of these two children welcomed the teacher, even though he knew that the teacher was a Christian.

One day, the teacher asked the father if he could give him a wall calendar. He explained that the calendar had a scripture on it. The father accepted the calendar and hung it on his wall. One scripture verse was on it. The father was aware of this verse day after day and month after month. Slowly, God's Holy Spirit did His work. The words on the calendar began to penetrate the father's heart. The message began to make sense to this man, who had been a Hindu all of his life. One day, the father was convicted of his sin, and he became a believer in Jesus.

Now this new believer has a fellowship of believers meeting in his home. He regularly attends training sessions to help him be a good leader.

The Word of God is true. Just one verse can bring light into the dark Hindu world of false teachings.

What verse is God using in your life? What verse will you share with a friend?

—R. AND K.C., SOUTH ASIA

Father, YOUR WORD IS TRUTH. IT PENETRATES TO THE HEART. THANK YOU THAT YOUR WORD IS HAVING A POWERFUL INFLUENCE ON HINDU FOLLOWERS. SHOW ME A VERSE TODAY TO SHARE WITH A FRIEND. *Amen.*

A miraculous repair

"The things that are impossible with people are possible with God."
Luke 18:27 (NASB)

The audiocassette player in the old car was broken, but we still had a couple of music tapes and a copy of "God's Story," an audiotape presenting the gospel in Arabic, between the seats. As we journeyed toward the capital city, the armed soldier with his machine gun on his lap leaned forward from the backseat and insisted that we play some music. Our Arabic was limited, so we demonstrated the problem by placing a music tape into the player. When the cassette did not work, he continued to insist that we try another tape. To appease him, we put in the tape of "God's Story." Imagine our surprise when the tape miraculously played!

As we traveled toward our destination, the soldier acknowledged his delight as he listened, and we prayed. He heard Bible stories of creation, Noah and the Flood, Abraham, the Hebrew Exodus and all the events leading up to the birth of Jesus. As we observed his facial expressions in our mirror, we were able to catch his occasional affirmative nod. The soldier eventually placed the machine gun on the seat beside him.

When the first side finished playing and we turned the tape over, the cassette player stopped working. However, we approached our destination at the same time. The soldier thanked us for the ride, took his machine gun and got out of the car. We believe that God planted some seeds in this young man's heart. We have never seen that soldier again, but we rejoice in knowing that all things are possible with God.

—A. AND A., NORTHERN AFRICA AND THE MIDDLE EAST

You are the God of possibilities, AND I THANK YOU FOR ALLOWING THIS YOUNG SOLDIER TO HEAR YOUR WORD. PUT OTHER CHRISTIANS IN HIS PATH AS YOU CONTINUE TO CALL HIM TO SALVATION. USE TAPES OF BIBLE STORIES TO SPEAK TO OTHERS ACROSS THE WORLD TODAY. *Amen.*

"I have not heard this"

"For everything that was written in the past was written to teach us, so that through endurance and the encouragement of the Scriptures we might have hope." Romans 15:4 (NIV)

Meseret (MESS-uh-ret) is a widowed woman with seven children. She works hard and rests little, like many women in the Horn of Africa. Her life is filled with hand-washing clothes, grinding grain, collecting firewood and caring for her children. But despite these harsh realities, Meseret sustains a beautiful smile and a love for others.

She follows a religion where there is no assurance of salvation. Perhaps if she is good enough, if she gives enough money to the poor, if she follows the rules, if she fasts properly, then she *might* earn passage to heaven. She adheres to a faith that emphasizes rituals and traditions, rather than a personal relationship. She does not know the experience of talking with Jesus, for her religion does not acknowledge that Christ made a way to come into the very presence of God. Meseret loves the Bible as a symbol, but she does not know what the Word of God says. She often listens to religious leaders read the Bible in a language she doesn't understand.

Meseret agreed to listen to the stories of the Bible. We first listened to the creation story, and she began to weep. She exclaimed, "I have never heard this before. God is the Creator; He is so good." Scripture had come alive for Meseret, and I was reminded again of the Word's power.

God's Word is not to be treated lightly just because we have heard it so often. Applying what we read or hear is the only way it is alive in us.

—J.L., NORTHERN AFRICA AND THE MIDDLE EAST

Father, MAKE THE WORD ALIVE TO ME TODAY AS I MEDITATE UPON IT, AND MAY I BE CHANGED AS A RESULT. USE YOUR MIGHTY WORD IN THE LIFE OF MESERET AND PEOPLE LIKE HER IN NORTHERN AFRICA AND THE MIDDLE EAST. *Amen.*

Is all religion the same?

"We know also that the Son of God has come and has given us understanding, so that we may know him who is true. And we are in him who is true—even in his Son Jesus Christ. He is the true God and eternal life." 1 John 5:20 (NIV)

It's 4 a.m. I try to ignore the call to prayer coming from the local mosque. I manage to doze for a while, but I hear little bells ringing and smell the pungent incense drifting through the apartment window next door. The Hindu mother is doing her morning prayer, called a *puja* (POO-jah).

As I walk to the market, I notice three shop owners with turbans wrapped on their heads, each a different color. These men are Sikhs (seeks), members of a prevalent religion in India. When home again, the doorbell rings. The neighbor girl shyly smiles as she brings me food offerings made to her gods. In Hindu culture, this is an extreme compliment. The little girl extends her hand that holds tiny pieces of coconut, rice, nuts and grain wrapped in newspaper. I say, "Thank you, but I cannot eat now." She beams and runs away.

Finally, I go to a new acquaintance's house for dinner. Over dinner, she says that she was "born" a Christian. The concept of being born into a religion without personal decision is common. I share scriptures about how one must make a choice to follow Christ.

The encounters illustrate the vast array of religious beliefs. Yet the most common statement heard is, "It's all the same anyway. I can pray to Jesus or Allah or Ganesh. They are all just incarnations of the same thing." The deception is real.

As I threw away the gifts of food offered to idols, I realized that the Word is what will make a difference in this hard place.

—C., SOUTH ASIA

Father, MAY THE WORD GUIDE WORKERS IN SOUTH ASIA SO THAT THEY WILL KNOW WHEN AND HOW TO PRESENT IT. PREPARE AND SOFTEN HEARTS SO THAT THE SOWING OF THE WORD WILL TAKE ROOT, GROW AND PRODUCE MUCH FRUIT. I ASK THAT YOU WOULD BRING A GREAT HARVEST TO NORTH INDIA. HELP ME TO BE A WITNESS TO OTHERS THAT JESUS IS THE ONLY WAY TO YOU. *Amen.*

Before it's too late

"We proclaim Him, admonishing every man and teaching every man with all wisdom that we may present every man complete in Christ."
Colossians 1:28 (NASB)

God has led our team to saturate our country door-to-door with the Bible. The Bible only has been available in the language of our Muslim people group for three years.

I never know what reaction to expect from the person behind a door. Will the resident be hostile or receptive? On one unusual visit, the occupant came slowly to the door and opened it in the same way. The man was weak, and his skin was darkly tinted yellow, most likely due to liver disease. Compassion and urgency stirred within my spirit.

My partner and I held the story of the only hope for this man. As we gave him the New Testament, I prayed that he would open it and receive the gift that would spare him from an eternity separated from Christ. He was too weak for us to share the gospel with him, but we pointed out areas in the Gospel of John for him to read, praying he would read them.

This experience was a picture of the urgency that Paul spoke about in Colossians 1:28. Men need to be warned so that they might be presented "complete in Christ." Colossians also talks about "redeeming the time" so that we make time count for the gospel (Col. 4:5, NKJV). There are so many heartsick people whom we walk by every day on the streets. My desire is to love them like Christ loves them and never be too busy to share His hope with them. We do not know which one of them might step out into eternity next.

—KIM, CENTRAL AND EASTERN EUROPE

Heavenly Father, I PRAISE YOU THAT YOUR WORD IS BEING TRANSLATED INTO MANY, MANY LANGUAGES. PENETRATE THE HEARTS OF THE LOST WHO READ THE WORD IN THEIR HEART LANGUAGES FOR THE FIRST TIME. I PRAY SPECIFICALLY THAT YOU WILL OPEN THE EYES OF THIS MUSLIM PEOPLE GROUP IN CENTRAL AND EASTERN EUROPE SO THAT THEY MAY UNDERSTAND THE TRUTH. *Amen.*

Open to God, regardless of comfort

"First seek the counsel of the LORD." 1 Kings 22:5b (NIV)

We were at the last town of our journey and were contemplating going home a day early. Our trip had been harsh, and I honestly didn't like the last town.

I was wearing some clean clothes, ones that I had hand-washed and let air-dry for days. Not five minutes of being in that town, a cement block came down from the top of a construction site and landed in a mud pit two feet from me. I was coated in mud but uninjured. When I found a bathroom to clean up, it was equipped with a communal washing barrel full of cold water. I laughed hysterically.

Leaving one day early seemed reasonable. We were supposed to meet with a Christian in this town, but we had an incorrect phone number. Before booking transport, I prayed, "Lord, if there is anything else that You would have us to do or anyone that You would have us meet, please show—" I had not even completed my prayer when a voice asked, "Are you Christian?" Surprised, we turned to meet a young national named Suk (sook), a missionary from the people group we target who also was trying to spread the gospel!

He invited us to go with him to villages in the area. We were able to share Jesus with many. Suk also informed us of other villages closer to where we live. Without this believer, it would have taken much research to locate them.

God is at work. Any Christian with a willing heart can join Him.

—A WORKER IN SOUTH ASIA

Father, I CONFESS THAT I HAVE ALLOWED MY OWN NEEDS OF COMFORT TO PREVENT ME FROM MINISTERING TO OTHERS. I CONFESS THAT "NOT WANTING TO GET INVOLVED" IS A MOTIVATING FACTOR FOR REFUSING TO SEE NEEDS AROUND ME. HELP ME TO SEEK YOUR COUNSEL FOR THE MINISTRY THAT YOU DESIRE FOR ME TO DO. BRING THE GOSPEL TO THIS UNREACHED PEOPLE GROUP IN SOUTH ASIA. *Amen.*

Good news in the mail

"Already he who reaps is receiving wages and is gathering fruit for life eternal; so that he who sows and he who reaps may rejoice together. For in this case the saying is true, 'One sows and another reaps.' I sent you to reap that for which you have not labored; others have labored and you have entered into their labor."
John 4:36–38 (NASB)

Often, as seed sowers, we do not see immediate results. Scripture reminds us that at the proper time, we will reap a harvest. It is still a challenge when you long for millions to come to faith in Christ.

On a trip to Taipei's Lung Shan Temple (TIE-pay's lohng SHAN temple) with a group of volunteers, we met a Chinese couple named Jimmy and Sue. They have a home in Taiwan and one in the States. Jimmy had come to consult the local "gods" regarding a health issue that could not be resolved in America.

A volunteer shared the gospel with Jimmy, but he wasn't interested. When offered an English-language Bible, Jimmy said his English was not very good. The volunteer told Jimmy he would send him a Chinese Bible when they returned to the States, which he did. A year later, the volunteer still hadn't heard from Jimmy.

The volunteer returned to Taiwan a year later. We went to Lung Shan Temple, and I asked him if he thought we might encounter Jimmy. He was unsure but felt the need to pray. We didn't find Jimmy.

After the volunteer returned to the States, he received a surprise letter from Jimmy. "I am a born-again, baptized Christian. Thanks for sending the Chinese Bible," he wrote.

Praise God for giving us the privilege of knowing how this story ended. Never give up—God is always at work!

—K.C., EAST ASIA

Father, I PRAY FOR _____ TODAY. GIVE ME PATIENCE TO CONTINUE TO LIFT THIS ONE'S NAME TO YOU FOR SALVATION. GIVE CHRISTIAN WORKERS ENCOURAGEMENT WHEN THEY DON'T SEE FRUIT SO THAT THEY WILL TRUST YOU FOR THE HARVEST. *Amen.*

Alima is introduced to God's Word

"The LORD *is near to the brokenhearted and saves those who are crushed in spirit." Psalm 34:18 (NASB)*

Working in her garden with her daughters, Alima (ah-LEE-mah) realized that she needed seeds. I gave her some when I found out, and frequent visits began. When prayerwalkers were in the village, we prayed with Alima, at her request, that she would have peace in her heart.

Later, Alima's husband died. During her four-month grieving period, the Holy Spirit led me to visit her. I said I would return to teach her God's Word in order to soothe her heart.

The first teaching visit, Alima invited a friend. Grasping truth, both women were excited when they didn't have to pay to hear the stories. They asked if they could hear more every day.

Often it was just Alima, but at times, Souliman (SUE-lee-mahn), an old, partially blind man, would come. Alima usually repeated phrases to the old man and even would add commentary! Both were entranced by the Old Testament prophecies. I asked, "What will He be called?" Alima responded, "Wonderful." Then in her own language, she gave a name for Him that had not been in the prophecies, "The fulfillment [completion] of the promise." Her words were pure revelation, as I had never used that term. Alima then wanted to know when He would come. "We will see," I replied.

Souliman asked if these stories would be told everywhere. I answered that I would tell anyone who wanted to hear.

Alima said, "My heart was crushed, and these stories are repairing it. All I want to do is follow God's path. Everyone needs to know this."

—A WORKER IN WEST AFRICA

Father, YOUR WORD BRINGS HEALING TO BROKEN SPIRITS. CONTINUE TO SOOTHE HEARTS IN WEST AFRICA. *Amen.*

What is your response, Alima?

"For the wages of sin is death, but the gift of God is eternal life in Christ Jesus our Lord." Romans 6:23 (NIV)

Once Alima (ah-LEE-mah) and the old man began hearing the stories of Jesus, they wanted more. Concerning the story of Nicodemus, the concept of "new birth" was as strange for them as it was for Nicodemus. After the parable of the sower, they were perplexed that anyone might *not* choose to follow God's way.

About God's kingdom, I questioned, "Can sinners enter heaven?" "No," they said. "It is as if you are traveling and don't have your identification card. If the police stop you, you will be in trouble. To get into heaven, you must have your card, and sinners don't have a card."

I explained that those who believe in Jesus will enter the kingdom. "We are all sinners," I said, "so if sinners cannot enter heaven, no one can enter."

When the story of Jesus feeding the 5,000 was told, the old man proclaimed that only God could do such a thing. This was a breakthrough, because Muslims believe that no one is equal with God and consider it blasphemy to say that Jesus is God.

Alima's two daughters listened and agreed that Jesus is the Christ. As an illustration, I took an orange out of my pocket and said, "I can believe that this orange is good for me. But until I pick it up and eat it, it does me no good. You believe that Jesus is the Savior. But until you accept Him for yourself as the sacrifice for your sins, you are not saved and the Holy Spirit cannot come into your heart. Will you do this?"

—A WORKER IN WEST AFRICA

Oh Father, REVEAL YOURSELF THROUGH CHRONOLOGICAL BIBLE STORYING IN WEST AFRICA! *Amen.*

Jesus is the only way for Alima

"For behold, darkness will cover the earth and deep darkness the peoples; but the LORD will rise upon you and His glory will appear upon you. Nations will come to your light." Isaiah 60:2–3a (NASB)

Alima (ah-LEE-mah) looked at the old man and said, "Souliman (SUE-lee-mahn), what are we going to do?" The old man said, "The Father and the Son are the same."

"Can't we just accept Christ in our hearts?" asked Alima, afraid of the response from her Muslim family. I was hesitant to answer. The Holy Spirit would have to convict them of trying to hold on to Islam.

Alima, Souliman and her daughters then confessed Christ as Savior. They were still troubled, probably a sign of the genuineness of their conversions and conviction by the Holy Spirit about Islam.

We began discipleship lessons the next day. They seemed somewhat nervous and expected a list of rules. Actually, the list was this: the assurance of being God's child, being free in Christ, praying, loving one another and loving Jesus. By the end of the day, they readily admitted their faith in Christ and expressed joy.

Another day, I asked, "Who walks in darkness?" Alima said, "The Mohammedans. They say we can't know Jesus as Savior. But Jesus is the truth and the only way."

One daughter said, "At night before I fall asleep, I think about Jesus. It is as if He is knocking at the door saying, *Let Me come in and talk to you!*"

I replied, "That is the Holy Spirit. The Bible says that Jesus stands at the door and knocks, and whoever will let Him come in, He will come in and be with him. You have opened the door to your heart, and now He is there to talk to you."

She grinned from ear to ear.

—A WORKER IN WEST AFRICA

Thank You, Father, FOR THE REDEMPTION OF ALIMA'S FAMILY AND FRIEND. ALLOW THEM TO GROW STRONG IN THE FAITH, EVEN WHEN PERSECUTED BY MUSLIMS. BRING YOUR WORD TO MUSLIMS ALL OVER WEST AFRICA SO THEY WILL SEE THAT JESUS IS THE TRUE WAY OF SALVATION. *Amen.*

A love letter

"Today, if you hear his voice, do not harden your hearts." Hebrews 4:7b (NIV)

God has allowed me an opportunity to befriend a young Muslim girl, S., from a Middle Eastern country. I vividly remember the day she said, "I want to spend more time with you, but I don't want to speak of Jesus anymore."

My heart was crushed, but I told her that I would not speak of Christ unless she initiated the conversation. Later, we traveled to visit some Christian friends. Before our arrival, I began feeling ill, so she assisted me to their house. Everyone gathered to comfort me. My friend touched S. on the shoulder and asked if she would like to pray for me in the name of Jesus. In a shaky voice she replied, "Yes, but I don't know how. Please help me."

She began repeating the prayer of my Christian friend, asking Jesus to heal me. Moments later, I felt my strength return, and S. was astonished that our prayers had been answered so quickly.

Later, S. saw a Bible on the table. She glanced through pages. We offered her a Bible in her own language. She accepted and randomly opened to Hebrews 4:7 and read out loud: *"Today, if you hear his voice, do not harden your hearts"* (NIV). We shared that God was speaking to her. Up until that night she would not accept a Bible, but she took a Bible home and she heard God, through His Word, directly speaking to her heart. She began to read His love letter to her.

—CHERYL, WESTERN EUROPE

Heavenly Father, YOU CHOOSE TO DEMONSTRATE YOUR POWER AND LOVE IN MANY WAYS. I THANK YOU THAT YOUR WORDS ARE LIFE AND SPEAK TO THE HEART. USE YOUR WORD IN WESTERN EUROPE TO SHINE TRUTH TO THOSE WITH HARDENED HEARTS. *Amen.*

Taking off orange robes

"So will My word be which goes forth from My mouth; it will not return to Me empty, without accomplishing what I desire, and without succeeding in the matter for which I sent it." Isaiah 55:11 (NASB)

When my wife and I began volunteer service, we were given a vivid demonstration of the truth of this verse. As trained teachers of English as a foreign language, we were requested to teach English to Buddhist monks.

Teaching Buddhists was a new challenge. After visiting a Buddhist monastery, called a *wat* (waht), we discovered that monks are extremely hungry to improve their English, and they love stories.

We made friends with the monks at one particular *wat*. Not knowing how they would react, we chose the Bible as material for the class. We prayed and wrote brief lessons, starting with Genesis.

Our major emphasis was helping them pronounce words correctly in short, easy sentences. We modeled the sentences and answers for the class to hear, such as, "Who made the world?" "God made the world." Then one monk would turn to another monk and ask, "Who made the world?" The monk would answer out loud, "God made the world." Around the entire class, the question and answer traveled. They heard every question and answer many times.

After 134 Bible stories, some monks were ready to take off their orange robes and believe God's Word. One former monk is now teaching an English class and has been able to lead 25 people to Christ.

God uses His Word to accomplish His desires, and He wants Buddhists to come to Him.

—G. AND E., PACIFIC RIM

Lord God, I PRAISE YOU THAT YOUR WORD IS THE POWER OF GOD UNTO SALVATION FOR ME, FOR BUDDHISTS AND FOR ALL PEOPLES. THANK YOU FOR EMPOWERED WITNESSES, TRUTH PROCLAIMED, LIVES TRANSFORMED, SAFFRON ROBES EXCHANGED FOR ROBES OF RIGHTEOUSNESS AND ONGOING EVANGELISM AMONG BUDDHISTS WHO SEEK TRUTH. *Amen.*

Appropriately clothed

"Therefore, as God's chosen people, holy and dearly loved, clothe yourselves with compassion, kindness, humility, gentleness and patience."
Colossians 3:12 (NIV)

As I strode down the sandy road toward my friend's home, I was quoting "compassion, kindness, humility, gentleness and patience." I wanted to wear this "clothing" that God had provided. If I truly and completely clothe myself with His spiritual gifts, what difference will that make in my ministry? How will it affect the evidence of Christ in my life? How will that bring glory to God and cause some of these people to desire truth?

Arriving at my friend's home, her children ran out to greet me. After I was welcomed, I sat on a mat and tea was prepared. Building relationships with people so that they will be willing to accept the good news is important. My friend is poor and shares the best she has with me. I have the riches of heaven at my disposal and desire to share them with her. Physically, I am wearing clothing appropriate to her culture so that I will not offend her people. Spiritually, though, I need to be clothed with compassion, kindness, humility, gentleness and patience so that I can reach her people with His love.

As I see the overwhelming spiritual darkness and poverty, the enemy tempts me to become discouraged. Discouragement's companions of selfishness, impatience and lack of compassion have the potential to become my attire. I must guard myself against wearing these filthy rags rather than the glorious gifts of my Lord. How I wish for God's rich apparel for my friend, her family and her people!

—SHARON, WEST AFRICA

Father, MAY MY CLOTHING ALWAYS BE THAT OF COMPASSION, KINDNESS, HUMILITY, GENTLENESS AND PATIENCE. MAY I NEVER WEAR RAGS, BUT ONLY THE CLOTHES OF RIGHTEOUSNESS. USE MISSIONARIES IN WEST AFRICA TO PROCLAIM THE GOOD NEWS THROUGH THEIR LIFESTYLE AND THEIR WORDS. *Amen.*

A great desire to own the Word

"The law of Your mouth is better to me than thousands of gold and silver pieces."
Psalm 119:72 (NASB)

Fulbe (FULL-bay) Muslims have great respect for their Korans. Korans are wrapped in plastic bags for protection.

When giving a Muslim a portion of the Bible, we show care. If we handle it carelessly, a person might think it's not valuable. So it is with prayer that we ask for payment when we distribute a Bible or portion. There is a Fulbe expression, *"Ko e hoore Kudhol"* (koh HOE-ray KOO-dohl), which literally means "on a blade of grass," implying that whatever one believes is appropriate can be given as payment.

I used this expression to "sell" a copy of Genesis and Exodus to "Andrew." I met Andrew on the road, and he asked, "When are you going to come to my village and teach?" That got my attention. He mentioned that he listened to Christian radio and that he wanted a Bible.

Later, I walked to his village to "sell" him a copy, but he was not home. Afraid to leave the Bible with his wife because of the trouble it might cause him, I returned home with the copy. We finally met, and carrots were exchanged for the Bible.

Andrew's friend asked for one, too. This man could not wait, so he walked five miles to my house. He was a little embarrassed at his great desire to own a copy. Andrew later showed up with his younger brother, who also wanted a copy!

God is at work in the lives of these men through His valuable Word, and one day, He will bring them to Himself.

—ROBERT AND RHONDA, WEST AFRICA

God of the Bible, THANK YOU FOR YOUR PRECIOUS WORD, WHICH IS MORE VALUABLE THAN SILVER OR GOLD! PUT AN INSATIABLE DESIRE FOR YOUR WORD INTO THE HEARTS OF THE FULBE MUSLIMS AND MUSLIMS ALL OVER THE WORLD. HELP ME TO OBEY YOUR WORD AS A TESTIMONY OF MY RESPECT AND LOVE. *Amen.*

Stay tuned next week for...

"We did not follow cleverly invented stories when we told you about the power and coming of our Lord Jesus Christ, but we were eyewitnesses of his majesty."
2 Peter 1:16 (NIV)

We had fun attending the International Storytellers Convention in Jonesboro, Tennessee. One of the best storytellers was a Methodist minister who had won his state's liar's contest five times. He told enthralling tall tales. The tent full of listeners hung on his every word.

It's easy to remember the gist of a story, with its surprising twists and turns. It's the same in the foreign country where we minister. In an oral culture, our friends learn through stories.

Our mobile eye clinic/witnessing team tells true stories to our waiting patients. I love watching their faces as our team tells the stories of the Bible. Will Adam and Eve really eat the forbidden fruit? What will happen to Isaac? Will Abraham really kill this son of his old age, this miracle boy? Will Joseph yield to Potiphar's wife? We always stop at the moment of greatest suspense, so that they will return to hear more. I love to hear them beg to hear the end of the story. I love hearing that they went home and told their relatives the stories.

These stories are not fodder for a liar's contest. These stories are wonderfully true and have great spiritual insight. Our greatest joy is to watch people latch onto the meanings and pray to the great God who made the heavens and the earth rather than calling on other spirits that they feared in the past!

Even though I've heard Bible stories all my life, there's always a new truth that I can apply to my current situation.

—A WORKER IN THE PACIFIC RIM

Father, BECAUSE YOU KNOW US, YOU KNEW THAT WE WOULD LOVE STORIES. THANK YOU FOR THE STORIES OF THE BIBLE THAT SPEAK TO THE HEART. MAY MANY COME TO CHRIST IN THE PACIFIC RIM AS A RESULT OF THE CHRONOLOGICAL BIBLE STORYING METHOD USED BY MISSIONARIES. *Amen.*

A man in a white robe

"I will pour out my Spirit on all people. Your sons and daughters will prophesy,
your young men will see visions, your old men will dream dreams."
Acts 2:17 (NIV)

Did you ever wake up remembering a dream? It's interesting how sometimes we forget our dreams, while other times they seem so real. The Bible speaks of dreams and visions; but in our sophisticated world, many dismiss the idea that God still speaks to us this way!

In South Asia, people are open to the idea of receiving messages from God in dreams. While walking in a rural area of my country with volunteers, an old lady, bent with age, started yelling at us. She was very excited! She told us that a man in a white robe appeared to her in a dream and told her that if she came to the river that day, she would find men who would give her God's Word. She repeatedly yelled, "Are you the men?" We gave her a Bible in her language. She hugged it and said that all her life she had been seeking God's Word and that she would read it to her children and grandchildren. When they knew God's Word, she said, she could then die in peace.

An hour later, we saw a man running toward us. We learned that he also had a dream telling him where he would find strangers that day with God's Word. When we gave him the Bible, he held it up over his head and shouted, "Thank You, God, for sending me Your truth today. May I be worthy to read and understand it."

Does God still speak to people in dreams? God often speaks to unreached people groups by this method.

—A WORKER IN SOUTH ASIA

Dear Lord, SPEAK TO THE LOST OF SOUTH ASIA IN DREAMS, IF THAT IS HOW THEY WILL INITIALLY LISTEN TO YOU. GIVE THEM A DETERMINATION TO SEEK YOUR WORD, AND MAKE YOUR WORD AVAILABLE TO THEM IN THEIR LANGUAGES. *Amen.*

The wonder of the Word

"They're speaking our languages, describing God's mighty works!"
Acts 2:11b (MSG)

A large tree had grown up at the edge of the road, its branches winding outward and down as a result of the prevailing wind of the region. The little shade provided was sufficient to cover one table with rustic benches. The larger branches supported a tarp, which provided shade over one more table. Under the tarp, two Wayuu (WHY-you) women were cooking goat, plantains, yucca and *arepa* (ah-RAY-pah) (cornmeal-based bread). Even with the constant breeze, the heat was demobilizing. The women had cloths tucked into the front of their dresses with which they constantly wiped their faces. The meat and a choice of plantains, yucca or *arepa* were served in a paper bag.

While waiting more than two hours for customs to open for our border crossing, three Wayuu boys left the side-of-the-road restaurant and approached the truck. One of them was trying to sound out the Wayuunaiki (WHY-you-NIE-key) word written on the side. He made out the words *Suwarala kai* (sue-wah-rah-lah kigh-EE), which mean "new day/fresh beginnings." As we talked, I discovered that he went to school and could read Spanish. I showed him a copy of the New Testament in Wayuunaiki and asked him to read the title. His face was a study in concentration as he sounded out the letters. All at once, he listened to what he was saying and understood. His voice grew heavy with emotion, and he softly translated, "The Story of Jesus Christ."

May we all be awed when confronted with God's Word in our own language.

—KAYE, SOUTH AMERICA

Heavenly Father, LET ME SHARE THE AWE OF YOUR WORD TODAY AS YOU SPEAK TO ME THROUGH IT. MAY YOUR WILL BE DONE IN THE TRANSLATION OF THE BIBLE IN EVERY LANGUAGE. *Amen.*

The power of a tract

"All Scripture is Godbreathed and is useful for teaching."
2 Timothy 3:16a (NIV)

At unexpected times, we learn how God uses His Word through tracts. The waitress at the coffee shop says she saves the tracts received and shares them with her mother.

The parking guard at the botanical garden boasts that he now has a sizeable stack that he shares with others, principally young people. However, he gave the tract with a beautiful rosebud as a peace offering to his wife on Mother's Day to make up for an argument and separation. Their relationship has been peaceful these past months. His nephew, a teenage soccer player, swings his brown, muscular legs straight out on a park bench to read his Bible portions.

Edith at the copy shop reads hers at quiet moments at work. Her work companion requests one, too.

At times as a tract is given to one person, notably the bag boys at the grocery or service station, someone else appears alongside expressing a desire for one. A bag boy began smiling when he realized what was in his hand; then with a big grin and a handshake, he said, "I am an evangelical, too."

This week I was not very fast in getting a tract ready for the street boy at the traffic light. I pressed only a coin in his hand. He then looked at me and said, *"y el papelito?"* (ee ehl pah-pah-LEE-toh) ("And the paper?"). He left the car reading his tract!

Praise God, His Word keeps going from one to another like a chain, a tract chain!

—JUDI, SOUTH AMERICA

Heavenly Father, USE CHRISTIAN TRACTS TO TOUCH THE LIVES OF MANY IN EVERY COUNTRY OF THE WORLD. PROVIDE TRANSLATORS FOR TRACTS IN MANY, MANY LANGUAGES. *Amen.*

God's Word cannot be destroyed

"The word of our God stands forever." Isaiah 40:8b (NASB)

Volunteers and a missionary distributed 4,000 Bibles by walking into Muslim villages with backpacks full of the Word.

In one village, a team met "Mamoon" (mah-MOON). They shared the gospel and left 14 Bibles, one given to Mamoon. Then the Christian worker gave Mamoon his address.

Two weeks later, Mamoon showed up at the missionary's house in the capital city. Three local *imams* (EE-mahms) (Muslim pastors) forcibly collected 13 of the Bibles. Before a crowd, they proclaimed that the Bibles were false. They opened to Luke 2 and read, "Mary's husband Joseph." One *imam* said, "We know that Mary was a virgin when she gave birth to the prophet Isa (EE-suh). This Bible says otherwise." The Bibles were burned.

The *imams* found the missing Bible with Mamoon. They demanded his Bible, but Mamoon refused, saying, "Let me read it first. If I find mistakes, I will give it to you." The *imams* petitioned Mamoon's father, but the father said, "Give my son two days. If he hasn't returned it, you are free to do with him as you wish."

Mamoon then fled to the missionary's home. He asked to be taught. During Mamoon's four months of discipleship, his mother wrote a letter advising her son not to return home because she feared for his life.

Mamoon accepted Christ and was baptized. Not heeding warnings, he went back to his village. There a large crowd gathered as he read Luke 2 and explained the story of the virgin birth of Isa (Jesus).

Today, a church exists in Mamoon's village. Two of the *imams* are members of this church. Mamoon has planted another 40 churches, all among Muslims.

—A WORKER IN SOUTH ASIA

Father, THANK YOU THAT YOU UPHOLD ME WITH YOUR HAND IN DIFFICULT TIMES OF PERSECUTION FOR MY FAITH. GIVE MUSLIM-BACKGROUND BELIEVERS STRENGTH TO SHARE YOUR WORD WITH MANY PEOPLE IN THIS DISTRICT OF SOUTH ASIA. *Amen.*

I will fear no evil

"Even though I walk through the valley of the shadow of death, I fear no evil, for You are with me; Your rod and Your staff, they comfort me."
Psalm 23:4 (NASB)

Alone at the house, I heard a quiet entry. As I turned around, an unknown man grabbed me from behind. With a knife, he demanded money. I screamed; he squeezed my windpipe. Holding the knife on me, he walked me through each room, and I gave him whatever money I knew about.

Then he took me into the bedroom, where he attempted to do what every woman fears the most, but God protected and delivered me.

As he let go of me, I told him, "God loves you. He loves you more than anyone. He has plans for your life, plans to give you a future and a hope." He told me to stop talking, but the Holy Spirit compelled me to speak.

Commanding me to stay seated on the bed, he went through the house in search of more money. A Bible was on the bed, and God directed me to Psalm 23. I prayed and read aloud. My quiet times prior to this incident had been centered on God's names. As I sat, I claimed the different facets of His character.

He is El Roi, the God who sees. *"The eyes of the LORD are in every place, watching the evil and the good"* (Prov. 15:3, NASB). He is Jehovah-Shammah, the Lord is there. He is Jehovah-Raah, the Lord is my Shepherd. *"Yea, though I walk through the valley of the shadow of death, I will fear no evil: for thou art with me; thy rod and thy staff they comfort me"* (Ps. 23:4, KJV).

The man left. God is in control.

—SARAH, CENTRAL, EASTERN AND SOUTHERN AFRICA

Father, THANK YOU FOR PROTECTING THIS JOURNEYMAN FROM FURTHER HARM. I PRAY, JEHOVAH-SHAMMAH, THAT YOU WILL PUT HEDGES OF PROTECTION AROUND SINGLE WOMEN MISSIONARIES AS THEY MINISTER IN INTERNATIONAL COUNTRIES. I ASK IN THE NAME OF JESUS THAT SATAN WILL NOT BE ABLE TO TOUCH THEM. *Amen.*

Korans are thrown in the river

"Remove the false way from me, and graciously grant me Your law."
Psalm 119:29 (NASB)

"What is happening to our religion? Muslims in the capital city are throwing their Korans into the dumpsters. In one district, Muslims with their *imam* are throwing their Korans into the river," said a Parliament member addressing an assembly in South Asia, 1999.

Deciding to investigate the second event, a missionary visited the village where Korans were thrown into the river. He quickly confirmed the story. The *imam* (EE-mahm) (Muslim pastor) had declared that the Koran had not benefited them. A church in America quickly replaced the Korans with Bibles.

Islam is experiencing its own reformation. The Koran was only in Arabic until recently, when the king of Saudi Arabia commissioned it to be translated into all languages. As a result, Muslims are reading the Koran and discovering that what they have been taught is not aligned with the Koran. They are also finding verses that exalt Jesus to be the most revered prophet, if not more than a prophet.

The largest church-planting movement among Muslims is taking place in this South Asian country. Church planters are seeing about 160 Muslims baptized daily as a result of showing Jesus from the Koran. Imran 3:42–55 reveals Jesus' incarnation, righteousness, power over disease and death and position at God's side in heaven. The Koran is only being used as a bridge to the gospel. On average, Muslims who discover Jesus as Savior discard their Korans within two weeks and turn completely to the Bible.

The truth of Jesus is being discovered, and God's Word in many languages is revealing the evidence.

—A WORKER IN SOUTH ASIA

Father, ONLY YOU ARE TO BE PRAISED WHEN PEOPLE TRADE THEIR KORANS FOR BIBLES. MAY YOUR WORD BE A LAMP UNTO THEIR FEET. GIVE ME AN OPPORTUNITY TO SHARE YOUR WORD WITH A MUSLIM IN MY COMMUNITY. *Amen.*

Something like an arrow

"For the word of God is living and active. Sharper than any double-edged sword, it penetrates even to dividing soul and spirit, joints and marrow; it judges the thoughts and attitudes of the heart." Hebrews 4:12 (NIV)

Every Friday night, Rogelio (roh-HEL-ee-oh), a master woodcarver from northwestern Mindanao (men-dah-NOW), sat with his friends in a dark corner of the local market. There is not much entertainment in the remote area, so usually he and his *barkada* (bar-KAH-duh), the local term for a group of close friends, would sit around drinking, laughing and telling jokes.

An American man and his Filipino companions began teaching from the Bible. Even though Rogelio was not interested, there was nothing better to do, so he and his *barkada* began to listen. This continued for a number of weeks with little real interest or change in Rogelio. One night, the Bible teacher began to teach the story of the Ten Commandments. Rogelio had carved many idols for people in his area. But when he learned that it was a sin to make and worship idols, he said "something like an arrow" pierced his heart. From that night forward, Rogelio began paying close attention to the teaching.

Several weeks later, Rogelio repented of his sins and prayed to receive Jesus as Lord. In fact, Rogelio was so convicted that he publicly confessed every sin that he knew he had committed!

Hands that once carved idols now create beautiful guitars and life-like figures for Nativity sets. As a leader in the church, Rogelio is training with others to teach the Bible stories that changed his life.

God's Word is a tutor to lead many to Christ.

—DEBBIE, PACIFIC RIM

Heavenly Father, THANK YOU FOR YOUR WORD, WHICH PIERCES THE VERY HEART AND BRINGS CONVICTION. MAY I READ YOUR WORD TODAY WITH ALERTNESS AND REPENT FROM ANY SIN. USE YOUR POWERFUL WORD TO TOUCH THE LIVES OF THE UNSAVED IN THE PACIFIC RIM. *Amen.*

A God of hope

"Now may the God of hope fill you with all joy and peace in believing, so that you will abound in hope by the power of the Holy Spirit." Romans 15:13 (NASB)

After feeling rotten for several days, I went to the doctor to learn that I had amoebas again. He prescribed amoeba medicine and hormones and told me to quit nursing my 11-month-old baby. A few weeks went by without much improvement. There was something strangely familiar about my symptoms. Sure enough, the pregnancy test came back positive.

I walked into my doctor's office and said, "Here's the diagnosis." He read the lab report and gravely looked up. "You should have an abortion. The amoeba medicine and the hormones you took are contraindicated during pregnancy. They could cause serious birth defects."

I made it home before completely falling apart. I picked up my devotional book, and Romans 15:13 jumped right off the page at me. I prayed, "Okay, God, this was a complete surprise, but it wasn't an accident. You have given us this new life. It was Your idea, and we rejoice in it whether there are birth defects or not."

Another voice whispered in my ear, *But what will happen to your ministry if you are tied down by a child who requires a lot of attention?* God's Spirit so completely overwhelmed me in that moment that I replied, "It isn't my ministry. It's God's. If He wants me to use my time taking care of this child, then that's what I have to do."

I returned to my doctor to refuse the abortion and to tell him why. Twenty-four years have passed since that time. Today our daughter, Rebecca, is a short-term missionary.

—HELEN, MIDDLE AMERICA AND THE CARIBBEAN

Heavenly Father, YOU HAVE A PLAN FOR EVERY CHILD IN THE WOMB. THANK YOU THAT REBECCA WAS GIVEN THE OPPORTUNITY TO FULFILL YOUR PLAN. I PRAY FOR MISSIONARIES TODAY WHO ARE EXPECTING A BABY. KEEP THEM HEALTHY, GIVE THEM STRENGTH AND USE THEIR CHILDREN TO OPEN DOORS FOR MINISTRY. HELP ME TO INFLUENCE OTHERS TO GIVE AN UNBORN CHILD A CHANCE TO LIVE. *Amen.*

Muslim meets "angel"

"They were ... destitute, afflicted, ill-treated (men of whom the world was not worthy)." Hebrews 11:37–38a (NASB)

At age 9, Abdul (AB-dool) was sent to the *madrassa* (muh-DRAH-suh), a school for boys, to read and memorize the Koran. He was dedicated but began to have many questions. The first time Abdul questioned the Koran's authority, he was beaten. Nevertheless, he later voiced his concern about the meaning of a passage. This time he was banned from the *madrassa* and sent home disgraced. A note on the *madrassa's* bulletin board stated, "Abdul is a sinner boy, and anyone who talks to him will also be shamed."

Branded with dishonor, the boy's father built a shack for Abdul. For three years no one was allowed to talk, touch or look at him. His mother would bring his meals and slide them through a hole in the door.

One day Abdul drank poison with the intent to die. His mother heard his vomiting and rushed him to the hospital. Not long after his return from the hospital, he again attempted suicide.

At age 13, his solitude was over, but still he was treated as cursed. One afternoon while walking on a road, a foreigner in a rickshaw asked Abdul if he needed a ride. The man actually spoke to *him*. Riding on the rickshaw, Abdul touched the foreigner's arm to see if he was an angel. They rode to the missionary's home. Abdul left with hope in his heart and a New Testament.

Abdul read John 3:17, which said that God did not condemn him. That night he realized that the God of the Bible loved him, and he accepted His grace.

A vibrant evangelist, Abdul now shares God's Word and love.

—A WORKER IN SOUTH ASIA

Father, THANK YOU FOR YOUR WORD, WHICH REVEALS YOUR LOVE, YOUR GRACE AND YOUR WILL. SPEAK YOUR TRUTH INTO MY LIFE TODAY. EMPOWER ME TO SHARE YOUR WORD WITH THE PEOPLE IN MY COMMUNITY. *Amen.*

The not-so-wet Bible

"The grass withers, the flower fades, but the word of our God stands forever."
Isaiah 40:8 (NKJV)

Every week I travel to Bella Esperanza (BAY-yah es-pear-RON-zah) (Beautiful Hope), where a new church is forming. The final obstacle in reaching this community is stepping from rock to rock in order to cross a small river. Doing this at night makes the river crossing more complicated.

One night, the river was flowing swiftly. While crossing, I slipped and fell into the water. The water was not overly deep, so I was fine. However, I dropped my Bible, and it was carried away. I searched the bottom of the river around me but finally gave up.

When I arrived at my destination, dripping wet, I described what had happened. I was certain that my Bible was a pile of mush by then. However, one of the men in the Bible study insisted on going back to find the Bible. The fellow walked out on a log that was about 40 feet downriver from where I fell in and felt around under the water. Feeling something smooth, he pulled it out—it was the Bible! Amazingly, the Bible was only wet on the outside. The inside pages were completely dry!

During the Bible study, the people stared in amazement at the Bible, which had withstood the river. The people repeatedly commented about how God had protected His Word.

Over time, the people in this group accepted Christ as their Savior and are now working to start new churches. They experience the same protection of God, which He once expressed to them through a Bible.

—EDWIN, SOUTH AMERICA

Father God, YOUR WORD IS PRECIOUS AND SPEAKS OF LOVE AND LIFE. MAY MANY STUDY THE BIBLE IN SOUTH AMERICA AS MISSIONARIES GO TO GREAT LENGTHS TO BRING YOUR MESSAGE OF GOOD NEWS. *Amen.*

Overflowing joy

"For the word of God is living and active." Hebrews 4:12a (NIV)

We teach from the Gospel of Mark in our English-as-a-Second-Language classes. Most of the students are Muslim, Catholic, or practice the traditional worship of their ancestors. Even though Mozambicans speak Portuguese, many people want to learn English to improve their job opportunities, so they don't mind that we use the Bible in class. As the students study Scripture to learn grammar and vocabulary, the Holy Spirit works in their hearts. It's exciting as they ask questions about Jesus.

One student, Pedro, belonged to a family that practices folk Islam, a mixture of Islam and traditional African practices, including ancestor worship. Pedro was a good student who was curious about the Bible. Several times, he stayed after class to talk. I gave him some verses to read at home.

One day, Pedro said, "Teacher, I think that Jesus is the only way to have life." He went on to tell me that his family was opposed to him being a believer, but he had decided to give his life to Christ anyway.

Pedro was the first of the English students to come to Christ. He was full of joy! I jokingly named him the "English-school evangelist" because he spent his free time in our little library sharing with any student who came by. Several of them came to know the Lord through Pedro's sharing.

Do you have that same overflowing joy as Pedro? What are you doing with it? The Word of God is living and active and waits to be shared.

—KATIE, CENTRAL, EASTERN AND SOUTHERN AFRICA

Father, MAY I OVERFLOW WITH THE JOY OF THE LORD SO THAT PEOPLE WILL WANT TO KNOW WHY I'M DIFFERENT. LET YOUR WORD FLOW FROM MY MOUTH, AND LET IT PENETRATE THE HEARTS OF UNBELIEVERS AROUND ME. USE ENGLISH CLASSES ACROSS THE WORLD TO BE AN OPPORTUNITY TO SHARE CHRIST. *Amen.*

MARCH V

Prayer

Our emphasis in this month's series of devotionals is prayer. I can't think of a more fitting follow-up to January's emphasis on God's character and February's emphasis on God's Word. If we have little confidence in God's character and His Word, why on earth would we have any confidence in prayer? Confidence in prayer is exactly what I'm praying God will use this entry to help infuse.

In last month's introduction, I shared a scripture I'd like us to reconsider now from a different perspective. First John 5:14–15 reads, "*This is the confidence we have in approaching God: that if we ask anything according to his will, he hears us. And if we know that he hears us—whatever we ask—we know that we have what we asked of him*" (NIV). Reread this verse carefully. What is the specific "confidence"? That God hears us when we pray in His will.

Let's get one obstacle out of the way quickly: our erroneous belief that God's will for us is tighter, narrower, more constrained and certainly more boring than our own. We have allowed the thief of humanism to convince us that God's will is sacrificial at best. God's will for our lives is so much broader than ours that the two are incomparable. He has more planned for us than our eyes have seen, our ears have heard and our minds have ever imagined (1 Cor. 2:9). Yes, God calls us to sacrifice lesser things, but only so that He can make room for greater things. Lasting things. Things that matter, as my grandmother would say, more than "a hill of beans." We can hardly have confidence in prayer if we aren't convinced that His will for our lives exceeds our own.

The specific confidence John tells us we can have in prayer is that God actually hears us. "And if we know that he hears us ...". Dear one, do you know that God hears you? Do you have absolute confidence that your prayers are heard? I fear one reason that much of our praying feels powerless is that we've based it on hope alone. In other words, we hope God hears us, but we aren't really sure. Multitudes surmise that prayer is better than nothing and that if it does happen to work, they'll be glad they did it. Others equate it with little more than positive thinking instead of a pointed petition to the living and listening Creator and Possessor of all.

As Jesus prepared to call Lazarus from the grave, He *"looked up and said, 'Father, I thank you that you have heard me. I knew that you always hear me'"* (John 11:41–42, NIV). Can you imagine how different our prayer lives would be if we "knew that [God] always [hears us]"? What if Christ showed up, robed and crowned, in the chair next to where you have your prayer time and said, "Go right ahead, child. I'm listening"? How differently would you pray? I love the reference in John 11:41 to Christ looking up as He talked to His Father. Christ knew that He was talking to the God of the universe and that all the resources of heaven and earth were at His disposal. That's why He had the confidence to raise the dead!

You might reason that Christ could have confidence that He was heard because He always prayed in God's will. I may be about to say something that almost seems heretical, but I'm going to take the chance of raising eyebrows because I believe Scripture backs it up: Many of us are making God's will harder to find than it is. If we have an active relationship with God and expose our hearts and minds fairly regularly to God's Word, our prayers are very often going to fall within the bounds of God's will. John 15:7 lends this support: *"If you remain in me and my words remain in you, ask whatever you wish, and it will be given you"* (NIV). In other words, the words of God work dramatically to conform our desires to the will of God. That's what the Psalmist meant when he told us that if we'd delight ourselves in God, we'd receive the desires of our hearts (Ps. 37:4). The more God overtakes our passions and fills our minds with His words, the more readily we can pray and have what we desire.

Is that old obstacle creeping up in your mind again? Are you thinking how much shorter God's will makes your prayer list? Check out Scripture! God's people prayed about every subject under heaven. Their petitions weren't just religious in nature, nor were they always strictly eternal in significance. Just as many were for here-and-now provisions and immediate earthly challenges. You need look no further than the Psalms to see the limitless categories of prayer that God obviously heard well enough to record them in Holy Writ. David prayed about friendships, enemies, betrayals, fears, passions, needs, wants, aggravations, irritations and disappointments. And God heard every word because each flowed from a heart aflame with Him.

Quit making this thing so hard! Even if you and I don't get our words right, if our hearts are right, God hears them. Do you sincerely have a heart for God? Are you regularly consuming His Word and pursuing an intimate relationship with Him even though none of us can claim to have "arrived" (Phil. 3:13)?

Then pour out your heart to Him. Pray, knowing He hears you! As He holds our hearts, He'll remold their desires more closely to His own, and His will for our lives will start finding us.

—*Beth Moore*

Peace of mind

"You answered me when I called to you; with your strength you strengthened me." Psalm 138:3 (GNT)

When my family felt called to Africa, I had misgivings. Images of starving children, deadly snakes, spiders and incurable diseases most concerned me. As God gently wooed us toward the African soil, I realized that most of my fears were unfounded and that with every possible danger, there was plenty of prevention available.

To combat malaria, we hung mosquito nets above all our beds. The net is nothing more than a giant piece of mesh draped from ceiling to floor over one's sleeping quarters. It's thin, delicate and not so attractive. Yet I want that net hanging over my head on hot African nights for peace of mind.

As much faith as I put in that gossamer sheet, I know it can't protect me against the real dangers in the dark. The Word of God plainly states that our struggle is not against flesh and blood, but against spiritual forces of wickedness (Eph. 6:12). As badly as I want to protect my children, true peace of mind doesn't come from a mesh curtain, but from prayer. The greatest insurance available is the mighty power tucked away in a praying heart. While we are not guaranteed the results we want, we are guaranteed something even greater: God's undivided attention, God's unyielding power and God's perfect will displayed right before our eyes.

I trust my mosquito net on still African nights, because in my heart I believe it is the safest guard against disease. But the true reason I rest peacefully is that I know my nightly pillow prayers are the greatest covering.

—KELLEY, CENTRAL, EASTERN AND SOUTHERN AFRICA

Dear Lord, THANK YOU THAT PROTECTION FOR MY FAMILY AND LOVED ONES COMES FROM YOU. HELP ME TO TRUST YOU IN ALL THINGS, AND GIVE ME GRACE TO FACE DIFFICULTIES. *Amen.*

Turning a heart

"I planted, Apollos watered, but God was causing the growth."
1 Corinthians 3:6 (NASB)

Upon arriving for our assignment, we enrolled our four children in the local primary school. Each day we passed mums, dads and grans escorting their children to and from school. Smiles and greetings were scarce as families scurried about their daily routines. We soon realized the best way to enter any new culture was by actively loving their children.

A few mothers soon joined me weekly to pray for the school, instructors and the head teacher. Soon we saw the need for an after-school Bible club. Surprisingly, a few national believers discouraged the idea. Many knew the head teacher's harsh views toward Christianity.

Following much prayer, I met with this teacher. My proposal for an extracurricular club was heard favorably. Upon my departure, she exclaimed that she had been prepared to deny our request but had a change of heart. Days later, a Christian teacher and the school secretary offered to assist with the club. Both ladies had been praying for three years that God would increase His presence in their school. We knew God had answered prayers.

God's presence has settled on the school every Thursday afternoon for the past three years. More than 80 students have heard, "Jesus saves." Though they are in the land of great Christian heritage, these students aren't aware of a personal God who loves them. Ten percent of these students recently committed their lives to Him, following a *JESUS* film viewing.

Prayer is the first step of any project, any encounter or any ministry.

—LISA, WESTERN EUROPE

Father, THANK YOU FOR THE PRAYERS THAT CHANGED THIS SCHOOL. I PRAY THAT YOU WILL CAUSE THE SPIRITUAL GROWTH FOR THESE YOUNG STUDENTS WHO HAVE NOW PROFESSED CHRIST. BRING THE UNITED KINGDOM BACK TO ITS SPIRITUAL HERITAGE SO THAT THE NEXT GENERATION CAN KNOW YOU PERSONALLY. *Amen.*

God's heart revealed in a life of prayer

"Devote yourselves to prayer, being watchful and thankful."
Colossians 4:2 (NIV)

As a two-year worker in India, I find that God continually reveals my need to have a life of prayer. My partner and I spent a week visiting a remote village and praying for every family. Traveling up and down the steep terrain in monsoon season often left us in the mud. Out of desperation, I prayed that God would keep our feet from slipping. Neither of us slipped the rest of that week. He showed me that I should *pray through even the small things.*

With this insignificant prayer answered, I decided to pray for my asthmatic partner's lungs. Hiking was hard enough without breathing difficulties. Upon reaching another village, my astonished partner said that she didn't use her inhaler once during our climb. God showed me that I should *always expect a response.*

At the end of our stay in this village, we were exhausted. I prayed that God would bring someone to pray for us. At the first house we visited, God not only led someone to pray for us, but He gave a word to us through a believer. She told us to continue to travel to remote villages to share the gospel without fear because many would be saved. Through this He showed me that I should *never be afraid to pray big.*

Pray through even the small things, for He governs all aspects of our lives; *pray always expecting a response,* for He answers; and finally, *never be afraid to pray big,* for He displays His awesome power.

—A WORKER IN SOUTH ASIA

Father, THANK YOU FOR THE AWESOME PRIVILEGE OF PRAYER. THE LESSONS LEARNED BY THIS MISSIONARY ARE TRUE, ALTHOUGH MY ACTIONS DON'T ALWAYS REINFORCE THESE TRUTHS. I PRAY ABOUT _____, AN INSIGNIFICANT THING THAT NEEDS YOUR GUIDANCE. *Amen.*

Joy in prayer

"Even those I will bring to My holy mountain, and make them joyful in My house of prayer." Isaiah 56:7a (NASB)

Prayer, especially intercession, was not something I equated with joy. Yet God promises to make me joyful in prayer. Four years ago, He graciously showed me what I had been missing.

I was aware of the faithlessness of my prayer life. The redemption of the people around me seemed impossible! I'd pray consistently for a week and then drop off into complacency for a month. It was certainly *not* joyful.

What I didn't recognize is that intercessory prayer is a battlefield. Living in this large city where a physical battlefield rages, I repeatedly charged out into this spiritual war zone unarmed. I'd stagger back shortly afterward, wounded and weary. Finally, I prayed that God would train my hands for spiritual warfare.

There's only one *offensive* weapon in the armor of God—His Word. As I began to pray Scripture, I knew that I was praying God's will. As a result, I began to win hand-to-hand combat with the enemy. Like any soldier returning victorious from battle, my reward was joy!

God tells us that He will bring us to prayer. Even if I fail to pray with discipline, God persistently invites me to join Him in prayer. I simply need to be faithful to pray whenever He brings prayer-worthy subjects to mind. By building up an arsenal of scriptures in my heart, I can now intercede anytime. This has freed me to a life of praying "without ceasing" (1 Thess. 5:17, NASB).

One of my greatest joys now is praying for seemingly impossible things.

—C.H., NORTHERN AFRICA AND THE MIDDLE EAST

Heavenly Father, TEACH ME MORE ABOUT INTERCESSORY PRAYER. THANK YOU FOR YOUR PERSISTENT INVITATIONS TO JOIN YOU IN PRAYER. THANK YOU FOR ANSWERING THE IMPOSSIBLE, BECAUSE I KNOW THAT ALL THINGS ARE POSSIBLE WITH YOU. *Amen.*

A fast answer to prayer

"I love the LORD, because He hears my voice and my supplications. Because He has inclined His ear to me, therefore I shall call upon Him as long as I live." Psalm 116:1–2 (NASB)

I was scheduled to meet American volunteers for dinner. Planning to take a taxi into town, I left about 15 minutes before the meeting time. As I closed the door behind me, my heart sank as I realized that I had locked my money and keys inside. Walking into town would take 45 minutes, so all I could do was pray for the Lord's help to get there on time.

I jogged my way to the road and heard a sound clamoring behind me. *Whoosh!* An old man riding a motorcycle with a rickety sidecar attached flew past me down the narrow road. Then, for no apparent reason, the man roared to a stop about 20 feet in front of me. He turned in his seat, looked me straight in the eyes and waved for me to come.

My heart pounding, I heard him shout, "Where do you want to go?"

"I don't have any money," I shouted back, fairly sure he would drive off.

The driver gave me a toothless grin and replied, "No problem. Where do you want to go?"

I told him my destination, and the man pointed at his empty sidecar. I hopped onto the little seat and white-knuckled the handle as the man took off toward town. Ten minutes later, we arrived in town. As I rushed to the meeting place, the team was walking up. I couldn't stop smiling the entire evening, thankful to serve a real God who hears and answers even our smallest requests.

—A WORKER IN EAST ASIA

Father, THANK YOU THAT YOU HEAR AND ANSWER OUR SMALLEST, MOST INSIGNIFICANT REQUESTS. YOU ARE TRULY A GOD WHO CARES FOR OUR EVERY NEED. PROVIDE THE SMALL NEEDS OF WORKERS TODAY AS THEY SEEK YOU FOR HELP. *Amen.*

Breakdown

"And I want you to know this, dear brothers: Everything that has happened to me here has been a great boost in getting out the Good News concerning Christ."
Philippians 1:12 (TLB)

It isn't unusual for us to travel more than 100 miles across rugged roads in one day. Sometimes we are in areas where there are no roads, just a walking path. It's a miracle that we don't have more truck problems than we do. But when a breakdown does happen, it causes quite a stir in our lives.

One day, I was traveling to some smaller villages when the truck broke down. I had a truck full of students, and everyone had his or her own idea on what the problem was. Nothing we "fiddled" with seemed to work. That's when I finally decided it was time to pray. We asked God to help us.

Not more than five minutes later, a man walked out of nowhere. He stopped along the path to see what our problem was. We found out that he was a mechanic from the capital city, Lusaka. I let out a resounding "Praise God!" as he looked at the truck.

As the mechanic worked, I learned more about him and began sharing the gospel. By the time the truck was repaired, our personal mechanic had accepted Jesus into his life.

We piled back in the truck and went on our way. The students kept talking about the breakdown and mentioning how sorry they were about the whole thing. I turned to them and said, "God allowed this to happen so that this mechanic would come to hear about Jesus."

Situations happen all the time—what do we do with them?

—MIKE, CENTRAL, EASTERN AND SOUTHERN AFRICA

Heavenly Father, HELP ME TO SEE WHAT I ENCOUNTER TODAY AS OPPORTUNITIES TO GROW AND TO SERVE YOU. PUT MISSIONARIES IN THE PATHS OF THOSE WHO NEED YOU. THANK YOU, LORD, THAT YOU GLORIFY YOURSELF THROUGH SITUATIONS THAT WE DON'T EXPECT. *Amen.*

I'll pray about it!

"And whoever welcomes a little child like this in my name welcomes me."
Matthew 18:5 (NIV)

A colleague suggested that I start a children's ministry. I said, "I'll pray about it," but I didn't want to do it. I had ideas of what I could do for God, but none included children. My two homeschoolers kept me busy enough!

After several months, I realized I was putting limits on God. Did I want to do His will? Or did I want Him to bless *my* ideas? Finally, I prayed, "I'll do *whatever* You want."

Soon, four neighborhood girls asked me to teach them English. I taught a few simple phrases. They learned easily and wanted more. Thinking their Muslim parents couldn't argue about the song "God Is So Good," I sang it for them. They quickly memorized the words and tune. Then they exclaimed, "We want you to teach us *all* the time!" I agreed that they could come to my house for another lesson.

Terrified, I planned a simple English lesson, but I also prepared a Bible story in their language. I didn't want to teach English without somehow drawing them to Jesus. Would parents complain and say I was trying to "Christianize" their children? Would we get in trouble with the local government?

I prayed, but I still felt unsure. Finally, God let me know that I was following His desire. Accented voices began singing "God Is So Good" in front of our home. English club became a regular class for children. I didn't want to do it, but God changed my heart.

—M., PACIFIC RIM

Father, FORGIVE ME WHEN I FOLLOW MY OWN PLANS RATHER THAN SEEKING YOU FOR YOUR WILL. HELP MISSIONARIES TO BE SENSITIVE TO YOUR GUIDANCE IN MINISTRY SO THAT THEY WILL JOIN YOU WHERE YOU'RE WORKING. *Amen.*

Kidnapped!

"The LORD is my light and my salvation—whom shall I fear? The LORD is the stronghold of my life—of whom shall I be afraid?" Psalm 27:1 (NIV)

After several months in language school, we drove to a neighboring country to visit our future home. A few hours into our journey, a car occupied by four men brandishing an automatic rifle and a pistol pulled us over. Three of them got into our car, forcing us into the backseat.

Our four children were between 3 months and 9 years old. The two oldest were terrified, but they calmed down as their father spoke with them. I grabbed the baby out of her car seat on my way to the back of the car. She and our 3-year-old son napped almost the entire time. He even snuggled up next to one of the hijackers!

My mind was reeling as I considered all that could happen. I experienced a new understanding of praying "without ceasing" (1 Thess. 5:17, NASB). God gradually calmed my frantic thoughts as I pleaded with Him to spare us. His peace pervaded our hearts, and I finally came to the conclusion that if I had to die, I wanted Him to be glorified somehow.

However, God saw fit to end the event in a different way. After two hours, the men drove us a mile off the road, took some of our things, let the air out of a tire and left us. How we thank God! They only took one of our two spare tires, so after changing the flat, we were able to go back home.

We praise Him for protecting us. Truly He is our light, our defense and our salvation.

—CARA, CENTRAL, EASTERN AND SOUTHERN AFRICA

Father, YOUR WORD SAYS, "THE RIGHTEOUS CRY AND THE LORD HEARS AND DELIVERS THEM OUT OF ALL THEIR TROUBLES" (PS. 34:17, NASB). THANK YOU THAT YOU PROTECTED THIS FAMILY. I PRAY THAT YOU WILL WATCH OVER MISSIONARIES ALL OVER THE WORLD TODAY. PROTECT THEM FROM THE EVIL ONE. GIVE THEM PEACE AND SAFETY. *Amen.*

"I guess God speaks Japanese"

"You are the light of the world." Matthew 5:14a (NASB)

Our family was moving to another city in Japan. We had hoped that our friends, a Japanese Christian couple, would continue the ministry started in Nagasaki (NAH-gah-SAH-kee), but they were afraid of losing their apartment because of their faith.

That night, our usually cheerful newborn couldn't sleep. Each time she woke, I cried out desperately, "Lord, why is Bethany waking up? And while I'm at it, Lord, won't You please give my friend a dream that convinces her to open her home for You? That her husband can lead this group? Oh Father, speak to her!" Without my knowledge, my sleepless husband was praying the same.

The next morning, my friend called and said that she had a dream. "There was something written on the ground in Japanese. It said Matthew 5 and Ga-something. I guess God speaks Japanese," she said.

When the husband returned from work, this couple read Matthew 5 and Ga-something (Galatians!). Paul said in Galatians 1:10 that if he were still seeking the approval of men, he wouldn't be a servant of Christ. And the Sermon on the Mount, found in Matthew 5, touched their hearts about being leaders of the Bible study.

Today, despite relentless attacks from the enemy, this couple's ministry is much stronger than ours ever was in Nagasaki. They have never lost a student, their apartment or a friend. When this couple was afraid of what man might do to them due to their faith, God assured them that He was with them no matter the consequences.

—KATHY, PACIFIC RIM

Lord, I PRAISE YOU THAT IN THE DARK NIGHT OF OUR FEARS, YOU OVERCOME OUR DOUBT. THANK YOU FOR HONORING THE PRAYERS OF YOUR PEOPLE AND CONFIRMING THE PROMISES OF YOUR WORD TO EMPOWER OBEDIENT SERVANTS IN JAPAN WHO ABANDON ALL TO FOLLOW YOU. *Amen.*

Divine intervention

"So I tell you to believe that you have received the things you ask for in prayer, and God will give them to you." Mark 11:24 (NCV)

We live in a gateway city of Europe where immigrants and refugees come to begin a new life. Many come from lands where they have had no religious freedom. Some come to study or to work; others are fleeing persecution. In areas where we see satellite dishes on buildings, we will find a diversity of people from other lands. We prayerwalk these areas regularly, asking God to show us a person of peace, someone in need, or a place where we can minister.

We felt led to prayerwalk in a certain community. As we walked, we prayed that God would lead us to a person searching for Him.

The temperature grew colder, the wind blew harder and it began to rain. We continued to walk because we were still waiting for God to show us the person who needed Him. Not many people were out, because of the weather.

Then we saw a man who was picking up clothing for the Red Cross. While talking with him, he told us that he was searching for God. God answered our prayers! We told this man that our meeting was no co-incidence, but rather God's divine intervention. When we offered to study God's Word with him, he agreed.

A few days later, we met for our first Bible study. His search for God continues, and each day he moves a step closer to knowing God personally.

Sometimes we are so surprised when God answers our prayers, yet He delights in giving us the desires of our hearts.

—J.J., WESTERN EUROPE

Thank You, LORD, FOR KEEPING MISSIONARIES FAITHFUL TO PRAY AND WALK THE AREAS YOU INDICATE. THANK YOU FOR ANSWERING THESE PRAYERS. GIVE ME A BURDEN TO PRAY WHILE I WORK THROUGH MY OFFICE, SCHOOL, HOME OR COMMUNITY TODAY. *Amen.*

I'll open the gate for you

"Enter His gates with thanksgiving." Psalm 100:4a (NASB)

Tabay (tuh-BUY) is a beautiful, unreached pueblo in the mountains of Venezuela. Our team had this pueblo on our hearts after one visit. Two groups of volunteers prayed over this town, and everyone wondered what God might be doing.

On an investigative trip around Tabay, we came to a red locked gate meant to keep wanderers like us out. I told my friend, "We need to get through that gate." I was partly referring to the spiritual barrier that the gate represented.

Weeks later, my family traveled to Tabay to prayerwalk. We asked God to guide us. While there, a friendly man approached us with a microphone. He wanted to interview the "strangers" for the radio.

Our new radio friend knew almost everyone in town and was more than willing to introduce us. He even agreed to play some Bible stories on the radio. Then God chose to bless us in an even more special way.

Our radio friend wanted us to meet the president of the local farmers' association. After a 20-minute drive on mountain roads, we came to a red locked gate. It was the very gate I had seen before! Getting out of the car, our new friend simply said, "I'll open the gate for you."

God cleared that path for us to join His work in this area. A Bible study started with the farmers behind that gate, and now the president of the farmers' association, the "gatekeeper," has accepted Jesus.

Gates and doors open by prayer.

—TOM, SOUTH AMERICA

Father God, ACCORDING TO YOUR WORD, WHATEVER WE ASK IN PRAYER, BELIEVING WE HAVE RECEIVED IT, WILL BE OURS. LORD, I PRAISE YOU THAT UNREACHED PEOPLE GROUPS THROUGHOUT THE WORLD ARE BECOMING OPEN AND RESPONDING TO THE GOSPEL BECAUSE OF THE PRAYERS PRAYED IN FAITH FOR THEIR SALVATION. *Amen.*

Breaking the bonds through prayer

"A voice is calling, 'Clear the way for the LORD in the wilderness; make smooth in the desert a highway for our God.'" Isaiah 40:3 (NASB)

"Little Mecca." It beckons people from this vast desert region to search for the power they believe dwells in the ancient shrine.

Imagine yourself as a prayerwalker in this town. You step off the bus, and the air is dry and hot. A woman with a veil draped from her head to her waist walks through the crowds to reach the shrine, where she hopes to be healed of her barrenness. Some of the people you pass are suspicious of you, while others won't make eye contact. Some just look sad. You think of Jesus, the giver of joy; but even if you spoke their language, they would not easily recognize the truth that His name represents.

All of a sudden, several villagers rush toward you. Excitedly, old men, women and shoeless boys and girls gleefully tell the news: A crippled boy has just been healed at the shrine! Yesterday he couldn't walk, but today he runs. And the name of Christ is never mentioned. Why would God allow this witchcraft to be affirmed through a miracle? He speaks quietly to your heart, *This is not the end of the story. It is only the beginning.*

These people are not hopeless. The Lord has brought you here to pray for people who have never heard His name. Your step upon this sand becomes even more determined as you begin your prayerwalk. You are ready to prepare the way of the Lord.

Prayer will change Central Asia—if only you will pray.

—"ELIZABETH CARMICHAEL," CENTRAL ASIA

Dear Father, I DO PRAY FOR THE PEOPLE OF CENTRAL ASIA WHO DO NOT KNOW YOU. I PRAY THAT THE BONDS THAT SATAN HAS FASTENED ON THESE MUSLIMS WILL BE BROKEN. GIVE ME A BURDEN TO REMEMBER THESE WHOM GOD LOVES IN THIS REGION SO THAT I WILL PRAY REGULARLY FOR THEM. *Amen.*

"You have come!"

"By day the LORD went ahead of them in a pillar of cloud to guide them on their way and by night in a pillar of fire to give them light, so that they could travel by day or night." Exodus 13:21 (NIV)

It took seven hours on a hot, smoke-filled bus to find the small town hidden deep within the mountains. God's assignment for us was to prayerwalk in this unreached village.

My co-worker and I began the short trek through the winding narrow roads. Believing that God had gone before us, we trusted Him to direct our steps. We turned into an alley while praying and noticed an elderly lady running toward us. She was speaking to us in the local dialect, exclaiming, "You have come! You have come!" Her face was radiant, and her dark, almond-shaped eyes filled with tears. She embraced us and escorted us to her home.

The unadorned shack provided shelter for four family members, chickens, mice and the family treasure—a pig. While sipping on Chinese tea, we learned that this grandmother was indeed a believer in Christ! She had come to know Him two years prior through relationship with a Christian teacher. Since the teacher's departure, there had been no one to disciple or even fellowship with the grandmother. She had been reading the only portion of Scripture she owned.

For two years she had prayed to the Most High God for a visit from believers. She knew we were the answer to her enduring prayers! All afternoon we prayed, sang, shared Scripture and laughed together. She served us the only thing she had—a piece of watermelon.

God answered the prayers of this believer while answering our prayers that He would guide us.

—S.H., EAST ASIA

Father, THANK YOU FOR YOUR PROMISE THAT YOU ARE WITH ME ALWAYS. I PRAISE YOU, EMMANUEL, "GOD WITH US," THAT YOU HAVE GONE BEFORE ME AND KNOW EXACTLY WHAT I WILL EXPERIENCE ON THE JOURNEY WITH YOU! GIVE ME KINGDOM EYES TO SEE WHERE YOU ARE AT WORK AND A HEART TO OBEY WHEN YOU SPEAK. *Amen.*

Written on His hands

"Can a woman forget her nursing child and have no compassion on the son of her womb? Even these may forget but I will not forget you. Behold I have inscribed you on the palms of My hands." Isaiah 49:15—16a (NASB)

It's about 3 a.m. The death wails from a neighbor's house wake me. Who has died? Is it a baby? Someone we know? About once a week this happens in our village. But so far, it hasn't lost its effect on us.

I begin to pray for the family, as they are inconsolable and without hope. Then I move on to pray for the village and the entire people group, dozing and waking again until morning. I rise with a heaviness of spirit. Later in the day, I sit with this family for a while. They are always a bit surprised to see me, even more surprised that I will eat the roasted grain, drink the little cups of strong black coffee and sit with them on the floor.

These people have become the object of my intercession. My husband and I strategize and agonize over how to get involved in their lives in ways that yield deep relationships. We celebrate little triumphs like spiritual conversations with a friend that lead to talking about Jesus. But we find our greatest hope comes from Scripture. God has said that Jesus' blood has purchased men *"from every tribe and language and people and nation"* (Rev. 5:9, NIV). Some of the people whom we've grown to love and others we don't even know will join in worshiping Jesus in eternity. They *will* come to Him. He knows who they are. Their names are written on His hands.

A God who knows us is the only One to love and serve.

—CANDICE, NORTHERN AFRICA AND THE MIDDLE EAST

Heavenly Father, YOU TRULY ARE THE ONLY ONE WHO CAN GIVE HOPE TO THOSE WHO HAVE ONLY KNOWN HOPELESSNESS. I PRAY SPECIFICALLY FOR THE UNREACHED PEOPLE GROUPS WHO LIVE IN NORTHERN AFRICA AND THE MIDDLE EAST. BRING DEEP RELATIONSHIPS BETWEEN CHRISTIAN WORKERS AND NATIONALS OF THIS REGION SO THAT THE TRUTH OF YOUR WORD CAN BE SHARED. *Amen.*

Believe and receive

"And all things you ask in prayer, believing, you will receive."
   Matthew 21:22 (NASB)

When our team relocated to Burkina Faso (ber-KEE-no FAH-so), we prayed for God to open doors for His Word. He answered that prayer with a friendship between another woman and me. During one visit, she shared that her family members were religious leaders. They had spread Islam from the Ivory Coast to Burkina Faso, and even into Mali (MAH-lee). Suddenly, I realized she was a missionary, but from a different religion!

At the same time this relationship was blossoming, another team member felt God calling her to live in a nearby village. This was a key village in our strategy, but how could she actually live there?

One day, my new friend told me about her relatives in the village. "What village would that be?" I asked. Sure enough, it was the same village where my teammate felt called. Then the woman said, "Would you like to visit there? My brother is sick, and I would like to see how he's doing."

My teammate went with us so that she would be introduced to the villagers. Several weeks later, a prayerwalking team from the States came. We asked the Father to allow our teammate to move to that village.

As the prayerwalkers, my friend and our teammates sat with my friend's relatives, I felt the strength of silent prayers being said. We were not surprised when our teammate was invited to live in the sick brother's courtyard.

We believed and we received. We are now asking that God will bring the people of this village to Himself.

—DIANE, WEST AFRICA

Father, I PRAY THAT PEOPLE IN THIS VILLAGE AND IN THE SURROUNDING AREA WOULD SEEK TRUTH. MAY THEY HEAR YOUR WORD AND SEE JESUS IN THE CHRISTIAN MISSIONARIES WHO LIVE AMONG THEM. *Amen.*

Living Water discovered

"But whoever drinks of the water that I will give him shall never thirst; but the water that I will give him will become in him a well of water springing up to eternal life." John 4:14 (NASB)

There is usually a clear view of the Himalayas from where I live, although I serve in the flat floodplain of the Ganges (gan-JEES) and the Brahmaputra (BRA-mah-POO-trah) Rivers.

One day after going to the airport, a friend and I decided to drive toward the mountains. I spotted a bridge, so I pulled the car over and we walked to the peak of the bridge. The beauty of the mountains was inspirational. Five waterfalls spilled out the mineral-rich mountain water. I prayed that the "Living Water" would also flow into this land, where more than 90 percent of the people are Muslim.

As we looked over the water and up the Khasi (CAUSE-ee) Hills, we could hear the sounds of a bazaar in a small town below reached only by ferry. My heart was filled with compassion, and I prayed that He would bless the people with the knowledge of Jesus.

Within a month, the national evangelist working with our team shared some exciting news about two Muslim religious experts whom he recently led to the Lord. The two lived in different villages but became friends as they both sought "real" truth. They would meet halfway between their villages once a week in a mosque located in the same small ferry town beneath the bridge. God is good! One of these men is ready to spread the gospel, even if it brings persecution.

God invited me to pray that day on the bridge for the people below, and I never dreamed that I would see what He had already begun.

—E.M., SOUTH ASIA

Father, MAY THE COUNTRY OF BANGLADESH DRINK LIVING WATER THROUGH YOUR SON JESUS. MAY YOU USE NATIONALS TO SPREAD TRUTH TO THE MANY MUSLIMS AROUND THEM. REMIND ME TO PRAY OFTEN FOR THE SPIRITUAL CONDITION OF THIS LAND THIRSTY FOR TRUTH. *Amen.*

Volunteers and prayer make a difference

"Then you will call upon Me and come and pray to Me, and I will listen to you."
Jeremiah 29:12 (NASB)

There are about 5,000 Marense (muh-RON-say) people in Burkina Faso (ber-KEE-no FAH-so). A few years ago, a missionary couple heard that the Marense were totally without the gospel. Needing help, the couple invited college students to go from village to village to prayer-walk and to lay the groundwork for what was to come.

Later that year, two-year missionaries moved into Marense villages to live primitively. These young people faced these living conditions with excitement and enthusiasm, and they began to learn the Marense language and culture. As they progressed with the language, they began to tell Bible stories, beginning with the Old Testament and chronologically working their way through the Bible. The Marense people adopted them, making them a part of their families and village life. They attended weddings and funerals, walked to the market and used opportunities to share their faith with the people.

The next summer, 100 volunteers and 25 summer missionaries worked with the young adults to share Christ with 95 percent of the Marense. Through drama, music, the *JESUS* film and sports events, the gospel was presented. As a result, 50 of the Marense came into the kingdom of God. Now these new believers are walking miles to surrounding villages to be witnesses to their own people.

College students called on the name of the Lord for a people group they had never seen. Prayer broke the hard ground of this land so that those who followed would be able to plant the seeds and see God reap the harvest.

—TIFFANY, WEST AFRICA

Father, I PRAY FOR THE MARENSE AND OTHER PEOPLE GROUPS OF BURKINA FASO TO HEAR THE GOSPEL THROUGH VOLUNTEERS AND TWO-YEAR MISSIONARIES. MAY THERE BE A GREAT HARVEST IN THIS AREA. RAISE UP VOLUNTEERS TO SPEND TWO WEEKS IN AREAS THAT ARE LOST, SO THAT THE GOSPEL CAN BE BROUGHT. *Amen.*

Whatcha prayin' about?

"I urge, then, first of all, that requests, prayers, intercession and thanksgiving be made for everyone. ... This is good and pleases the Lord our Savior who wants all men to be saved and come to the knowledge of the truth."
1 Timothy 2:1, 3–4 (NIV)

Dressed in a fireman's hat, suspenders, shorts and rain boots, the 4-year-old missionary kid spots a small flame burning beneath the guards' teapot. "Bobby" runs to extinguish it. In his excitement, he trips and lands headfirst onto the prayer mat where two Muslim guards kneel.

Not even stunned by the fall, Bobby kneels with his hands clasped ready to join the prayer session. He looks up at the bewildered men and says, "Daddy told me that when you do that talk and stand up and down a lot, you guys are praying. So whatcha prayin' about? Did you know that Jesus loves you and Daddy says that's why we pray? So don'tcha know what you're prayin' about? 'Cuz you haven't answered me."

Prayer is serious business for a Muslim. One must pray five times a day while facing the distant holy city of Mecca. Devout Muslims are never without their prayer beads, and they repeat the Koran and a prayer over and over in Arabic, even though most do not understand this language.

All over Bobby's city, when the call to prayer sounds over the loudspeakers, Muslims cleanse themselves with water so they can pray. Some men go to the mosque, but most pull out their prayer mats and do it right where they are. Inside homes, women do the same.

As prayer time ends with the guards, Bobby pats the men's shoulders and says, "Don't worry. My family will pray for you tonight so tomorrow, you'll know whatcher prayin' about."

—SUE, WEST AFRICA

Father, YOU SAY IN YOUR WORD THAT IF WE CALL UPON YOU AND PRAY TO YOU, YOU WILL LISTEN. THANK YOU THAT YOU ARE A PERSONAL GOD WHO GIVES ME THE PRIVILEGE TO SPEAK WITH YOU. OPEN THE EYES OF MUSLIMS SO THAT THEY WILL SEE THAT JESUS IS THE ONLY WAY TO YOU. *Amen.*

"Tireless" prayers

"God did extraordinary miracles." Acts 19:11a (NIV)

Rogers finished a course on evangelism simultaneously with completing medical school. He prayed God would use all of his training for His glory. The government offered him a position working with 30 different tribes in an area where many had never heard of Jesus.

This region of the Democratic Republic of the Congo was isolated. To get anywhere, Rogers hopped on the back of a small motorcycle driven by a Muslim man. The small motorcycle easily was maneuvered through overgrown walking paths. When they arrived at a river, they carried the motorcycle across a log bridge.

One day, they had a flat tire in the middle of nowhere. Knowing they could be stuck for days, Rogers said to the driver, "We can't fix this tire, but God can. Take it off."

Rogers lifted the flat above his head and said, "God, we can't fix this tire, but You can—so fix this tire." He then told the driver to put it back on the bike and pump it up. The driver followed orders but thought the doctor had lost his mind, especially when Rogers ordered him to continue driving on the flat tire.

They drove slowly for the first half mile and gradually picked up speed. By the end of the day, the twosome traveled almost 60 miles on the "flat" tire. The driver thought Rogers was a magician, but the doctor explained that his God answers prayers.

Word about the miracle spread throughout the province. Every village the pair visited wanted to hear about the "God who answers prayers." By the end of the 21-day trip, many came to Christ, including the driver.

—RUSTY, CENTRAL, EASTERN AND SOUTHERN AFRICA

Thank You, Father, THAT YOU CHOSE TO MEND A FLAT TIRE FOR YOUR GLORY. ALLOW THIS TESTIMONY OF YOUR GOODNESS TO BE REMEMBERED BY MANY. THANK YOU FOR THE MIRACLE OF NEW LIFE THAT YOU OFFER TO EACH PERSON WHO BELIEVES IN YOUR SON. PROVIDE FOR MISSIONARIES WHEN TRANSPORTATION PROBLEMS OCCUR SO THAT GLORY CAN BE GIVEN TO YOU. *Amen.*

A daughter's lesson on faith

"I pray that the eyes of your heart may be enlightened, so that you will know what is the hope of His calling, what are the riches of the glory of His inheritance in the saints, and what is the surpassing greatness of His power toward us who believe." Ephesians 1:18–19a (NASB)

We have all questioned our faith at one time or another. So it was with our daughter, Rebekah. She asked how we know that our God is the real God. How do we know that our Bible is more real than the Koran or others? I did my best to explain to her and reminded her that our God answers prayer. She verbalized that only once had God ever answered prayer in her life. We prayed that God would show Himself to her.

The very next week, something began happening to my eye. Because we were traveling to the Philippines from Japan, there wasn't time to see a doctor. My husband and children prayed over me. Rebekah paid unusually close attention to my eye during the next few days. In the Philippines, I had an opportunity to receive medications, but I believed God was saying, *Wait, Deborah. I'm using your eye to teach Rebekah something of Myself.* He chose to heal me, and Rebekah was amazed.

On the way to our final destination, somehow luggage fell off the bus. Four suitcases were found on the road but would only be returned for a reward. Rebekah said that she hoped her suitcase would not be retrieved, because someone else would have to do without. My husband and I marveled at her outlook. God was using these two circumstances to reveal Himself to her.

Is your faith your own? Do you share others' experiences, or do you share what God is doing in your life? He desires a personal relationship with each of us.

—DEB, PACIFIC RIM

Heavenly Father, I PRAY FOR MISSIONARY KIDS TODAY. MAY THEY HAVE THEIR OWN PERSONAL FAITH IN YOU AND NOT DEPEND ON THE FAITH OF THEIR PARENTS TO BRING THEIR OWN SALVATION. SPEAK TO EACH ONE TODAY WHO IS OLD ENOUGH TO UNDERSTAND YOUR REDEMPTIVE PLAN. CAUSE THEM TO EXAMINE THEMSELVES TO SEE IF THEY ARE IN THE FAITH. *Amen.*

Seeing the power of God

"The effective prayer of a righteous man can accomplish much."
James 5:16b (NASB)

Civil war pummeled Ivory Coast, West Africa. When the fighting began, doctors fled. That was how one Toura (TOUR-ah) village found itself without modern medicine. An epidemic swept through, killing dozens of children.

Among the victims was 4-year-old Rebecca, the daughter of Clarice and Zo, two of only three Christians there. "If your God is so powerful, why did Rebecca die?" the villagers asked Clarice, taunting.

"If your fetishes are so powerful, why did your children die?" Clarice answered. "The Bible says it rains on the righteous and the unrighteous alike."

Months later, illness struck Clarice, and she fell into a coma. Zo's father, Lee, summoned the medicine men to work magic over his daughter-in-law. Zo refused the witchcraft. Lee was furious and told the medicine men, "Just leave. We'll let my son and his Christians pray, and we'll see how powerful their God is!"

Zo and Christians from another village prayed. They knelt on the dusty floor of the two-room home, laid their hands on Clarice's motionless body and cried out to God. As they prayed, Clarice opened her eyes!

The next day, there was another miracle. After hearing about Clarice's recovery, Lee put on his nicest robe, picked up his cane and walked six miles to the other village. There, he thanked each Christian who prayed. This man who had persecuted Christians was now honoring them.

Today, Clarice is back working in her fields. Her life has been a testimony to many of the power of prayer to the true God.

—SUSAN, WEST AFRICA

Father, THANK YOU FOR THE MIRACLE OF CLARICE'S RECOVERY. PLEASE DO YOUR WILL IN THE LIFE OF HER FATHER-IN-LAW. I PRAY THAT THERE WILL BE MANY NEW BELIEVERS ADDED TO THIS VILLAGE AS THE RESULT OF THE TESTIMONIES OF THESE FEW BELIEVERS. THANK YOU FOR THE POWER OF PRAYER. *Amen.*

One smart donkey

"This is the confidence which we have before Him, that, if we ask anything
according to His will, He hears us. And if we know that He hears us in whatever
we ask, we know that we have the requests which we have asked from Him."
1 John 5:14–15 (NASB)

It was harvest time when Mrs. Tendai's (ten-DIES) donkey went missing. She searched everywhere and even reported the missing animal to the local police. When it was evident that her donkey had simply disappeared, she began praying that it would return.

Due to lack of good seed, fertilizer and sufficient rain, Mrs. Tendai's harvest that year was small, and she had little money to buy food for her family. Several months later, her prayers were more about God providing "daily bread" than finding the donkey. The family's maize meal supply was depleted. Would God answer her prayers for food?

The next morning, when Mrs. Tendai walked out of her hut, she was amazed to see her donkey standing there with a 100-pound bag of maize meal on its back! She was happy to see the donkey but afraid to use the maize meal since it wasn't hers.

Eventually a story was pieced together that a man had stolen her donkey and used it to do his labor. One night after grinding his corn, he went to the beer hall to drink, leaving the donkey burdened down with the maize meal outside. The donkey realized that he was not far from home and decided to return to where he would be taken care of and fed. The thief, wishing to remain anonymous, did not claim his maize meal, so Mrs. Tendai was able to use it to feed her family. God had answered both of her prayers in a very unusual manner!

—DONNA, CENTRAL, EASTERN AND SOUTHERN AFRICA

Heavenly Father, YOU ARE A GOD WHO LOVES JUSTICE, AND YOU MAKE A CASE FOR THE POOR. THANK YOU FOR HEARING THE PRAYERS OF THIS AFRICAN WOMAN. MAKE A WAY FOR YOUR CHILDREN TO EAT DURING THESE DIFFICULT DAYS IN ZIMBABWE. SHOW ME HOW I CAN HELP THE POOR IN MY COMMUNITY. *Amen.*

A life transformed

"Is not this the one who used to sit and beg?" John 9:8b (NASB)

Each week, I lead a Bible study with Asian believers. As I began our study of John, a new believer entered the room and shyly took a seat. She seemed very distracted, often rocking back and forth while laughing. After the lesson, one of the students explained that she was mildly retarded and abused. My heart cried out to God for this young girl.

The next week, she returned and I asked if she would like to pray. She nervously shook her head. I learned that she believed God couldn't use her. I immediately began to encourage her. I shared the story of Jesus healing the blind man. I could see her expression change as she intently listened to the words.

Several weeks later, the group prayed for this girl, asking God to heal her from a medical problem that had existed for years. The very next day, her physical problem was healed. I began to see God slowly working in her heart. She began to softly respond during our studies about what God was teaching her.

One day, I again asked her if she would like to pray out loud. This time she prayed, pouring out her heart to God. One believer shared that God was using the young woman to witness in a clear way, stating that Jesus died on the cross for us all.

Everyone who knew her before asks, "How can this be the same girl?" She simply says, "Jesus is alive and lives in my heart."

—CHERYL, WESTERN EUROPE

Thank You, precious Lord, THAT YOU LOVE THE GREATEST AND THE LEAST AND ALL THOSE IN-BETWEEN. YOU ARE JEHOVAH-RAPHA, THE GOD WHO HEALS. *Amen.*

We all scream for ice cream!

"Each time he said, 'No. But I am with you; that is all you need. My power shows up best in weak people.' Now I am glad to boast about how weak I am; I am glad to be a living demonstration of Christ's power, instead of showing off my own power and abilities." 2 Corinthians 12:9 (TLB)

God is always teaching me about trusting Him to provide. I often learn through my friend, an Indian woman who lives in the Democratic Republic of Congo. She has five children and makes a meager living. Her husband is in jail in Dubai (do-BIE). Her faith is simple yet remarkable. She trusts in God to provide *everything*—and I do mean everything.

In the Congo, the sidewalks roll up around 6 p.m., and everyone just stays at home. It's during this time that my friend prays and teaches her children about God's power to provide. One night, she shared that her stomach ulcer was painful. She also mentioned that ice cream might help settle it down. But the family didn't have money to buy ice cream— if the stores had even been open. Besides, finding ice cream in the store is a challenge!

One of her kids asked what he could do. My friend replied, "Let's pray for my stomach and pray that God would provide for my need."

Her 6-year-old prayed earnestly for ice cream. Ten minutes later, the phone rang. A neighbor called to say he had leftover ice cream from a party and wanted to know if they could use it.

My friend sang the "Hallelujah Chorus" and told her neighbor, who was not a Christian, that the ice cream was a direct answer to prayer. On the phone, she told the story of how God provides for her family—even for the simple things like ice cream.

—DEBBIE, CENTRAL, EASTERN AND SOUTHERN AFRICA

Jehovah-Jireh, YOU ARE THE PROVIDER OF MY NEEDS. THANK YOU THAT I CAN TRUST YOU IN THIS AREA OF MY LIFE. CONTINUE TO SHOW YOUR GOODNESS TO THIS DEAR SISTER IN THE DRC AND OTHERS LIKE HER. *Amen.*

Whom will I serve?

"Choose for yourselves today whom you will serve ... but as for me and my house, we will serve the LORD." Joshua 24:15 (NASB)

She's having a baby!

There was no better news to my ears than to hear that a woman in one of my Bible study groups was pregnant. It was such exciting news that I cried. The women and I had been praying for this for a very long time. The news also just "happened" to reinforce our study points for that session: the power of God, how God answers prayers and how we need to choose whom we are going to serve each day.

In the past, this woman and another woman were both desperate to become pregnant after years and years of trying. They went to the witch doctor seeking some drugs or amulets to bring fertility to their wombs. Babies are signs of blessing on their households, as well as insurance that they will be taken care of when they are old. Children are very important in Africa.

After hearing about Jesus, both women decided to stop taking the medicine from the witch doctor and to trust in God. We spent hours and hours praying for the two to become pregnant. Now both women have been blessed with a pregnancy—showing the power of God and showing that He answers prayers. These women chose to serve God instead of the witch doctor, and the entire village knew their choice.

Each day, we are faced with the same question of whom we will serve. Choosing to serve the living God is the better way.

—SUZIE, CENTRAL, EASTERN AND SOUTHERN AFRICA

Father, I CHOOSE TO SERVE YOU TODAY. I PRAY THAT MISSIONARIES WILL CHOOSE TO SERVE YOU TODAY ALSO AND NOT FOLLOW HUMAN AGENDAS. BREAK STRONGHOLDS THAT THE TRADITIONAL WITCH DOCTORS HAVE OVER PEOPLE IN AFRICA. MAY PEOPLE GROUPS TRUST YOU INSTEAD. *Amen.*

Show them My power

"You are a God who sees." Genesis 16:13a (NASB)

While working in a remote area in Central Asia, I visited a refugee camp of 50 to 60 families. No one had food; most of the children were lethargic and ill. Everyone was asking me if I could help.

I was invited inside one of the plastic 4 x 8 foot tents. Inside, a woman severely ill and blinded lay very still. "I'm not a doctor, nor a nurse. I am not able to do anything," I announced. By this time, a crowd had gathered. Immediately, I sensed in my spirit, *You can do something; you can pray. Show them My power.* I thought, *Not here, Lord, not now. It is too dangerous.*

After getting permission, I was allowed to pray over this woman. Through tears, I prayed, "Use this, oh Jesus, to show these deserted people that You see them, You hear them. Heal this woman in Jesus' name!" As I walked out of the tent, I said, "I don't know what I can do for you, but this I do know. God hears you, and He sees you. Call out to Him. He will give you hope."

Two days later, upon returning to the camp, many ran to greet me proclaiming, "He heard us; He saw us!" The day after I had prayed, two different organizations brought bread, oil and needed supplies. I looked up to see the previously sick woman walking toward me completely healed!

In later months, at least three of these ladies have become believers. These refugees from all over Afghanistan saw God's power and message of hope.

—ROBIN, CENTRAL ASIA

Father, YOU ARE EL ROI, THE GOD WHO SEES! THANK YOU FOR THE POWERFUL DISPLAY OF YOUR LOVE ON THESE REFUGEES IN AFGHANISTAN. LET THEM SEE JESUS THROUGH CHRISTIAN AID WORKERS. LET THEM EXPERIENCE THE POWER OF PRAYER. *Amen.*

A miracle for God's glory

"But Jesus took him by the hand and raised him; and he got up."
Mark 9:27 (NASB)

"Can you come pray?" Meryl asked us to visit her hospitalized 2-year-old nephew. A week earlier he had quit eating, developed diarrhea and then began vomiting. In the hospital, he became more lethargic.

By this time, all her family had gathered in despair. The doctor said that nothing else could be done and that even if the boy began to improve, it would take many days for him to regain strength.

Accompanied by another friend, we walked quietly into the room. The small child's eyes were closed, and only the smallest whisper of breath could be heard as he suffered on the bed. After greeting the family, we held hands and began praying quietly. Through tears, we asked God to give life back to the boy. In this atheistic country, the majority of the people believe that there is no God. Yet, in that hospital room, all hearts were turned to Him—those who knew Him as Savior and those who did not. After praying, we hugged his parents and grandmother and departed.

Meryl didn't call for several days, and we feared the boy had died. Then she told us an amazing story. By late afternoon of the day of our visit, the child roused; and by evening, he ate some rice porridge. By the next morning, he was sitting up, eating and drinking. The doctor was baffled. The following day, his mother carried him back to the village, while her entire family rejoiced over her son's new gift of life!

—A WORKER IN CHINA

Heavenly Father, YOU TRULY ARE A GOD WHO PERFORMS MIRACLES FOR YOUR GLORY! MAY THIS ANSWER TO PRAYER BE SHARED FOR GENERATIONS, AND MAY MANY IN THIS VILLAGE COME TO CHRIST. *Amen.*

Healing body and soul

"And the prayer offered in faith will make the sick person well: the LORD will raise him up." James 5:15a (NIV)

After a week of seeing patients in several Miskito (mees-KEE-toh) villages, the medical team stopped in Waspam (wahs-PAHM) to spend the night.

The next morning as we packed to head home, a lady with a baby came to the church gate. I ran to the gate seeing her urgency and found this baby in severe respiratory distress. Taking the 18-month-old from the mother, I called the other nurses and immediately started an IV and antibiotics. We prayed as we worked, begging God to save this child. The mother told us that she had been on her way to the health clinic when she realized that the baby was dying, so she ran to the church. The pastor and other team members gathered around to pray for the baby.

After doing everything we could do, we had to leave to return to Puerto Cabezas (PWER-toh Kah-BEY-sahs). A pediatric intensive-care nurse on the team told us that even in the most modern facilities in the States, a child whose lungs sounded like this would die. We walked the mother and child home, took out the IV and prayed once more. Our hearts were heavy when we left.

Two weeks later when I visited Waspam, the pastor told me that the baby had lived! The church continually visited the family after we left. As the baby improved, the mother and extended family began attending church, and several family members were to be baptized the following week.

God does not just heal bodies; He heals souls!

—VIOLA, MIDDLE AMERICA AND THE CARIBBEAN

Father, YOU ARE THE GREAT PHYSICIAN! THANK YOU THAT YOU NOT ONLY HEAL BODIES, BUT YOU ALSO HEAL SOULS. I PRAY THAT YOU WILL BE WITH MEDICAL MISSIONARIES TODAY AND THAT YOU WILL PERFORM MIRACLES BEFORE THEIR VERY EYES IN ORDER TO BRING GLORY TO YOUR NAME. *Amen.*

God is in control

"Be anxious for nothing, but in everything by prayer and supplication with thanksgiving let your requests be made known to God. And the peace of God, which surpasses all comprehension, will guard your hearts and your minds in Christ Jesus." Philippians 4:6–7 (NASB)

Our three young sons accompanied us to the mission field in 1986. I never thought about the day that our family would be separated by thousands of miles. The day our oldest son left for college was a heart-wrenching day.

One day, the call came. "Mom, if ever I wished that I could be back home, it is today," he said in a weak voice.

"What's wrong?" I asked.

"Mom, I am so sick," came the reply.

"Honey, go to the infirmary on campus and call us back as soon as you return," I said.

As I hung up the phone, I began to cry out to the Lord. "Father, my son is hurting and I am not there. He needs someone to care for him. He needs a mama's care. Please, God, take care of my precious son."

Several hours later, he called. "Mom, you won't believe what happened! I went to the infirmary, and I was so sick that they sent me on to the doctor's office. When the doctor came into the room, she was shaking her head. She put her hand in her pocket and she pulled out one of our prayer cards! Mom, it had my picture on it! Mom, she worked with you on a medical team in Guatemala! She took great care of me and even gave me the medicine."

Did God answer my prayer? Yes! Does God care about all the things that happen in our lives? Yes! And His answer is more than I even thought to ask!

—MARGIE, MIDDLE AMERICA AND THE CARIBBEAN

Father, YOU KNOW MY NEEDS BEFORE I EVEN ASK. THANK YOU FOR ANSWERING THE PRAYERS OF THIS MISSIONARY. FILL THE VOID OF MISSIONARY COUPLES WHOSE GROWN CHILDREN ARE IN THE STATES. WATCH OVER THOSE COLLEGE MISSIONARY KIDS AND BRING ADULTS INTO THEIR LIVES WHO WILL SPEND TIME WITH THEM. *Amen.*

Prayerfully willing

"Trust in the LORD with all your heart and lean not on your own understanding; in all your ways acknowledge him, and he will make your paths straight."
Proverbs 3:5–6 (NIV)

When we "adopted" the Kabyle (kuh-BEEL) Berbers as our ministry focus, my husband began developing friendships throughout France and Northern Africa. I remained in France to take care of our five young children. I begged the Lord to open doors for me to bond with Kabyle Berbers as well.

If I had seen how God was going to answer that prayer, I might not have voiced it! I was involved in a tragic car accident, which left the baby of my Kabyle language partner unconscious in the hospital. The baby had a fractured skull and displaced skull bones.

How could I live knowing that I had been responsible for the handicap or death of an innocent child? Was this the end instead of the beginning with the Kabyles? Reciting Proverbs 3:5–6, I gradually began to "trust in the LORD" with all my heart. God assured me that this event was allowed for His glory.

As I prayed with the Kabyle mother, we claimed healing for her child in Jesus' name. As we finished praying, the hospital called to report that the doctor decided to cancel the scheduled operation. The skull bones miraculously moved back into place and the fractures were healing. There was no rational medical explanation!

This was the beginning of a faith walk alongside this young Kabyle mother. She renounced her involvement in the occult and turned to Jesus.

God accomplishes His purposes in ways we don't always understand. We just need to be prayerfully willing to accept His plan.

—S.G., NORTHERN AFRICA AND THE MIDDLE EAST

Father, MANY CHRISTIAN WORKERS EACH YEAR ARE INVOLVED IN ACCIDENTS. I ASK THAT YOU WOULD PROTECT THEM FROM HAVING SERIOUS CAR OR BICYCLE ACCIDENTS. THANK YOU FOR HOW YOU HEALED THIS INFANT AND BROUGHT GLORY TO YOUR NAME. *Amen.*

Thy will

"Going a little farther, he fell with his face to the ground and prayed, 'My Father, if it is possible, may this cup be taken from me. Yet not as I will, but as you will.'"
Matthew 26:39 (NIV)

The shaman told Sunny that she wouldn't live to her 40th birthday. She was under a curse. A doctor prescribed several medicines to treat the life-threatening blood clot in her head. She endured intense headaches and constant depression. Sunny's only child, Siti (SIT-ee), encouraged her mother to talk to the American in their neighborhood.

Siti heard about Jesus at my house. Finally, she convinced her mother to talk with me. Sunny asked, "What is the difference between the resurrection of Jesus and the ascension of Jesus?" Every few days, Sunny would visit and ask questions.

Sunny began to read the Bible with me. One week, we studied about the betrayal and death of Jesus, including His prayer at Gethsemane. He said, "Not as I will, but as you will" (Matt. 26:39, NIV). Attracted to Jesus' prayer, Sunny prayed that she would accept God's will.

A few nights later, Sunny had an unusual dream. A tall man, wearing white garments, came to her. He poured ice-cold liquid over her head. As it chilled her whole body, he said, "You are healed." She woke up cold and bewildered. Who was the man? Was the dream from God? Was she really well again?

Sunny decided that whether or not she was healed, she believed that Jesus is the Savior, her Savior. When the expensive pills had run out, Sunny went to the doctor for a checkup. The blood clot was gone! The Muslim doctor said it was impossible. Sunny said, "No, it's an answer to prayer."

—M., PACIFIC RIM

You hear, O Lord, THE DESIRE OF THE AFFLICTED; YOU ENCOURAGE THEM AND LISTEN TO THEIR CRY. THANK YOU THAT YOU ANSWERED SUNNY'S PRAYER. I PRAY THAT YOU WILL USE MIRACULOUS HEALINGS TO BRING MUSLIMS TO CHRIST IN THE PACIFIC RIM. *Amen.*

APRIL **V**

God's Grace

None of us will miss the invitation to be bitter. It will be hand-carried, special delivery to our front doors by the devil himself with God's name signed at the bottom of it ... in the devil's handwriting. Satan scrawls his own anonymous note at the bottom of it: *Look what He's done to you after all you've done for Him!*

Satan knows nothing will disintegrate our effectiveness more dramatically than bearing a deep offense toward God. The more we trustingly expose our hearts and minds to God, the deeper the offense can go when we get our feelings hurt at Him. This is certainly true of those who have surrendered their lives to serve God, no matter what side of the ocean they're on.

In the introduction of this book I asked you to consider a number of ways missionaries are just like the rest of us who call ourselves Christians. We also bear some obvious differences. Let's distinguish between "us" and "them" for a moment. (Consider "them" the kind of folks who have written these devotionals.) I am what religious language would call a "layperson," just like many of "us." I'm not on a church staff, and I'm not a missionary by vocation like "they" are. While *many* of "us" may have given our lives, our futures and our plans to God, *all* of "them" have. So?

So, the deeper the emotional exposure to God, the deeper the wound can plunge when a servant sustains a hurt. A person who offers God little more than a few hours on Sunday and a blessing over a meal doesn't have the same potential for devastation toward God when something terrible happens. And Satan knows it. For this reason, we can be confident that Satan picks on "them" even more than "us." He knows they've fully exposed themselves. They are out on a limb so far with God that if someone cuts it off, they have nothing left. Satan does everything he can to convince them after all they've done for God, He has been unfaithful to them. Satan actually has no power to cut the limb, but the sound of the saw in our spiritual ears can be enough to make us jump.

This entry is a plea on their behalf for a very specific kind of prayer: prayer against bitterness. Our focus this month will be on the glorious grace of God. Many verses speak to me about the unmerited favor of God, but one comes most readily to mind as we pray God's lavish grace over our brothers and sisters on the international field. Hebrews 12:15 says this: *"See to it that no one misses the grace of God and that no bitter root grows up to cause trouble and defile many"* (NIV). The King James Version makes the relationship between missing the grace of God and bitterness much clearer with the wording "lest *any root of bitterness springing up trouble you*" (emphasis mine). The profound implication is this: God will always offer the grace we need in any tribulation or tragedy not to become bitter; but if we miss it or refuse it, bitterness can become so deeply rooted that many are defiled.

Make no mistake. Satan is constantly on the lookout for what he can do to one that can affect many. The more deeply exposed the believer is to God, the more deeply the enemy tries to plant bitterness because he knows how many might eat from its poison fruit. I have had the privilege of studying and worshiping with hundreds of missionaries and hearing their personal stories. Trust me when I tell you that many of "them" have suffered deep agonies. Certainly, so have many of "us," but theirs can be a little more complicated. After all, they've made so many sacrifices ... and is this what they get in return? I'm thinking of Lyn from the Philippines, whose husband was killed by a terrorist's bomb. I'm thinking of another dear sister who was nearly raped in her home in Africa. Another who lost her child. I could tell you story after story, each of them representing a hand-delivered invitation from Satan to become bitter.

Why do the righteous suffer? Ah, this is a question as old as mankind. Not coincidentally, it is also the question posed by the book of the Bible many scholars believe to be among the first penned: the Book of

Job. Based on the final summaries of the tumultuous book, Job never knew that a battle was raging in the heavenlies over his aching head. He had no idea that the contest was over whether or not he would remain faithful under the worst of circumstances. Had he known, surely the competitor would have roused within him and he would have gladly won one for the team. Instead, all he ever figured out on this earth was that God was huge. When Job finally saw his Redeemer and learned what was at stake in his suffering, can you imagine how thankful he was that he passed the test?

Dear servant of God, whether you're an "us" or a "them," far more is going on around you than meets the eye. A war is raging in the heavenlies. Glory is at stake. You will not miss the test. None of us will. But will you miss the grace when the test comes? Keep drinking deeply and daily from the wellspring of God's grace. Form the habit of living on it so that you'll not be tempted to do otherwise when suffering comes.

One day we'll understand, and until then, we must trust. Keep exposing yourself. Keep offering God your all. Go as far out on the limb as you can. Christ is the Branch that no one can cut out from under you.

—*Beth Moore*

Value despite flaws

"He saved us, not on the basis of deeds which we have done in righteousness, but according to His mercy, by the washing of regeneration and renewing by the Holy Spirit, whom He poured out upon us richly through Jesus Christ our Savior." Titus 3:5–6 (NASB)

In a small town high in an Andean (AN-dee-an) valley, exquisite wool rugs are made entirely by hand. Freshly shorn sheep's wool is first washed in a vat of water heated over an open fire. Detergent is added to remove natural oils and grime as a wooden paddle is used to stir. The workers then rinse the wool in the river.

Then, the craftsmen examine the wool. They set aside the purest white wool to be used in its natural color. The wool that is not pure white is placed in a vat and heated again. Dye is added to the flawed wool to make the bright colors needed.

After the dye process, the wool is hand-spun into thread. The finished rug will have at least 60,000 hand-tied knots per square meter. Brilliant masterpieces of color and design are made of the pure wool and the wool that was once flawed. The dye covers the flaws and makes the wool attractive and useful.

I look at my life and see many failures. However, just like the wool that could not meet the standards of pure white, I can still have value. God has not only forgiven my sins, He covers my flaws with Himself, and I am made beautiful and useful. As I daily submit to Him, I become part of the design of His perfect will.

There is no one of us whose life is too flawed with sin to be used by God. Our value comes not from who or what we are, but from what God makes of us.

—DONNA, SOUTH AMERICA

Father, I CANNOT BEGIN TO TELL YOU HOW GRATEFUL I AM THAT YOU FORGIVE ME AND LOVE ME DESPITE MY FLAWS. I AM MADE CLEAN AND PURE AS A RESULT OF THE SACRIFICE OF YOUR DEAR SON. MAY I NOT WALLOW IN MY FAILURES, BUT TRUST YOU TO MAKE ME IN THE IMAGE OF JESUS. *Amen.*

Flushing out the secret things

"Wash away all my iniquity and cleanse me from my sin." Psalm 51:2 (NIV)

We woke to the worst flood in our South Asian city in eight years, discovering a river where our street used to be. Curious, my husband and I put on our raincoats and flip-flops and waded through the neighborhood.

We saw several interesting sights. One car tried unsuccessfully to get through a flooded intersection, and an older couple came out in their pajamas to help push the car. An iron rail fence was covered with snails, slugs and leeches. A fist-sized frog scrambled to get over a low wall into a safe yard. A scary eight-inch centipede swam into our driveway, giving me major heebie-jeebies. And a fish swam by the driveway—honestly! The flood seemed to bring things out that normally stay hidden or unobserved.

The Holy Spirit is a lot like floodwaters. When the Holy Spirit "rains" down, He flushes out the things in us that try to remain unseen. The power behind the flood is mighty, and nothing is safe unless it has a firm foundation on which to stand. As we yield ourselves to the Holy Spirit's power, the embarrassing moments are revealed; the slimy, creepy things are flushed out; the heebie-jeebies of our lives get exposed; and sometimes a few surprises float out and we say, "Look at that! How did that get there?"

As the floodwaters pass by, we need to be careful not to allow those things to creep back in our lives. Because of Jesus and His shed blood on the cross, we have a way to be cleansed from all our sin.

—T.D.F., SOUTH ASIA

Holy Father, EXPOSE THE CREEPY THINGS, THE UGLY THINGS THAT ARE IN MY LIFE. I TAKE TIME NOW TO EXAMINE THOSE THINGS SO THAT I CAN CONFESS THEM TO YOU. THANK YOU FOR YOUR FORGIVENESS AND FOR THE PRECIOUS BLOOD OF JESUS, WHICH CLEANSES ME FROM SIN. *Amen.*

The hyena and the woman

"Be of sober spirit, be on the alert. Your adversary, the devil, prowls about like a roaring lion, seeking someone to devour." 1 Peter 5:8 (NASB)

Telling stories communicates basic biblical truths in Swaziland (SWAH-zee-land). After my husband tells a Bible story, he often tells an African animal story that illustrates the same truth.

After the story about Adam and Eve and the first sin, he told a story about a hyena's encounter with an African woman and her three children. The hyena was sleeping by the road with some rattles around his feet. A woman and her children wanted to see him dance, shaking the rattles. The hyena agreed to do so if she would give him a piece of the dried meat she was carrying. One thing led to another, and he ate not only all of her meat, but also the woman and her children. The hyena was like Satan. He tempts us with something fun or beautiful but ends up destroying us.

When my husband pretended to be the hyena dancing again for more meat, the children in the room laughed. Everyone especially laughed when the pastor, who was translating, danced like the hyena. The women gasped when the hyena ate the woman in the story.

Who would have thought that something so silly would affect people so much? At the end, the pastor gave an invitation, and a young man came forward. He was like the woman in the story—he had danced with the devil too long and wanted to follow God.

Are you dancing with sin and in danger of being eaten? God is waiting for you to follow Him.

—R.G., CENTRAL, EASTERN AND SOUTHERN AFRICA

Heavenly Father, THANK YOU THAT YOU PERFECT, CONFIRM, STRENGTHEN AND ESTABLISH ME ACCORDING TO YOUR WORD. HELP ME TO RESIST THE DEVIL AND TO FLEE FROM HIM. I PRAY THIS SAME PRAYER FOR MISSIONARIES TODAY. LET THEM FLEE FROM SIN. *Amen.*

The ugliness of partiality

"Circumcise your hearts, therefore, and do not be stiff-necked any longer. For the LORD your God is God of gods and Lord of lords, the great God, mighty and awesome, who shows no partiality and accepts no bribes."
Deuteronomy 10:16–17 (NIV)

I had known the quiet woman for only a few months, but already I respected her. Her father had died young, and she was the primary breadwinner for her family. She worked hard and sought to honor her mother. After a missionary led her to the Lord, she also lived her life for Jesus. She was pleasant and had a true servant's heart.

She went to church, yet even there the dividing lines were drawn. As a poor girl born into a low Hindu caste of street sweepers, few greeted her with handshakes and warm embraces.

I had been bedridden for more than a week. I was too weak to go to the nearest medical facility. I struggled to swallow water, and I ate and drank nothing else. My body and mind were too exhausted to read Scripture or even to pray. My family was continents away, and friends did not know what to do to help me improve.

Then the young woman came to my bedside. I was happy to have her there. She placed her hand on my forearm and went directly to the Lord in prayer, asking for my healing. The next morning, I was well.

How grateful I am to the Lord that the woman whom so many reject placed her hands of prayer on me!

Although it is easy to judge other believers for their treatment of this woman born in humble circumstances, I had to ask myself the shameful question, *Do I have any prejudice in my heart?*

—CHELE, SOUTH ASIA

Heavenly Father, YOU LOVE ALL PEOPLE THE SAME. YOU SHOW NO PARTIALITY. FORGIVE ME OF ANY PREJUDICE IN MY HEART AS I CONFESS IT AS SIN. MAY I LOVE AND REACH OUT TO THOSE THE WORLD SHUNS. *Amen.*

A good washing

"Wash me thoroughly from my iniquity, and cleanse me from my sin. For I know my transgressions, and my sin is ever before me. Against You, You only, I have sinned. ... Then I will teach transgressors Your ways, and sinners will be converted to You." Psalm 51:2–4a, 13 (NASB)

One evening just before sunset, we were walking back to the van after shopping in the marketplace. As I walked, I failed to see a huge hole in the sidewalk that was not covered by concrete. In a matter of seconds, my entire leg was in the sewer!

The man nearby and my husband came quickly to help. A curious crowd of at least 30 men had formed around us, probably because I had broken the monotony of the day with something exciting. I could smell the stench of the waste and felt the thick, black muck on my leg up to my knee. A crowd gawked at me while I was covered in sewage. This was definitely an initiation into culture!

Later as I thought about this mishap in the sewer, the event became funny to me as well as a learning lesson. I truly needed deep cleansing after this experience! I scrubbed and scrubbed to get all that filth removed. I realized how foul I smelled after falling in the sewer and how thankful I was after a thorough washing.

Comparatively, I also need deep cleansing when I sin. I cannot imagine how the stench of my sin lingers until I confess and allow a holy God to wash me clean. God says that when I confess my sin, He is faithful and just to cleanse me from my sin (1 John 1:9). This forgiveness is available to all who believe in Him.

—PATTI, SOUTH ASIA

Holy Father, I CONFESS MY SINS OF _____ . FORGIVE ME, FATHER, FOR THESE SINS. DELIVER ME FROM THE EVIL ONE, WHO SEEKS TO MAKE ME STUMBLE. BRING CHRISTIAN WORKERS TO REPENTANCE AS WELL SO THAT THEIR MINISTRIES MAY NOT BE HINDERED. *Amen.*

Scapegoat

"He is to lay both hands on the head of the live goat and confess over it all the wickedness and rebellion of the Israelites—all their sins—and put them on the goat's head. He shall send the goat away into the desert in the care of a man appointed for the task. The goat will carry on itself all their sins to a solitary place."
Leviticus 16:21–22 (NIV)

We were going through the Bible orally in a village in Tanzania (tan-zan-EE-ah). When we came to the concept that the high priest was to put the people's sins on the scapegoat in Leviticus 16, no one understood. I explained that everyone's sin was put on the head of one scapegoat. The people of Israel confessed all of their sins and sent the goat away into the desert, carrying the burdens of his people. This allowed everyone else to be forgiven.

As the picture became clearer, one of the men spoke up. "We have a custom just like that," he said. During colonial times, it was customary for 20 young men to go out to fight the colonists and enemy tribes. Many times, they killed one or more of their enemies. The German authorities would then come hunting for the perpetrators with hopes of punishing the guilty ones.

For the good of the tribe, the elders chose one of the young warriors to accept the punishment. They told the authorities that this one warrior alone did the killing. The colonialists would take away the warrior to hang him for the crimes of his people. He was their scapegoat and allowed the clan to be forgiven.

At that moment, I wanted so desperately for the Barabaig (bah-rah-BIGE) people to understand that there is no forgiveness of sin without the spilling of blood. Jesus is God's perfect scapegoat, and His blood has already been spilled.

—DAN AND PEGGY, CENTRAL, EASTERN AND SOUTHERN AFRICA

Blessed Jesus, THANK YOU THAT YOU WERE THE ULTIMATE SACRIFICE FOR MY SALVATION, AND I NO LONGER NEED TO LOOK FOR A SCAPEGOAT. FATHER, GIVE UNDERSTANDING TO THE BARABAIG PEOPLE OF TANZANIA OF WHAT JESUS DID FOR THEM. *Amen.*

Coming to the cross

"'And it shall come to pass in the last days,' saith God, 'I will pour out my Spirit upon all flesh: and your sons and your daughters shall prophesy, and your young men shall see visions and your old men shall dream dreams.'" Acts 2:17 (KJV)

"Kai-li" (KIGH-lee) felt he had no choice but to be in a gang. Most Miao (Mee-OW) villages are safe, but his town in Southwest Asia was not. He had been robbed and threatened too many times. As part of a gang, though, things were looking up. The other gangs feared him, for he was a fighter.

To be Miao meant that Kai-li grew up in a family who worshiped their ancestors and lived in fear of evil spirits. He never heard the name of Jesus or knew of His power. But that was about to change.

One night, in a dream, Kai-li saw a cross by the river. He picked it up, and a beam of light fell upon him from heaven. He began to dance in it. The next day after the dream, Kai-li's roommate came in holding a cross. Kai-li exclaimed, "You found that by the river, didn't you?"

He had! Kai-li asked if he could have the cross, and he set out to discover what it meant. Then one night, he had another dream. A tall angel came to his door and told him the message of the cross.

Not long afterward, there came a knock on Kai-li's door. When he opened it, a tall foreigner was standing there. Kai-li exclaimed, "You're the one! Tell me how I can know the message of the cross!"

Kai-li gave his life to Christ and has led many gang members to Him. Together, they've started a new "gang" of Miao Christians who are leading others to Him.

—A WORKER IN EAST ASIA

Lord and Master, YOU HAVE TOLD US THAT IN THE LAST DAYS, PEOPLE WILL HAVE DREAMS AND VISIONS TO BEGIN THEIR JOURNEY TO FIND YOU. MAY WORKERS BE USED TO EXPLAIN THE MEANING OF THE DREAMS SO THAT THE ONES YOU ARE CALLING WILL HAVE ANSWERS TO THEIR QUESTIONS. MAY YOU CALL MANY OF THE MIAO PEOPLE GROUP TO TRUST IN YOU. *Amen.*

When I saw the cross, I was home

"And I, if I be lifted up from the earth, will draw all men unto me."
John 12:32 (KJV)

God has been so gracious to us by giving us a beautiful place to live in a 77-acre coffee plantation.

One day, Caleb, our 8-year-old son, and three of his friends went exploring through the coffee plants. When they were ready to come home, they were not sure which way to go. They decided to go up one of the hills, but they still could not see the house. Then Caleb had the idea of climbing trees in order to see farther. After climbing several trees along the way, he yelled out to his friends, "I see the cross!"

In hopes of having a good harvest each year, our landlord had constructed a large white cross on one of the hills near our house because he believed that Mary, Jesus and God would bless his efforts. So when Caleb saw the cross, he knew which direction to head. When he retold the story, he commented that when he was up in the tree and saw the cross, he knew that he was home.

What is the compass you use to guide you and your loved ones? What is your home? Are you sure that the path you are on today will lead you to the eternal home with God?

Jesus said, "And I, if I be lifted up from the earth, will draw all men unto me." Caleb saw the cross, and it represented home, safety and the right to say, "I once was lost, but now I am found."

—JEFF AND KAREN, MIDDLE AMERICA AND THE CARIBBEAN

Father, I PRAISE YOU THAT YOU SENT YOUR SON TO DIE ON THE CROSS FOR MY SINS. THANK YOU THAT HE ROSE AGAIN. THANK YOU THAT AS A RESULT, ANYONE WHO BELIEVES IN HIM CAN HAVE ETERNAL LIFE! MAY I NEVER STRAY FROM THE CROSS. MAY I ABIDE IN YOU. *Amen.*

The true sacrifice, once and for all

"Now once at the consummation of the ages He has been manifested to put away sin by the sacrifice of Himself." Hebrews 9:26b (NASB)

Our Muslim neighbors were preparing for Eid Al-Adha (EED ul ODD-hah), a yearly commemoration of Abraham sacrificing an animal instead of his son "Ishmael." The most important preparation is buying a cow or goat to sacrifice. Salesmen go up and down the streets with cows or goats decorated with painted horns and strings of flowers around their necks.

Our landlord purchased two expensive cows for the ceremony. The requirement is that one sacrificed animal only covers the bad deeds of seven persons, so since he had 10 children, two cows had to be bought. That night he proudly invited us to see the live cows.

The next morning, Muslim men gathered together to pray and kill the cows. I had been in prayer most of the morning, and with the impending slaughter, a somber feeling was in the air. I stayed in the landlord's house with all of the women while my husband and sons curiously watched in the yard. The *imam* (EE-mahm) (Muslim pastor), who came to kill the cows, held in his hand the names of our landlord and his family members. I could hear the moaning of the cow as its throat was cut. The landlord's son, covered in blood, walked passed me and with a big smile said, "It is finished."

That statement sent chills up my spine as I remembered the words of Jesus on the cross, the *true* sacrifice for sin. The lostness here is heartbreaking. As we share about Jesus, we pray that truth will be revealed.

—JANESSA, SOUTH ASIA

Heavenly Father, THANK YOU THAT YOUR SON, JESUS, DIED FOR MY SINS. NO LONGER ARE SACRIFICES NECESSARY, SINCE HE DIED ONCE FOR ALL. I PRAY THAT TRUTH WILL BE REVEALED TO THESE MUSLIMS IN THIS COMMUNITY OF SOUTH ASIA. MAY THEY HEAR ABOUT AND BELIEVE IN THE SON, WHO WAS SACRIFICED FOR THEM. *Amen.*

Jesus paid it all

> *"Salvation is found in no one else, for there is no other name under heaven given to men by which we must be saved."* Acts 4:12 (NIV)

To religious persons where I live, heaven is a lofty dream. They believe that good deeds and others' prayers help them climb their way up to heaven. The better a person, the closer to heaven one is at death. The concept of salvation by grace is foreign, as they think it is earned.

My pastor and I were meeting with a friend to discuss her recent conversion and her understanding of her decision. Using 10 coins as an example, we posed the following scenario to her: "You are a sinner, and your debt to God is 10 złoty (ZLOT-ee). How much are you going to pay, and how much is God going to pay?"

She was confused and asked for clarification.

"For example, will you pay the full amount?" We pushed all the coins toward her. "Or will God pay the full amount?" We pushed the coins away from her. "Or will you pay half and God pay half?" We shifted the coins into two piles of five złoty each. "How much of the 10 złoty must you pay to get yourself to heaven, and how much of your debt must you let God pay?"

Smiling, my friend placed her hands on the coins and pushed them into one pile. She said, "I want God to pay it all!"

My heart jumped for joy as I realized that she was not relying on herself for salvation. We cannot earn our salvation, for only God's grace can save us!

—MICHELLE, CENTRAL AND EASTERN EUROPE

Father, THANK YOU THAT I AM SAVED BY GRACE AND NOT BY MY WORKS. THANK YOU THAT THE LORD JESUS CHRIST PAID MY DEBT ON THE CROSS. BRING UNDERSTANDING IN AREAS OF CENTRAL AND EASTERN EUROPE, WHERE MANY BELIEVE THAT THEY MUST EARN THEIR SALVATION. *Amen.*

Reaching those difficult to love

"And he said to them, 'But now, whoever has a money belt is to take it along, like-wise also a bag, and whoever has no sword is to sell his coat and buy one.' ... They said, 'LORD, look, here are two swords.' And He said to them, 'It is enough.'"
Luke 22:36, 38 (NASB)

As usual, the disciples did not get it. Earlier, Jesus had promised that He would be with them on their journey. Although they had taken no money, clothes or weapons, all their needs had been provided. While He was with them, no harm could touch them. But now Jesus was say-ing that He was about to be taken away from them, and they did not understand it.

Just as promised, Jesus was killed within a few hours of speaking those words. He lay in the grave three days, but He rose from death. Shortly thereafter, He sent His Holy Spirit to live in us. We now have the assurance that God will protect us, providing for us regardless of where we are or how things look.

The most incredible experience of my life was going on a nine-day trip to find a group of fanatical Muslims. I took nothing but a Bible and another book. I went intending to rely totally upon the kindness of strangers and promises of God. The Lord really came through for me. I was the first foreigner who spoke their language ever to visit them. They have heard the gospel now and want to learn more. If God's promises did this for me, He will most certainly be there for you!

May the Lord be with you today. May you love those who are dif-ficult to love. May you forgive others. May your light blast the darkness around you. God is with you!

—DANIEL, CENTRAL ASIA

Father, THANK YOU THAT YOU ARE WITH ME, THAT YOU PROTECT AND PROVIDE FOR ME. I DO NOT NEED TO BE AFRAID IN WHATEVER YOU CALL ME TO DO, FOR YOU ARE WITH ME. PROTECT CHRISTIAN WORKERS TODAY IN CENTRAL ASIA AS THEY SHARE WITH MUSLIMS WHO HOLD ANTI-CHRISTIAN VIEWS. LET THESE MUSLIMS SEE JESUS IN THEM. *Amen.*

Easter Saturday

"You are among us, O LORD, and we bear your name; do not forsake us!"
Jeremiah 14:9b (NIV)

Easter Saturday. Between the cross and the light of resurrection. The tomb. It is easy to believe that darkness prevails when you are in the tomb. For months, we passed the spirit houses in the corners of yards, buildings and parks. We saw the sacrifices and gifts of flowers and food. The smell of incense became familiar to us. Grief weighed heavy on our hearts, as we had just arrived in this country where people were bowing down to idols made with their own hands.

On Easter Saturday, we set out for the park for our morning exercise. As we rounded the curve in the track, we couldn't miss the monks' orange robes. A special ceremony was in progress.

We walked in silence, wondering how to respond. We decided to prayerwalk on our second lap. The group was chanting. We kept praying and walked briskly.

As we entered the next stretch, we saw another group of people. With shining faces, they were clapping and singing joyfully! Even though we weren't proficient in the language, we recognized the tune as they sang in their native tongue, "When the roll is called up yonder, I'll be there!"

Thanks be to God that He continually reminds us that the victory has already been won! The tomb and the darkness do not prevail. He will not forsake the people of this country. He longs for all of us to bear His name with the same assurance of this group of Christians pushing back the darkness in the park.

—W.S., PACIFIC RIM

Father, THANK YOU FOR THE VICTORY OF OUR RISEN SAVIOR OVER DEATH! THANK YOU THAT YOU HAVE RAISED US INTO NEW LIFE IN JESUS! BRING AWARENESS OF YOUR SON TO BUDDHIST MONKS IN SOUTHEAST ASIA. *Amen.*

No greater sacrifice

"But God demonstrates His own love for us in this: While we were still sinners, Christ died for us." Romans 5:8 (NIV)

Blood sacrifices are a real part of life in South Asia. Every year to commemorate Abraham's willingness to sacrifice his son, Muslims offer sacrifices in an effort to please God. Goats, cows and the occasional camel are herded through the city and taken to stockyards to be inspected by potential buyers. Only those animals without blemish are considered worthy.

We had the opportunity to see this festival when we were invited to a friend's home. The atmosphere was somber as they sought to earn one step closer to heaven. We were given special food while we waited for the sacrifice. After the men returned from the mosque, we were led outside to a small alley where the sacrifice would take place.

It turned out that we could not proceed down the path without stepping over the animals that had already been sacrificed. The prescribed Muslim way to sacrifice an animal is to slit its neck and then let it bleed to death. Blood and the stench of death was everywhere. Men, women and children looked on eagerly as the animals were slaughtered. The men doing the slaughtering chanted in Arabic, "God is great, God is great."

Although these sacrifices are futile, they are a very graphic reminder of how God sent His Son into this world to save us from our sins. He knew we could never offer any sacrifice that would be able to bridge the gap between Himself and us, so He offered the sacrifice for us.

—A.B., SOUTH ASIA

The sacrifice of Your only Son IS MORE THAN I CAN COMPREHEND. THANK YOU FOR HIS BLOOD SACRIFICE, WHICH TAKES AWAY MY SIN, PAST, PRESENT AND FUTURE. I PRAY ESPECIALLY TODAY FOR THE PEOPLE OF SOUTH ASIA. BRING LIGHT IN THE MIDST OF DARKNESS SO THAT THEY MIGHT KNOW OF THE TRUE SACRIFICE FOR THEM. *Amen.*

How far is far?

"As far as the east is from the west, so far does He remove our transgressions from us." Psalm 103:12 (ESV)

I hadn't thought about it, but *far* is a long way—from one horizon to the other such that the eye has trouble focusing. I have been to Mongolia, and it is the same! By jet, it isn't *far* across Mongolia; but by Russian Jeep, it is far.

Russian Jeeps were built for torture. People buy a fixable machine for a modest sum of money. This is practical for a country with little money and a lot of rough terrain. When one breaks down on the steppes, mountains or desert, it's not long before someone can fix it or someone will come along in another Jeep to help out.

Mongolia's few roads defy description. The pavement extends only a short distance in four directions from the capital. If one needs to go where the road doesn't, then usually someone has had the same idea, so one can follow tracks.

Jeep drivers can get anywhere with no signs, no maps and no real roads. So if we plan to go on a trip in a Jeep with a Mongol driver, we hang on, hope for no breakdowns and avoid running out of gas because for that, we will have to go *far*.

The Bible tells us about *far*. Psalm 103:12 says that God loves us so much that when we accept His great love, He forgives us and removes our sins as *far* as the east is from the west. Friends, that is *far*. I guess He has been to Mongolia.

—A WORKER FROM EAST ASIA

It is incomprehensible, Father, THAT YOU REMOVE MY SIN AS FAR AS THE EAST IS FROM THE WEST. ALL I CAN SAY IS THANK YOU. MAY I SHOW THE SAME LOVE AND FORGIVENESS TO OTHERS AS YOUR EXAMPLE. *Amen.*

Be imitators of God

"Be imitators of God, therefore, as dearly loved children and live a life of love, just as Christ loved us and gave himself up for us as a fragrant offering and sacrifice to God." Ephesians 5:1–2 (NIV)

Many Muslim friends ask me, "How can you believe that you can sin and still go to heaven?" I explain that it *is* my sin that separates me from God, but a sacrifice was made for my sin.

Sometimes, I have a hard time fathoming it myself. Why does God bother with me, and why does He still want to use me when I do wrong? What is it that makes Christianity different than any other religion? The answer is *grace*.

I once believed that grace meant simply forgiving others, because Christ forgives us. I have come to see that grace affects my whole way of thinking. Muslims believe there is no grace and that salvation is the result of good works. As a result, they live a life of rules and fear.

Am I living a life valuing grace? I am learning that how much I appreciate and accept God's love and grace is how well I show it and give it to others. I see how my appreciation for God's love and grace affects how I forgive, how I respond to others and what my attitude is throughout the day.

Living in grace means that I am not living under a list of rules—the law condemns me. But because of God's grace that covers me, I am no longer condemned. My obedience comes out of love, not duty, as a result of His amazing grace.

Where does your obedience come from? Are you demonstrating God's love to others?

—C.B., NORTHERN AFRICA AND THE MIDDLE EAST

Gracious Father, MAY I LIVE UNDER GRACE RATHER THAN REVERTING BACK TO LIVING UNDER THE LAW. THANK YOU FOR AMAZING GRACE THAT YOU DEMONSTRATED IN YOUR SON, JESUS. USE CHRISTIAN WORKERS TO SHARE THE GRACE OF GOD WITH MUSLIMS AND OTHERS WHO ARE BOUND BY FALSE TEACHINGS SUCH AS SALVATION BY WORKS. *Amen.*

Words reflect the heart

"The one who guards his mouth and tongue keeps himself out of trouble."
Proverbs 21:23 (HCSB)

During our second semester in language school, our 5-year-old son, Robert, started kindergarten where he was the only English-speaking student. His Portuguese skills weren't very good. The second day, however, he came home very excited.

"My teacher speaks English," he said.

"How do you know?" we asked. "What did she say?"

"Robert, I don't want to have to tell you again—please sit down and be quiet!" he answered proudly.

We laugh as we remember this conversation with our son. As an innocent child, he did not realize how much he was revealing about his own misbehavior in the classroom.

But what about us adults? Do we also let our tongues get us into trouble? Do we regret a hasty comment and wish we could retrieve it? Do we reveal what we are really like as we ramble on or gossip to those around us? Do we talk when we should be listening? Do those around us listen to us or tune us out, knowing we will have nothing valid to say? Do we use our tongues to cut down others, causing them pain and sorrow?

Although the tongue is little, it is very powerful. It can be used to encourage, comfort and instruct those around us. It can share the gospel with the lost. Or it can be used to destroy, criticize, slander or deceive others. How will we use our tongues today? It is a daily decision to allow God to control the tongue.

—E.H., SOUTH AMERICA

Heavenly Father, PUT A GUARD ON MY MOUTH TODAY. FORGIVE ME SPECIFICALLY FOR SAYING_____WHEN I SHOULD HAVE OFFERED KIND AND POSITIVE WORDS. I REALIZE THAT MY WORDS ARE A REFLECTION OF WHAT IS IN MY HEART. HELP ME TO SPEAK AS JESUS WOULD SPEAK. *Amen.*

Fruit bearers

"When the harvest time approached, he sent his slaves to the vine-growers to receive his produce." Matthew 21:34 (NASB)

As a missionary, the phrase "harvest" in this verse intrigued me. I began to examine some cross-references of what the Bible calls "harvest" or "season of fruit." I came to Mark 11:13–14, which tells the story about Jesus cursing a fig tree. The fig tree had a lot of "showy leaves" from a distance, but when Jesus began to look for real fruit, there was none.

In Eastern Europe, there is an abundance of Orthodox churches with gold cupolas and ornate crosses atop. In fact, the casual visitor might think, *Why do we need missionaries here? There are plenty of churches with crosses.* These are the "showy leaves from a distance"; in reality, there is great spiritual hypocrisy and fruitlessness.

But cursing the tree? Isn't that a little harsh? Isaiah 5:2, 4 says that God *expects* fruitfulness. Judgment is always the case for worthless fruit. The Lord's way is personal relationship-building, not personal kingdom-building. It's a good reminder to examine our own lives and ministry. Are we abiding in Christ to produce real fruit, or are we producing showy leaves?

As a believer, I try to balance what I do for God and my relationship with God. In societies where 1 percent of the population knows Christ, it's easy to get drawn away from a deep walk with God.

In her book *Empowered! Claiming the Power of the Holy Spirit*, Esther Burroughs writes, "We are humbled when we recognize the working of the Holy Spirit in and through us. When the Spirit chooses us as a vessel to point to Jesus, we become the *fruit bearers*, not the fruit producers."

—B.B.H., CENTRAL AND EASTERN EUROPE

Father, MAY I BE A FRUIT BEARER, NOT A SHOWY FRUIT PRODUCER. MAY MISSIONARIES IN CENTRAL AND EASTERN EUROPE ABIDE IN YOU SO THAT YOU CAN WORK THROUGH THEM. *Amen.*

Cleaning the grooves

*"Jesus answered him, 'If I do not wash you, you have no part with Me.' Simon
Peter said to Him, 'Lord, not my feet only, but also my hands and my head.'
Jesus said to him, 'He who has bathed needs only to wash his feet, but is com-
pletely clean.'" John 13:8b–10a (NASB)*

My dining room table has a small, decorative groove that circles the entire table. It looks nice, but just as with all small ruts, it collects crumbs
that fall in the groove. Sometimes, when I have company, I will put a
tablecloth on the table. This keeps the crumbs from getting into the
groove and covers any crumbs that I didn't clean before. Sometimes,
though, I will use a lacy tablecloth that has small openings, and sure
enough, crumbs get through to the groove until I decide to clean again.

For my regular cleanings, I wipe off the table, wash it and polish it.
Sometimes, though, I look closely and decide that it's time for the scrub
brush to really dig deep into the groove.

Thinking about this table, I can easily make a parallel to my own life.
Some sins I will instantly recognize that I need to confess and repent
from. Sometimes my armor is solid, and my spirit is protected against
sin and temptation. However, at times my armor has tiny openings that
let sin through. These crumbs may not be overt sin but rather a general
acceptance of worldly ways, without questioning them in light of God's
Word and God's values. That's when God tells me that it's time for me
to look at the groove in my life in order to scrub away the sin. The days
with the scrub brush may be rough, but afterward, I feel clean.

—BETTY, CENTRAL AND EASTERN EUROPE

Father, REVEAL ANY SIN IN MY LIFE NOW. FORGIVE ME FOR _____.
I CONFESS IT AS SIN. CLEANSE ME FROM ALL UNRIGHTEOUSNESS AND HELP ME IN THIS AREA
SO THAT I WON'T CONTINUE TO SIN. I PRAY THAT THE PEOPLE GROUPS IN CENTRAL AND
EASTERN EUROPE WILL HAVE AN OPPORTUNITY TO HEAR ABOUT JESUS SO THAT THEY, TOO,
MAY HAVE NEW LIFE. *Amen.*

Removing idols

"But the high places were not taken away; the people still sacrificed and burned incense on the high places." 2 Kings 12:3 (NKJV)

We often encounter new believers who still have idols or other pagan objects in their homes. On one occasion, we were discipling a married couple. While touring their apartment, we discovered their idol shelf in a back bedroom. After we showed them scriptural teachings on idols, they were determined to remove the shelf immediately.

The idol shelf was removed with a screwdriver, and all its implements were tossed into a box. We patched the holes in the wall with putty, and the new believers placed a cross over the patching just to make it clear where their loyalty rested. Then the husband boldly walked outside and smashed the head off the idol with a hammer as his curious neighbors stared in disbelief.

While cleansing their home of the pagan objects, I reflected on my life. How many "high places" do I still have in my own life? God revealed to me the stronghold of pride in my heart. Instead of relying on God's power, I often summon my pride and tell myself, "I can do this." When criticized by others, instead of turning to Jesus, I soothe my pride by saying to myself, "Who cares what they think?"

Pride was getting me deeper in sin and further away from God's powerful grace. My idol, pride, wasn't sitting up on a shelf; it was hidden deep in my heart. It will take more than a one-time smash with a hammer to remove pride. It requires *daily* confession and repentance for me to take away this "high place."

—A WORKER IN CHINA

Heavenly Father, RIGHT NOW, I SMASH THE IDOL OF_____
AND WILL DAILY DO THIS UNTIL IT IS OBLITERATED. I PRAY THAT YOU WILL CONVICT ME IMMEDIATELY WHEN MY RELATIONSHIP IS NOT RIGHT WITH YOU AND THAT I WILL OBEY THE COMMAND, "YOU SHALL NOT PUT ANY OTHER GODS BEFORE ME." GIVE WORKERS THE WISDOM TO TEACH NEW CONVERTS ABOUT DESTROYING PAGAN IDOLS. *Amen.*

Hunger in the light

> "You are all sons of the light and sons of the day. We do not belong to the night or to the darkness. So then, let us not be like others, who are asleep, but let us be alert and self-controlled." 1 Thessalonians 5:5–6 (NIV)

I am always amazed by what I learn from the ladies I teach on this great continent of Africa. I am convinced that they teach me more than I could ever teach them.

I had been struggling with overeating. I was teaching from 1 Thessalonians 5:1–11, and God showed me through some Ugandan women that I was not taking my problem totally to Him. As these spiritually growing women and I read the Scripture together, the Spirit encouraged me to ask the ladies how Jesus keeps them alert and how He assists them in staying in the Light. A very thin, malnourished woman who had joy written all over her face said, "When I am hungry, I go to the Lord and ask Him to take the hunger away and He does. He takes the hunger away. Jesus can fill the void of hunger."

You *did* notice that the lady did not ask for food, didn't you? She asked God to take the hunger away. This lady's faith spurred the other ladies, but oh, was I ever convicted! How long has it been since I felt hunger? I'm talking about that real gut-wrenching physical hunger. Do I dare go to the Lord for such a thing as hunger? *Yes*, I should go to the Lord about anything, even my problem of overeating.

Let us stay alert in our Lord moment by moment, seeking Him in all things. He cares for all our needs.

—SANDY, CENTRAL, EASTERN AND SOUTHERN AFRICA

Father, I BRING TO YOU MY NEED OF_____. HELP ME TO BE FREE FROM THIS BONDAGE. IN THE NAME OF JESUS, DO A WORK IN MY LIFE IN THIS AREA. I PRAY THAT YOU WILL BREAK STRONGHOLDS IN THE LIVES OF MISSIONARIES TODAY. *Amen.*

Contaminated no longer

> *"Therefore, since we have been justified through faith, we have peace with God through our Lord Jesus Christ. ... You see, at just the right time, when we were still powerless, Christ died for the ungodly. ... But God demonstrates his own love for us in this: While we were still sinners, Christ died for us."*
> Romans 5: 1, 6, 8 (NIV)

Being new in the city of Jerusalem, I was culturally inept. Used to greeting people I met on the street, I quickly learned that many of my Orthodox Jewish neighbors wouldn't greet me in return. Being a Gentile woman makes me unacceptable in a religious sense. While shopping in the Old City, a Muslim shopkeeper assisted me in a store. In completing the transaction, I thanked him and thoughtlessly extended my hand, whereupon he solemnly explained that he was on his way to prayers and could not touch me.

Religiously, I am considered a contaminant to the people I live among. As I replayed these experiences in my mind, I saw my sinfulness in a fresh way. Yet new gratitude came for the Holy One. He is not defiled by me. Instead, in grace, He has actually imputed His own righteousness to me.

Several months after these experiences, my husband and I were walking when a man in Orthodox Jewish dress stopped us, asking if we loved God and knew how to pray. We affirmed our love for God, explaining that we pray to Him through Jesus the Messiah. He asked us to pray for him, saying that he needed to find peace with God. Finding a place where he wouldn't risk being seen with us, we prayed for him. As we prayed, he reached out and held our hands.

Knowing one needs peace with God strips us of pride in the presence of each other and the One who died for us.

—A WORKER IN NORTHERN AFRICA AND THE MIDDLE EAST

Holy God, YOU ARE RIGHTEOUS AND I AM A PERSON OF UNCLEAN LIPS. THANK YOU THAT YOU HAVE REACHED DOWN AND TOUCHED ME ANYWAY. THANK YOU FOR YOUR MERCY. USE WORKERS IN ISRAEL TO SHARE THE GOOD NEWS ABOUT THE MESSIAH, THE SAVIOR OF THE WORLD. *Amen.*

Failure and forgiveness

"You are a forgiving God, gracious and compassionate, slow to anger and abounding in love." Nehemiah 9:17c (NIV)

My friend "VaTate" (vah-TAH-tay) was admitted to the hospital on the same day as his death. His daughter-in-law was also ill, but she remained at the hospice with a broken femur bone.

When I found out, I decided to visit the daughter-in-law. She lay on a grass mat on the hospice floor. I knelt beside the mat and shared my condolences about her father-in-law, her sick husband and herself. Inside I was angry with myself for not visiting them earlier.

I had thought to visit earlier, knowing VaTate was not well, but for the last few days I had made every excuse not to go—the heat, the flies, the stench, the pain and the suffering. So I missed the burial of my friend. In fact, I found out that no one went to VaTate's burial since all his relatives were ill. I felt like a failure.

"Lord," I prayed, "please redeem my mistakes and forgive me for this. I knowingly chose my own comfort over You."

VaTate had become a Christian. Every time I visited him, I found him sitting in his broken chair, too swollen to eat or sleep but hungrily devouring God's Word in his Lozi (LOW-zee) Bible. Happily, he would say, "I am trusting Christ alone!"

I failed my friend the week he died, but thankfully he was not trusting in me. He was trusting in the One who never fails. Sometimes I feel like a big flop, but praise God, I know that Jesus forgives my failures.

—STACEY, CENTRAL, EASTERN AND SOUTHERN AFRICA

Father, FORGIVE ME WHEN I CHOOSE MY OWN COMFORT INSTEAD OF OBEYING YOU. THANK YOU FOR CLEANSING ME OF MY SIN AND FORGIVING MY FAILURES. USE MISSIONARIES IN WESTERN ZAMBIA TO BRING THE LOZI TO CHRIST SO THAT THEY MIGHT KNOW THE LOVE AND MERCY THAT YOU OFFER. *Amen.*

Busted!

"He will not always accuse, nor will he harbor his anger forever; he does not treat us as our sins deserve or repay us according to our iniquities."
Psalm 103:9–10 (NIV)

Contravening a "No Entry" sign results in a big fine and three penalty points; I found out three months after receiving my host country's driver's license. I foolishly drove through a small section of road that had posted "No Entry." A month before, this road was a two-way road. The police were patrolling, waiting for drivers like me to drive the wrong way down this street. As my husband eloquently put it, "You were busted."

With a three-point ticket in hand, I sat behind the wheel trembling and praying I would make it back home without any more penalty points. A total of six points results in losing the license.

I praise the Lord for the lessons learned. As I washed dishes that night, the thought came: *the reason this hurts so bad is because there will be a record of it.* The points are there to remind others and me that I broke the law.

However, God isn't like this. Once I confess my sin, He casts it far from me and remembers it no more. God doesn't keep penalty points.

But the Lord also gently revealed that I have a tendency to keep penalty points on people. They're called grudges. He loves me freely and without points, and He wants and expects me to love in the same way, freely and without conditions. This can only be done through His Holy Spirit living in me. *"Love your neighbor as yourself"* (Gal. 5:14, NIV) translates as "Love people as I do, without penalty points."

—SHAUNA, WESTERN EUROPE

Father, FORGIVE ME WHEN I BEAR GRUDGES AGAINST OTHERS. I SPECIFICALLY PRAY THAT I WILL NO LONGER BEAR A GRUDGE AGAINST_____. CONVICT MISSIONARIES TODAY IF THEY ARE HOLDING A GRUDGE SO THAT THEY WILL CONFESS, FORGIVE AND SEEK FORGIVENESS. *Amen.*

Not afraid to be real

"I will turn their mourning into gladness; I will give them comfort and joy instead of sorrow." Jeremiah 31:13b (NIV)

Africans are very transparent people. They do not fear their emotions, nor do they hide them. Tonight I witnessed unrestrained mourning over someone's misfortune, and it has forever changed me.

The 13 women who huddled in my living room to watch the *JESUS* film quickly became absorbed in the story. Did they think Jesus really spoke their tribal language as the actor on television? Did they think He was white-skinned and blue-eyed, as the gentle-faced actor happened to be? Did they know someone was acting, that he was not really being nailed to a wooden plank? Over and over I heard muttered, "So sorry, so sorry!" in their language as they witnessed an innocent man being mistreated and abused by a nasty crowd of hypocrites. At times the women turned their heads, as it was inappropriate for them to watch the Son of God hanging half-naked from a tree. They dabbed their eyes as they heard, "My God, My God, why have You forsaken Me?"

These simple African women were completely enthralled by a video I've seen many times. When the crucifixion was over and they realized Jesus was not dead, the room brightened. Faces lit up and hands clapped, drums beat, and we sang praises to a risen Savior.

Yes, the Africans are influencing me. They are shaping me more than I ever imagined. I am not afraid of feelings anymore. I'm unashamed to weep, knowing my sorrow will be turned to joy.

—A WORKER IN CENTRAL, EASTERN AND SOUTHERN AFRICA

Dear Lord, LET MY HEART ALWAYS BE TENDER TO THE ACCOUNT OF THE CRUCIFIXION OF JESUS, AND GIVE ME BOLDNESS TO SHARE HIS DEATH AND RESURRECTION WITH THE PEOPLE I ENCOUNTER TODAY. *Amen.*

How can I know when I'm saved?

"If you confess with your mouth Jesus as Lord, and believe in your heart that God raised Him from the dead, you shall be saved." Romans 10:9 (NASB)

"How can I know when I'm saved?" Sabine looked up from the Bible with tears in her eyes. The others in the Bible study, which meets deep in the Bavarian Forest of Germany, looked at me and smiled. After only a few weeks of attending, Sabine was hungry for what the Bible said.

I asked, "Sabine, do you believe that Jesus Christ is God's Son, that He died on the cross and rose from the dead for you?"

"Yes, I really do!" she said, nodding.

"Do you put your complete trust in Jesus Christ alone for your salvation? Do you believe that Jesus Christ is the only One who can save you?" I asked.

"Yes," Sabine replied.

"Sabine, are you sorry for your sins, and do you want to turn from your sins right now and put your faith in Jesus Christ alone?"

"Yes." She lowered her head.

"Sabine, are you asking Jesus Christ to forgive you, save you, give you eternal life and be the Lord of your life right now?"

"Yes! More than anything else!" she cried.

"He just did!" I excitedly explained. "Jesus Christ just saved you!"

Sabine sat very still for a few seconds, looked up and exclaimed, "He did! He really did! Now I understand what you all have been talking about the past weeks! Jesus has saved me!"

Later that night, I said to my wife, "That is what it is all about! I love my job."

—WAYNE, WESTERN EUROPE

Thank You, Lord, FOR SABINE'S CONFESSION OF FAITH. I PRAY THAT YOU WILL ALLOW HER TO SHARE JESUS WITH MEMBERS OF HER FAMILY AND COMMUNITY. GIVE MANY OPPORTUNITIES FOR MISSIONARIES TO SHARE CHRIST WITH PEOPLE WHO LIVE IN GERMANY. SPEAK THROUGH ME TODAY, FATHER. *Amen.*

The one step to knowing Christ

"Those who obey his commands live in him, and he in them."
1 John 3:24a (NIV)

"How do we come to know Christ better?" I asked a new Christian. Answering humbly, the young African said, "By doing what Jesus tells us to do." Surprised, I was reminded that day of the very important foundation of the Christian life.

Obeying Jesus Christ is the very basis of life. Simply put, when we obey Christ, we live in Him. When we live in Him, we will know the very mind of God.

If we become centered on laws, rules and regulations rather than just simple obedience of Christ's words, then the particulars of the Christian life turn into a source of stress, worry and argument. Spiritual-improvement books or plans, instead of Christ, are sought after to clear up the problems. Over time, we tend to lose sight of that which brings us truly in step with Christ.

Jesus has come to give us life. The young African believer may not have known the commands of the Bible at this point in his life, but he knew from where his life came. He also knew that obedience was the key to gaining knowledge of the Savior, who gave him new life.

Knowing Christ doesn't come from a five-step plan, a self-help book or a list of rules. It is gloriously found in following our Savior and obeying His words.

Nothing more needed to be said to the young, new Christian at the moment. I sat back and smiled in affirmation, realizing the simple truth that had just been spoken.

—DANIEL, CENTRAL, EASTERN AND SOUTHERN AFRICA

Father, MAY I LIVE SIMPLY BY OBEYING YOUR COMMANDS SO THAT I CAN FOLLOW THE EXAMPLE OF JESUS. YOU HAVE ORDAINED YOUR PRECEPTS, THAT WE SHOULD KEEP THEM DILIGENTLY. I KNOW THAT I CAN KEEP MY WAY PURE BY KEEPING TO YOUR WORD. I PRAY THAT MISSIONARIES WILL OBEY YOU AND NOT STRAY FROM YOUR WORD. *Amen.*

Three days from hell

"And He shall wipe away every tear from their eyes; and there shall no longer be any death; there shall no longer be any mourning, or crying, or pain; the first things have passed away." Revelation 21:4 (NASB)

The emaciated, young African man leaned against the hut on the cool winter day. I walked down the path nearby with volunteers and a national pastor. We were visiting people who'd seen the *JESUS* film and had responded to the gospel. A relative of the emaciated man interrupted our progress and asked us to pray for him. Hesitantly, I acquiesced to his request.

As we approached the hut, I realized immediately that this man was in the last stages of AIDS. Stanley looked older than his 36 years. His wife had died the year before. His lone son sat nearby. Stanley's eyes were filled with despair. As I placed my hand on his shoulder, I remember the thought that invaded my prayer—he was a skeleton. I sensed a need to pray not for his physical state, but for his spiritual condition. We shared some tracts and left Stanley to rest.

During the night, I awoke three times with Stanley on my mind. I prayed and knew that we must see him again. Stanley was in the same place the next morning. We inquired as to whether he'd read the tracts, and we shared the gospel. Stanley repented and turned to Christ!

Three days later, I learned of Stanley's death. Amazed at God's timing, I realized that while family mourned his passing, Stanley rejoiced!

The crying, the pain, the mourning and the tears punctuate the urgency surrounding those enduring the AIDS pandemic. Jesus takes hopeless desperation and exchanges it for hope in heaven.

—D. RAY, CENTRAL, EASTERN AND SOUTHERN AFRICA

Father, BRING CHRISTIANS TO WITNESS TO THOSE DYING OF AIDS SO THAT THEY WILL HAVE HOPE FOR ETERNITY IN HEAVEN. HAVE MERCY ON SUB-SAHARAN AFRICA, WHERE UP TO 8,500 PEOPLE PER DAY ARE DYING FROM THIS DREADED DISEASE. *Amen.*

From bugoy to new creation

"I will give them an undivided heart and put a new spirit in them; I will remove from them their heart of stone and give them a heart of flesh."
Ezekiel 11:19 (NIV)

One of the elements of a church-planting movement is the active involvement of laypeople sharing the gospel and participating in new church starts. In Zamboanga del Norte (Zam-bow-AHN-gah del NOR-tay), Philippines, 30 men are trained to teach the Bible using the chronological storying method. Many of these men are new believers, and most have very little formal education.

R.B. is one of these men. He was known as *bugoy* (boo-goy), the local term for a bad boy. R.B. drank, smoked, gambled and was a womanizer. A group of local pastors and a missionary began to teach the Bible in R.B.'s village. After hearing the gospel presented through the chronological Bible storying method, he gave his heart to Jesus. Now he is active in sharing the gospel and how it changed his life. R.B. has even planted several new churches. Friends and neighbors in his village have been amazed at his lifestyle change.

What makes R.B. special is that he is blind! Due to cataracts in both eyes, he can't see. This has not stopped him from sharing God's Word. His son guides a horse, which carries R.B. to rural places that have not heard the good news. R.B. has memorized the Bible stories and the scriptures for each. God is using R.B. to open the eyes of the spiritually blind!

It doesn't matter what our past was before salvation or what our disabilities may be now; God can use us to lead others to His Son.

—DEBBIE, PACIFIC RIM

Father, YOU CHANGE LIVES AND LOVE ME NO MATTER WHAT I'VE DONE IN MY PAST. THANK YOU FOR THE EXAMPLE OF R.B. USE HIM AND OTHERS LIKE HIM TO SPREAD THE GOSPEL AND PLANT CHURCHES IN THE PHILIPPINES. *Amen.*

Removing the veil

"But their minds were made dull, for to this day the same veil remains when the old covenant is read. It has not been removed, because only in Christ is it taken away. Even to this day when Moses is read, a veil covers their hearts. But whenever anyone turns to the Lord, the veil is taken away. ... And we, who with unveiled faces all reflect the Lord's glory, are being transformed into his likeness with ever-increasing glory, which comes from the Lord."
2 Corinthians 3:14–18 (NIV)

She walked the dusty streets of her home country covered by a *burqa* (BER-kah) that adorned her beautiful face. She was in bondage to a religion that kept her from knowing the love of the Creator.

While fleeing her country with most of her children, she found herself in a land of freedom. She cast aside the veil that covered her face, but there was only one way to remove the veil from her heart. God's love for her was greater than any government, language barrier or obstacle. With unveiled face, she met the God of the universe.

After months of discipleship, she addressed her need to be baptized. What a party it was as 13 of us gathered together in the home of one of our teammates to baptize her and another believer! A fellow Christian from her country baptized them and prayed in their heart language! What a sight to see, as well as the sound of the Lord praised in a language of this unreached people group, of which very few have heard the good news.

With "unveiled" faces, God's children are being transformed into His likeness with ever-increasing glory from the Lord!

—A WORKER AMONG REFUGEES AND IMMIGRANTS, WESTERN EUROPE

What a joyful celebration IN HEAVEN IT MUST BE, LORD, WHEN ONE IS DELIVERED FROM THE BONDAGE OF DARKNESS INTO YOUR KINGDOM. PLEASE WORK THROUGH YOUR MISSIONARIES TODAY TO DRAW REFUGEES AND IMMIGRANTS IN WESTERN EUROPE TO YOURSELF SO THE VEIL THAT COVERS THEIR HEARTS WILL BE FOREVER REMOVED. *Amen.*

What's your temperature?

"Never be lacking in zeal, but keep your spiritual fervor, serving the Lord. Be joyful in hope, patient in affliction, faithful in prayer. Share with God's people who are in need." Romans 12:11–13a (NIV)

Three times in fewer than 12 hours, strangers—unsolicited—took my body temperature. At 1 a.m., as I checked into the transit hotel at an international airport, a hotel desk clerk stuck a digital thermometer in my ear. All clear.

Then, about 9:45 a.m., as I exited the airplane in the capital city of another country, masked nurses stopped me and turned my head toward a camera that took my temperature without touching me, showing the results on a computer screen. I checked out okay.

Again, about 11:25 a.m., as I entered immigration at another airport, nurses slapped a strip on my forehead. Acceptable.

Three times various officials checked to make certain that I did not have SARS (Severe Acute Respiratory Syndrome) before letting me go on my way.

All this temperature taking, however, made me wonder about my spiritual temperature. My body temperature was low enough to pass the checkpoints, but what is my spiritual temperature? Do I still have that high temperature for the Lord? Do I have His passion for the lost, for the tasks He has given me to do and for Him?

I hope that I'm never found lukewarm, but that I will seek out the lost and share the reason for living, and that I will approach every task He gives me with unswerving thanksgiving, joy and faithfulness. To do anything less, I am without excuse, for I know the secret for keeping my spiritual fervor lies simply in taking time daily to be with my Savior.

—CHELE, SOUTH ASIA

Heavenly Father, MAY YOUR HOLY SPIRIT FILL ME WITH GOD'S BURNING PASSIONS, HELPING ME TO MAKE THE MOST OF EVERY OPPORTUNITY AND TO BRING GLORY TO OUR WORTHY LORD. MAY I CHOOSE TO ABIDE IN JESUS AND NEVER LOSE MY FIRST LOVE FOR HIM. *Amen.*

MAY V

Witnessing

Our emphasis this month is witnessing. Yep. I'm talking about sharing our faith with people who might rather we kept it to ourselves. As much as many of "us" (laypeople) would like to leave the witnessing to "them" (missionaries), we just can't find the biblical grounds to get away with it. Witnessing is listed on the divine job description of every single believer no matter what our talents or spiritual gifts. Effective witnessing has two requirements.

First, we need something to say. The most effective, unforced witness isn't canned. It flows automatically from what we've personally witnessed. In other words, the more I witness God, the more effectively I'll witness to others. Don't get me wrong. I am a fan of evangelism training, but unless the right words are mixed with the authenticity of an ever-fresh witness of God's activity, it falls flat. *The New Testament Lexical Aids* define "witness" as: "One who has information or knowledge of something; hence, one who can give information, bring to light, or confirm something."

If my relationship with God is current and lively and I am continuing to see His activity and marveling over His greatness, I have something living and active to testify about. We all understand the concept. When we're especially close to our spouses, children or friends, we tend to talk about them twice as much. The same is true in our relationships with God. When He and I are close, I can hardly stand for someone else not to know the joy of loving Him.

When we live on fresh revelation, our lives become breathing confirmations. Listeners can sense whether or not we are convinced and caught up in what we're sharing. Our game face is a pretty dead giveaway. When our relationship with God gets stale and we've witnessed little of His activity in recent days, our words are empty and our spiritual mood sours. We know something's out of kilter when we find ourselves sharing the good news in a bad mood. We've all had seasons when we didn't feel strongly about sharing our faith because, frankly, we didn't have that much to share. We want God to keep our experience with Him current and our vision of Him sharp. No one can witness like a true witness.

Fresh encounters with God may give us plenty to say, but having the guts to say it is the next challenge. I've suggested that the first requirement of effective witness is something to say. The second requirement of effective witnessing is the power to say it. Even with the current motivation of a lively relationship with Christ, witnessing can still be uncomfortable. Oh, for crying out loud, let's go ahead and admit it. It can even be embarrassing. Not all of us are talkative, and even those of us who are can find "cold calling" (first-encounter witnessing) intimidating. Here's the good news for sharing the good news: Witnessing doesn't just come naturally. It comes supernaturally. See for yourself.

"But you shall receive power (ability, efficiency and might) *when the Holy Spirit has come upon you, and you shall be My witnesses in Jerusalem and all Judea and Samaria and to the ends* (the very bounds) *of the earth"* (Acts 1:8, AMP).

Effective witness is supernaturally empowered. The Holy Spirit Himself makes us able, efficient and mighty as witnesses. He offers the power. We just offer the volume. Even when we think we've butchered a presentation, if we were sincere and God was in it, He will render it effective. Leave the results to Him. He's the One who draws. We'll never be so good at blowing it that we mess God up.

—*Beth Moore*

Beginning with one

"You are the light of the world. A city on a hill cannot be hidden. Neither do people light a lamp and put it under a bowl. Instead they put it on its stand, and it gives light to everyone in the house. In the same way, let your light shine before men, that they may see your good deeds and praise your Father in heaven."
Matthew 5:14–16 (NIV)

One thing you can count on in Asia is that the electricity will go out. A prudent homemaker has a candle (and matches) in every room for such occasions. One night when the power went out, my husband and a friend stepped out onto the balcony into the pitch darkness: no house lights, no streetlights, no lights from cars or motorcycles, just darkness. They faced a hill some distance away, which was peppered with houses. As they watched, one candle was lit, and they saw its small light shine. Two more were lit, then five more, then 20 more. At an increasing rate, the hill became illuminated with small lights.

Sometimes, our family feels overwhelmed at the task before us, especially when we focus on the many lost people in our target group. There just isn't enough time in each day to impact every life by ourselves. But we have chosen to pour our lives into a few believers who have a strong influence in the community. These few, in turn, are each discipling several new believers, who will disciple several more and so on, spreading the Light. Even Jesus chose only 12, knowing that those 12 would impact their own people as well as other nations surrounding them. He knew our human limitations.

Using His example of discipleship, many more will be added to the kingdom at an increasing rate. That's what I hope for—the rapid spread of the gospel, starting with just one: me.

—ANGIE, SOUTH ASIA

Heavenly Father, WHAT A GRACIOUS GOD YOU ARE TO GIVE US A PATTERN OF DISCIPLE-SHIP TO FOLLOW THROUGH YOUR SON. MAY I INVEST MY TIME INTO A FEW WHO WILL MAKE MORE DISCIPLES AND THEN BEGIN THE PROCESS AGAIN. GIVE CHRISTIAN WORKERS AND NATIONAL BELIEVERS THE SAME VISION IN SOUTH ASIA. *Amen.*

Condemned

"Whoever hears my word and believes him who sent me has eternal life and will not be condemned; he has crossed over from death to life." John 5:24 (NIV)

"Show me Your handiwork," I had prayed moments before. My heart danced at the thought of walking alongside God Almighty, anticipating the wonders of His handiwork. I expected Him to show me faces. I would look into the eyes of each person, seeing them as He sees them. I'd see how special they are and be inspired to pray for these magnificent displays of His handiwork.

And that's when I saw it. The dingy bus lumbered past me from where I stood on the sidewalk. Not a seat was left unfilled, and the eyes of each prisoner seemed to gaze vacantly at me through the windows. These were the faces of those condemned. Their guilt was indisputable and their sentences issued—punishment by death.

On that bus rumbling away was God's handiwork. Each passenger was lovingly knit together by His hands. Did they even know where they were headed? They seemed to simply resign themselves to the journey ahead. They didn't know that they had a choice. They didn't know that there is One who wants to free them. If only they'd call on His name ...

"How, then, can they call on the one they have not believed in? And how can they believe in the one of whom they have not heard?" (Rom. 10:14, NIV).

It was the first time I'd seen them, but now I know they are all around me. How is it that I hadn't noticed them before? Maybe I had never taken the time to look.

—A WORKER IN CENTRAL AND EASTERN EUROPE

Father, THERE ARE MANY THAT I ENCOUNTER EACH DAY WHO HAVE NOT CHOSEN YOU, WHO ARE HEADED TOWARD ETERNITY WITHOUT YOU. PLEASE INTERVENE AND USE ME AND FELLOW BELIEVERS TO SHARE THE GOSPEL IN MY COMMUNITY. MAY MISSIONARIES SENSE THE URGENCY TO SHARE IN CENTRAL AND EASTERN EUROPE. *Amen.*

Meeting people where they're at

"For though I am free from all men, I have made myself a servant to all, that I might win the more; and to the Jews I became as a Jew, that I might win Jews."
1 Corinthians 9:19–20a (NKJV)

Bathhouses are popular in South Korea. There are pools of water at different temperatures, places for a massage and saunas. The men are separate from the women. As a person sits in a pool or scrubs himself or someone else with a rough rag, conversation occurs. In order to build relationships, missionaries have had to overcome cultural barriers to utilize an opportunity for evangelism. A key missionary principle is, "Adapt to the culture as much as possible without compromising any biblical principles."

Sometimes following God's purpose means giving up your own comfort. Members of the East Sea Team in Ulsan (ool-SAHN), South Korea, found this to be true when they volunteered to help a small church develop relationships with senior adults in its community. After a worship service and lunch, church members and other senior adults boarded a bus to a spa. During the hour-long ride, an International Mission Board worker, Martha, befriended a Korean grandmother and led her to Christ.

At the bathhouse, Martha sat by another grandmother. They discussed grandchildren, aging and weather. When Martha offered to scrub her back, the grandmother was impressed that an educated woman would offer to do such a thing. She listened intently to Martha's witness and gave her heart to Jesus. The gentle scrubbing of the grandmother's back helped open her calloused heart to Jesus.

God sometimes calls us out of our comfort zone. Jesus, who humbled Himself to become a man, is our example in reaching the lost.

—GRACE, PACIFIC RIM

Father, USE ME TODAY TO SHARE CHRIST WITH SOMEONE, EVEN IF IT'S OUT OF MY OWN COMFORT ZONE. HELP ME TO REACH OTHERS ON THEIR LEVEL. GIVE MISSIONARIES OPPORTUNITIES FOR SITUATIONAL WITNESSING IN UNREACHED AREAS. *Amen.*

A significant contact

"I planted, Apollo watered, but God was causing the growth."
1 Corinthians 3:6 (NASB)

Research shows that it takes seven to 12 significant contacts for anyone, especially a Muslim, to become a Christian. I was blessed to be one in the life of a Middle Eastern lady whom I call Star.

Others working in my country of service had earlier met and baptized Star. She had been a successful hairdresser in her homeland. Her husband, a university professor, asked to store some boxes of test papers in her salon. When the police arrived for those boxes, she discovered they really contained antigovernment documents. Her husband fled. She was arrested, imprisoned, beaten and raped before the police declared her innocent. She and her 6-month-old daughter escaped by donkey over the mountains. They sought official refugee status in the country where we met.

Star would often come to my home for a Bible study, a meal or just to get away from the refugee center. Every time she heard domestic violence in the center, she relived the horrors of those beatings. She and her daughter frequently ended up staying two or three nights with me.

She began to mature in her faith as she read her Bible, prayed, led a friend to Christ and sent Bibles to her home country. I am grateful that I could be one of the significant contacts in Star's life. I am even more grateful that she has become one of the seven to 12 Christian contacts in the lives of others.

Are you a "significant contact" in the life of another?

—MARGARET, WESTERN EUROPE

Thank You, Lord Jesus, FOR SAVING STAR'S LIFE, IN SO MANY WAYS. THANK YOU THAT YOU ASK US TO SIMPLY SOW OR WATER ... AND THAT YOU ARE THE ONE WHO GIVES THE INCREASE. MAKE ME SENSITIVE TO THE WAYS THAT I CAN BE A "SIGNIFICANT CONTACT" IN THE LIVES OF OTHERS. *Amen.*

Lost coins

*"Or suppose a woman has ten silver coins and loses one. Does she not light a lamp,
sweep the house and search carefully until she finds it? And when she finds it, she
calls her friends and neighbors together and says, 'Rejoice with me; I have found
my lost coin.' In the same way, I tell you, there is rejoicing in the presence of the
angels of God over one sinner who repents." Luke 15:8–10 (NIV)*

To become more familiar with Fulani (foo-LAHN-nee) culture and
language, my husband and I built a grass hut in a bush village. We spent
at least one night there each week and tried to do things as closely as
possible to the way the Fulani live.

I cooked our meals over an open fire. A single pot held up by large
rocks cooked most of our food. We often slept outside under the stars
like the rest of the village. We used kerosene lanterns for our light.

One night, as we prepared for bed, my husband laid his long shirt
(like those worn by Fulani men) over the end of our stick bed. As the
shirt flopped forward, some coins fell onto the floor of our hut. We immediately started looking for the coins with the little bit of light shining
from the lantern. Almost as soon as the coins hit the sand floor, they
sank deep into the loose sand, making them impossible to find. We
searched but were amazed at how the coins quickly disappeared!

The incident reminded us of the parable about the woman and her
lost coin. Our lost coins reminded me of our lost Fulani neighbors. Jesus sees them and knows each of them by name. How He must rejoice
when one of them is found!

There are many people around you who are lost: neighbors, teachers, internationals in the community and colleagues at work. Where are
your lost coins, and are you finding them?

—SHELLEY, WEST AFRICA

Heavenly Father, I PRAY FOR MISSIONARIES WHO ARE WITNESSES OF JESUS TO THE FU-
LANI PEOPLE GROUP OF WEST AFRICA. GIVE THEM STRENGTH, ENDURANCE, WISDOM AND
FREEDOM TO SHARE CHRIST WITH THE LOST. MAY I REACH OUT TO THE LOST AROUND ME
SO THAT MORE CAN COME INTO YOUR KINGDOM. *Amen.*

New life?

"How, then, can they call on the One they have not believed in? And how can they believe in the One of whom they have not heard? And how can they hear without someone preaching to them? And how can they preach unless they are sent?" Romans 10:14—15a (NIV)

After evangelism training in rural areas of Mozambique, we split into teams to share from home to home. I was on a team with an American volunteer and two Mozambican believers. We were in the middle of nowhere with 10 to 15 minutes of walking between houses.

At the last house, we were invited to sit with an elderly couple and some teenagers. I asked the old man if he had ever discovered new life. He said, "There is no such thing as new life. There is only suffering and pain."

With his permission, I began to share about Jesus, an unfamiliar name to them. One of the teenagers, named Carlos, was especially attentive. I asked how we could have eternal life, and Carlos answered, "I'm not sure why, but I think it's through this Jesus." We continued talking about the gospel, and the couple and several teenagers wanted to give their lives to Christ.

After we prayed, Carlos looked at me and said, "I've had this thing in my heart for a long time. You told me today the answer I was looking for."

That "thing in his heart" was the Holy Spirit seeking him. However, there was no way for Carlos to know what to do unless someone came and shared the truth with him.

How many others around the world have "this thing in their heart"? They are waiting ... are you willing to go and share as a volunteer or missionary? Are you willing to pray?

—KATIE, CENTRAL, EASTERN AND SOUTHERN AFRICA

Oh, Father, MAKE A WAY FOR THESE PEOPLE IN REMOTE PLACES TO HEAR ABOUT THE ONE WHO GIVES NEW LIFE, THE ONE WHO GIVES ETERNAL LIFE. BRING VOLUNTEERS, NATIONAL BELIEVERS AND MISSIONARIES TO THESE AREAS THAT THE WORLD HAS FORGOTTEN. *Amen.*

Identifying with others

"I have become all things to all men, that I may by all means save some."
1 Corinthians 9:22 (NASB)

Our Muslim landlord and family invited us to their home village for three nights. Their hospitable relatives welcomed us. The family had two houses, and they allowed us to stay in the smaller one. My husband, our three boys and I slept in one bed with no mattress, as is culturally acceptable.

Food was prepared in a mud stove, which is basically a hole in the ground. I had not brought enough clothes, so we washed our clothes in the pond. The more we lived like them, the closer our relationship became.

The second night, I was reading a Bible story by candlelight to our boys at bedtime when Arifa (ah-REE-fah), our landlord's 15-year-old daughter, came in the room. Since she understood English, she listened as I read and prayed.

Later, Arifa and I sipped tea and listened to a Christian music cassette of mine. When she heard the words to one of the songs, she said, "I've heard of Him before." After some discussion about Jesus, she asked to read my Bible when she returned to the city. I gave it to her gladly.

When Paul said, "I have become all things to all men," I believe he meant for me to eat their food, drink their water, sit with them and sip tea, use their "squatty potty," accept their hospitality, wash my clothes in their ponds and let my children play with their children. I want to become all things to all men so that some might be saved.

—JANESSA, SOUTH ASIA

Father, YOU SENT YOUR SON TO BECOME ONE OF US. THANK YOU FOR THE EXAMPLE OF JESUS AS I REACH OUT TO OTHERS. GIVE CHRISTIAN WORKERS THE PERSEVERANCE TO BECOME ALL THINGS TO ALL MEN SO THAT SOME MIGHT BE SAVED. *Amen.*

Don't push

"Be humble and gentle. Be patient with each other, making allowance for each other's faults because of your love." Ephesians 4:2 (NLT)

A friend of ours became a Christian, although he had grown up as a good Muslim by reading the Koran and praying five times a day. He had married a Muslim wife and had pleased his family.

After our friend's conversion, he decided not to push his wife to accept his new beliefs. He was open about following Christ, and she was allowed to continue living as before—but life did not stay the same.

Our friend's life changed drastically as his relationship grew with the Lord. His wife silently noticed a more generous man, a man committed to her and their children—not only in providing food and shelter for them, but in spending time with them.

As our friend hungered for more of God's Word, he began to spend more time with one particular foreign Christian family. At first, his wife was apprehensive. She had never met any foreigners before—especially not any who spoke her heart language. Eventually, she ventured out of her home to meet them for tea. She later reciprocated with a meal in her home.

As our friend's love for Christ overflowed, he shared the good news. One day, his wife overheard as he told a friend stories from the Bible. She stood hidden from view, listening intently. Once the visitor left, she scolded her husband for not telling her these stories. She wanted to hear them, too!

Our friend learned an important lesson: "Don't push, and allow God to work in His time!"

—L., NORTHERN AFRICA AND THE MIDDLE EAST

Heavenly Father, I PRAY THAT I WILL NEVER "PICK GREEN FRUIT." HELP ME NOT TO BE PUSHY ABOUT MY FAITH, BUT TO BE OBSERVANT AND SENSITIVE IN THE TIMING OF SHARING ABOUT CHRIST. GIVE CHRISTIAN WORKERS THIS SAME DISCERNMENT TODAY, ESPECIALLY IN NORTHERN AFRICA AND THE MIDDLE EAST. *Amen.*

A new song

"He brought me up out of the pit of destruction, out of the miry clay; And He set my feet upon a rock making my footsteps firm. And He put a new song in my mouth, a song of praise to our God; Many will see and fear, And will trust in the Lord." Psalm 40:2–3 (NASB)

I recently spent two years working with an unreached ethnic-minority people group, scattered throughout Asia. It was there in a small village surrounded by mountains, rice fields and bamboo that this song begins.

Xiang (SHE-ahng) and I met obscurely one morning when he came bolting out from his house and hollered, "Come over and sit awhile!" After sitting down and getting acquainted, I spotted a dusty guitar in the corner of the room and asked him to play. As soon as I asked, he filled the room with melodic beauty.

Music was the cornerstone of our relationship in the months following. One night, after singing our way into the late hours of night, Xiang received God's gift of salvation, praying in his own language. The following day he wrote a song of praise to God, just as the young poet David did coming out of his own "pit of destruction."

Xiang is a man of influence in his village, so when he sang a new song of a Creator God previously unheard of, many were intrigued. Belonging to a people that are Buddhist, his song was different from their cultural traditions. Yet, since he bridged his message using music, many listened and responded to the lyrics.

Xiang met two other believers a few months later. They now worship and write songs together as they bear witness to each other and to their village of what the Creator God has done for them.

—A WORKER IN EAST ASIA

Creator God, THANK YOU FOR THE GIFT OF MUSIC! CONTINUE TO USE MUSIC TO BRING THIS PEOPLE GROUP AND OTHERS IN EAST ASIA TO CHRIST. *Amen.*

Filling the earth

"You looked, O king, and there before you stood a large statue ... a rock was cut out, but not by human hands. It struck the statue on its feet of iron and clay and smashed them. Then the iron, the clay, the bronze, the silver and the gold were broken to pieces at the same time and became like chaff on a threshing floor in the summer. ... But the rock that struck the statue became a huge mountain and filled the whole earth." Daniel 2:31, 34–35 (NIV)

We work with an ancient people whose ancestors were at Pentecost. Among the 12 million in this country, there are fewer than 200 believers in this group, one of the most unreached peoples in the world.

One day, an unbelieving friend in this people group mentioned a news item about volunteer Christian workers arrested for possessing Bibles in my friend's mother tongue. This language is different than the national language and is suppressed, even though it is legal to speak and read it. When I asked him to comment, he said, "They [the majority] are very afraid of these things. They are afraid that my people will believe because we are so sick of them and Islam. We have suffered assaults for more than 1,000 years, and they have come from other nations acting in the name of Islam."

May it be! Even though there are only a few believers in this city, we can be sure that the kingdom of God will one day fill the earth.

How would our lives be different if we lived as if the hellish gates that guard the captives could not withstand the onslaught of God's kingdom through His messengers (Matt. 16:17–18)? Pray for the destruction of God's enemies: the rulers, authorities and powers of evil (Eph. 6:12). Rejoice, for He is victorious!

—WORKERS IN CENTRAL ASIA

Father, I CONFESS THAT I HAVEN'T FULLY GRASPED THE LOSTNESS OF OTHERS. HELP ME TO LIVE LIKE I AM FULLY CONVINCED THAT YOUR KINGDOM WILL ONE DAY FILL THE EARTH BECAUSE YOUR MESSENGERS ARE BRINGING THE GOOD NEWS. USE WORKERS IN THIS SENSITIVE AREA IN CENTRAL ASIA TO LEAD MANY TO CHRIST. *Amen.*

Planting seeds

"And the seed whose fruit is righteousness is sown in peace by those who make peace." James 3:18 (NASB)

The parable of the sower was part of my Bible reading one morning. This reading reminded me that only a few seeds actually produce fruit, but those few seeds are worth all the effort.

My dad has cared for a small garden year after year, ever since I can remember. He does not do this out of necessity—he tends to the plants simply because it is one of his passions in life. He plants every year, knowing that his efforts may not be successful. Many variables, such as weather conditions, are simply out of his control.

I cannot say that I have seen all the results that I have hoped for as a missionary, although I believe many students that we have shared with have received Christ. It is sometimes discouraging, however, to see that many have not continued with consistent Bible study.

Today, a few students sat by me, and we began talking. One of them expressed interest in Bible study, so I began sharing the gospel with her and her friends. Three or four of them listened as I shared. I'm not sure they really understood the essence of the gospel, but they seemed interested in learning more.

I don't know what will happen to this "seed" I planted today, just as my dad didn't know how his garden would produce. One thing I know for certain—nothing will grow if I don't plant. I am here to share the gospel, so that is what I will continue to do.

—KEVIN, PACIFIC RIM

Father, HELP ME TO BE MINDFUL OF THE SEEDS THAT I PLANT RATHER THAN FOCUSING ON THE HARVEST. THE HARVEST IS IN YOUR HANDS. I PRAY THAT MISSIONARIES, ALSO, WILL CONTINUE TO PLANT THE SEEDS OF THE GOSPEL AND LEAVE THE REST UP TO YOU. *Amen.*

Restaurant evangelism

"Now he who plants and he who waters are one; but each will receive his own reward according to his own labor." 1 Corinthians 3:8 (NASB)

There is a tourist area in Buenos Aires (BWAY-nos AIR-ees), Argentina, where one can eat authentic food and see a demonstration of the "tango." Often, we take visitors to this area called LaBoca, especially to a restaurant where the owners recognize us.

One day, the manager approached us and asked if we would be willing to translate the menu into English so that the tourists could better understand it. The request was comical to us since our Spanish is not that good, but we agreed to do it. At that time we left a Christian tract with one of the waiters, one of the dancers and one of the managers, not knowing if they would be read.

When we finally translated the menu, we returned to the restaurant. As we left, one of the waiters approached us. He said that he had read the tract and given his heart to the Lord.

Soon afterward, we returned to the restaurant with a volunteer group and several of our missionaries who were fluent in Spanish. The same waiter approached us again, and we asked other missionaries to interpret for us. Again the waiter said that he had accepted Christ after reading the tract and that he was teaching his family about Jesus.

What a thrill to know that although our language was limited, God used a simple tract to win others to Him. A gospel tract is such an easy witnessing tool to give to someone for a clear gospel message.

—RALPH AND JUDY, SOUTH AMERICA

Father, USE TRACTS AND OTHER CHRISTIAN LITERATURE TODAY IN MANY PARTS OF THE WORLD TO BRING PEOPLE TO JESUS. WE PRAY THAT YOU WOULD INSPIRE MISSIONARIES TO WRITE TRACTS IN LANGUAGES THAT HAVE NO TRACTS AVAILABLE. SHOW ME SOMEONE TO WHOM I CAN POSSIBLY GIVE A TRACT. *Amen.*

Lead by example

"And you should follow my example, just as I follow Christ's."
1 *Corinthians* 11:1 (TLB)

Going 20 miles probably sounds like no big deal, but to get to Maofwe (mah-OH-fway), Zambia, those 20 miles take more than three hours by car. As we travel, it isn't uncommon to see people who want a ride flagging us down. On this particular day, I had several students with me, but there was still enough room for one more passenger. When a young man flagged us down, I offered him a ride.

As the new passenger sat in the truck, I began telling him about Christ. He had a lot of questions, but for the next two hours, he listened to the story of Jesus. Just before dropping him off, the man accepted Christ and repented.

The students and I went on to our meeting. On our way home, I picked up another person on the side of the road. Before I even had a chance to say anything, the students began telling this stranger of Christ's love and all that He had done in their lives. Praise the Lord, this passenger also accepted Christ before parting the truck.

Before dropping off the students, I mentioned how blessed I was when they witnessed to a total stranger. One of the students said, "Well, after I saw how you did it, I figured that anyone could do it like that. So why shouldn't I do it, too?"

We often learn by example, and others learn by our example. What kind of example do we demonstrate?

—MIKE, CENTRAL, EASTERN AND SOUTHERN AFRICA

Heavenly Father, MAKE ME AN EXAMPLE OF CHRIST TODAY IN EVERYTHING THAT I DO. ALLOW ME TO INFLUENCE OTHERS TO MAKE CORRECT CHOICES AND TO LIVE GODLY LIVES. LET MISSIONARIES BE POSITIVE EXAMPLES TO YOUNG BELIEVERS WHO WILL CONTINUE TO SPREAD THE GOSPEL. *Amen.*

First haircut

"Your beauty should not come from outward adornment, such as braided hair."
1 Peter 3:3a (NIV)

When our son was born, we were still "green" in this culture, so we didn't realize the traditions that went with baby hair. Our son was born with long, thick blond hair. I hate to confess, but I strutted around with my boy as if we had been blessed from on high since he had so much hair.

It impressed no one in our new culture. Actually, we were the topic of neighborhood gossip since they think baby hair is dirty and needs to be shaved at 6 weeks of age.

When my son was pushing 5 months old, and his "birth" hair was still lingering, one brave woman confronted me. I realized that if it would help us to fit in better by cutting his hair, what was the big deal?

So with a beard trimmer, we gave our son a crew cut as I tried to save the hair scraps. Then I cried! I didn't do a very good job, so I tried to touch it up with the trimmers, only making it worse. His hair now looked like I had taken a lawn mower right down the center. I was horrified! But when my friends saw it later that afternoon, they said, "Oh, that looks *soooo* good."

I guess a little scalping won't matter in heaven if it means those friends can listen to my stories about Jesus without being distracted by all that blond hair! The Lord chooses funny ways to humble me.

—T., PACIFIC RIM

Father, FORGIVE ME WHEN I STUBBORNLY HOLD ON TO THINGS THAT DON'T REALLY MATTER, THINGS THAT PREVENT OTHERS FROM POSSIBLY COMING TO CHRIST. SHOW ME ATTITUDES, TRADITIONS OR HABITS THAT MAY BE STUMBLING BLOCKS TO OTHERS. AND HELP MISSIONARIES TO FIT INTO THEIR NEW CULTURES WITHOUT COMPROMISING THE THINGS THAT YOU HOLD AS IMPORTANT. *Amen.*

Spiritual gossip

"And they all continued in amazement and great perplexity, saying to one an-other, 'What does this mean?'" Acts 2:12 (NASB)

We began using a new method of training nationals to start church-planting movements in South India. We found that evangelists were sharing the gospel with family members of new believers, rather than the new believers taking the responsibility of leading their families to Christ.

Thus, we began training evangelists to teach new believers to imme-diately share their faith. The evangelist would also train them to teach those they led to Christ to share the gospel. This approach enabled the number of people sharing Christ to grow exponentially.

An immediate breakthrough occurred. Some evangelists started seeing 20 times more people come to Christ than when they were do-ing all the evangelism themselves. There were so many Hindus coming to Christ that new churches and Bible study groups were being orga-nized rapidly.

An evangelist said that in one village of India, so many new believers were sharing their faith and training others to share Christ that people were calling what was happening a "spiritual gossip." The village was amazed and perplexed to see their fellow Hindus not only coming to Christ, but immediately leading others to Christ and training them to share their faith. Christianity was spreading rapidly, just as fast as gossip!

Are we using this method, or are we relying on our pastors to win people to the Lord? Do we share with our lost relatives or neighbors, or do we beg the pastor to give them a visit? The responsibility is ours.

—B.B., SOUTH ASIA

Heavenly Father, MAY I TAKE THE RESPONSIBILITY TO WIN THE LOST TO CHRIST AND TO TRAIN THEM TO SHARE THEIR FAITH. YOU HAVE COMMANDED ME IN YOUR WORD TO MAKE DISCIPLES. I PRAY ALSO THAT CHURCH-PLANTING MOVEMENTS WILL RAPIDLY CONTINUE IN SOUTH INDIA AND ALL OF SOUTH ASIA. *Amen.*

Setting captives free

"So shall my word be that goes out from my mouth; it shall not return to me empty, but it shall accomplish that which I purpose." Isaiah 55:11 (NRSV)

In the land of Namibia (nah-MIB-ee-ah), we traveled to remote villages, where most practice ancestor worship and traditional tribal religion. We visited homes and presented the gospel when permitted.

At one street, we again sought the Lord's guidance. From behind a wire fence, two men called to us. They were prisoners at a jail and asked if we would come in to talk. We knew that dealing with police officers and paperwork would take a long time. So, regretting that we couldn't visit at that point, we prayerfully handed the men some tracts in their language.

Before we could leave, a man outside the fence stopped us. Dressed in plain clothes, he told us that he was a police officer. The translator openly explained what we were giving to the prisoners. To our surprise, the officer said, "You must come to my home and tell me about Jesus." He led us to his home behind the jail.

In the yard, the man listened intently to the gospel through the translator. I silently prayed for him the whole time. To our joy, he asked Jesus to be his Lord! But what he said next brought tears to our eyes. "I've been waiting for someone to tell me about Jesus," said the officer.

The prisoners we met now have someone on the "inside" to explain the tracts and tell them about Jesus. What "prisoners" do you know who need to be set free? Will you share the key to life today?

—M.M., CENTRAL, EASTERN AND SOUTHERN AFRICA

Father, I PRAY THAT YOU WILL MAKE A WAY FOR PRISONERS ALL OVER THE WORLD TO HEAR THE GOSPEL. THROUGH THE OFFICER IN NAMIBIA, BRING THE GOSPEL TO THE JAIL WHERE HE WORKS. HELP ME TO SET A CAPTIVE FREE TODAY THROUGH MY WITNESS. *Amen.*

Facing the fear of witnessing

"With your help I can advance against a troop; with my God I can scale a wall."
Psalm 18:29 (NIV)

In a predominantly Muslim country, our team's goal is to put a New Testament in every household. Many volunteers assist as we go door to door, a method that can be intimidating. There are many fundamental Muslims who are not happy with us giving out the Scriptures. Each time a team comes, I pray for a courageous man who can do the talking while I interpret.

One day, the team leader assigned the sweetest, most soft-spoken couple in the group to be with me. It was hard not to outwardly show my disappointment. I immediately went to be alone to talk with my Father. I told Him that there was an obvious mistake, since I didn't want to be the leader. God gently reminded me how His Son did not go back to heaven (His comfort zone) until His task was complete. I returned to my teammates.

The first door we knocked on brought a woman who said nothing when we offered her a Bible. She left us in the doorway feeling uncomfortable. We heard her talking loudly in another room in the house. She returned to us and said, "No." Her hatred was visible.

That was not a good start. The next two hours took a complete turn. We gave away 60 Bibles! We could only praise our Father.

Our journey on this earth is not guaranteed to be an easy one. Our prize in heaven will be giving glory to the One who endured the cross for us.

—KIM, CENTRAL AND EASTERN EUROPE

Father, I PRAY THAT YOU WOULD DISPEL ANY FEAR THAT I MIGHT HAVE TO SHARE JESUS WITH _____. GIVE COURAGE TO MISSIONARIES AND VOLUNTEERS AS THEY WITNESS ACROSS THE WORLD. *Amen.*

Your name will be "Liseli"

"The people living in darkness have seen a great light; on those living in the land of the shadow of death a light has dawned." Matthew 4:16 (NIV)

There was an air of excitement all around Sefula (seh-FOO-la) and especially at my small home. The Lozi (LOH-zee) king was coming to attend the church services and to eat at my house! As far as I knew, the king usually did not visit a private home.

The day came when the king entered my home. During the introductions, I explained in the Lozi language that I was a missionary and that my name was Gerri. In SiLozi (see-LOH-zee), the name Gerri sounds like "Jelly" because it is hard for them to pronounce the "r" sound. So I boldly asked for a Lozi name, which I found out later was against protocol. The king was humored, and he answered with a smile, "I'll think about it."

Before the end of the visit, the king said, "My wife and I have decided upon a name for you. It will be 'Liseli' (lee-SEH-lee). It means 'light.' Just as the sun gives light and life to plants, animals and people, I want God's Word to be life and a light to the people of Western Province."

I was stunned and pleased to receive this blessing. After the king left the room, a lady seated nearby privately said, "Ah, you are a very lucky woman to be given a name by the king."

Luck? No! God knew that I would be given the name Liseli, and as I let the excitement of the moment sink in, I realized that His true "light" must shine through me to the Lozi.

—GERRI, CENTRAL, EASTERN AND SOUTHERN AFRICA

Almighty God, I PRAY THAT YOU WOULD PLACE GOD-FEARING PEOPLE OF WISDOM IN PLACES OF LEADERSHIP IN SOUTHERN AFRICA. MAY YOUR WORD GO FORTH BOLDLY, O LORD, TO BE LIFE AND LIGHT AMONG THE LOZI PEOPLE AS YOU STRENGTHEN THOSE WHO CARRY YOUR MESSAGE. *Amen.*

Too late

"Go out and train everyone you meet, far and near, in this way of life ... Then instruct them in the practice of all I have commanded you."
Matthew 28:19–20a (MSG)

The hot sun is merciless as it beats down upon the procession of men and women slowly walking on the dusty trail. At the head of the procession, a coffin is born by eight tribal leaders of a Wayuu (WHY-you) clan who interchange during the four-hour trek to the burial site. The man being carried in the coffin was a tribal leader, but foremost, a singer. He sang of life and the daily happenings of his family clan. He sang of death, darkness and forever wandering in the between world. He was adept at playing many of the Wayuu tube and whistle instruments. The sounds of birds and turkeys, wind and rain flowed from his instruments while his talented fingers and lips moved over them.

The sounds heard today are mournful with heart-wrenching sobs and gut-level groans. This gentle man believed in God, but he believed that after making the Wayuu and giving them their land, God walked away and left them alone. He was never told of the God who loves and cares about every detail of his life. Although from a tribe that is based on an intricate payment system, he didn't hear or understand that Jesus paid to set him free. He died too soon. The oral Bible stories came too late ... for him.

Determination to reach those around us before it's too late is real. We never know when a loved one, acquaintance or friend might die. Today is the day for salvation.

—KAYE, SOUTH AMERICA

Father, GIVE ME AN OPPORTUNITY TO SPEAK TO SOMEONE TODAY WHO NEEDS TO HEAR ABOUT JESUS BEFORE IT'S TOO LATE. LET THE GOSPEL BE SPREAD IN THIS AREA OF SOUTH AMERICA, AND MAY MANY OF THE WAYUU COME TO CHRIST. *Amen.*

Pork chops, anyone?

"And as it is appointed for men to die once, but after this the judgment."
Hebrews 9:27 (NKJV)

Isn't it great how God uses humorous situations to get people to think about Him? One day, our English Bible study class discussed salvation. We read from the manual in English, then Mike and James explained the meaning in English and Korean. The concept of salvation for the Christian was explained and compared to the Buddhist concept of salvation through reincarnation. Buddhists believe that if a person does good works, then he will come back as a better or richer person. If a person's bad works outweigh the good, then that person could be reincarnated as an animal, even a pig.

Questions arose as fodder for discussion. If someone were to be reincarnated as a pig, how does the pig break out of the bad cycle and redeem itself? Can a pig do good works? And what happens if the pig is used for food and consequently eaten? Needless to say, the futility of the Buddhist faith was made evident.

After class, we left with the men to eat lunch. When we arrived at the cafeteria, the meal for the day was pork! Laughter overcame us, but we finally managed to eat our lunches. I'm sure most of the men are still thinking about that lesson on salvation.

We thank God for this funny occasion. May God's Word reveal truth to those walking in the darkness of false religion. May the lost grasp the truth that we are saved by grace and not by works.

—GRACE, PACIFIC RIM

Righteous and true Father, MAY THE FUTILITY OF FALSE RELIGIONS BE MADE EVIDENT TO THOSE IN THE PACIFIC RIM. MAY SALVATION BY GRACE BE REVEALED BY THE HOLY SPIRIT. THANK YOU THAT SALVATION IS NOT EARNED, BUT THAT I AM SAVED BY YOUR GRACE. *Amen.*

The difference Jesus makes

"And we know that in all things God works for the good of those who love Him, who have been called according to His purpose." Romans 8:28 (NIV)

Linda came to the Bible study deep in mourning, having suffered her second miscarriage the previous week. How could she be a good wife if she couldn't bear a child? She was even angry with her mother for giving her life.

Her friend, who was a believer, kept encouraging Linda to seek God. Reluctantly, Linda came to the Christian's house, quiet and fearful. Two weeks later, she came again ... and a little hope crept into her voice.

A month later, we were invited to the home of another believer who had invited several students to watch the *JESUS* film. Linda was also there. At the end of the film, the host extended an invitation to accept the Lord. It was a quiet moment, full of promise and expectations. Yet the students seemed completely disinterested. But a meal had been planned, so they felt obligated to stay. As we discussed the movie, they said how impossible it was that God could have come to earth as a human.

But there was a difference in Linda. She said quietly, "When they prayed that prayer, I prayed with them. Now I believe, too." She didn't allow the taunting words of the students to take away her joy in Christ.

That week she wrote her mother a letter thanking her for giving her life. She said she didn't know what the future held, but she now had confidence that Jesus would help her face it. She also thanked her friend for not giving up on her.

—A WORKER IN CHINA

Father, YOU HAVE A PURPOSE IN EVERYTHING THAT COMES MY WAY. HELP ME TO FIND HOPE IN HOPELESS SITUATIONS, AND HELP ME TO GIVE OTHERS HOPE THROUGH JESUS. *Amen.*

Apathy revealed

"The thief comes only to steal and kill and destroy; I have come that they may have life, and have it to the full." John 10:10 (NIV)

As my eyes fell to the bundle in her arms, I could not hide the alarm on my face, although I desperately tried. The mother, covered in her religious black, sat quietly, submissively, sullenly. Her bearded husband seemed unaware that his family was in the midst of crisis, but she knew.

Death soon would steal her child from her arms. The babe's sunken eyes, taut skin and shallow breaths were evidence. My stomach sickened, and my heart cried out to God.

In their culture, her husband would not have permitted us to converse. Besides, words would not have been adequate to comfort her. After our meeting, she went home expecting to bury her firstborn within a day, and I went home to cry.

I asked God, "Why?" Then, in the solitude, He spoke to my heart and asked me, *Why do you cry for the physically dying, but do not show the same grief for those who are spiritually dead? Why did it take a dying babe in a mother's arms to bring your attention to her lostness? Why do you pass by a single soul without bringing his or her needs before Me?*

Until then, I was unaware of my growing apathy, and His questions jolted me. My prayers and tears of intercession quickly turned to those of repentance. How I thank God that He has forever etched in my memory the face of a dying child so that I shall not forget that He longs to give life to dying souls.

—CHELE, SOUTH ASIA

Father, FORGIVE MY FREQUENT APATHY SHOWN TOWARD A LOST WORLD. I PRAY THAT YOU WILL USE THIS ILLUSTRATION IN MY LIFE TO HELP ME GRASP THE REALITY OF LOSTNESS. MAY I HAVE A PASSION TO SHARE CHRIST WITH THE LOST, ZEAL TO FINANCIALLY SUPPORT CHRISTIAN WORKERS OVERSEAS, AND AN OVERWHELMING DESIRE TO PRAY FOR PEOPLE GROUPS OF THE WORLD WHO HAVE NOT HEARD THE GOSPEL. *Amen.*

A willing heart

"But God chose the foolish things of the world to shame the wise; God chose the weak things of the world to shame the strong. ... Therefore, as it is written: 'Let him who boasts boast in the Lord.'" 1 Corinthians 1: 27, 31 (NIV)

We were new missionaries arriving in a large city. While waiting to disembark the plane for our first glance of Africa, my 9-year-old son said, "Mom, have the camera ready. I want you to take a picture of the first person I tell about Jesus."

In the weeks that followed, we continued to talk with our children about witnessing. God often reminded me of the words my son spoke our first day on this continent.

One day, we were invited to go ice-skating at a local mall. The kids laughed that their first time ice-skating was in Africa. After a while, I noticed my son and another boy standing in the middle of the rink having a serious conversation. Eventually, my son rushed to me.

"I was nervous, but I knew I had to do it," my son said. He asked the other boy if he knew how to get to heaven. The child said no. My son then told him about Jesus, sharing the ABCs of salvation that he had learned in Vacation Bible School and several verses he had memorized.

I listened, absolutely amazed. Why? Because our son has learning disabilities that often make conversation difficult for him. So when he shared Jesus, I *knew* it was God working through him. God simply used a willing heart.

Are we an example of sharing with others before our children? Are we teaching our children to share their faith? God can do this through us, and He is willing.

—JOYE, CENTRAL, EASTERN AND SOUTHERN AFRICA

Heavenly Father, MAY I BE OBEDIENT TO YOUR LEADING TODAY WHEN AN OPPORTUNITY ARISES TO SHARE MY FAITH. HELP ME TO BE SENSITIVE TO YOUR SPIRIT. MAY MISSIONARIES AND I NEVER SHARE IN ARROGANCE OR IN OUR OWN STRENGTH, BUT LET US BE VESSELS OF YOUR COMPASSION AND LOVE WHEN WITNESSING. *Amen.*

"You have a twin"

"'And you will seek Me and find Me, when you search for Me with all your heart. And I will be found by you,' declares the Lord." Jeremiah 29:13–14a (NASB)

As I prayerwalked, an African man, who is taller than I, approached me. This experience was unusual, since I'm six foot nine. Instantly, a common bond was formed. By our next meeting, Usman (OOS-mahn) and I were talking about spiritual things.

Usman is a devout Muslim. Knowing that I am a Christian, Usman still enjoys my company as I enjoy his.

As our friendship developed, Usman invited me to meet his family. At first, they were reserved, but eventually God gave me favor with them. One brother purposely chanted the Koran or his prayers in my presence. Other brothers confronted me about my faith, but God gave me such grace that, later, they were more cordial. Villagers would say, "Ah, sa seek; am nga seek" (ah sah-sek ahm in-gah sek), meaning, "Your twin; you have a twin." Even his cautious mother said, "You behave just like my son," and she started to call me her son as well.

Amazingly, Usman accompanied me to a meeting with 30 Wolof (WOOL-off) men who follow Jesus. A Christian radio broadcaster then began to speak, and Usman heard the Word of God. It wasn't long before Usman was debating points as he defended Islam. It reminded me of the apostle Paul before his conversion.

Meeting Usman was no coincidence. He is continuing to discuss the Word of God with me and has heard testimonies of former Muslims who could not find truth in the Koran. I look forward to the end of the story.

—WADE, WEST AFRICA

Holy God, THANK YOU THAT YOUR SPIRIT IS MIGHTILY AT WORK IN THE LIVES OF USMAN AND OTHERS LIKE HIM WHOM YOU ARE DRAWING TO YOURSELF. I PRAY THAT EACH DAY TRUTH WILL BE REVEALED TO MUSLIMS AROUND THE WORLD AND THAT THEY WILL HAVE A DESIRE TO WORSHIP THE TRUE GOD WITH EVERYTHING THEY HAVE. *Amen.*

Just in time

"And Jesus said unto him, 'This day is salvation come to this house. ... For the Son of man is come to seek and to save that which was lost." Luke 19:9–10 (KJV)

Within the dark interior of the mud hut, an elderly woman lay on a straw mat with a thin blanket pulled up to her chin. Her face was wrinkled by years of exposure to the hot Kalahari (kah-lah-HA-ree) Desert sun. She was dying.

The eldest daughter was expected to tend to her mother's needs in these last hours. According to the daughter, her mother had not known of a single Christian coming to their village during her lifetime. I realized that she had never heard the message of salvation. I apologized that no Christian had come before to share with her mother.

Beneath the blanket, the elderly woman stirred. A thin, fragile arm appeared waving feebly in the air. She whispered in the Tswana (SWAH-nah) language, "I hear you, I hear you."

With a sense of the God-appointed moment, I knelt by her to share the gospel and the free gift of salvation that God was offering to her. Her thirsty soul drank in every word. By her own simple prayer, she received the gift. A look of peace settled over her countenance as though an arduous race was finished. She died a few hours later.

Surely angels in heaven rejoiced as the glory of God extended its reach and found a foothold in this forsaken village consumed by spiritual darkness. How many more are there who have not heard? This old woman heard just hours before her death.

Who in our family needs salvation before they die?

—GORDON, CENTRAL, EASTERN AND SOUTHERN AFRICA

Father, HOW MANY PEOPLE AROUND ME ARE TAKING THEIR LAST BREATHS? MAKE ME SENSITIVE TO THE NEED OF SALVATION FOR THE DYING. GIVE ME COURAGE TO SHARE WITH OLDER FAMILY MEMBERS WHO DO NOT KNOW YOU. BRING THE GOOD NEWS OF CHRIST IN REMOTE VILLAGES IN BOTSWANA, NAMIBIA AND ANGOLA. *Amen.*

Conversations

"Pray that I may proclaim it clearly, as I should. Be wise in the way you act toward outsiders; make the most of every opportunity. Let your conversation be always full of grace, seasoned with salt, so that you may know how to answer everyone." Colossians 4:4–6 (NIV)

We sat holding our cups of tea, chatting on a cold winter afternoon, just like ladies in the United States might do. My friend and I talked about a variety of things, including how her particular people group views women and children.

She is a Jat Sikh (jot SEEK). She told me that in their society, they feel women should stay at home and not work. Women are protected. For instance, her niece is not allowed to go out of the house much, except to go to school.

We talked about how being too strict on children can sometimes make them go wild later in life. Even though our two cultures are very different, there is common ground. She said, "Parents should not be so rigid. We need to give children some freedom." I agreed and added, "Parents should give freedom while still watching what their children do." She nodded in agreement.

I started to tell her how I had been rebellious as a teenager. I hadn't planned to tell her about myself, though I had been praying for an opportunity to share. But suddenly, I found myself giving my personal testimony in her language. I was a little nervous. When I finished, she told me, "I like to hear the things you have to say."

I'm still praying for her and using every opportunity to share. God seems to direct our conversations to Him at the most opportune times.

Do you allow God to be in control of your conversations?

—K.B., SOUTH ASIA

Father, DIRECT MY CONVERSATION TODAY. LET EVERY WORD THAT I SPEAK BE UPLIFTING AND SEASONED WITH GRACE. USE THE FRIENDLY CONVERSATIONS OF CHRISTIAN WORKERS WITH NATIONALS TO PRESENT THE GOSPEL, ESPECIALLY TODAY IN SOUTH ASIA. *Amen.*

Breaking the ice

"Behold, you will call a nation you do not know, and a nation which knows you not will run to you, because of the LORD your God, even the Holy One of Israel; for He has glorified you." Isaiah 55:5 (NASB)

After he had placed his carry-on in the overhead compartment, the neatly dressed middle-aged man took his seat next to me on the plane. I smiled and greeted him. Abruptly he stated, "So you want to talk. Are you with the CIA?" Surprised, I amazed myself with a quick comeback and retorted, "No. Are you?" That comment seemed to break the ice, and we both gave a hearty laugh that began a five-hour conversation between him, my husband and me.

During our discussion, the man stated several times that he had never shared his life with a perfect stranger before, especially on a plane, and did not understand why it was so easy to do so this time. He seemed to relax as he told about his wife's death, the horror of being left to raise three children and the anger with God for taking his wife, even though he claimed to be an atheist. After listening, God gave us the opportunity to share His love with him.

Amazingly enough, during the next couple of years, we were able to build a deep relationship with this man and his family. One Christmas, he gladly accepted a Bible. How we wish we could say that he had made a decision for Jesus, but we only know that the Father enabled us to love him and his family and to plant many seeds. We continue to pray for him and trust that he will eventually choose to follow Jesus.

—A. AND A., NORTHERN AFRICA AND THE MIDDLE EAST

Father, I PRAY SPECIFICALLY FOR THIS MAN AND HIS FAMILY, WHO HAVE FORMED A FRIENDSHIP WITH THIS COUPLE. BRING THEM TO SALVATION. OPEN DOORS FOR WORKERS IN NORTHERN AFRICA AND THE MIDDLE EAST TO BUILD RELATIONSHIPS. *Amen.*

In the midst of sorrow

"As the mountains surround Jerusalem, so the LORD surrounds His people from this time forth and forever." Psalm 125:2 (NASB)

During our second year in China, my husband and I were thrilled to discover that we were expecting for the first time. As the second trimester approached, our joy turned to fear as I began to miscarry. We went to the local hospital to have a sonogram performed, and our eyes filled with tears as the doctor searched without success for a heartbeat.

With heavy hearts, we made hasty preparations to travel to another country with better health care. During our flight, we felt the warm presence of the Lord in an intense way.

I miscarried the baby as we flew to our final destination. Our hearts grieved as we struggled to come to grips with the loss of this tiny life. Being thousands of miles away from family was especially hard. Even though we didn't understand why this had happened, we felt the Father's love and knew that He would somehow use this loss for His glory.

After we returned home, many of our local friends came to visit us. As we shared about the loss of our unborn child, something changed in our relationships. We were no longer just "the foreigners" who dress funny and like to eat strange foods, but we had now become people like them who experience loss. Unlike them, however, our loss was not without hope. We were able to testify to our unbelieving friends about the faithful, loving God we serve, who gives joy in the midst of sorrow and hope in place of loss.

—A WORKER IN CHINA

Father, BE WITH WORKERS TODAY WHO ARE EXPERIENCING LOSS OR TRAGEDY. HELP THEM TO SEE YOUR PURPOSES DURING TRIALS. HELP ME TO ALSO KNOW THAT JOY COMES AGAIN AFTER TRAGEDY. *Amen.*

Earthly tents and heavenly bodies

"For we know that if the earthly tent we live in is destroyed, we have a building from God, a house not made with hands, eternal in the heavens. For in this tent we groan, longing to be clothed with our heavenly dwelling."
2 Corinthians 5:1–2 (NRSV)

In the village of Nintenga (nen-TANG-uh), another missionary and I met a man named Idrissa (ee-DREE-sah), who asked if we could purchase a tent for him. A tent was bought, and we brought it to him a few weeks later. We began to show him how to set up the tent. When we finished, he said, "When are you going to teach me and my household the Jesus path?"

I remembered the passage in 2 Corinthians about our bodies being like an earthly tent. We shared that our earthy bodies are temporary, just like the tent. If we follow Christ, when we die we will receive a new body that cannot break or get hurt. Christians long to have that new body—to be with Christ—because we know this is "very much better" (Phil. 1:23, NASB).

After sharing about our earthly bodies, my fellow missionary told the story of Jesus and Nicodemus in John 3. She explained that the only way to obtain eternal life is by being born again. Nicodemus wondered how he could enter his mother's womb again, but Christ was talking about being born of the Spirit. We told Idrissa that to have eternal life, he must be born again through believing in Jesus.

Then Idrissa said, "The tent you brought was sweet, but the words you have just shared are better than sweet." Wow! May Idrissa understand the truth he heard and see that he can experience the sweetness of God for all eternity by trusting in Christ.

—TARA, WEST AFRICA

Father, MAY THE "JESUS PATH" BE SOUGHT BY WEST AFRICANS SUCH AS IDRISSA. PROTECT AND GUIDE YOUNG TWO-YEAR MISSIONARIES WHO ARE WILLING TO GIVE UP COMFORTABLE LIVES TO BRING THE GOSPEL TO THE LOST. *Amen.*

The harvest is rotting

"Behold, I say to you, lift up your eyes, and look on the fields, that they are white for the harvest." John 4:35b (NKJV)

A country divided by civil war and vast numbers of refugees descending on the capital city made the situation look bleak at best. Because of government restraints, we could not work with refugees or hold the orphans or evangelize the lost.

My selfish prayer was, "Lord, what can I do here? Did You bring me here to drive me insane? The fields haven't even been plowed or planted. How can there be a harvest? The government does not allow evangelism. When will there be a harvest in this dry and weary land?"

I cried these words, wanting God to answer immediately. In reality, I wanted Him to remove me. I heard no voice.

I went to worship at a new place. Upon entering, I noticed people from many nations—Americans, Europeans, Africans and people from the many tribes of my new home. Maybe this land *had* been plowed and planted.

Attached to the wall hung a ragged sign. It read: *The Harvest Is Rotting.* My heart was overcome with conviction. The refugees nobody wanted, the orphans who did not exist in the eyes of the government and the strict laws about religion encouraged complacency, but the words on the wall woke me.

The harvest is rotting. The harvest my Lord proclaimed ready is rotting, because I had focused on limitations and lost sight of the Lord. The harvest is ready. Am I going to stand by while they "rot" because the passion in my heart has been replaced with fear?

—D.S., Northern Africa and the Middle East

Lord of the harvest, may I not stand by while others rot. May I speak words of peace, words from the Word, so that those around me can understand who Your Son, Jesus, is. Use Christian workers in Northern Africa and the Middle East to bring in the harvest for Your glory. *Amen.*

Waiting and waiting

"Then he said to his disciples, 'The harvest is plentiful but the workers are few. Ask the Lord of the harvest, therefore, to send out workers into his harvest field.'"
Matthew 9:37–38 (NIV)

"A few years ago I had a dream that the prophet Jesus was teaching on a hilltop to thousands of people. He healed many and gave them a book of truth. As I watched, my heart was burdened deeply with a problem that only I knew. Jesus looked across the crowd, into my eyes and answered my problem. He did not speak aloud, but He spoke directly to my heart, filling me with peace.

"Later in my dream, Jesus approached me on the street and told me to follow Him. I followed Him all the way to a church, where He motioned for me to enter. At first I would not, because I am a Muslim. Jesus was so compelling, though, that I finally entered. He told me to sit and wait, because someone would meet me there soon. Then He disappeared. I waited and waited for hours, but nobody came. Finally I left."

When Gail finished telling her dream, I could barely contain my excitement. God had prepared her to receive truth. She only needed someone to befriend her and explain the gospel. Several months later, Gail trusted in Jesus.

I am haunted, however, by the way Gail's dream ended. I wonder how many seekers of God are ignored by church members? How many others live in countries where access to the gospel is extremely limited? Have my busyness or my feelings of inadequacy left someone waiting? In His mercy, the Holy Spirit prepares people's hearts to hear truth, but He calls us to actually speak it.

—JOY, CENTRAL ASIA

Father, IT GRIEVES ME TO THINK THAT I HAVE KEPT SOMEONE WAITING TO HEAR THE GOS-PEL. OPEN MY EYES TO OPPORTUNITIES TO GREET VISITORS AT CHURCH, NEW NEIGHBORS, STUDENTS AND OTHERS WHOM I MEET. GIVE CHRISTIAN WORKERS THE URGENCY, TOO, TO SEEK OUT THE LOST IN ORDER TO DEVELOP RELATIONSHIPS WITH THEM. *Amen.*

JUNE V

—

Persecution

—

My daughter, Melissa, told me the other day that she watched a talk-show host interview one of her favorite actresses. The actress made a comment that disappointed her so much that Melissa said she'd never respect her again. Somehow the subject of the world's troubles came up in the interview, and the celebrity quipped that she never watched the news because she didn't want to know. There's a name for that: voluntary ignorance. The worst kind.

You and I who are stateside don't want to suffer from the same sad malady. Some serious stuff is going on in and around the family of God, and we need to know about it. This month, our emphasis is on persecution. The human ego is so grotesquely large that we tend to think that the state of our own personal lives is the state of most lives.

The state of the Western church is very unlike the church in the rest of the world. In Matthew 24, Christ prophesied that a great escalation in persecution would take place toward the time of His return and the *"end of the age"* (v. 3, NIV). The ninth verse reads, *"Then you will be handed over to be persecuted and put to death, and you will be hated by all nations because of me"* (NIV). That's the bad news.

The good news comes a few verses later: *"And this gospel of the kingdom will be preached in the whole world as a testimony to all nations, and then the end will come"* (v. 14, NIV). At the same time the testimony of Jesus Christ is permeating every single people group, the persecution of Christians will dramatically escalate. The church of Jesus Christ in the latter days will doubtless experience the worst of times and the best of times. Christ will pour out His Spirit even as the enemy rises up in furious persecution against His Bride.

We don't have to look to the future for these events. Prophecy is being fulfilled right under our noses. Jerry Rankin, president of the International Mission Board, tells me that the Great Commission (disciples in every nation, according to Matthew 28:19–20) is a reachable goal in the lifetime of any middle-aged believer. At the same time, the IMB, as well as many other missions organizations, has never felt the sting of persecution and death like it has in the last few years.

Even in the midst of such escalation, what missionaries in persecuted areas personally experience is still only an ounce of what they are forced to watch indigenous believers experience. I have seen missionaries sob as they testify to the suffering of some of their converts. The witness of missionaries in countries where the gospel is opposed often places those to whom they witness at far greater risk than themselves. Imagine the complication of knowing that your witness might lead to the end of a person's earthly life but to the beginning of his eternal life!

The persecuted church is one of the greatest realities of our time. Very harsh things are happening to some of our own brothers and sisters in Christ. Many are dying. Many are purposely starved. Many are beaten. Many lose their jobs and their homes and sometimes even their children if they don't renounce their faith. Can you imagine?

But we must! First Corinthians 12:26 reminds the body of Christ: *"If one part suffers, every part suffers with it"* (NIV). We have a responsibility to know what is going on in our own family. We cannot hide our heads under the sand. We must pray. Not only because it may often be all we can do, but because it is by far the most powerful thing we can do. Big things happen when small people ask big things of a big God.

You will have many opportunities to read about the persecuted church this month, but don't for a moment dread it. Some of the sweetest, most moving stories you'll ever hear come out of persecution. The only reason that God puts up with an iota of persecution against His people is because its harvest can be great. Just listen to the testimony that came out of the first wave that broke out against the early New Testament church: *"On that day a great persecution broke out against the church at Jerusalem, and all except the apostles were scattered throughout Judea and Samaria"* (Acts 8:1, NIV).

God also allows a measure of persecution against His church because its flames can be purifying. Refining. Wise indeed is the Western church to reach out to the persecuted brothers and sisters in other nations. Ours is coming.

—*Beth Moore*

One voice, one dream

"If you confess with your mouth the Lord Jesus and believe in your heart that God has raised Him from the dead, you will be saved." Romans 10:9 (NKJV)

Taken to the *madrassa* (muh-DRAH-suh), a school for boys, at age 5 by his parents, Raja (rah-jah) was trained early to be a leader in a mosque. When he was older, a local Christian woman visited his school and was allowed to speak briefly to the students, but Raja angrily shouted and forced her to leave.

That night, he had a disturbing dream. He dreamed that he was in his family's house. Suddenly, the house was surrounded with people who slowly kept moving closer to his house. The people were angry with him for running off the Christian woman. This dream deeply disturbed him. As a result, Raja became curious about Christianity.

Several years later, Raja wanted to become a doctor. He received training from Dr. Shah, who was a converted Muslim. Dr. Shah helped Raja study the passages in the Koran that spoke about Isa (Jesus). Raja learned and accepted that Isa was righteous, honorable and knows the way to heaven. Through this discipleship, Raja believed in Jesus and was baptized.

As a doctor, Raja gives medicine to his patients but never fails to pray for healing in the name of Isa. He is now writing a book to Muslims so they can understand that Isa is the only way to heaven.

The courage of one Christian to risk everything to speak to Muslim boys was a radical step. Stepping out in faith to share the gospel is what it takes to give the least likely to convert the chance to consider Jesus.

—A WORKER IN SOUTH ASIA

Father, THANK YOU FOR THE COURAGE OF ONE VOICE DECLARING SALVATION THROUGH THE MESSIAH, JESUS, IN THIS SOUTH ASIAN SCHOOL. GIVE BOLDNESS TODAY TO CHRISTIAN WORKERS IN THIS REGION OF THE WORLD SO THAT THEY MAY SHARE THE GOSPEL WITH MUSLIMS, BUDDHISTS, HINDUS AND OTHER PEOPLE WHO TRUST IN FALSE RELIGIONS. *Amen.*

God has done it

*"Why do you boast in evil, O mighty man? The lovingkindness of God endures
all day long." Psalm 52:1 (NASB)*

There is a wealthy, influential Muslim man who has sworn to destroy our Christian fellowship. Because of his efforts, believers have been arrested, extorted and harassed, in addition to trying to be forced into recanting. For months, we had been praying that God would touch this man's heart. His persecution has been a terrible burden. Although I had never done this before, I began praying Psalm 52. This psalm has much more to do with cursing enemies than praising God.

One day, this man called for several of our group's leaders to explain themselves, their faith and their witness. This man had threatened that within two weeks, his power would be seen by the Christians. We prayed that he would see God's power.

When our brothers appeared before the man, he was confused, ashamed and not able to respond to the answers given! Several other civil and religious authorities present spoke in support of the Christians' right to freedom of religion. The outcome was better than we expected. We knew that many people worldwide were praying during this meeting.

We don't know what scheme this man might have in the future, but we are praying for victory against Satan and those he would use to try to thwart God's plans. In the meantime, as in the last verse of Psalm 52, *"I will give You thanks forever, because You have done it, and I will wait on Your name, for it is good, in the presence of Your godly ones"* (v. 9, NASB).

—D., WEST AFRICA

Heavenly Father, PUT IN THEIR PLACES THE MIGHTY MEN WHO THINK THEY CAN THWART YOUR PLANS. YOU WILL NOT BE MOCKED. ALLOW THE GOOD NEWS TO PENETRATE THIS MUSLIM AREA OF WEST AFRICA SO THAT THE TRUTH WILL BE KNOWN. *Amen.*

Confessing Jesus before others

"Everyone therefore who shall confess Me before men, I will also confess him before My Father who is in heaven." Matthew 10:32 (NASB)

Ali (ah-LEE) glanced to his right and then to his left to make certain that no one was close enough to hear what he was about to say. He then leaned forward and whispered into my ear, "I have been a Christian for three years. I have been keeping it a secret from my family in Africa and my friends here in France."

I was shocked, and my reaction showed! I had just presented the gospel and my personal testimony to Ali minutes before. Here we were, two foreigners standing in the middle of a French open-air market, and Ali stunned me with his secret. "Why?" I asked.

Ali explained. "Years ago, a Christian friend led me to Christ in Senegal just before my arrival here in France to work." Then with a look of shame he said, "I was afraid that if I told my Muslim family about my newfound faith, they would take my wife and children from me. I was afraid that I would never be allowed to see them again when I returned to Africa."

Ali regularly fellowships with Christian believers in France as he worships, prays and studies the Bible. He now says, "My strength is getting larger; I think I am ready to declare my faith to my family in Africa when I return. But I am still afraid of what might happen."

Declaring our faith is not always easy to do, but as Christians, how can we keep silent?

—TONY, WESTERN EUROPE

Father, MAY I NEVER BE ASHAMED OF CONFESSING YOU BEFORE OTHERS. GIVE ME COURAGE WHEN I NEED IT. GIVE NEW CONVERTS FROM STRICT RELIGIOUS BACKGROUNDS THE BOLD-NESS TO DECLARE JESUS TO FAMILY AND FRIENDS. *Amen.*

A light in the village

"He is a Light to reveal God to the nations." Luke 2:32a (NLT)

As he sat in the jungle, R.C. thought, *When they discover my body beside the footpath one day, who will mourn me?* An image of a man came to mind that stirred hope within his heart. R.C. had seen the face of a missionary.

He knew the risk of talking to a Christian. Soon after his encounters with the missionary, R.C. became the first Christian among his people.

He decided to introduce Christ to his village by becoming the best husband, father and neighbor. He looked for people who were seeking truth. He developed relationships and then shared his faith.

R.C. was unlike anyone in the community. Although he had not publicly announced that he was a Christian, many came to that conclusion after hearing him explain the true beliefs of the Christian faith so skillfully. People were even saying they no longer believed Christians were infidels!

The council decided they would force R.C. to recant or be ostracized from the village. R.C. was prepared for this day. They asked, "Are you an infidel Christian?"

R.C. said, "Brothers, no matter what I say, you will not like it. Therefore, I will not answer, but I will continue to live my life as I have lived it for many months. Examine what I say and do each day. And then, you tell me: Am I an infidel, or do I serve the one, true God?"

R.C.'s story is one in progress. Even though R.C. is being ostracized, villagers have seen the difference Christ has made in the first convert.

—R.B., PACIFIC RIM

Heavenly Father, STRENGTHEN THESE NEW BELIEVERS IN THE PACIFIC RIM AS THEY ARE REJECTED BY THEIR ISLAMIC VILLAGES. LET THE TESTIMONIES OF THEIR CHANGED LIVES SPEAK TO OTHERS ABOUT THE POWER OF THE ONE, TRUE GOD. *Amen.*

Theirs is the kingdom of heaven

"Blessed are those who are persecuted because of righteousness, for theirs is the kingdom of heaven." Matthew 5:10 (NIV)

The Book of Acts records early church history. After the stoning of Stephen, the first Christian martyr, the eighth chapter begins, *"On that day a great persecution broke out against the church"* (v. 1, NIV). Jesus told his followers to expect persecution. In John 15:20, He says, *"If they persecuted me, they will persecute you also"* (NIV). Since Christians don't experience persecution much in the Western world, we sometimes think it doesn't exist.

It was a wonderful day for 15 new believers in a South Asian village. Having accepted Jesus as their Savior, they were now baptized—the first believers in their area! They had been warned of possible persecution, and two days later it happened with a vengeance. An angry mob came to their homes and beat them all—men, women and children. Then the mob burned their homes and took all of their possessions that had survived the fires. Three men were hospitalized, one of them in a deep coma. Many prayers were offered for these families, especially for the man in the coma.

Two days later, this man awoke from his coma and praised God for his healing! All of the hospitalized men witnessed to others, saying that if they had to die, it was okay, because they now knew Jesus. The hospital staff talked among themselves about the miracle they had seen. They began asking, "Who is this God these men are talking about?"

In South Asia, persecution of Christians is real. So is the faith of these new believers!

—A WORKER IN SOUTH ASIA

Father, KNOWING YOU IS LIFE AND PEACE. PLEASE GIVE STRENGTH AND COURAGE TODAY TO BELIEVERS AND CHRISTIAN WORKERS IN SOUTH ASIA AS THEY SHARE THE GOSPEL. BRING MUCH FRUIT AS A RESULT OF THEIR FAITHFULNESS TO OBEY AND FOLLOW YOU NO MATTER THE COST. *Amen.*

Jailed for a purpose

"You intended to harm me, but God intended it for good to accomplish what is now being done, the saving of many lives." Genesis 50:20 (NIV)

An evangelist named Lay smuggled 150 cassettes and 40 cassette players into a closed country, coinciding with the Chinese New Year. He got across the border but then ran into problems. The transport person betrayed him and went to the police. The police arrested him and sent him to a prison for questioning.

Officials tried to call central headquarters to see what they should do, but no one answered due to the holiday. Then the head of the police station wanted *every* message on *every* tape examined. Lay heard the tapes being played all over the prison as the police listened to the gospel.

In Lay's cell, he saw a hole that looked big enough through which to escape. He prayed, asking God if he should try to escape. Two small birds flew through the hole and sang. Then they flew back out. He felt it was a sign that he would be freed, so he should not escape on his own.

In the morning, the head of the police spoke with him. He made Lay sign a paper saying he would never bring tapes across the border again, and then he fined him.

In the end, a better plan could not have been made to get the gospel to the police in this prison. There is no telling where those tapes will end up as they are passed out to more police or maybe sold in the black market. It is possible that many more will hear the cassettes than had been previously planned.

—V., PACIFIC RIM

Heavenly Father, YOU TURN INTO GOOD WHAT OTHERS MEANT FOR EVIL. CAUSE THESE POLICEMEN TO THINK ON THE WORDS THAT THEY HEARD ON THE CASSETTE TAPES. SEND THESE TAPES MANY PLACES SO THAT YOUR WORD CAN BE HEARD BY MANY MORE THAN ANYONE INTENDED. *Amen.*

Persecution in the Middle East

"Rejoice that you participate in the sufferings of Christ, so that you may be over-joyed when his glory is revealed." 1 Peter 4:13 (NIV)

When I'm discouraged by thinking about how difficult it is for Muslims to come to the truth, the Lord sends someone into my life who has come to Christ. One such person is my electrician, who was trained in Germany. While in Europe, he became a Christian. Before he returned to his home country in the Middle East, he told his family of his decision to follow Christ. Consequently, the family waited for him at the airport upon his return, bringing law officers to have him imprisoned. He is now out of prison and working as an electrician, but he has been disinherited by his family and experiences discrimination in his profession. In spite of all this, he is a joyful witness to others.

Another young man, Mohammed, became a believer and dynamic witness. He visited another country in the Middle East and distributed the Word. The group that he was with became so effective at spreading the Word that militant Islamic groups decided to put a stop to their work. They murdered Mohammed by placing a bomb in his apartment. He was buried in that country, because his family had disowned him and refused to accept his body.

God's perspective of persecution is revealed in Philippians 1:21: *"For to me, to live is Christ and to die is gain"* (NIV). I do know that the Lord is working in the Middle East, and I'm thankful for the fruit that I see occasionally. When discouragement comes, God finds a way to personally demonstrate His faithfulness.

—P.A.F., NORTHERN AFRICA AND THE MIDDLE EAST

Faithful Father, YOU ARE IN CONTROL EVEN WHEN I'M DISCOURAGED OR WHEN I THINK THAT MY CHRISTIAN WITNESS FALLS ON DEAF EARS. I PRAY FOR CHRISTIANS WHO ARE BEING PERSECUTED ALL OVER THE WORLD, ESPECIALLY IN THE MIDDLE EAST TODAY. MAY YOU GIVE THEM COURAGE AND STRENGTH TO FACE THEIR PERSECUTORS. MAY THEY FEEL YOUR PRESENCE TODAY. *Amen.*

All nations will worship

*"All nations whom thou hast made shall come and worship before thee, O Lord;
and shall glorify thy name." Psalm 86:9 (KJV)*

Through four inches of snow, a group of dedicated believers came to the small apartment, and it was my first time to worship with them. The sacrifice these Christians had made to assemble together was astounding.

I looked around the room and wondered about their stories. Their parents had been immigrants. The 75 gathered in this room were persecuted believers. Eighty-five percent of them were unemployed because they were Christians. The language these people spoke daily was not their heart language. But when they gathered to praise God, they sang in the language of their hearts.

The Word of God was preached in one language and translated into their heart language. I sat attentively, not understanding everything that was said. Nonetheless, God spoke to me. Three heart languages were heard worshiping God. He understood every one of them. Truly God desires worship from every tribe, tongue and nation.

As we were concluding worship, the electricity went out in the apartment. They were so focused on praising Him that no one paid any attention to the darkness that had suddenly engulfed the room. It convicted me that in my own church in the States, we probably would have tried to get the power back on before finishing the song.

God wants us to worship and glorify Him, and He wants us to do so from our hearts. I learned much from this persecuted group of believers. I learned much about worship and the majesty of God.

—STAN, SOUTH AMERICA

Dear Lord, ACCEPT MY WORSHIP OF YOU FROM MY HEART. CREATE IN ME A PURE HEART TO WORSHIP YOU IN SPIRIT AND IN TRUTH. *Amen.*

Left for dead

"And others experienced mockings and scourgings, yes, also chains and imprisonment." Hebrews 11:36 (NASB)

Faithful believers who have endured persecution, beatings and even death to take the gospel to the unreached have planted many of the churches in the areas where we serve. Pastor Joseph's story is one of thousands typical of the pioneer church planters of South Asia.

Joseph is from a Hindu family in Orissa (or-ISS-ah), India. When the gospel was first brought to his village, he and his wife became believers. Soon the whole village became known as a "Christian village," so Joseph and his wife decided to move to another village that had not heard the gospel. They built their house and witnessed to their new neighbors of the love and forgiveness of God.

Eventually, the people threatened to beat Joseph if he did not leave, but Joseph and his wife stayed and continued to share Christ. One day, some men forcefully took Joseph to the middle of the village and said, "We are going to kill you right here." Joseph replied, "If you kill me here, God will build a Christian church on this spot." The men decided to take him outside the village. Dragging him to an empty field, they were reluctant to kill him, but they beat him severely.

Joseph lived through the beating, and he and his family remained in the village. Soon the people began to respond to the gospel. Today there is a Christian church of 20 families. Their church building stands on the spot where the persecutors left Joseph to bleed to death.

—J. AND D., SOUTH ASIA

Heavenly Father, PROTECT NATIONAL PASTORS IN SOUTH ASIA TODAY AS THEY RISK EVERYTHING FOR THE CAUSE OF CHRIST. MAY I NOT BE COMPLACENT TO THE PERSECUTION OF BELIEVERS IN THE WORLD AND EVEN MY OWN COUNTRY. ACCOMPLISH YOUR WILL THROUGH THESE CHRISTIANS WHO LIVE IN COUNTRIES THAT DESPISE JESUS. *Amen.*

Four questions

"That I may know Him, and the power of His resurrection and the fellowship of His sufferings, being conformed to His death." Philippians 3:10 (NASB)

This was the second group of leaders we had trained in two weeks. The training had been going well even though many of the believers were young: some young in years and some in their faith. A couple of them were only 15 and 16 years old. Some had only been Christians for a few months.

The teaching for the morning was on baptism, and a 15-year-old girl wanted to be baptized. She had been a believer from a young age but had never been immersed.

Four questions are asked during a baptism: (1) Do you believe in Jesus? (2) Has He forgiven your sins? (3) Do you promise to walk with Him always? But there is one more question.

I watched and listened to the father, who would be performing the baptism. Calmly, and with much joy, he asked the first, second and third questions. Then I heard a surprising question. The father asked the fourth question, "When they come into our house and take us away, when they beat us and try to get us to deny Him, will you still follow Jesus?"

There before my eyes, a father was asking his daughter to be willing to be persecuted for her faith in Christ and to be willing to see him persecuted for his faith. With a sense of awe, I prayed that I might be more like them. I think they understood more clearly what the Father felt when He sent His Son to die for us.

—A WORKER IN CHINA

Lord, THANK YOU FOR REMINDING ME THAT MY ABILITY TO KNOW YOU AND THE POWER OF YOUR RESURRECTION IS DEPENDENT ON MY WILLINGNESS TO BE ONE WITH YOU IN SUF-FERING AND DEATH. GIVE COURAGE TO THESE CHINESE BELIEVERS AND MULTIPLY THEIR WITNESS. *Amen.*

No denying

"Take my yoke upon you and learn from me, for I am gentle and humble in heart, and you will find rest in your souls." Matthew 11:29 (NIV)

The people of the Lake Victory islands believe in witchcraft and underworld spirits. They practice traditional tribal religions and regularly worship idols. On these islands live mostly outcasts—thieves, prisoners, people kicked out of the mainland villages.

Christian work in this remote area is slow, as most simply add Jesus Christ to all of their other beliefs and gods. However, the Holy Spirit continues to work in the hearts of young believers. Often they are kicked out of their homes and sometimes even beaten because of their faith.

One of our friends had been a Christian for about a year when she began to experience abuse from her husband. Her husband still worshiped idols. He continued to reject Jesus Christ, stating his Islamic faith as the reason.

During the fast of Ramadan (rah-MUH-don), our friend's husband built a shrine next door to their mud home. At the prodding of Muslim leaders, the husband demanded that his wife worship with him at the shrine or be beaten.

Late one evening, the husband beat his wife when she refused to worship his god. After hearing enough screaming, some neighbors came to rescue her and gave her shelter for the evening.

A couple of days later, she came to talk to us. She shared that she told her husband that no matter how much he beat her, she would not deny her Savior, Jesus Christ. She was willing to die before worshiping any other.

Are we willing to do the same?

—A WORKER IN CENTRAL, EASTERN AND SOUTHERN AFRICA

Heavenly Father, YOU ARE A GOD WHO SEES. BRING PEACE TO THE HEARTS OF THESE WOMEN IN UGANDA WHO ARE FORSAKING THE FALSE GODS TO WORSHIP YOU ALONE. I PRAY FOR THE SALVATION OF THEIR HUSBANDS. USE MISSIONARIES IN UGANDA TO BRING THE GOSPEL TO THOSE WHO ARE LOST. *Amen.*

Not keeping silent!

*"So is my word that goes out from my mouth. It will not return to me empty,
but will accomplish what I desire and achieve the purpose for which I sent it."*
Isaiah 55:11 (NIV)

A young man recently converted from Islam to Christianity after hearing about Christ through a summer English team in the capital city. He obtained a small portion of the Scriptures before returning to his little village far away from any other believers. His uncle discovered the book and took it to read for himself so that the young man would never be able to read from it again.

Several months later, I made a trip to this small village to do some mapping and prayerwalking. Through a series of out-of-the-ordinary events, God put this young believer in my path. He and his friends invited me to lunch. The first thing he asked me was whether I was a Christian. Being cautious not to offend a Muslim, I replied, "I'm a follower of Jesus Christ." He told me that he, too, was a follower of Christ.

Later he invited me to a nonreligious class that he taught. At one point, the word "cross" came up in the discussion, and he explained to his students the crucifixion of Christ as an example of "cross." Although he had signed a contract not to mention religious things in class, he could not keep silent!

A few months later, I was able to give him some praise tapes and more of the Scriptures in his language. He continues to grow in his faith by leaps and bounds, even as he stands alone in his little village daily carrying the cross of Christ.

—A WORKER IN CENTRAL ASIA

Father, THANK YOU FOR THIS YOUNG BELIEVER AND OTHERS LIKE HIM IN COUNTRIES WHERE CHRISTIANS ARE PERSECUTED TO THE EXTREME. GIVE THEM YOUR STRENGTH. TAKE AWAY ANY FEAR FROM MISSIONARIES AS THEY SERVE YOU IN THESE COUNTRIES. GIVE ME BOLDNESS TO SHARE MY FAITH, NO MATTER THE CONSEQUENCES. *Amen.*

No longer afraid

"For you did not receive the spirit of bondage again to fear, but you received the Spirit of adoption by whom we cry out, 'Abba, Father.'" Romans 8:15 (NKJV)

Four years ago, people in Socorro's small mountain village had been afraid even to accept a tract or a New Testament when Christians visited their *pueblo* with the good news. The people had little or no knowledge of God's Word and believed that reading the Bible would cause insanity. There was real fear of being rejected by friends and family by attending Bible studies with evangelicals.

Socorro knew all too well that local sentiment was against her participation in weekly Bible studies. Her neighbors asked her why she wanted to keep one foot in Bible study and the other foot in traditional religion. Didn't she know that too much Bible study would make her crazy?

But Socorro enjoyed learning the deeper truths she was finding in God's Word. She was being challenged in some of her long-held traditional beliefs by what she saw clearly taught in the Bible. Instead of going crazy, she was becoming strong in the Word. One day, she realized that she needed not just religion, but a relationship with God through Jesus Christ. Socorro gave her heart to Christ.

After serious thought and prayer, Socorro found herself standing waist-deep in the river for baptism. Even though her head had never been under water in her life and she couldn't swim, Socorro looked me in the eyes and firmly answered, "I am not afraid."

Facing her fear and trusting in Jesus brought the freedom in Christ that she desired.

—KEN, SOUTH AMERICA

Glorious Lord, ACCORDING TO YOUR WORD, YOU DO NOT GIVE US A SPIRIT OF FEAR, BUT OF POWER, LOVE AND SELF-DISCIPLINE. I PRAY THAT NEW BELIEVERS WHO HAVE HAD THE COURAGE TO DENOUNCE THEIR TRADITIONAL RELIGION AND PUBLICLY PROFESS THEIR NEW LIFE IN YOU WILL GROW IN THE KNOWLEDGE OF YOUR WORD AND BECOME POWERFUL, LOVING, DISCIPLINED WITNESSES IN THEIR COMMUNITIES. *Amen.*

As you go

"And you will be called the repairer of the breach, the restorer of the streets in which to dwell." Isaiah 58:12b (NASB)

It happened rather by accident that Marcus read the paper posted inside of our front door that serves as a reminder of why we are in China:

As you go ...
Can you BREAK a yoke?
Can you FEED the hungry?
Can you HELP the homeless?
Can you CLOTHE the naked?
Can you SATISFY the afflicted?
Can you LIFT up a needy brother?
Will you REFRAIN from cursing?
Will you GIVE yourself?
(based on Isaiah 58)

Marcus spent the holiday with us and tearfully prepared to return home. Our friend paid a high price for his newfound belief in Jesus. He had been forced out of a good-paying job, disowned by his family and pressured to move away from his hometown because of his faith.

A few days after Marcus's visit, he saw a battered man beside the road, looking in the garbage for food. Marcus could only think, *Can you feed the hungry?* Marcus fed the man, treated his wounds, gave him a place to stay until he recovered and bought him a ticket to Guangzhou (gwang-JOH). The man told Marcus that he had not met a man as good in China. Marcus shared the gospel with the man, and he repented.

Considering the words of the poem helped Marcus focus on another's needs rather than on his own difficulties.

—A WORKER IN CHINA

Father, HELP ME TO BE ONE WHO REPAIRS AND RESTORES THE LIVES OF OTHERS THROUGH JESUS CHRIST. HELP ME NOT TO FOCUS ON MY PROBLEMS. ENCOURAGE CHINESE CHRISTIANS WHO ARE PERSECUTED FOR THEIR FAITH. *Amen.*

In the crossfire

"Some trust in chariots, and some in horses; but we will remember the name of the Lord our God." Psalm 20:7 (NKJV)

You may have read of the wars between the rebel forces and the government of the Philippines. Perhaps you prayed for the safe release of missionary hostages.

Grace and a friend traveled to a remote island to survey needs in a small fishing village known for its hostility to strangers, hoping to be able to one day live and minister among them. The team shyly entered, was welcomed and miraculously received an invitation to stay. Grace began to teach health care and basic sanitation. A community water pump installed by a team of Christians delighted everyone. Soon, Grace was able to teach Bible stories chronologically. Before long, there were 30 new believers among a people group where no known believers have ever been!

Why now? A newfound village friend explained, "Our children are afraid of outsiders. They always hide when strangers come. But the day you arrived, they surprised us all and ran out to greet you. The food we prepared for you that first day was poisoned; we meant to kill you. But you didn't even get sick! We *knew* that God must be with you!"

Some months after the conversions to Christianity, the whereabouts of the 30 new believers is unknown because of the current war. Even though the missionaries don't know where they are, we do know that God is with them. They are learning to trust the Father of their newfound faith. They depend upon the prayers of other believers around the world.

—JANET, PACIFIC RIM

Father, YOU KNOW WHERE THESE BELIEVERS ARE. PROTECT THEM. HELP THEM TO GROW IN THEIR FAITH. PROTECT MISSIONARIES IN THE PHILIPPINES FROM KIDNAPPINGS OR BEING IN THE CROSSFIRE. CONTINUE TO BRING THE GOSPEL TO THESE VILLAGES WHERE THERE ARE NO KNOWN BELIEVERS. *Amen.*

A return to a village

"You have heard that it was said, 'Love your neighbor and hate your enemy.' But I tell you: Love your enemies and pray for those who persecute you, that you may be sons of your Father in heaven." Matthew 5:43–45 (NIV)

Geo was quietly rejoicing as he fervently preached the gospel of Christ to the group sitting in front of him. The 40-year-old man could not resist thinking back 25 years earlier when he was in this exact spot.

In those days, he accompanied his grandfather and uncle as they traveled up and down the river, preaching the gospel. Their goal was to tell the story of Jesus in every village, but they were rejected and driven out of each one.

He remembered this village of the Saramaccan (sair-ah-MAH-can) people group. His grandfather had led the village medium to Christ. The respected medium destroyed his fetishes and materials used in magic rituals. The villagers became so furious, however, that they threw rocks at young Geo and his relatives.

The three jumped into their boat and were able to make it safely back home. Later that same night, however, those offended villagers raided Geo's village. All the villagers were pulled from their huts. When the men found Geo's grandfather, they brought him out, whipped him with a chain from a chainsaw and poured tar over his gaping wounds. Geo ran and hid in the jungle to watch.

Now it was 25 years later, and Geo was back in the same village where he had been rejected. During the years, God worked in Geo's heart to forgive that village. He reminded them of the event 25 years ago and extended an invitation to follow Christ. That night, 30 Saramaccans trusted Jesus as Savior.

—TIM AND JUDY, MIDDLE AMERICA AND THE CARIBBEAN

Faithful Father, THANK YOU FOR THE FRUIT BEING PRODUCED TODAY AMONG THE SARAMACCAN PEOPLE AS A RESULT OF THOSE WHO SUFFERED PERSECUTION AND CHOSE THE POWER OF FORGIVENESS. I PRAY THAT YOUR WORD WILL SPREAD RAPIDLY THROUGHOUT SURINAME AND THAT BIBLE-BELIEVING CHURCHES WILL BE ESTABLISHED AND MULTIPLY. Amen.

Precious in His sight

"Precious in the sight of the LORD is the death of His saints."
Psalm 116:15 (NIV)

Abdul (AB-dool), a new believer in Christ, was trapped by a group of older youth who decided to beat the Christian to death. A local politician walked by and convinced the boys they would bring trouble to the entire community if they killed Abdul. They spat on Abdul as they left.

Hearing about the beating, Rafik (RUH-feek), Abdul's classmate, took his injured friend to his home. Over the course of several days, Abdul told Rafik all about his faith in Jesus. Rafik accepted Christ and was baptized. Abdul told Rafik, "Yesterday I was one, today we are two, and tomorrow we could be 200."

A relative of Rafik was sent to talk to him and Abdul about recanting. Two weeks later, Rafik journeyed to the relative's village. Upon his return, he shared with Abdul that he had led seven families to Christ, a total of 36 people.

The two began to travel and share God's love, beginning first with their families and slowly reaching their friends. A church-planting movement started.

Muslim converts from surrounding districts came to Rafik's bamboo house to receive discipleship training. Late one February night in 2003, Rafik answered a knock on his door. Fundamentalist Muslims rushed in and stabbed Rafik to death.

Even after this martyrdom, Abdul remains in the area leading the movement. International Mission Board missionaries have adapted Abdul and Rafik's method of Muslim church planting to their work. As a result, 363 new church plants and 4,797 baptisms during a two-year period have been reported.

—A WORKER IN SOUTH ASIA

Heavenly Father, MAY MANY COME TO CHRIST AS A RESULT OF THE DEATH OF THIS PRECIOUS BELIEVER, RAFIK. STRENGTHEN ABDUL AND OTHERS LIKE HIM IN SOUTH ASIA FOR SHARING THE GOSPEL. USE OUR MISSIONARIES IN THIS REGION TO PARTNER WITH NATIONALS TO MULTIPLY CHURCHES. *Amen.*

A reminder of His faithfulness

"Though the fig tree does not bud and there are no grapes on the vines, though the olive crop fails and the fields produce no food, though there are no sheep in the pen and no cattle in the stalls, yet I will rejoice in the LORD, I will be joyful in God my Savior. The sovereign LORD is my strength; he makes my feet like the feet of a deer, he enables me to go on the heights." Habakkuk 3:17–19 (NIV)

We had prayed for children for years with no success. We could identify well with Sara and Hannah, but the pain didn't go away. As we began the process of adoption, we encountered obstacle after obstacle: the cost, the travel as we are missionaries in Spain trying to adopt from Guatemala, the time away from our work and the endless paperwork.

God opened one door at a time, first providing some adoption grants, then providing approval from our missions agency to go to Guatemala and then providing money to pay for part of the travel. Once in Guatemala, what should have been a six-week experience turned into a seven-month trial of our faith and perseverance as we faced problem after problem. Our paperwork was rejected five or six times for random reasons, and we were about at the end of our rope.

Yet in the midst of it all, God reminded us of His faithfulness. He showed us that we could be thankful even though things did not happen in the timing we had desired. He showed us that even though we did not yet have the final adoption decree, He was worthy to be praised. Our faith had to grow to be able to still believe that God would work out the impossible.

He did work everything out in His timing. After a year of difficulty, we are back in Spain with our two precious children!

Even though ... *"yet I will rejoice in the LORD"*!

—CATHIE, WESTERN EUROPE

Father, YOU ARE A GOD WHO MAKES THE IMPOSSIBLE HAPPEN. GIVE ME PATIENCE TO WITHSTAND TRIALS. MOLD ME INTO THE PERSON I NEED TO BE. *Amen.*

Life insurance

"The righteous cry out, and the LORD hears, and delivers them out of all their troubles." Psalm 34:17 (NKJV)

Living in a country that is less than 0.01 percent Christian is a daily spiritual battle. As believers living in South Asia, we are constantly praying for God to use us to penetrate the darkness and to protect us as we serve.

One day, my husband was traveling in a remote area. As he was waiting at a bus stop to return home, a few young guys began talking with him. When the bus arrived, my husband said his goodbyes and decided to give one of the young men a book about the life of Christ. Seeing the book, the man became extremely angry that anyone would dare give him a book about Christ. He threatened to kill my husband! He and his friend then followed my husband onto the bus. The angry guy sat next to him, and the other guy sat across from them.

My husband called me on his cell phone, told me the situation and asked me to pray. Several co-workers were with me, so we prayed for his safety and for God to work in this young man's life. Thirty minutes later, my husband called to tell me that about 20 nuns had just gotten on the bus. The angry young man told him that having the nuns present was his life insurance. He wouldn't do any harm with these women around. Not only did God protect my husband from harm, but the young man's friend read the book about Jesus for the duration of the three-hour ride. Praise God for hearing us when we call!

—APRIL, SOUTH ASIA

Heavenly Father, PROTECT WORKERS TODAY IN AREAS IN WHICH HOSTILITY AND VIOLENCE ARE SHOWN TOWARD CHRISTIANS. MAY YOUR ANGELS SURROUND THEM. DELIVER THEM FROM THOSE WHO SEEK TO HARM THEM. THANK YOU FOR YOUR PRESENCE AND FOR THE PROMISE THAT YOU ARE ALWAYS WITH US. *Amen.*

A seeker of God

"'Behold, I am the LORD, the God of all flesh; is anything too difficult for Me?'"
Jeremiah 32:27 (NASB)

Moses came to our home to introduce us to "Solomon" and one of his wives. By lantern light, I could see that Solomon was dressed in fine Anii (AHN-ee) Muslim clothing and learned that he was the prince and future king of his Anii village. His clan originated from the Ashanti (ash-AHN-tee) people of Ghana, who were Christians, but his family had been Muslim for generations.

Solomon began asking, "If being Anii is being Muslim, then why were our ancestors Christians?" Solomon also observed that fellow Muslims often prayed for curses on their neighbors, but Christians prayed for blessing on others.

Solomon and his two wives wanted to learn what it meant to follow Jesus. Finally, they attended a service where he heard someone praising Jesus Christ in his own language. It was Moses, who had offered his assistance as a translator. Solomon approached Moses, ecstatic to hear the gospel preached in Anii.

The next morning, Moses shared with Solomon and his wife stories from the New Testament. When finished, Moses brought him to me.

As Solomon finished this story in my front yard, I began with Genesis 1:1 and told the great events of the entire Bible. I asked Solomon what his decision would be. He chose to trust Jesus as Savior. I asked, "Are you prepared for the persecution that is sure to come with your new life in Christ?"

Solomon looked me in the eye and stated, "Pastor, when you have Jesus Christ, other problems become meaningless."

—A WORKER IN WEST AFRICA

Our great God, THANK YOU FOR THE LIGHT THAT HAS COME TO THE ANII PEOPLE. MAY IT SHINE BRIGHTLY, AND MAY THE DARKNESS FLEE FROM IT. MAY I REMEMBER THAT PROBLEMS ARE MEANINGLESS WHEN I HAVE JESUS. *Amen.*

When understanding is absent

"Father, I want those you have given me to be with me where I am, and to see my glory, the glory you have given me because you loved me before the creation of the world." John 17:24 (NIV)

The deaths came one right after another—a missionary colleague, a pastor friend, another missionary and national believers martyred by their own neighbors. The deaths made no sense to me. Each man was in the prime of his service unto the Lord, honoring Him and bearing fruit for His kingdom.

I could not understand why the Lord would allow the deaths of these godly men. However, as I read John 17:24, it became clear that their deaths were the desire of His heart.

Jesus finished His work on earth and then went into the presence of the Father. His desire then was that His disciples would finish the work that He had given them to do so that they could be with Him and see His glory.

From my earthly perspective, I saw that these men still had much work to accomplish for the Lord and that their deaths had left that work incomplete. However, I would have thought the same about the timing of Jesus' death had I been there to witness it. Certainly those in His inner circle looked upon the cross and thought their Master's life had been taken prematurely. Yet it was while He was on the cross that Jesus declared, "It is finished."

From heaven's perspective, the men who died had finished the work that the Lord had given them to do and were ready to be with Jesus. God is still sovereign, even though I don't always understand His plan.

—CHELE, SOUTH ASIA

Heavenly Father, I CAN'T FULLY UNDERSTAND IN MY HUMAN MIND THE DEPTH OF THE SUFFERING OF YOUR SON, JESUS, AS HE DIED ON THE CROSS FOR ME. I DON'T UNDERSTAND WHY BELIEVERS ARE MARTYRED. BUT I KNOW THAT YOU ARE SOVEREIGN AND THAT YOUR PURPOSES WILL BE REVEALED. GIVE GRACE TO THOSE YOU ALLOW TO GO THROUGH THIS KIND OF SUFFERING. *Amen.*

"It is time for a change"

"Not that we are adequate in ourselves to consider anything as coming from our-selves, but our adequacy is from God." 2 Corinthians 3:5 (NASB)

God has truly shown us that He is working among the Herero (hah-RARE-roh) people. It was getting late in the day, and I was wondering if we really had time to make another stop in Talismannis (TAL-iss-MAN-iss) before heading back to where we were going to spend the evening. We were deep in the bush, two hours from our destination, knowing that it was not safe to be traveling on these roads after dark due to the many animals that graze by the side of the road at night.

Just out of Reitfontein (REET-fon-tain), we saw a woman and a child hitchhiking. We knew the woman was Herero because she was wearing the traditional Herero dress with the headdress fashioned into what resembles cattle horns. We picked her up and found out she was traveling to her home in Talismannis. Since we had a captive audience, I started to present the gospel through my interpreter on this trip.

We arrived in Talismannis before finishing the gospel presentation, and to our surprise, the woman invited us to her house to finish pre-senting the gospel. "If I [become a Christian]," she said, "then I will lose many friends, and things will be different around here." Then she added, "It is time for a change around here."

We were exuberant as she put her faith in Jesus. We returned to where we were staying for the evening before nightfall, not having to worry about the danger of encountering unseen animals in the road.

—MARVING, CENTRAL, EASTERN AND SOUTHERN AFRICA

Father, FOR THOSE WHO SACRIFICE RELATIONSHIPS WITH OTHERS TO FOLLOW YOU, I PRAY THAT YOU WILL GIVE THEM GRACE. BRING THE GOSPEL TO THE HERERO PEOPLE IN NAMIBIA, AND BRING YOUR MESSENGERS TO SHARE THIS GOOD NEWS. LORD, ENABLE ME TO VALUE MY RELATIONSHIP WITH YOU ABOVE ALL OTHERS. *Amen.*

Jailhouse discipleship

"But someone came and reported to them, 'Behold, the men whom you put in prison are standing in the temple and teaching the people!'" Acts 5:25 (NASB)

"Sam," a national church planter, and an International Mission Board missionary, had planted 18 churches among village Muslims. Before locating to a different area, Sam prayed that God would give him access to influential community leaders.

After Sam's first day of preaching in the new area, a mob of angry Muslims pulled him out of his hotel. The police soon arrived, arrested Sam and placed him in prison. The missionary quickly went to the jail. The visiting room was chaotic and crowded. Finally, the missionary squeezed his way to the cell bars. He yelled to Sam, "We are doing everything we can to get you out. How are you doing?" Sam yelled back, "Don't worry about me. My discipleship class is going great!"

Because it was an election year, Sam found himself in prison with many political leaders from the opposition party. Sam preached to them for 11 days until he was released.

At his trial, Sam declared before a packed courtroom what God had done in his life and that Jesus was the only Savior. Seeing a riot developing, the judge adjourned the court. Later, Sam was invited to the judge's home to tell this good news to the judge's family. The judge dismissed the charges.

Since then, local government leaders have permitted evangelists to preach. Within 18 months of this event, more than 200 Muslims were baptized and seven churches started. God turned a potentially upsetting circumstance into an opportunity to evangelize.

—A WORKER IN SOUTH ASIA

Heavenly Father, HELP ME TO RECOGNIZE YOUR HAND AT WORK, GRANTING MY HEART'S DESIRE EVEN WHEN THE ANSWER TO MY PRAYERS IS NOT COMFORTABLE. STRENGTHEN, ENCOURAGE AND SUSTAIN SAM AND YOUR OTHER WORKERS IN SOUTH ASIA AS THEY SHARE YOUR WORD WITH THE 350 MILLION MUSLIMS IN THAT REGION. *Amen.*

Labeled as an infidel

"With prayer and fasting, committed them to the LORD, in whom they had put their trust." Acts 14:23 (NIV)

We decided to join the annual fast, Ramadan (rah-MUH-don). This is a ritualistic fast that Muslims hope will assist them in attaining eternal life. Our reason for fasting was to focus our prayers on neighbors and friends so that they would come to Christ.

The fast from food and drink begins before sunrise. Muslims are not allowed to eat again until about 6 p.m. Most get up at 3:30 a.m. to eat a big breakfast and drink. We, however, didn't always make it up before dawn. We woke up hungry. We made it, though, to the end of daylight.

One day, at a store counter, two girls asked me a few questions just to be polite, and then one girl asked if I was an infidel. She was shocked when I asked her to explain that to me. Her friend punched her hard in the arm.

I was upset on my walk home. I felt like I was doing this fast for nothing! Why did I want to identify with these people when they only see me as an outsider with no value?

We try to reflect on what people said to Jesus during His time on earth and how misunderstood He was. We don't even begin to measure up to Him in trying to identify with the people He came to reach, but we're beginning to sense His being "despised and rejected" (Isa. 53:3, NIV). Even though He made great efforts—the greatest—to reach them, not all welcomed Him.

—J.J., PACIFIC RIM

Father, ENCOURAGE MISSIONARIES TO PERSEVERE IN BRINGING THE LOST TO CHRIST. ALLOW THEIR MORAL AND UPRIGHT LIVES TO BE SEEN AS THEY LOVE OTHERS IN THE NAME OF JESUS. INCREASE THEIR LOVE FOR THE PEOPLE GROUPS AROUND THEM, EVEN DURING PERSECUTION. *Amen.*

God still moves

"Not that we are sufficient of ourselves to think of anything as being from our-selves, but our sufficiency is from God." 2 Corinthians 3:5 (NKJV)

Usually in South Asia, it takes months, sometimes years to have an op-portunity to clearly share the gospel. Even then, the possibility of that person accepting the Lord is unknown and highly unlikely. We were astounded when we were given the opportunity to lead several semi-nars with nationals from the mountain areas. We were definitely not prepared for the heart-wrenching tales of commitment to our Lord.

One man had walked two days to get to a bus so that he could then ride three hours to the seminar. Another man shared that in his village, a small group of believers had come together in faith. Unfortunately, the Buddhist majority of the village said that they must renounce their faith or be immediately banished from the village. Of the 15 members of the fellowship, three refused to renounce their faith, which resulted in banishment from their homes forever. The man who told the story was one of the three.

A pastor told of preaching in another village where he was com-manded by village elders to stop immediately. He continued teaching, however, and the elders decided to hire terrorists to kill the believers. That night, the national army arrived unexpectedly, and the terrorists were unable to do their job. The believers were then able to escape.

It became apparent that God is working in South Asia, even if we aren't aware of what is happening. When progress is not evident, we remember these stories of God drawing nationals to Himself.

—D. AND J., SOUTH ASIA

Heavenly Father, YOU ARE THE ONE RESPONSIBLE FOR THE GROWTH OF YOUR KINGDOM. HELP ME NOT TO BE DISCOURAGED WHEN I DON'T SEE IMMEDIATE RESULTS OF SPIRITUAL SEEKING OR GROWTH OF INDIVIDUALS AROUND ME. IN AREAS WHERE MOST PEOPLE REJECT YOU, ENCOURAGE WORKERS TO TRUST YOU AND NOT GIVE UP. *Amen.*

Trusting God

"But as many as received him, to them gave he power to become the sons of God, even to them that believe on his name." John 1:12 (KJV)

A group of believers crossed Lake Victoria to reach one of the main islands. They walked 45 minutes to visit a Muslim village in an effort to share God's Word.

Five women sat outside a mud home in the shade. They invited the visitors to stop and chat. These women wanted to hear about Jesus.

After sharing, the believers offered an invitation to accept Jesus Christ as their Savior, but the women refused. While they believed the gospel message, they were afraid of their husbands. If the women accepted Jesus, their husbands would beat them or force them to leave. The women asked, "If we accept Jesus, who would take care of us? Who will take care of our children? And where will we live?"

The believers reassured the women that God knew their problems and that they should put their trust in Him. However, the women stood firm in their decision to reject Jesus. At each home visited, the response was the same.

As the believers prepared to leave the island, a lady ran to them saying she wanted to hear about Jesus. The believers shared with her. She hesitated and asked who would give her a place to live when chased away by her husband. The believers advised her to trust in God to see her through any problem. This one woman stepped out in faith to accept Jesus as her Lord and Savior.

Are you willing to follow Christ—even when it means definite hardships are on the way?

—A WORKER IN CENTRAL, EASTERN AND SOUTHERN AFRICA

Father, NO MATTER THE PERSECUTION, I PRAY THAT YOU WILL GIVE ME THE COURAGE AND STRENGTH TO FOLLOW YOU EVERY DAY. GIVE THIS WOMAN AND OTHERS LIKE HER A DETERMINATION TO CHOOSE YOU EVEN WHEN IT MEANS HARDSHIP. GIVE THEM GRACE AND MEET ALL THEIR NEEDS. I WOULD ASK THAT MANY IN THIS AREA OF UGANDA WOULD CHOOSE YOU. *Amen.*

A grandmother's heart opened

"Anyone who will not receive the kingdom of God like a little child will never enter it." Luke 18:17; Mark 10:15 (NIV)

Like all new believers in Muslim Central Asia, my young friend Vera was anxious for her family members to know and love Jesus as she did. Although she initially experienced a great deal of persecution from her family, over time their hostility faded.

Vera's constant prayer was for all of her family members to become believers. She was especially eager for her elderly grandparents. She had not seen her relatives for two years while she was attending university in a distant city. So imagine the family's happy excitement when Vera told them that we would visit them in their village!

Vera is the oldest of many grandchildren in her family and has always been a favorite for her lively, loving spirit. It was not surprising that troops of relatives arrived to welcome Vera and her friends at her grandmother's home. The happy reunion lasted well into the night as everyone caught up on news.

The next day, a moment came when most adults were out of the house, but children of all ages continued scampering in and out. In the relative quiet, Vera concentrated on her grandmother, carefully telling her the story of salvation through Jesus. At that moment, the Holy Spirit opened her grandmother's heart, and she accepted Jesus as her Savior. As we led her grandmother in a prayer of repentance and faith, I looked up and saw that Vera's teenage cousin, Kevin, was unexpectedly praying along with us. God does more than we could ever dream or imagine!

—JANET, CENTRAL ASIA

Heavenly Father, AS NEW MUSLIM CONVERTS SHARE THEIR FAITH WITH FRIENDS AND FAMILY MEMBERS, GIVE THEM COURAGE AND A CLEAR MESSAGE. I PRAY FOR _____ TODAY, AN ELDERLY FAMILY MEMBER OR FRIEND WHO NEEDS JESUS. USE ME TO SHARE BEFORE IT'S TOO LATE. *Amen.*

The last laugh

"But God chose the foolish things of the world to shame the wise; God chose the weak things of the world to shame the strong. He chose the lowly things of this world and the despised things—and the things that are not—to nullify the things that are, so that no one may boast before him."
1 Corinthians 1:27–29 (NIV)

"Sherman" is a humble pastor with a heart for God. His village in Central Asia didn't have a reliable water source, so God laid it on his heart to dig a well. However, the local Muslim leaders opposed the well because a traitor to the Muslim faith was behind it.

Sherman was nearly stoned and constantly harassed. Muslim leaders spread rumors that Sherman would poison the well water or Allah would strike a person dead if he drank from it.

Because of the village's need for water, the officials told the leaders to stop bad-mouthing the well. They grudgingly complied publicly. Yet secretly they arranged for a truckload of rocks to be dumped on the site where the well was to be drilled. What they didn't know was that the engineers had been to the site earlier that day and decided to dig the well on the other side of the street!

A few months later, the project was completed and villagers celebrated the provision of water. Sherman gave full credit to the Lord. There were a few in the crowd, however, still wiping egg from their faces. That pile of rocks across the road became a monument to the foolishness of man and the awesome power and humor of God.

God allows the wise to be shamed by what the world considers foolish people. Sherman didn't consider retribution. The antagonistic leaders shamed themselves. God got the glory!

—S.H., CENTRAL ASIA

Heavenly Father, THANK YOU FOR WATCHING OVER THIS WELL PROJECT. MAY YOU USE IT TO BE A CONSTANT TESTIMONY OF YOUR GOODNESS, AND MAY MANY COME TO CHRIST AS A RESULT. FATHER, WHEN I DESIRE TO GET REVENGE ON OTHERS, MAY I BRING GOOD TO OTHERS, EVEN TO THOSE WHO WRONG ME. *Amen.*

What can man do to me?

"We say with confidence, 'The Lord is my helper; I will not be afraid. What can man do to me?'" Hebrews 13:6 (NIV)

Although several hundred people attended the meeting about endurance in persecution, some were prevented from coming by authorities. Three groups were detained and questioned in three separate regions for several days. Two of the groups were then released.

However, the third group was not freed. One of our lay leaders was in this group. Just before the time of the meeting, a fight arose in that area over an attempt to prevent some of our people from attending the conference, and a number of our newest Christians were involved. In the course of events, a chief was badly injured, and he later died during the time of the detainment of our friends. The young leader detained was not even present when the fight occurred. He called us from the jail to say that he feared for their lives.

The new Christians attending the conference were distressed about what happened to their friends. Even though he was afraid, one of the leaders who attended the meeting said to the group, "The only way to stop these things is to stop sharing the gospel, and we can't do that. I won't let people keep me from doing what God has given me to do."

After several days of negotiations, the third group was released! The lay leader who spoke boldly at the meeting told me of a dream he had in which God said, *My beloved child, don't be afraid. They can only touch flesh and blood, but you belong to Me.* This dream gave him peace.

—D., WEST AFRICA

Father, WHAT CAN MERE MAN DO TO ME WHEN YOU HAVE MY LIFE IN YOUR HANDS? ENCOURAGE THESE BELIEVERS IN WEST AFRICA WHO ARE BEING PERSECUTED FOR THEIR FAITH. GIVE BOLDNESS TO CHRISTIAN LEADERS SO THAT THEY WILL CONTINUE TO SHARE THE GOSPEL. *Amen.*

Will I forgive my persecutors?

"Bless those who persecute you; bless and curse not." Romans 12:14 (NASB)

The local religious leader began to stir up the townspeople against a new follower of Jesus, a young man called N. Stones were gathered, and the villagers rushed to lay hold of N., dragging him to the predetermined place for stoning. Just as the first stones were raised in the villagers' hands, a sudden storm with a mighty wind and rain materialized. The deluge drove the villagers away. N. was shaken, but unharmed. This angered the religious leader even more, and he made a plan with others to try again. Several days after the attempted stoning, the same young men seized N., holding him down while they kicked him, beat him and cut his throat. The young victim survived this brutality and was hospitalized.

We visited N. in the state hospital, offering legal advice and medical assistance. I told him, "This is illegal and is against your nation's constitution. We can go to the state prosecutor, who will assist you."

His response, however, was, "Thank you for your offer of help, but the Bible says to forgive those who persecute you. I am going back home and will visit with those who beat me. I will tell them that God forgave my sins. I forgive them."

I was amazed at the spiritual maturity of this young believer. God revealed that even though a believer might be new in his faith, he is empowered by the Holy Spirit to withstand such persecution and to forgive. I was humbled by his example and resolved to learn from new believers.

—A WORKER IN CENTRAL ASIA

Heavenly Father, PLEASE MAKE THESE YOUNG BELIEVERS STRONG WHEN THEY ARE PERSECUTED FOR YOUR SAKE. I PRAY THAT THE FORGIVENESS SHOWN WILL WIN OTHERS TO CHRIST. I PRAY THAT I, TOO, WILL BLESS AND FORGIVE THOSE WHO PERSECUTE ME OR MY LOVED ONES. EVEN NOW, I FORGIVE MY ENEMIES AND PRAY FOR AN OPPORTUNITY TO FORGIVE THEM PERSONALLY. *Amen.*

JULY V

God Working

Every day this month we're going to see some visible prints of the invisible hand of God. He is at work, you know. Not all of us get to see it so plainly. One of my friends on the mission field serves on a small Muslim island where her husband and children are the only other Christians she knows. Their day-in, day-out mode of evangelism is being a good neighbor and slowly changing negative perceptions of American Christianity. Their calling demands tremendous patience and hospitality in the midst of unimaginable isolation.

I used to picture all missionaries in bands of close-knit brothers and sisters of the faith laboring side by side. They didn't have the comforts of the United States, but I imagined they had a very uncommon companionship with one another that could make up for it. Certainly this is an accurate picture of some locations.

I was floored, however, when I learned that one solitary couple might serve the more sensitive areas of the world, posing the largest security risks. Often the places where only a few missionaries serve are also the places of fewest obvious believers. Can you imagine how often they must wonder if their efforts make any difference? Some of them have served for years in fundamentalist Muslim or Hindu communities where they've seen a rare convert if any.

We don't have to be on the mission field in a Muslim country to feel isolated. My favorite places to serve in the United States are those regions farthest from the Bible Belt. I have no greater honor than serving people who feel overwhelmed and terribly outnumbered. They desperately need and readily respond to encouragement. I'm not sure Satan uses anything more effectively in the daily grind of ministry than discouragement. Surely he tempts devoted believers who are isolated and outnumbered to ask themselves, "Is anything working? Is God even working?"

God is working. You can count on it. Not coincidentally, the kinds of service that stand to make the monumental differences are the same kinds that demand the most faith. More succinctly: the most difference demands the most faith. Dear one, we have to exercise faith to participate wildly in what God is doing in our generation. We can't just exercise energy, sweat and tears. It is still impossible for 21st century believers to please God without faith (Heb. 11:6).

I am greatly concerned for evangelicals like me in our generation. I am convinced we are caught in a stronghold of unbelief. Among many reasons are at least these two:

1. We are so far removed from the days of wonders in the early New Testament church that we've forgotten what God can do.
2. We are turned off by, if not scared to death of, the sensational extreme of the current faith movement.

As for the latter, I don't think God is going to allow us to use the other extremists as an excuse for our lack of faith. As for the former, though His kingdom agenda admittedly evolves, God is still who He says He is, and He can still do what He says He can do. I am convinced that a paramount reason we see so little of the stunning, miracle-working hand of God is because we've accepted the visible as the possible and the possible as the probable. In other words, God can do what we've seen Him do, and we can believe Him to do what He'll probably do anyway. What kind of faith is that?

I'm not picking on you. Actually, God picked on me. I was the biggest offender of all because I cut my theological teeth on a hypercessation interpretation of the New Testament, which says that miraculous and phenomenal works of God have ceased in our day. I had wonderful teachers and tutors in those days, and the great majority of what I learned I still believe with all my heart. However, my "stand" had paralyzed my faith. I believed God readily did what we'd seen Him do with our own eyes. I loved God, served Him and sought Him with all my heart. Then one day He nearly hammered me to the ground with a harsh rebuke for not believing Him. That was about seven years ago, and He and I have been working on my weak faith ever since.

God taught me a way to pledge my faith to Him every single day through five statements. I taught these in the Bible study *Believing God*, but I want to share them in this book as well because they've meant so much to me. I believe that these five statements encompass virtually everything God calls us to believe in His Word:

1. God is who He says He is.
2. God can do what He says He can do.
3. I am who God says I am.
4. I can do all things through Christ.
5. God's Word is alive and active in me.

I always conclude the five statements by making a verbal commitment: "I'm believing God."

I want to challenge you to give these statements a try. Say them every single day. I can be completely overwhelmed by a challenge, and as I spit these statements out of my mouth, I can feel faith rising up in me. I have never seen God work as blatantly as I have since He challenged me to believe Him instead of just believing *in* Him. I've quit being so safe and sterile about what I ask. The primary question that precedes my request is simply this: Is it biblical? Nothing has had a greater impact on my approach to God and to daily living than raising both my sword of the Spirit (Scripture) and my shield of faith (belief).

God *is* still working in our generation. Faith is how we join Him.

—*Beth Moore*

Desperate and dependent

"Now faith is being sure of what we hope for and certain of what we do not see.
This is what the ancients were commended for." Hebrews 11:1–2 (NIV)

"Where God's glory is gaining a foothold, Satan will not sit idle. Die to self, Margie. Dependence = power = God's glory. Be desperate and dependent. Walk by faith, embrace the unknown and watch the deliverance of God. We'll pray. God's in control!"

Tim's e-mail message challenged me as I prepared for the production of an evangelism video in Guadeloupe (gway-day-LOO-pay). Sheets of rain were falling. The majority of the video content needed to be recorded in the rain forest. Even a light rain could ruin the electronic equipment. The video shoot could not be rescheduled.

As the director, the decision was in my hands to cancel or continue. I knew that God had developed this project from the beginning. "Walk by faith. Die to self. Be desperate and dependent." The litany continued in my mind.

The equipment was unloaded from the van, and we hiked to the location. The rain increased. A decision must be made. "Walk by faith. God's in control." It was time to remove the equipment from the cases. The rain did not slow. "Faith." I opened the lid of the first case and removed the camera. At that exact moment, the rain stopped! For six and a half hours, we remained in the rain forest. Not one drop of rain fell ... until the equipment was safely put away. And then the heavens opened again. We were drenched, but not the equipment. "Watch the deliverance of God." God received the glory—rain and shine!

—MARGIE, MIDDLE AMERICA AND THE CARIBBEAN

Father, YOU SO DESIRE US TO HAVE FAITH. INCREASE MY FAITH. HELP ME TO ACTIVELY BELIEVE THAT YOU ARE IN CONTROL IN ALL SITUATIONS. STRENGTHEN THE FAITH OF MISSIONARIES, AND CONTINUE TO SEND THEM AN ENCOURAGING WORD THROUGH E-MAILS, LETTERS AND YOUR WORD. *Amen.*

A plea for help

"Let your light so shine before men, that they may see your good works, and glorify your Father which is in heaven." Matthew 5:16 (KJV)

As I was pulling out of my driveway one morning in Toluca (toh-LOU-kah), Mexico, my next-door neighbor knocked on my car window and made motions for me to stop. I had lived next to Bill and Marisol for six months.

They knew I had lost my dear husband and oldest daughter in a swimming accident a year earlier and had repeatedly expressed their admiration for the peace and contentment that my other children and I demonstrated daily.

I quickly rolled down the window of my car and heard Bill's plea. "My wife and I are having some real struggles," he said. "We know that you are close to God and know a lot about the Bible. We have seen what that has done for you and your family. Could you come tonight to our house and offer some solutions for us?"

Of course, I immediately accepted the invitation. My children and I had already made plans for that night, but each one of my kids agreed to stay home and pray for my meeting with our neighbors.

That night, two more souls were saved at the house next door, and my children had a part in that event. It was my privilege to open God's Word and share the solutions from God. Bill spontaneously dropped to his knees, and Marisol followed. They offered sincere and heartfelt prayers of repentance and acceptance of God's provision for their lives.

Late that evening, I celebrated with my three great partners in ministry—my children.

—GLORIA, MIDDLE AMERICA AND THE CARIBBEAN

Father, YOU SEE THIS DEAR WIDOW WHO IS STILL MINISTERING WITH HER CHILDREN TO PEOPLE IN MIDDLE AMERICA. BLESS HER MINISTRY AND FAMILY TODAY. USE OTHER SINGLE MISSIONARIES TO MAKE A DIFFERENCE IN THE SOULS OF OTHERS. *Amen.*

Voice in the night

"And they said, 'Cornelius the centurion, a just man, one who fears God and has a good reputation among all the nation of the Jews, was divinely instructed by a holy angel to summon you to his house, and to hear words from you.'"
Acts 10:22 (NKJV)

The woman awoke startled. She frantically glanced around the dark room. No one was there, yet she knew she had heard a voice speak clearly. Confused, the Muslim woman fell back on the foam mattress. She closed her eyes and heard the voice again. *Okay,* she thought to herself. *I'll do what You say.*

The next morning, she sent a child to the exact location in her dream. There, the child met me walking down a dirt path. The child said there was someone wanting to see me. I thought it was a case of mistaken identity—especially since I had never walked down this path before. However, the child was so insistent that I finally followed.

Once we neared the home, a Muslim woman ran out to greet us. Before anyone could shake hands in introduction, she blurted out, "Tell me about God!" I smiled and asked, "How did you know that I was a Christian when we don't even know each other?"

The Muslim woman recounted the dream that she had the previous night. "This voice told me to send a child to meet a woman walking down the dirt path at the exact time you were walking there," she said. "It then told me to ask this woman about God, and then I would know the truth."

Knowing that many Muslim converts come to Christ through dreams, I began to share. I thanked God for the "voice in the night" that encouraged her to hear and accept the truth of Jesus.

—A WORKER IN CENTRAL, EASTERN AND SOUTHERN AFRICA

Father, THANK YOU THAT YOU SPEAK IN THAT STILL, SMALL VOICE. OPEN MY EARS TO HEAR AND OBEY YOU. THANK YOU THAT YOU ARE SPEAKING TO THE UNREACHED IN RWANDA. GIVE ME A HEART FOR THE MUSLIM PEOPLE AND AN OPPORTUNITY TO BE YOUR WITNESS. *Amen.*

God causes the growth

"So then neither the one who plants nor the one who waters is anything, but God who causes the growth." 1 Corinthians 3:7 (NASB)

The Lord recently led a team of four missionary friends in Central Asia to obtain permission from the government to move to limited access areas where large numbers of Ewe (YOU) people live. We believed that the Ewes had not heard the gospel before. Immediately, a door opened to one of these areas, and two single women went to a city where tens of thousands of Ewes were living.

I was one of those women. We thought we would be the first to share truth. A month after our move, I received a knock on my door. It was my dear Ewe friend, Elizabeth, accompanied by her husband. Because I had talked about Jesus with Elizabeth, she thought I might like to see a book someone had given her a long time ago. The book was an old copy of the Ewe translation of the Gospel of Luke. I was amazed! The Father had brought this truth to Elizabeth long before His laborers had come to the area.

Eighteen months later, I was looking for some movies that I could watch to enhance my listening capabilities in the difficult Ewe language. What movie did my teacher and I stumble upon in a rental shop in the heart of a Ewe village? The *JESUS* film! It was the original movie, including the invitation to follow Jesus. What's more, the DVD that the movie was burned on had been worn with use. The truth of God was being spread all over the city. What a faithful God we serve!

—"ELIZABETH CARMICHAEL," CENTRAL ASIA

Praise You, Father, FOR PUTTING YOUR MESSAGE INTO THE HANDS OF THOSE WHO SEEK YOU. I PRAY THAT YOUR SPIRIT WILL CONTINUE TO REVEAL TRUTH AND TO CONVICT AS YOU BRING TO THEIR REMEMBRANCE THE VISUAL IMAGES AND WORDS THAT THEY SAW AND HEARD ON THE FILM. CONTINUE TO PREPARE THE WAY FOR YOUR SON TO BE RECEIVED IN THE CITIES OF CENTRAL ASIA. *Amen.*

Arranged friendships

"For the truth about God is known to them instinctively. God has put this knowledge in their hearts." Romans 1:19 (NLT)

"Naomi," a Muslim teenage girl, worked in a salon where I visited. I felt a bond with her and prayed silently that God would build a friendship between us. Naomi began to share with me about a decision she needed to make: whether to quit her job at the salon (her only source of income) or remain there with a boss who beat and abused her.

I discreetly asked if I could pray for her, and Naomi nodded. I asked God to protect her from her boss and then asked the Spirit to unveil her heart from the grasp of Islam.

We kept in touch, and eventually she visited. I gave Naomi an Arabic Bible and showed her passages explaining the gospel. I shared with her how Jesus changed my life. I told her that the Bible was sacred to me and that Jesus was everything. Naomi listened and then told me about her recent dream.

In her dream, she came upon a man dressed in white, standing in front of her. Naomi said she was frightened, until the man opened His arms and beckoned her to come to Him. She immediately felt peace. The man was Jesus. Naomi said that she knew both the Bible and Jesus would be sacred in her life one day as well.

To bring the lost to Christ, we need to be willing to share with whomever God brings into our path. I'm now waiting for the next friend God brings my way.

—ROSALYN, NORTHERN AFRICA AND THE MIDDLE EAST

Father, THANK YOU THAT YOU GIVE CHRISTIAN WORKERS OPPORTUNITIES TO SHARE JESUS WITH THOSE WHOM THEY MEET IN THEIR COMMUNITIES IN THE MIDDLE EAST. GIVE THEM COURAGE TO BUILD RELATIONSHIPS IN COUNTRIES THAT ARE ANTAGONISTIC TOWARD CHRISTIANS. USE ME TO SHARE WITH A PERSON WHOM YOU BRING INTO MY PATH THIS WEEK. *Amen.*

Miracles still happen

"For nothing will be impossible with God." Luke 1:37 (NASB)

It's a miracle that we return safely to our hotel room each evening during a week of training others! We ride the local rickshaws to our seminar site and sit high up on a slanted seat, planting our feet in such a way so as not to slide right off into the street. The driver works hard, pumping his bicycle in front of us. There aren't many cars, but that is not to say there isn't a lot of traffic. The streets are jam-packed with foot traffic, bicycles and thousands of rickshaws. Cows meander here and there. I have watched as my driver maneuvered around all obstacles, human and otherwise, safely ... but only just! I'm too old to get anxious anymore. I watch in wide-eyed wonder as we twist and turn, dodge and dart through every busy intersection. It is a miracle!

But a greater miracle is to see the changed lives that Jesus Christ makes. Today I talked with a former Muslim cleric of a mosque. Two years ago this cleric came to truth; he met Jesus Christ. His wife did also. He led Muslims before, but now he leads the growing number of people who believe in Jesus. His former friends and family at the mosque cannot imagine why he would forsake their religion. They cause him great distress and many problems. But for him to talk eagerly to me, a woman, with a big smile on his face as he tells me about his new life in Christ, is a miracle.

—D., SOUTH ASIA

Heavenly Father, THANK YOU FOR THE MIRACLES, BIG AND SMALL, THAT TOUCH MY LIFE EACH DAY. PLEASE PROTECT MISSIONARIES DURING THEIR TRAVEL. MAKE THEM A BLESSING TO THE PEOPLE THEY SERVE. LORD, SPEAK TO MUSLIM IMAMS SO THAT THEY WILL SEARCH FOR YOU, THE ONE, TRUE GOD IN YOUR WORD, THE BIBLE. *Amen.*

Putting words in one's mouth

"Now then go, and I, even I, will be with your mouth, and teach you what you are to say." Exodus 4:12 (NASB)

An opportunity came for me to fill in as a Bible study teacher. My student would be a national woman named "Alice." However, I was anxious because of my inadequacies in the local language.

The first time that Alice and I met, I shared the story of the fall of Adam and Eve. Alice's two older daughters listened in: one intently, the other less conspicuously from across the room. Remarkably, the language came as easily as if I'd been talking and understanding in my own language. After the story, we prayed and sang a worship song together. I drove home that day filled to overflowing! It was the most encouraging thing that had happened to me since we'd come to this land.

The next day, the Lord confirmed His miracle of the day before as I sat in my neighborhood park and struggled to converse and understand my friends with whom I speak every day. The day before, God Himself had provided above all that I had dreamed or imagined (Eph. 3:20).

The next week, after another clearly communicated Bible study in Alice's kitchen, we ended with a song from the Psalms. As we walked into the living room, we found Alice's husband, "Mark," crying. "I'm looking for the truth in both the Koran and the Bible," he said. When I asked him if he would be interested in studying the Bible with my husband, he said yes.

As we pray for Mark's repentance, we trust the Father to communicate through us as we share His Word.

—LISA, CENTRAL ASIA

Heavenly Father, YOU MADE MAN'S MOUTH, AND YOU CAN PUT THE WORDS AND LANGUAGES INTO THE MOUTHS OF THESE MISSIONARIES. HELP THEM TO LEARN LANGUAGES QUICKLY. GIVE ME THE RIGHT WORDS TO SAY TO _____ AS I WITNESS. *Amen.*

Going through open doors

"The LORD is close to all who call on him, yes, to all who call on him sincerely."
Psalm 145:18 (NLT)

Lydia had been asking spiritual questions, almost always without any prompting from me, and it opened a door to share more with her. She wanted to know about prophecies that Jesus fulfilled, about heaven and hell and if there really was a seventh heaven.

We met over coffee. I came prepared with a complete Bible in her heart language, ready to give it to her if the opportunity arose. As always, she started asking more questions. We talked about what a parable was, why four Bibles (she was referring to the four Gospels), what few stories of the Bible she was familiar with and so on.

After talking about the Bible, I asked her if she'd like one in her own heart language. She exclaimed that she would love to have one. I reached into my bag and pulled out the gift. Tears filled her eyes. "I'm so happy I could cry. My husband will be so excited, too," she said. I offered to read and study the Bible with her. She agreed on the spot.

It never ceases to amaze me how God draws people to Himself and how easy it is to walk through doors that God opens instead of forcing our way through closed ones. God alone calls people to Himself; we are just blessed to be part of the process.

Lydia and her husband are hungry for truth. Since childhood, they'd been taught lies about Jesus. She said that they see a difference in me. I look forward to the day we can celebrate Christ in them.

—A WORKER AMONG REFUGEES, WESTERN EUROPE

Father of love and wisdom, THANK YOU THAT YOU CREATE PEOPLE WITH A DESPERATE HUNGER AND LONGING THAT YOU ALONE CAN SATISFY. THANK YOU THAT YOU DRAW NEAR TO THOSE WHO CALL OUT TO YOU IN SINCERITY. I PRAY THAT WORKERS IN WESTERN EUROPE WILL HAVE THE OPPORTUNITY TODAY TO SHARE THE LIVING, POWERFUL WORD OF GOD WITH REFUGEES WHO HAVE RECEPTIVE, SEEKING HEARTS. *Amen.*

Bush emergency: 9-1-1!

"Do not be anxious about anything, but in everything, by prayer and petition, with thanksgiving, present your requests to God." Philippians 4:6 (NIV)

I feared the worst as I hung up the phone. A missionary had appendicitis. Deep in the bush with no available medical care, it would take two plane trips to get him to a city for surgery. It was my responsibility to get this man medical attention, but only the Father could help him in time. We were racing against the clock!

A few phone calls later, I was on a small plane and the family on another so that we could meet for the last leg of the journey. After landing, I rushed to the small four-seater plane to assess his condition. His face was a ghastly white, and he was dehydrated. After situating him on the larger plane, I prayed, asking God to take control of this seemingly impossible situation.

In the rush to get on the plane, not everyone had a passport. The authorities wouldn't let us take off. All we could do was pray for guidance as the missionary groaned in pain. Finally, after more than two hours, we were allowed to leave.

When we landed in the city, the airport was dark. Being after hours, local authorities immediately seized the passports that some of us had. After more begging and praying, we were finally allowed to take the patient to the hospital for emergency surgery.

Because of the faithfulness of our Father in answering prayers, the missionary made it in time. Praise God for taking care of His workers —especially when the clock is ticking.

—NANCY, CENTRAL, EASTERN AND SOUTHERN AFRICA

Father God, I PRAY THAT YOU WILL BRING HEALTH TO MISSIONARIES WHO NEED THIS PROVISION TODAY. IF THERE ARE ANY EMERGENCIES, ALLOW THEM TO BE HANDLED IN A TIMELY MANNER. *Amen.*

"Sure—get in!"

"You will make known to me the path of life; In Your presence is fullness of joy; In Your right hand there are pleasures forever." Psalm 16:11 (NASB)

Working in a new refugee center in Western Europe where sharing the gospel was difficult, my husband and I met D. from Northern Africa. One day, we arranged to take him out with us for a chance to develop a friendship. Upon leaving the center, my husband suddenly stopped the van. Four young refugee men from the camp were walking in the road, blocking our way.

Oh no, I thought, *they'll probably want a ride, and that will distract from our conversation with D.* I prayed, "Lord, please make these guys move out of the way so we can do Your work!" At that point, the four young men motioned for me to roll down my window.

"May we ride with you to town?" one of the Middle Eastern young men asked, in broken English. Wanting to say no, I surprised myself when I said, "Sure—get in!"

There was an awkward silence after we started on our way. Then one of the young men asked, "Excuse me, we want to know about Jesus. Do you know about Him? We were not permitted to ask in our country, but we want to know truth."

My husband and I were so surprised that I asked the man to repeat the question! We had thought that a roadblock was in our way a few moments before, but a miracle occurred when God put those men in our path.

A few months later, these four men became Christians. We never heard from D. again, but we know God is still constructing miracles.

—JODY, WESTERN EUROPE

Almighty God, I'M AMAZED THAT YOU EVEN PUT UP WITH US WHEN WE SET OUR MINDS TO A CERTAIN COURSE THAT IS NOT YOURS. I PRAY THAT THE SEEDS PLANTED IN D.'S LIFE WILL BE WATERED BY OTHER SERVANTS SO THAT HE WILL COME TO KNOW YOU. USE THESE FOUR MIDDLE EASTERN MEN TO SHARE CHRIST WITH THEIR COUNTRYMEN. KEEP MISSIONARIES SENSITIVE TO YOUR PLANS. *Amen.*

God-sized opportunities

"Now to Him who is able to do far more abundantly beyond all that we ask or think, according to the power that works within us." Ephesians 3:20 (NASB)

Meeting the head official of the people group I work with allowed me an unexpected, huge opportunity. So often I do not pray "big"; I settle for less, but God goes for "big."

While in the north of this South Asian region, a man named Karma introduced himself to us. Karma was eager to make our experience optimum. He set up meetings for us, and even though he was a Buddhist, he introduced us to other key officials, Christians in the community, and his personal friends and family. The greatest experience of all came when he utilized his contacts to get us into a forbidden land, the government-protected area of our people group. We had not planned on laying a foundation in that land during this first excursion. It was a blessing from the Lord.

The forbidden land is where our target people group live. It is off-limits to foreigners. The people are Buddhists and worship nature. The satanic strongholds of this place are very intense. We were warned by Christians outside this land that if the people heard that we were Christian, they would kill us, foreigner or not. With heavy hearts, we entered the area under the Lord's direction and under Karma's wing.

God also began a great work in Karma's heart. He was receptive when we shared the gospel with him, for he is searching for truth.

God taught me much on this trip about praying for "big" results and not settling for less.

—A WORKER IN SOUTH ASIA

Father, YOU HAVE ALREADY GIVEN KARMA A SEEKING HEART. BRING HIM TO YOURSELF AND CONTINUE TO GIVE OPPORTUNITIES TO MINISTER TO THIS HUGE PEOPLE GROUP THAT IS WITHOUT YOU IN THIS FORBIDDEN LAND. FATHER, ALSO I PRAY THAT I WILL NOT SETTLE FOR LESS THAN WHAT YOU INTEND. MAY I TRUST YOU FOR "BIG" OPPORTUNITIES FOR THE KINGDOM. *Amen.*

Seeing your "children" grow up

"For you know that we dealt with each of you as a father deals with his own children, encouraging, comforting and urging you to live lives worthy of God, who calls you into his kingdom and glory." 1 Thessalonians 2:11–12 (NIV)

Mary entered a church building in a Muslim country out of curiosity. There was no service there. That day, however, a group of national believers had chosen the same place to have time to pray as a group. As a result, Mary met Jesus.

Discipling Mary, I witnessed how the Lord helped her through difficult trials as she sought to be an active follower of Christ. I was able to stand beside Mary as she married another believer. Their marriage didn't come without difficulties from the families, but the Lord gave them peace to withstand opposition.

Having a Christ-centered home is not automatic, and Mary and her husband have struggled as they overcome cultural and religious barriers that are counter to God's direction for marriage. They have learned how much they need Christ to make their marriage work.

When we moved to another country, it was hard to leave my "children" in Christ. Did I really believe God would take care of them?

After almost six years of knowing Mary, she is expecting her first child. However, her last e-mail not only told me that she was going to have a boy, but that she was going to share with a person who was seeking to become a believer! I do not know which made me happier—the news of the boy or the new believer.

Investing our lives in relationships with others for the sake of Christ pleases the Father.

—C.B.G., NORTHERN AFRICA AND THE MIDDLE EAST

Abba, Father, YOU POURED YOUR LIFE INTO OTHERS THROUGH YOUR SON. I DESIRE TO BUILD RELATIONSHIPS WITH OTHERS FOR THE SAKE OF YOUR KINGDOM. I ALSO PRAY FOR CHRISTIAN WORKERS IN NORTHERN AFRICA AND THE MIDDLE EAST TO HAVE OPPORTUNITIES TO DEVELOP RELATIONSHIPS FOR YOUR PURPOSES. *Amen.*

Using whatever skills God gives

"Consequently, faith comes from hearing the message, and the message is heard through the word of Christ." Romans 10:17 (NIV)

I could tell the young boy was curious as I set up my equipment in the plaza. We didn't seem to be communicating well, and I soon realized that he was hearing-impaired. I didn't know sign language.

I was preparing an open-air gospel presentation using a blacklight assembly. It always drew a crowd. I preached on the cross of Calvary, illustrating the message on the sketchboard.

Volunteers had come to Veracruz (bear-ah-CRUISE) from two churches in my home county in the States, including my home church. We worked together to saturate the area with the gospel.

One of the volunteers was Shirley. She knew sign language and had prayed for at least one opportunity to use her skills during the mission trip.

After the presentation in the plaza, the hearing-impaired boy walked forward with others to indicate that he had prayed to receive Christ. I called out, "Shirley, come down here; I think the Lord has answered your prayer." With tears in her eyes, she knelt down and interpreted to the boy as I asked him various questions. He never took his eyes off her. Truly he had understood, and Christ had saved him.

That night, God not only faithfully answered Shirley's earnest prayer, but He allowed a little boy to understand the gospel and receive Christ. All the way from the United States, God brought Shirley there for that moment, for that divine appointment.

When we use what skills we have, God will bless them for kingdom purposes.

—LARRY, MIDDLE AMERICA AND THE CARIBBEAN

Father, USE MY SKILLS THAT YOU HAVE GIVEN ME TO MINISTER TO OTHERS. SEND MANY VOLUNTEERS TO THE UTTERMOST PARTS OF THE WORLD TO SHARE WITH OTHERS AND TO BRING MANY TO JESUS. I PRAY SPECIFICALLY FOR MINISTRIES TO THE HEARING-IMPAIRED WITH OUR MISSIONARIES AND VOLUNTEERS TO BE FRUITFUL. *Amen.*

Even in illness, He is with me

"For our light and momentary troubles are achieving for us an eternal glory that far outweighs them all." 2 Corinthians 4:17 (NIV)

That was the scripture I read the morning I was to check into the hospital in a foreign country. Within one week, my world had turned upside down. Throughout the summer, I had been having leg cramps that were waking me up in the middle of the night. One night I woke up in tears and decided that I'd had enough.

A doctor ran blood tests and asked, "Has anyone ever diagnosed you as having diabetes?" I was confused. I came to see the doctor because of leg cramps, and she was telling me something about diabetes? She referred me to a specialist, and I was on my way out the door.

I had been in Western Europe, working with refugees for less than a year. Diabetes was definitely not a part of my plans. The morning I went to the hospital, God gave me His sweet peace through 2 Corinthians 4:17. I knew from that moment on, everything would be okay. He reminded me that He created me and that He would take care of me as He always had.

As I look back, I see that God got my attention with the nightly leg cramps; otherwise, I would not have gone to the doctor. He placed me in a country that had good medical care so that all my needs could quickly be met. He was with me as I learned to eat differently and learned to take better care of myself. I am never alone, for He is always with me.

—MENDY, WESTERN EUROPE

Heavenly Father, WHEN THINGS SEEM TOO BIG FOR ME, REMIND ME THAT YOU ARE JEHOVAH-JIREH, MY PROVIDER. YOU ARE A FAITHFUL GOD. THANK YOU FOR YOUR GRACE TO ACCEPT THINGS THAT COME MY WAY. MAY MISSIONARIES ALSO PROVE FAITHFUL TO YOU AND BRING GLORY TO YOUR NAME DURING ILLNESS. *Amen.*

Faithful in the small things

"And who knows whether you have not come to the kingdom for such a time as this?" Esther 4:14b (RSV)

Often, huge accomplishments are made merely because people were in the right place in the will of God at the right time. Yet some people miss opportunities to make a difference because they fail to take small steps along the way.

Wendall and Jane came to Guatemala to minister to the Mam people. After having served nearly 40 years on the mission field and then retiring, they had plenty of other things to do. Instead, they made the decision to give us a month of their lives for ministry.

What happened during that month? They shared their faith in Guatemalan churches, helped to moderate and bring healing in a church situation, encouraged pastors, trained several readers for the Mam *JESUS* film and even assisted in the directing of the film, taught youth groups and led others to Christ. These are just some of the "ordinary" things that they did during one month. We are convinced that they were with us "for such a time as this."

This retired couple just wants to be useful to God. Is it any wonder that God does marvelous things through their lives?

What did we do last month? Are we dedicating minutes, hours and weeks to the little details that God puts in front of us to do? Or are we on the sidelines, waiting for something bigger to come along? May we be useful to His kingdom's work in whatever, whenever and wherever He deems to be "such a time as this."

—GARY, MIDDLE AMERICA AND THE CARIBBEAN

Father, YOU HAVE A PLAN TO USE ME AT ALL STAGES OF MY LIFE. HELP ME TO FOLLOW YOUR WILL EVEN IN THE LITTLE THINGS SO THAT I'LL BE READY FOR ANY OPPORTUNITY YOU HAVE TO USE ME. I PRAY THAT MANY RETIRED PEOPLE WILL VOLUNTEER FOR SHORT OVERSEAS MISSION TRIPS OR TWO-YEAR TERMS. *Amen.*

The thief's loss, your gain

"And as for you, you meant evil against me, but God meant it for good."
Genesis 50:20a (NASB)

We heard a wonderful story from a local pastor in Uberaba (oo-bare-AH-bah). It seems that some time back, a pastor friend of his felt led to buy a van in order to transport people to church. To help pay for the van, he would remove the backseats and do light delivery work. However, the van needed four new tires, and he had no money to purchase them.

One night while at church, the van was stolen. He had been praying for new tires, and now he had no van. Some of the members of the church tried to console him by saying that it was not God's will for him to have the van. Nevertheless, the pastor had faith that God would somehow use this for his good.

A few days later, the police called from a nearby town saying that they had caught the thief and had traced the pastor through the van's serial number. The pastor immediately caught a ride to that police station. He was surprised to find his van unharmed and with a set of new tires, new backseats and a radio installed! He told the police officer that although it was his van, the thief had evidently supplied the extras. The policeman said, "Well, I guess that is the thief's loss and your gain."

God turned the evil intentions of a thief into good for a faithful, prayerful pastor. He does the same for us as we trust Him to work things out for our best.

—MONTY AND JANIS, SOUTH AMERICA

Heavenly Father, YOU SEE THE BIG PICTURE OF MY LIFE. I PRAY THAT YOU WOULD TAKE HURTFUL EXPERIENCES OF MY PAST TO MAKE ME A BETTER PERSON TODAY, SOMEONE WHO TOTALLY DEPENDS ON YOU. *Amen.*

Behind the scenes

"But the plans of the Lord stand firm forever, the purposes of his heart through all generations." Psalm 33:11 (NIV)

I can look out from my fourth-floor window to see snow. It's fresh and clean—a miracle in this culture of hurt and hopelessness. My favorite miracle, other than snow, is Anna, one of my English students. I noticed her early on, because she brought her boyfriend to class one day.

After a few weeks of teaching, I received an e-mail forwarded from an American who had visited our city. The man told about his flight out of the country. He sat beside a young man from South Africa. As they talked, the South African spoke of his girlfriend whom he had visited. He said that she wanted to "bring Jesus back to this place."

As I read the e-mail, I began to wonder. The man who was writing wanted to ensure that someone in our city of 2 million made contact with this girl. Her name was Anna—my Anna!

The next week, I told Anna about the e-mail and asked if she would tutor me in Russian. Amazed at the happenstance, she said she had been praying for a job. As her story unfolded, I learned that a year ago, Anna was not willing to go to our English classes that met in a church. A friend convinced her to go, and her spiritual journey progressed.

Now Anna and I practice Russian and talk about life. It's obvious God has a special work planned for her. It will be through people like Anna that God will bring hope to hurting hearts—miracle by miracle.

—D.W.D., CENTRAL AND EASTERN EUROPE

Lord, THANK YOU FOR THE WORK YOU ARE DOING IN CENTRAL AND EASTERN EUROPE. PLEASE BRING MORE PEOPLE LIKE ANNA TO HELP MISSIONARIES IN THEIR WORK. I PRAISE YOU THAT THERE ARE NO COINCIDENCES FOR THE CHILDREN OF GOD. LORD, MAY YOUR PLANS AND PURPOSES BE MY PRIORITY TODAY AND EVERY DAY. *Amen.*

Hearing truth, seeking truth

"Live an exemplary life among the natives so that your actions will refute their prejudices. Then they'll be won over to God's side and be there to join in the celebration when he arrives." 1 Peter 2:12 (MSG)

Miriam was 10 years old and studying Islam, but she didn't believe it was the truth. A year later, she heard a radio broadcast in an Arabic dialect that she couldn't understand, but she discerned that the voice was speaking truth. She asked God to show her the way. Five years later, Miriam heard a radio broadcast in her language. The presenters talked about Jesus being the Son of God. She accepted Christ but didn't tell her family. She desired a Bible more than anything.

At the same time in a nearby city, Ahmed (AH-mud) was a practicing Muslim. His older brother, Lamine (lah-MAY-ah), was a believer and shared Jesus with him often. Ahmed refused to listen and was planning to kill Lamine for turning his back on Islam. After some troubles, Ahmed started searching for truth and asked his brother for a Bible. With Bible in hand, he traveled to a small town a few miles away in order to think. Miriam and her family lived there.

Walking down the road, Ahmed passed Miriam and began talking to her. Miriam told Ahmed that she was a follower of Jesus but that she'd never had a Bible to read. Ahmed said, "Here's a Bible." He handed her the Bible he had received earlier that day.

For the next two years, Miriam lived an exemplary life before Ahmed in friendship. Ahmed was won over to God's side. Today they are married, have two young sons and are bright lights shining for Jesus in Northern Africa.

—D.M., NORTHERN AFRICA AND THE MIDDLE EAST

Dear Lord, HOW WONDERFUL YOU ARE TO BRING YOUR WORD TO MUSLIMS! THANK YOU FOR MUSLIM BELIEVERS WHO ARE LIVING THEIR FAITH IN FRONT OF OTHERS. ALLOW OTHERS TO RESPOND TO THEIR TESTIMONIES. HELP ME TO BE AN EXAMPLE OF JESUS TO ALL THOSE WITH WHOM I COME INTO CONTACT TODAY. *Amen.*

God will make a way

"Being confident in this, that he who began a good work in you will carry it on to completion until the day of Christ Jesus." Philippians 1:6 (NIV)

Six years ago on a snowy winter day, I sat in a modest home in northern Bosnia and prayed with a Serbian young man named Sasha (SAH-sha) as he received Christ. Another missionary and I had met with Sasha and his parents on three occasions before, teaching them simple truths from the Bible. Soon after that visit, however, a war was brewing nearby, which forced Americans to leave this part of the country. We lost contact with Sasha, his parents and many others. I often wondered what became of Sasha through the years, and at those times, I prayed for him and his family.

So often we become weary when our efforts are stopped short by circumstances that are out of our control. As a missionary, we don't always see the results of growth among those we lead to Christ. But God remains faithful. I have learned that He is in control, and although we do not have the ability to fathom it, God knows the bigger picture for those lives He touches through us.

Six years later, I received an e-mail telling of someone named Sasha looking for me. Thanks to the e-mail and colleagues tracking me down, we have made contact again with this young man. What a wonderful blessing to finally hear about Sasha and what God has done in the lives of him and his family. Today, Sasha is attending Bible college in a Balkan country and has responded to God's call on his life.

—DONNA, CENTRAL AND EASTERN EUROPE

Father, IN THE MIDST OF INSTABILITY, WAR AND CONSTANT CHANGES, MAKE A WAY FOR NEW BELIEVERS TO GROW EVEN WHEN THEIR TEACHERS HAVE HAD TO LEAVE THE COUNTRY. GIVE THEM ACCESS TO YOUR WORD AND THE FELLOWSHIP OF OTHER BELIEVERS. GIVE ME AN OPPORTUNITY TO BE INVOLVED IN THE GROWTH PROCESS OF NEW BELIEVERS WITH WHOM I MEET. *Amen.*

Looking for the man of peace

"If a man of peace is there, your peace will rest upon him; but if not, it will return to you." Luke 10:6 (NASB)

Traveling to Muslim villages, I ask to speak to the leader. Inevitably, a crowd gathers to listen. Usually, God is working inside the heart of at least one individual. We call this individual the "man of peace." Through a dream, a tract found on the side of the road, a radio program or another way, the Spirit already has begun His work in the man of peace.

Two volunteers from Texas joined my first trip to discover a man of peace. We took a backpack with a change of clothes, snacks, a Bible, teaching pictures, tracts and the *JESUS* film. It is the God-given duty of the man of peace to take care of us.

The first day of our journey, we talked to everyone along the way, something we shouldn't have done. Jesus instructed His disciples not to speak to anyone when looking for the man of peace. We didn't receive an invitation to stay in a home. Before falling asleep at a government office guest room, two Muslim men knocked on our door.

They told us that missionaries had come four years previously. The missionaries couldn't speak their language but prayed in Jesus' name for one of the men's daughters who had a bad leg. A few weeks later, the daughter's leg was healed. In their language, I shared with them about Jesus. The next morning, the men took us to a home where 25 were gathered to see the *JESUS* film.

As a result of God locating men of peace, five small churches have begun.

—A WORKER IN SOUTH ASIA

Father, THANK YOU FOR THE PROVISION OF A "MAN OF PEACE" IN PLACES WHERE YOU ARE WORKING. USE THEIR CONVERSIONS AS THE CATALYST FOR MANY TO COME TO CHRIST. GIVE ME A SENSITIVE SPIRIT TO DISCERN THE PEOPLE WHOM YOU ARE DRAWING TO YOURSELF SO THAT I CAN SHARE THE GOSPEL WITH THEM. *Amen.*

The golden years

"To every thing there is a season, and a time to every purpose under the heaven."
Ecclesiastes 3:1 (KJV)

As a child, the Father gave me a desire to be on the international mission field. My parents opened our home to visiting missionaries and pastors, which provided exposure to the work. I secretly wanted to pack a bag and go home with all the missionaries.

I married at age 17 and became a mother at age 18. The Father blessed me with a marvelous Christian husband, three children and eight lovely grandchildren. My husband died at the age of 47 with cancer, and I have been a widow for 20 years.

The longing I had as a child turned to reality at 64 years of age. Now in China, working with college students, I'm in an area where age is highly respected. I have witnessed many young girls coming to faith.

I look back and realize that every portion of my life was preparation for the awesome privilege I now enjoy. For years I wondered why my Father waited so long, but I know that every event was necessary.

One important hurdle was preparing my children to release me to this task. I read in Exodus about Moses being challenged to be the leader of the Jewish people. He understood the calling and went to his father-in-law, saying, "Please, let me go." Jethro told him, "Go in peace" (Ex. 4:18, NASB). I am thankful that my children have said the same to me even though the separation is difficult.

God's timing is always perfect. He sees the parade from beginning to end. We only see the portion that passes by us.

--A WORKER IN CHINA

Heavenly Father, THANK YOU THAT YOU ARE USING SENIOR CITIZENS FOR SERVICE OVERSEAS. USE THEIR EXPERIENCE AND WISDOM TO MAKE A DIFFERENCE FOR CHRIST ALL OVER THE WORLD. GIVE THEM GOOD HEALTH AND SAFETY, AND GIVE THEIR CHILDREN THE GRACE TO RELEASE THEM FOR SERVICE. *Amen.*

Prepared for a place

"However, as it is written: No eye has seen, no ear has heard, no mind has conceived what God has prepared for those who love him." 1 Corinthians 2:9 (NIV)

"No, you can't turn the heat up. The reindeer will thaw!" my husband replied to my plea for more heat. "But my toes are 10 chunks of ice!" I grumbled.

We must have looked a sight, huddled in our coats in subzero temperatures as we drove along. In the back of our jeep lay a frozen reindeer carcass, which we hoped would not thaw on the eight-hour drive home from a northern village of reindeer herders.

God had called us from our home in Alaska to work among people in the northern reaches of Russia. Many discouraged us from moving there, saying it was too isolated and temperatures were extreme. Even our Russian friends had reacted in horror when we told them we were moving to such a remote area to work among reindeer herders. But we knew that God had prepared us for this place.

Hunting moose and caribou, fishing, and living on a homestead with no running water or electricity were just a few of our Alaskan adventures. Yet when God called us to international missions, I had despaired over qualities lacking in our lives: theological knowledge, missiological training and eloquent speech.

As I watched my husband wrestling with frozen reindeer meat, I had to laugh at my feelings of inadequacy. In God's eyes, it is often the most insignificant experiences that are the most valuable in His plan. By God's grace, we were perfectly fitted with the needed abilities to minister in Russia. All that is required for any of us is to follow Him.

—ROBIN, CENTRAL AND EASTERN EUROPE

Father, THANK YOU THAT YOU USE PAST EXPERIENCES TO PREPARE US FOR PRESENT AND FUTURE CIRCUMSTANCES. HELP MISSIONARIES IN DIFFICULT AREAS TO FACE EXTREME CONDITIONS WITH HOPE AND DEPENDENCY UPON YOU. HELP ME TO ALLOW YOU TO MOLD AND SHAPE MY LIFE ACCORDING TO THE SPECIFICATION OF YOUR PLANS AND PURPOSES. *Amen.*

A real missionary

"For to me to live is Christ, and to die is gain." Philippians 1:21 (ESV)

Missionaries are ordinary, everyday people. I grew up thinking they were superspiritual: that they didn't need money to live on because they had an extra dose of Jesus and that their kids were delighted to receive old clothes and ragged toys because they were somehow "different."

Now I know better. I fall under the category of "missionary," and I have one of those kids who is supposed to be different but really isn't.

I thought becoming a missionary meant that I would have great stories to tell that would wow my Christian friends back home. My story, however, is of an ordinary person, struggling to learn a foreign language, frustrated because there is no such thing as privacy where I live, and battling thoughts of criticism directed toward the people I am here to love. And my story is also about how God is changing this everyday gal, from the inside out, to live a life of divine proportions.

Mine is a marvelous story because He brought me all the way to East Asia to show me that I am complete in Him. He is teaching this weak individual, with human limitations and hang-ups, that His power truly is manifested in weakness. God's promises become real as I encounter the world outside or as I crack open the language book to study.

I am learning that it is not just about victories. It is also about obedience that costs, unrecognized sacrifices and unanswered questions. Ultimately, it is about following Christ.

—A WORKER IN EAST ASIA

Heavenly Father, THANK YOU THAT YOU TAKE ORDINARY PEOPLE LIKE ME AND USE THEM TO FULFILL YOUR PURPOSES. HELP ME NOT TO ELEVATE THE STATUS OF MISSIONARIES OR PEOPLE IN MINISTRY, BUT TO KEEP MY EYES FOCUSED ON THE ONE WHO IS RESPONSIBLE FOR ANY VICTORIES FOR THE KINGDOM. *Amen.*

Night school

"Commit to the LORD whatever you do, and your plans will succeed."
Proverbs 16:3 (NIV)

James, our security guard, was the first Ugandan we taught about the Bible and how to live the victorious life. He latched on to truth, and his life dramatically changed.

Months passed, and we watched him grow. James is shy and only has time to work and sleep. However, he desperately wanted God to use him. We knew God had big plans!

God soon revealed that James's ministry was right under his nose. Most guards for his security company ride in the back of one truck and are dropped off at their work sites. The ride to work was the perfect time for James to reach them with the good news.

James didn't waste any time. He knew the gospel had the power to change lives; after all, it changed his. He went from one guard to the next, telling of his faith and offering them the opportunity to take a Bible course with him. Many were truly interested in learning what the Bible had to say. Others were interested in doing the study only as a reprieve from the boredom of sitting alone all night. Their motives didn't matter—they were studying God's Word. This was an opportunity to feed their minds and hearts. God has the power to change lives.

James now runs a "school" with more than 1,800 students studying and memorizing Scripture each night as they guard a gate. Many are making decisions for Jesus Christ. God does much when a heart is willing!

—B.J., CENTRAL, EASTERN AND SOUTHERN AFRICA

Father, CONTINUE TO USE MINISTRIES THROUGH JOB CONTACTS ON THE MISSION FIELD. DEVELOP BIBLE STUDIES IN MY OWN COMMUNITY DURING LUNCH HOURS OF WORKING PEOPLE. *Amen.*

Go team!

"Each person is given something to do that shows who God is: Everyone gets in on it, everyone benefits." 1 Corinthians 12:7 (MSG)

Opportunities to be flexible sometimes develop into divine appointments. I experienced such an opportunity while driving to a youth English camp. The Lord showed me how He is working to plant churches among more than 18 million Isaan (EE-sahn) people of northeastern Thailand, who are less than 1 percent Christian.

Three other women shared the backseat of my truck: Granny, Tuk (TUKE) and Oi (OY-ee). Granny is the pastor's wife. Tuk is a new believer who was led to Christ by one of our missionary doctors, Doug. Oi is a youth who attended a volleyball clinic sponsored by missionaries Brent and Kathy.

Tuk excitedly shared about what she was learning in Bible study and how she became a Christian after receiving a tract and having truth explained by the doctor. Through all of Tuk's sharing, I noticed that Oi was sitting quietly between Tuk and Granny. When Tuk paused, I jumped in. I said, "Oi, do you remember the girl who said she was interested in following Christ at the last volleyball clinic?"

"It was me!" said Oi with a bright smile. "I prayed to become one of God's children." For the rest of the ride, the passengers got Oi's information and arranged to take her to church on the following Sunday. Now local believers like Tuk will tenderly care for Oi. It made me realize that no matter where we are in the Lord's harvest field, we're all on the same team, and the name on the back of our uniform is *Jesus!*

—HELEN, PACIFIC RIM

Father, HOW IT MUST PLEASE YOU TO SEE EACH INDIVIDUAL MEMBER EXERCISING HIS OR HER GIFTEDNESS IN THE BODY OF CHRIST TO IMPACT PEOPLE GROUPS SUCH AS THE ISAAN OF THAILAND, A PEOPLE WHO FOR CENTURIES HAD NOT HEARD THE GOSPEL BUT ARE NOW RESPONDING. MAKE CHURCHES AWARE OF SPECIFIC OPPORTUNITIES TO PARTNER WITH MISSIONARIES AND WITH NATIONAL BELIEVERS TO HELP BRING IN A HARVEST OF SOULS INTO YOUR KINGDOM. *Amen.*

Stop and celebrate

"I tell you that in the same way there will be more rejoicing in heaven over one sinner who repents than over ninety-nine righteous persons who do not need to repent." Luke 15:7 (NIV)

At the end of a typical Sunday in our Ugandan church, one of our members stood up to introduce her friend. As she explained who the guest was, the visitor stopped her in midsentence and whispered something in the member's ear. A huge smile erupted on the church member's face. She said, "My neighbor has decided to get saved today." It was no longer a typical Sunday.

The entire church became quiet. No one moved or made a noise—not even the children. We stood quietly as the guest moved near one of the prayer team members and was led in a prayer for salvation. As the prayer leader said, "Amen!" in a loud voice, we all began to applaud. Then the crowd burst into spontaneous songs and joyous laughter. The ladies began dancing in a circle around the new believer as drums banged in the background. We carried on as if this was the *first* person ever to come to Christ in our church.

I was reminded of Luke 15:7 and thought about the party going on in heaven at that very moment. Our church was celebrating so much for this sheep who was found that it's hard to even imagine the bigger celebration going on up above.

I prayed right then that God would continue to give Japadhola (chah-pah-DOHL-lah) Christians a tender heart for the lost. It also made me wonder, are we ready to stop everything, at any time, for anyone who wants to get saved?

—DAVID, CENTRAL, EASTERN AND SOUTHERN AFRICA

Father, I PRAY THAT I WOULD CONTINUE TO HAVE A HEART THAT IS TUNED TO GOD'S HEART, REJOICING IN EACH ONE WHO IS SAVED. GIVE THE JAPADHOLA CHRISTIANS TENDER HEARTS FOR THE LOST, AND MAY MANY IN THIS PEOPLE GROUP BE SAVED. *Amen.*

God works through an elephant

"Then God said, 'Let the earth bring forth living creatures after their kind: cattle and creeping things and beasts of the earth after their kind'; and it was so."
Genesis 1:24 (NASB)

An elephant from the circus escaped and walked along the busy highway in Manila, Philippines. It turned into a street near my house, and a chain on its foot got tangled around a post, causing it to be trapped in the middle of the road.

As animal lovers, Filipinos gave the elephant bananas and coconuts. This event gave us a unique opportunity to share Christ to the crowd that gathered around the elephant, proving once again that God can work in any situation.

The following morning, I followed my routine of going to the coffee shop to minister to businessmen eating breakfast. The many topics we discuss serve as a springboard for me to talk about faith in God. This morning's popular topic was the elephant. Someone mentioned how amazing it was that God created an elephant, which consumes 100 kilos of bananas a day.

That opened the way for me to share about God. I began by asking, "How does God create human beings?" and "Do you think that God loves us so much?"

Questions such as these do not cause the businessmen to feel threatened, but serve to bring them a step closer to faith in God. Every event that happens around me is an opportunity to witness. If God will take the unusual, such as an elephant, to lead to a testimony of Him, then anything is possible as an icebreaker.

—LONG AND *MARY, PACIFIC RIM

Gracious God, HELP ME NOT TO BE SO DISTRACTED THAT I NEGLECT THE DAILY OPPORTUNITIES TO SHARE YOUR LOVE WITH THOSE WHOM YOU SOVEREIGNLY PLACE IN MY PATH. I PRAY FOR AN EMPOWERING OF YOUR SPIRIT AND ENCOURAGEMENT FOR MISSIONARIES WHO FACE THE SEEMINGLY IMPOSSIBLE TASK OF REACHING THE URBAN MASSES WHO RESIDE IN MANILA, PHILIPPINES. *Amen.*

*MARY PHAM PASSED AWAY IN DECEMBER 2003
AFTER THIS DEVOTIONAL WAS SUBMITTED.

In the right place at the right time

"The king's heart is like channels of water in the hand of the LORD*, He turns it wherever He wishes." Proverbs 21:1 (NASB)*

A friend and I were walking on a residential street when two men approached us. Harmlessly, they asked my friend questions in Russian about me. I noticed we were standing beneath camera surveillance by an iron gate for what I guessed to be an Islamic political building. Then a third man approached. As introductions were made, I realized this building was his home and the two men were his guards. He then asked if I would help his family with conversational English. I told him I would pray about it.

To this he said, "I believe there is one God for all. My family has been praying for two years that God would send someone to us. Yes, please pray."

His words pierced my heart. I knew that the city had a mosque, which was an Arab cultural center, and that little was known about the Muslims of this region. Being curious if he was Muslim, I asked if he attended the cultural center. Confidently he replied, "Yes, I do. I own it." In fact, he was the spiritual leader! Recognizing God at work, I agreed to teach English to his family.

I didn't know when I entered his home that I entered into the world of one of the most influential leaders of an unreached people group. Being on mission with God means He will either take me to where I need to be or bring the need to me. My response of obedience may determine the turning of a king's heart and the eternal direction of a nation.

—BOBBI, CENTRAL AND EASTERN EUROPE

Thank You, Father, THAT YOU ARE WORKING IN PLACES LEAST EXPECTED. I PRAY FOR THE MUSLIMS IN THIS PEOPLE GROUP OF CENTRAL AND EASTERN EUROPE THAT THEY WILL HEAR ABOUT JESUS. I PRAY SPECIFICALLY FOR THIS FAMILY MENTIONED TO COME TO KNOW CHRIST. TODAY, GIVE ME DISCERNMENT ABOUT WHERE YOU ARE WORKING SO THAT I CAN RESPOND IN OBEDIENCE. *Amen.*

The key to friendship

"And whatever things you ask in prayer, believing, you will receive."
Matthew 21:22 (NKJV)

After 15 years in Thailand, our missionary family moved to Korea. Suddenly, I had no friends, no language skills and no way to minister. My neighbors lived behind high walls and spoke no English. I asked God to bridge the gaps between us. I was not prepared for His answer!

One day, a friend picked up my children to go to a concert. As they drove away, I looked forward to a quiet afternoon. Reaching for the keys to the security wall gate, I suddenly realized they were inside my house and that the only other keys were in my husband's pocket in another country!

I have many acquaintances around my neighborhood, although communication is extremely unintelligible. One by one, they gathered to assist me in my crisis, all enthusiastically suggesting ways to get back inside the gate. After several suggestions were discussed, a businessman I didn't know disappeared inside an adjacent house. Someone else led me by the arm to my front gate, talking with great animation. Before I could respond, the businessman reappeared—opening my gate from the inside. The "security wall" around the house apparently is not all I might wish, but I was too delighted to be back inside my house to be anything but grateful to my new friends.

I now have new status in my neighborhood. Everyone knows me. They smile and laugh when we meet on the street. One day soon, I pray I'll be able to introduce them to my friend Jesus.

—JANET, PACIFIC RIM

Lord, YOU BRING UNEXPECTED OPPORTUNITIES TO REACH OTHERS FOR CHRIST. I PRAY THAT MISSIONARIES WILL MAKE SURPRISING AND DELIGHTFUL CONNECTIONS WITH PEOPLE AROUND THEM SO THAT THE GOSPEL CAN BE SHARED. IN MY OWN LIFE, BRING AN OPPORTUNITY TO WITNESS TO _____. *Amen.*

"Get up and go"

"He replied, 'Blessed rather are those who hear the word of God and obey it.'"
Luke 11:28 (NIV)

The Anii (AHN-ee) are a Muslim people group, one of the 52 distinct people groups who live in Benin. We knew of only one Anii Christian, "Moses." He had become a Christian 11 years ago as he traveled to the neighboring country of Togo for itinerant farm work. There he met Baptist missionaries who shared the gospel with him. However, when he shared his decision with his family upon his return home to Bassila, Moses was ostracized and forced to flee to Togo.

Upon arriving in Benin, we met with national leaders to ask them to send their own missionaries to the Anii. We suggested Moses might fill that position. The leaders agreed to interview Moses, but we needed to locate him.

We traveled to Moses' former home in Bassila to ask his family if they knew where he might be. There, in the home from which he had fled 11 years ago, we found Moses praying for his family. He told me of a dream he had a week earlier. In the dream, he heard a voice repeatedly say to him, "Get up and go to Bassila; the pastor is seeking you." Moses thought that I was in America, but he obeyed the voice and came to his family, who now accepted him and even asked him to pray for their illnesses. God blessed our friend with restoration, and then Moses agreed to be sent as a missionary to his own people.

God fulfills His plans in amazing ways. He blesses immediate obedience, as was made evident in our friend's life.

—A WORKER IN WEST AFRICA

Father, IT AMAZES ME HOW YOU SPEAK TO YOUR CHILDREN. PROTECT YOUR SERVANTS AS THEY BRING TRUTH TO THIS PEOPLE GROUP IN WEST AFRICA. MAKE ME SENSITIVE TO YOUR VOICE AND GIVE ME AN OBEDIENT HEART. *Amen.*

Fruit from a seed

"And we know that all things work together for good to those who love God, to those who are the called according to His purpose." Romans 8:28 (NKJV)

In March 2003, a missionary colleague was killed at an airport in the Philippines, where he had gone to pick up another missionary family. He regularly helped others in this way. His usual work led him into the dangerous parts of the island, so continual prayers went out for him while he was engaged in these activities, but not so many while he was in the "safe" city where he lived!

The Lord had been blessing this man's work in tremendous ways as he and another missionary had been training 1,000 pastors and leaders to begin church-planting movements. All of us were questioning why our friend was killed at this time.

The week after the memorial service, my husband, Dan, was talking to a head official. When the official found out that Dan knew the missionary who had been killed and that he was a part of the same organization, he invited Dan into his office. In the conversation, Dan shared that this missionary had been willing to die for the Filipino people. Dan told him that he, too, was willing to die and had assurance that he would be with the Lord if he died. The captain said that he wished that he had that assurance, too. Dan then proceeded to share the gospel with this Filipino official and lead him to the Lord!

Salvation has come out of this tragedy. We know that other good things have happened, too, and that the Lord will keep revealing them to us.

—CARA, PACIFIC RIM

Father, ONLY YOU COULD BRING GOOD OUT OF TRAGEDY. THANK YOU FOR THE LIFE OF THIS MISSIONARY WHO DIED IN THE PHILIPPINES AT THE HAND OF TERRORISTS. CONTINUE TO LET GOOD COME FROM HIS DEATH. *Amen.*

AUGUST V

Contentment

I didn't choose the monthly themes. They basically chose themselves from the categories of subjects the missionaries reflected in their devotionals. The reason I'm letting you know I didn't choose them is that I'm about to talk to you about contentment. It's not that I'm not content. For crying out loud, I ought to be content. My bird dog lives better than most of the world's human population. It's just absurd talking to you about it in the company of the people who will address the subject for the next month.

I've noticed on a number of occasions, however, that God doesn't mind if I feel like an idiot. I get the idea that He thinks the ink of the Holy Spirit flows best through a humbled pen. So here's my shot at a subject I know virtually nothing about. My inexperience with more extreme challenges of contentment stems from the fact that I've never really lacked. I was raised on my father's meager military salary and, while we never had an extra dime, we had enough. When I married Keith, he made very little money, but as long as I could get popcorn and a coke at the movie, I thought we were sitting pretty. I drove our daughters around in an old station wagon with fake wood-grain siding, a bent antenna and a loose inside lining that hung down so far that it sat on top of my hair. Of course, if you've seen my hair, you know that it didn't have to hang terribly far. A Texas woman cannot be less than who she is. Yep, as long as I could roll my hair and match my lipstick to my outfit, life was fine by me.

To inhabitants of most Third World countries, Keith and I are rolling in cash. So are any of us in America literate enough to read this book. Most Western Christians don't know the first thing about biblical contentment. Then again, perhaps that's why in some ways we should be pitied. We are as addicted to more stuff as a cocaine addict is to his next snort. The more we have, the more we want. What we can't fit in our homes, we move into storage. What we can't pay for, we borrow. Relatively speaking, we have more and give less than any people in the world. And we—Western believers—are arguably the most discontented Christians in the world.

In Philippians 4:11–13, the apostle Paul wrote, *"I am not saying this because I am in need, for I have learned to be content whatever the circumstances. I know what it is to be in need, and I know what it is to have plenty. I have learned the secret of being content in any and every situation, whether well fed or hungry, whether living in plenty or in want. I can do everything through him who gives me strength"* (NIV).

Christians like me cannot say with the apostle Paul that we "have learned to be content whatever the circumstances" because most of us have been less content with plenty than we were with less. Ironically, excess only increases discontentment. Why? Proverbs 13:12 offers the perfect explanation: *"Hope deferred makes the heart sick"* (NIV). In other words, we set our hopes on the lie that if we could only have this or that, we will be content. If we get it (or him, her, them or there), we are astonished to realize that it still doesn't cut it. Our hope that we'd finally be happy inevitably defers, and our hearts are left sick. At least with less, we still have the fantasy. Those with more and more attend one funeral of expectation after another.

So would poverty make us content? Hardly! Simplicity would introduce us to contentment much sooner than either riches or poverty. Miserable "have nots" make miserable "haves." Unhappy singles make unhappy spouses. Contentment has little to do with what we have or lack. It is a state of mind. One that is far more often learned than suddenly attained, by the way. Check out the apostle's wording again: "I have *learned* to be content" and "I have *learned* the secret of being content" (emphases mine). The original Greek word comes from the same word as "disciple." Paul explained that Christ had used circumstances to disciple Paul in the art of contentment. Discovering the power and presence of Christ in every circumstance was the secret.

Both "haves" and "have nots" alike need discipleship in contentment. How can "have nots" learn to be content? I would not insult you by suggesting I know. I'll let some missionaries who have earned the right tell you. But how about the "haves"? How can those among us with plenty—who find ourselves addicted to more by a billion-dollar advertising industry—learn a little contentment? Two suggestions: Practice saying no to ourselves if just for the satisfaction of Spirit-empowered self-discipline. Second, give! Nothing brings the satisfaction of giving. If I'm feeling especially selfish, I know that I haven't been giving enough.

I lost my mind recently and wrote a check for a suit that was way over my price range. The salesperson hesitated just long enough for me to ask for the check back. I can't describe how good I felt walking out of that ridiculously expensive department store empty-handed. Had the discipleship lesson stopped there, I alone would have been helped. The next day I sensed God leading me to give away the money I was going to spend on that suit. I squirmed, then I submitted. Then I learned a secret.

—*Beth Moore*

Putting the pieces together

"LORD, you have assigned me my portion and my cup; you have made my lot secure. The boundary lines have fallen for me in pleasant places; surely I have a delightful inheritance." Psalm 16:5–6 (NIV)

On March 4, 2003, a terrorist's bomb took the life of my husband. Although I was not physically injured when the bomb exploded, my life blew up as if I were a thousand-piece jigsaw puzzle. In the weeks following my husband's death, the puzzle pieces seemed to lie upside down and untouched on the worktable. In time, however, God began to slowly turn over some of the pieces. When I tried to put the pieces together, the picture didn't make sense. After 37 years of marriage, I didn't know what the picture would look like without my husband.

One day I was complaining to the Lord that He hadn't given me the border pieces of my new life puzzle! How could I possibly make sense out of it if I didn't have a starting place? If I just had the border pieces, I thought, maybe then I could begin to see where to start putting my life back together. Then the Lord spoke to me through Psalm 16:5–6.

From these verses I saw that the boundary line of my life is God Himself. With God as the linked and locked border around me, I know I am secure. I am assured that the border lines of my life are in pleasant places, and I can look forward to a delightful inheritance. I can trust God to put the puzzle pieces of my life together—even as a widow and even though terrorists choose to do evil to others.

—*LYN, PACIFIC RIM

Thank You, Father, THAT YOU HAVE MY LIFE IN YOUR HANDS AND THAT IT DOESN'T HAVE TO MAKE SENSE TO KNOW THAT I AM SECURE. I TRUST YOU WITH MY LIFE IN TIMES OF CHAOS, DEVASTATION AND SHATTERED DREAMS. I PRAY THAT YOUR LOVE AND REDEEMING GRACE WILL DRAW EVEN THE PERPETRATORS OF TERRORIST ACTS TO YOURSELF, THE ONE FOR WHOM THEIR HEARTS UNKNOWINGLY SEEK. *Amen.*

* LYN'S HUSBAND, BILL HYDE, WAS KILLED BY A TERRORIST'S BOMB IN THE PHILIPPINES.

Dislocated

"And he sent you on a mission, saying, 'Go ...'" 1 Samuel 15:18a (NIV)

Dislocate: To displace from normal connections with another.

While helping with a sports camp, I dislocated my finger playing basketball. At first, it didn't hurt much. But it looked bizarre—until the doctor pulled it back into place.

My pilgrimage as a missionary has been a little like that finger. At times I felt out of place in my new country, disconnected not only from family, friends and all that was safe and comfortable, but also disconnected from other missionaries, since we serve on an isolated island.

Dislocation: Disruption of an established order.

My life in America used to be simple. But suddenly that changed when we moved to Western Europe. With a hurt finger, little things that used to be easy like making a bed were now difficult. Likewise, simple things become full of obstacles when in a new place. After seven months, my finger still was not the way it used to be. There were days when it ached, just like I ache to see my oldest daughter in the States. Every time I attempt to bend my pinky, no matter how hard I try, it won't conform without pain and effort. I suppose the Lord knew what would be involved in pulling a life into proper alignment with His!

Dislocate: To force a change.

Maybe this crooked finger of mine will serve as a visual reminder to me that my God can stretch, mold and use misshapen things to serve Him in whatever way He chooses.

—AMY, WESTERN EUROPE

Father, GIVE MISSIONARIES A SENSE OF BEING IN THE LOCATION THAT YOU'VE CALLED THEM TODAY. MAY THEY REST IN COMPLETE TRUST IN YOU AND IN PROPER ALIGNMENT WITH YOU. *Amen.*

Why the fly?

"Be careful for nothing; but in every thing by prayer and supplication with thanksgiving let your requests be made known unto God."
Philippians 4:6 (KJV)

Before coming to Africa as a missionary, I remember seeing African children on television with their wide eyes and protruding stomachs. What disturbed me most were the flies clinging to their faces. God had a lesson for me about flies, however.

Each morning in Zambia, as I go for my daily walk, I deal with pesky flies. They crawl all over my face, into my eyes and around my mouth. No insect repellent will keep them away.

This particular morning was no exception. After 15 minutes of walking, constantly batting at flies, I called to mind Philippians 4:6 (KJV): *"Be careful for nothing; but in every thing by prayer and supplication with thanksgiving let your requests be made known unto God."* So I prayed, but I still wasn't thankful. "God!" I cried. "These flies are bothering me! They make me not want to walk each morning!" I continued to complain.

Gerri, God said to my heart, *what makes you any better than the Lozi [LOH-zee] people? They walk every day with flies bothering them. And furthermore,* He continued, *you committed to identify with them. Did you mean what you said?* I began to think of how Jesus came to earth to become like us, yet without sin, and He certainly put up with more than a fly.

Why the fly? To remind me of how much God loves me. Now when I am bothered by this insect, I say to Him with humility, "Thank You, Jesus, for enduring much more than a pesky fly for me!"

—GERRI, CENTRAL, EASTERN AND SOUTHERN AFRICA

Lord Incarnate, MAY THE LOZI PEOPLE OF SOUTHERN AFRICA SOON UNDERSTAND THAT YOU ENTERED EARTH'S DOMAIN IN HUMAN FORM IN ORDER TO SUFFER AND DIE FOR THEIR SINS. THANK YOU, LORD, THAT BY YOUR GRACE, YOU TRANSFORM DAILY IRRITABILITIES INTO BLESSINGS OF SPIRITUAL TRUTH FOR OUR MISSIONARIES AND FOR US AS WELL. *Amen.*

Are you content?

"I am not saying this because I am in need, for I have learned to be content whatever the circumstances." Philippians 4:11 (NIV)

The Sudan sun blazed as we rode the all-terrain vehicle deeper into the dry and crackling bush. I felt sweat stream down my back as we traveled more than 200 miles. We were so isolated that many had never heard of Coca-Cola. The poverty in the region was evident. Finally, we reached our destination—a women's group of about 80. These Sudanese women gathered weekly to learn about hygiene and to hear stories of Christ.

The women seated us at the head of the group. A red drink made from local flowers was served. This drink probably cost the women their entire month's worth of wages to purchase the sugar. Yet they were happy to pool their resources for guests.

As we discussed hygiene, my friend explained the importance of cleanliness and washing one's clothes. Many seemed perplexed by the lesson. Finally, one of the women asked, "But what if you only have one dress to wear?"

The majority of the women spoke their agreement with this situation. My friend told each to wash her dress out at night and then hang it to dry while she slept. This solution brought smiles and approving nods.

I felt so convicted! Some days, I feel like I don't have anything to wear—yet these ladies only had one choice. In my prayer that day, I praised God for these women who truly had learned to be content in whatever circumstances they were given. I asked God to help me be more like them—content and willing to share.

—NANCY, CENTRAL, EASTERN AND SOUTHERN AFRICA

Oh, Father! FORGIVE ME WHEN I AM UNGRATEFUL FOR THE CIRCUMSTANCES YOU HAVE DESIGNED FOR MY SPIRITUAL GROWTH. I PRAY THAT I CAN TRULY SAY WITH PAUL THAT I'VE LEARNED TO BE CONTENT IN ALL THINGS. FOR THESE DEAR ONES IN SUDAN, I PRAY THAT YOU WILL MEET THEIR NEEDS AND GIVE THEM SPIRITUAL BLESSING. *Amen.*

Trusting God during unexpected circumstances

"Trust in the Lord with all your heart and lean not on your own understanding; in all your ways acknowledge him, and he will make your paths straight."
Proverbs 3:5–6 (NIV)

Direction. That's what we needed.

As a small child in my grandmother's lap, I had memorized Proverbs 3:5–6. During 51 years of life, I had repeated it often, but now I would be experiencing the reality of this promise.

After 28 years in corporate America, my husband's company downsized and his position was eliminated. We were stunned. We had been taught to praise God in our problems, so we began counting our blessings daily and praising God for a future assignment.

Immediately after the dismissal, we sent an e-mail to friends serving in Central Asia, asking for prayer. Their reply startled us! After words of comfort, they asked, "Would you consider joining our team? We need someone to do finances and run a guesthouse." Our reply was simple: "Tell us more."

When we learned the exact location of the assignment, we were overwhelmed. We read everything we could find on this country—a country broken after 24 years of war and a city barren from five years of drought. Then God spoke through a worship service, *Come and watch Me bring beauty from ashes* (Isa. 61:3). We decided to go.

Peace that passes understanding, joy in diverse circumstances, contentment in whatever state we are in—these are lessons to be learned only as we pass through life's experiences. While living in this country, God has promised us that He shall direct us as we trust Him. Whatever I might face, I know that God has it all figured out.

—A WORKER IN CENTRAL ASIA

Thank You, God, THAT YOU HAVE EVERYTHING FIGURED OUT! I PRAY THAT YOU WILL DIRECT MY PATHS AND THAT I WILL TRUST YOU COMPLETELY. YOU ARE WORTHY OF MY TRUST! STRENGTHEN THESE WORKERS IN DIFFICULT WAR-TORN COUNTRIES TO CONTINUE TO LEAN ON YOU RATHER THAN THEIR OWN UNDERSTANDING. *Amen.*

In the shadowlands

"The LORD is my shepherd; I have everything that I need. He lets me rest in green meadows; he leads me beside peaceful streams. He renews my strength. He guides me along right paths, bringing honor to his name. Even when I walk through the dark valley of death, I will not be afraid, for you are close beside me."
Psalm 23:1–4 (NLT)

I am a single woman working in a Chinese city alone, but God is with me in everything! When I first arrived in my city, I moved into my apartment and called my family to give them my new phone number. My mother's first statement was, "An ambulance has just picked up your sister. She will be dead by the end of the week." (She had been suffering with cancer for some time.) I didn't know what to do.

After investigating a way to get to the States, God led me to call home again. I said, "God, I can't. I know my sister is gone." However, I called and found out that my sister had just died. I talked to my mom for a while and then sat on my couch alone. I asked God, "Why am I here? I should be home with my family!"

Immediately there was a knock on my window. A young lady said, "I was told that I should come and see you. May I come in?" Totally unaware of what I was going through, she plopped down on the couch and said, "I have been searching for God. Can you tell me about the true God?" She accepted Jesus as her Savior that day.

I thanked God for reminding me why I live overseas and that I am never alone. Even when I walk through the valley of the shadow of grief, He is with me. Those who think I am a team of one can't see the One who stands beside me.

—A WORKER IN CHINA

Comforter and Friend, BE WITH WORKERS WHO ARE GRIEVING TODAY AND WHO HAVE FAMILY MEMBERS IN THE STATES WHO ARE AILING. GIVE WORKERS WISDOM TO KNOW WHETHER TO STAY ON THE FIELD OR TO COME TO THE STATES FOR A TIME. LET THEM FEEL YOUR PRESENCE AND STRENGTH. *Amen.*

My view

"He has sent me to comfort the brokenhearted and to announce that captives will be released and prisoners will be freed." Isaiah 61:1b (NLT)

Several years ago, the Lord made it clear that we should move from a nice house with a yard, trees and flowers to a lower-class house in a crowded neighborhood with no yard. This immersed us in a neighborhood where our people group lived. Now we have opportunities to share God's love and experience the culture on a daily basis. It not only helped us personally, but has also given us opportunities to train others to reach the lost.

While on a visit to the States, I visited a dear friend who lives on the dogwood trail in Knoxville. I was able to sit at her bay window and enjoy the view of her backyard in its autumn splendor. I couldn't help but contrast the view from her window with the view from my own dining room window overseas. There are no pretty trees to look at, only a wall.

As I sat in my friend's home soaking up the beautiful view, the Holy Spirit reminded me what is *truly* my view. My view is not the wall, but the children who walk by and often stop to chat with me through the window. My view is of the women who also wave and smile. My view is the men who politely nod their heads in greeting.

He showed me that my view is an eternal view. My hope and reason for living where I live is that many of those precious people will worship the Lord Jesus someday and be eternally in the presence of our loving Father.

—J.S., PACIFIC RIM

Father, I ACKNOWLEDGE THAT MANY TIMES WHAT IS IN MY VIEW IS MY OWN FAMILY, MY OWN PROBLEMS AND MY OWN SELFISH DESIRES. HELP ME NOT TO HAVE TUNNEL VISION, BUT TO EXPAND MY VIEW TO INCLUDE THE LOST AND THE NEEDY AROUND ME. ENCOURAGE MISSIONARIES TO KNOW THAT THE COMFORT THEY GAVE UP IN AMERICA IS WORTH THE COST FOR THE SAKE OF THE GOSPEL. *Amen.*

Embracing life

"So here's what I want you to do, God helping you: Take your everyday, ordinary life—your sleeping, eating, going to work, and walking-around life—and place it before God as an offering. Embracing what God does for you is the best thing you can do for him." Romans 12:1 (MSG)

Life is unpredictable. Many times the best-laid plans are changed or rerouted. And often the key to the entire situation is our response.

After taking time away from my normal ministry in order to plan a meeting for missionary women, I looked forward to returning to work. I missed the bright faces and warm friendships of the Muslims with whom I'm developing relationships. Most of them are refugees and strangers to Kenya. Many live in bad circumstances—cramming as many people as they can into one room. They are simply grateful for escaping the dangers of war and fighting in neighboring countries.

I was excited about receiving a volunteer to work with me as I got back into ministry. I started making big plans, but because of changes in my husband's responsibilities, I had to change and reroute my plans. The volunteer ended up working elsewhere, and God has provided a better opportunity than I could ever have imagined.

This response of "embracing what God does" must come from a surrender of our lives to Him. It's taking our everyday, ordinary life— sleeping, eating, working and walking-around life—and placing it before God as an offering. We must relinquish our rights and expectations to what we do and where we go. I will embrace what God has for me, knowing that in the act of warmly receiving and clinging to those things, it will be the best thing that I can do for Him.

May we embrace what God does and allows in our lives.

—P., CENTRAL, EASTERN AND SOUTHERN AFRICA

Father, YOUR WAYS ARE NOT MY WAYS, AND I PRAISE YOU THAT YOU KNOW BEST. MAY MISSIONARIES WHO EXPERIENCE CHANGE IN MINISTRY THIS YEAR DEPEND ON YOU TO GUIDE THEM. I ACCEPT WHAT YOU HAVE FOR ME TODAY, KNOWING THAT YOU WILL DIRECT MY PATHS. *Amen.*

That's why it went so well!

"Therefore do not worry about tomorrow, for tomorrow will worry about itself. Each day has enough trouble of its own." Matthew 6:34 (NIV)

Worry. People around me worry about education, marriage, finding a job, being successful, providing a good education for children, and the list goes on.

One day, I was with a local friend whose family had adopted me as their foreign child. I watched my friend that day as she offered bribes to get a job for her younger brother and as she and her mom fretted over the results of her brother's final exams. As she was making a phone call, I was impressed to pray for her. I felt led to share with her from Matthew 6:25–34 about how God cares even for the birds and flowers and how much more important we are to Him.

After she finished the call, I picked up a Bible, turned to the passage and asked her to read it. It immediately struck her in a powerful way. I told her that I had been praying for her while she was on the phone. She responded with, "That's why it went so well!" She then told her younger sister that she should learn more about the Bible from me.

On another occasion, I shared Matthew 6 with a friend who was worrying about her future. She asked me where I had heard it. I told her it was written in the Bible. Her response was that every time we met, I had to tell her the words again.

God continues to use His Word to open closed doors into the lives of local friends. Casting our cares on the Lord brings great freedom!

—A WORKER IN CENTRAL ASIA

Father, FORGIVE ME FOR WORRYING WHEN I KNOW THAT YOU HAVE EVERYTHING UNDER CONTROL. I CAST MY CARES ON YOU TODAY. THANK YOU FOR TAKING THEM. *Amen.*

An unexpected confirmation

"Have I not commanded you? Be strong and courageous. Do not be terrified; do not be discouraged, for the LORD your God will be with you wherever you go."
Joshua 1:9 (NIV)

While preparing to become a missionary to the Dominican Republic, Joshua 1:9 became special to me. I was excited about leaving but scared of the unknown. I had never lived outside of Alabama, but I knew this was God's will for our family. God is so good that He even gives us affirmations of His call on our lives.

After arriving in our new country, my 8-year-old son, Daniel, asked if he could have a small envelope, paper and pencil. A little while later, he delivered a note for my husband and me, telling me to wait until his daddy got home. Five minutes later, he begged me to read it. Here is what I read:

> Hello family,
> I am very happy to be with you. I like the DR very much. I love you very much.
> Love Daniel.

As I read the note, the most powerful words to me were: "I like the DR very much." What an affirmation from God that we are right where He wants us to be. He used a little boy to confirm His call to me!

Are you serving God where He wants you? Are you a little scared, as I was, of the unknown or of the commitment it means? God is so faithful to us, and He deserves our obedience.

—DANA, MIDDLE AMERICA AND THE CARIBBEAN

Father, MAY I ALWAYS SERVE YOU ACCORDING TO YOUR WILL. I AM COMMITTED TO SERVING YOU IN MY CHURCH, IN MY NEIGHBORHOOD, IN MY WORKPLACE OR SCHOOL, OR IN ANY WAY. STRENGTHEN AND CONFIRM THE CALL OF MISSIONARIES SO THAT THEY HAVE THE ASSURANCE THAT THEY ARE IN YOUR WILL. *Amen.*

Facing change

"There's far more here than meets the eye. The things we see now are here today, gone tomorrow. But the things we can't see now will last forever."
2 Corinthians 4:18 (MSG)

A few months ago I received an unusual request from my brother-in-law. He wanted me to buy a pair of Birkenstocks for my 11-year-old nephew. That wasn't unusual. What seemed unusual to me was that he requested clogs.

Clogs? "Do boys in the U.S. wear clogs?" I asked my husband. He shrugged, not knowing. "Do boys in the U.S. wear clogs?" I asked a career missionary colleague. I got the same vacant stare. "Do boys in the U.S. wear clogs?" I asked a 20-something two-year missionary fresh off the plane. "Yes," she replied, a bit surprised by my question.

So I bought my nephew Birkenstock clogs, and my anxiety level began to increase. I had that disconcerting, out-of-touch feeling about our impending furlough in the States. I resigned myself to the reality that I was going to look like a missionary.

It isn't just clothing styles that change during our time on the field. Hairstyles change. Products change. Technologies change. Music tastes change. Television themes change. Certainly, change is inevitable. To survive, we must all learn to cope with the many changes we face. But God wants us to do more than just cope. He wants us to experience His abundant life. He wants us to thrive. To do that, we must focus not on what is seen, but on what is unseen.

Focus on the big picture. Focus on eternity. It helps keep the change in perspective. I remind myself to experience abundant life and not to worry about the changes that I can't control anyway.

—ANN, PACIFIC RIM

Eternal Father, THE SAME YESTERDAY, TODAY AND FOREVER, THANK YOU THAT YOUR PLAN AND PURPOSES NEVER WAVER. IN A WORLD OF CONSTANT CHANGE AND FLUX, HELP ME KEEP MY EYES FIRMLY FIXED ON YOU TO SEE YOUR VISION AND WITH UNSHAKABLE RESOLVE, FOLLOW YOUR LEADERSHIP. *Amen.*

On the heights with Him

"Though the fig tree does not bud and there are no grapes on the vines, though the olive crop fails and the fields produce no food, though there are no sheep in the pen and no cattle in the stalls, yet I will rejoice in the LORD, I will be joyful in God my Savior." Habakkuk 3:17–18 (NIV)

Have you ever had one of those days when nothing seems to be going right? Of course you have! When my children experienced evacuation from the boarding school they were attending in West Africa, my daughter chose to return to the States and live with family members in Texas to finish her senior year. My son chose to attend a boarding school in another country that I would rarely get to visit. Less than two months after this sudden evacuation, my husband and I packed up our belongings and moved from the house we had lived in for nine years to head to a new destination.

One day, soon after moving to our new country, I was reading Habakkuk 3:17–18 and felt compelled to paraphrase it: "Though the electricity is sporadic and the water fails to drip, though the traffic is horrendous and I have to sit and sit, though Amber lives in Texas and Brandon boards in Dakar, yet I will rejoice in the Lord, I will be joyful in God my Savior." I had to smile as I went on to read, *"The Sovereign LORD is my strength; he makes my feet like the feet of a deer, he enables me to go on the heights."* (v. 19, NIV).

Has every day been perfect? No. Has the sovereign Lord been my strength? You bet! Have I gone onto the heights with Him? I think the choice is mine. Will I rejoice in the Lord no matter what? On the heights with Him—that's where I want to be!

—KRISTY, WEST AFRICA

Dear loving Father, MAY I FIND MY JOY IN YOU NO MATTER WHAT THE SITUATION AROUND ME MIGHT BE. MAY I FIND STRENGTH IN YOU TO MEET THE CHALLENGES OF EACH NEW DAY. TAKE ME TO THE HEIGHTS, LORD. LET ME WALK WITH YOU, AND MAY MANY OTHERS JOIN ME THERE! *Amen.*

Flexibility brings blessing

"By faith Abraham, when called to go to a place he would later receive as his inheritance, obeyed and went, even though he did not know where he was going."
Hebrews 11:8 (NIV)

During our training prior to our departure for overseas service, our assignment was changed three times. As soon as I studied one country, we were asked to consider another. Our colleagues called us "Mr. and Mrs. Flexible." I did not know that this would be indicative of our career. After 13 years on the field, we have lived in five different countries!

Each time we moved, I knew God's hand was there, even if it was a result of being "forced out" by other sources. We experienced God's blessings either through wonderful church-planting experiences or by enduring tough times and learning useful lessons for faith and ministry.

As Abraham, I never felt completely settled but always a stranger, even if it was during furlough time in the States. As a result, I have had a renewed appreciation for heaven and look forward to being settled there.

Here on earth, I am still learning to walk in faith. This last move was one of the hardest. We knew this land well, but we did not know what was in store for us! In the short time since our arrival, He is bringing people to us for sharing, discipleship and training. We are experiencing opportunities to mentor others to reach the majority population of the region. We are seeing the Lord call out individuals and families to serve in nearby countries where there is little witness.

Though we are still looking to that home above, we are experiencing heaven on earth as God draws His people together for the common task.

—C.B.G., NORTHERN AFRICA AND THE MIDDLE EAST

Father, THANK YOU FOR CHRISTIAN WORKERS WHO ARE SO FLEXIBLE TO YOUR CALL. GIVE THEM PATIENCE AND GRACE TO MAKE IT EACH DAY. BRING GREAT FRUIT IN EACH PLACE THAT THEY SERVE. HELP ME TO BE MORE FLEXIBLE TODAY. *Amen.*

Joy in a hopeless world

"Now may the God of hope fill you with all joy and peace in believing, so that you will abound in hope by the power of the Holy Spirit." Romans 15:13 (NASB)

When going through the process of becoming a missionary in 1993, I was asked what I hoped to communicate to the people of Ukraine (YOU-crane). I answered, "Hope."

When we arrived on the field, I was not prepared for the deficiency of hope quickly visible in the eyes of the people. Olga is one whom the Lord brought into our lives. My husband and I had witnessed to her for more than a year and were beginning to feel that we were getting nowhere.

One Saturday, she came to visit me. I was in the middle of typing a test for one of my boys, so I asked if I could finish before we talked. She sat down beside me in the study and talked to me while I typed. I was half-listening when I heard her say that she was coming to believe that one must have hope. I stopped typing and turned to her and said, "Yes, Olga, one must have hope, but that hope must be in Jesus Christ!" We went into another room and knelt by my son's bed, where the Lord brought her to Himself and gave her the hope that she was seeking.

We have been in Ukraine for nine years. Much has changed. But one thing is constant ... hopelessness. Spreading the gospel will silence the despair.

Living in countries where hopelessness is so prevalent often leads missionaries to feelings of hopelessness. We know we could not make it without the many prayers offered to the Lord on our behalf.

—DALESE, CENTRAL AND EASTERN EUROPE

Father, I PRAY THAT YOU WILL GIVE MISSIONARIES JOY IN THEIR SALVATION AND THAT THEY WILL BE ABLE TO SHARE THIS JOY SO THAT ALL PEOPLES WILL KNOW THE HOPE THAT IS IN JESUS CHRIST. I PRAY THAT MISSIONARIES AND I WILL NOT FALL INTO DEPRESSION. MAKE US A JOYFUL TESTIMONY TODAY. *Amen.*

Lay it all down again

"Commit your way to the LORD; trust in him and he will do this."
Psalm 37:5 (NIV)

Yesterday, I realized something through a progression of events.

First, we got kittens. This signified that we were "home" in our new country. A bit of settling in happens when you adopt pets. Then, for the first time in my life, I chose furniture.

The next day, in worship service, we sang a Michael W. Smith song. I choked out the words: "I lay it all down again ... to hear You say that I'm Your friend. Help me find the way. Bring me back to You. You're all I want. You're all I've ever needed. You're all I want. Help me know You are near."[1]

It's hard to say those words because I think I also want a bit more stability. Yet I sing the words, "You're all I want." Is my desire for Him bigger than my desire to stop moving? Is He really *all* I want?

I truly want to sing those words and to feel that they are true for me. I don't want to be a hypocrite ... but am I *really* content to "lay it all down again," as the song goes? It's a *very* difficult thing to be willing to say, "Yes, Lord, I will give up the furniture You just allowed me to select. I'll even be willing to get rid of the kittens we just adopted. I'm willing to disrupt our family life again."

All I know is that I need to be able to say honestly to Him, "You're *all* I want."

—D.B., CENTRAL ASIA

Father, WOMEN CHARACTERISTICALLY WANT STABILITY, BUT I PRAY THAT WOMEN WORKING OVERSEAS WILL SEEK THEIR STABILITY IN A RELATIONSHIP WITH YOU. GIVE THEM GRACE WHEN THEY MUST MOVE TO A NEW MINISTRY SETTING. HELP ME TO SEEK MY STABILITY FROM YOU RATHER THAN MY CIRCUMSTANCES. *Amen.*

1. Michael W. Smith, *Worship*, Reunion, 2001

At home with God

"Jesus replied, 'All those who love me will do what I say. My Father will love them, and we will come to them and live with them.'" John 14:23 (NLT)

After 36 hours on several different airplanes, my husband, two young children and I arrived on the other side of the planet—exhausted, excited and a little anxious. In thinking back, the journey we'd been on spiritually probably bridged a greater distance than the one we had been on geographically. We'd traveled many spiritual miles between the initial "Yes, Lord" to setting foot on international soil in Southeast Asia. Still it was my first time away from Arizona, which had been my home since I was five. On the whole, I had no complaints. It's just that everything in Southeast Asia was so different.

We were blessed to live close to our team members. Within the first month of our arrival, our team had a meal together at our neighbor's home. The children played outside as the adults finished the meal inside.

One of the older children asked my three-year-old daughter, "Where do you live?" We had prepared our daughter for many things, but her response had not been part of our preparations. She replied simply, "Well, it doesn't matter where I live, because Jesus lives in my heart."

Our daughter's words quickly reminded me of a truth that I had forgotten somewhere between the Los Angeles International Airport and Southeast Asia. Through her words, the Father reminded me that no matter where I live, He is there with me. What more do I need?

—SUSAN, PACIFIC RIM

Heavenly Father, GIVE ME A HEART THAT SAYS WHAT THIS PRECIOUS ONE SAID. WHEN I COMPLAIN ABOUT WHERE I LIVE OR WHERE I'M MOVING TO, REMIND ME THAT GEOGRAPHY IS UNIMPORTANT TO YOU. WITH YOU IN MY HEART, I'M AT HOME ANYWHERE. HELP NEW MISSIONARIES TO MAKE THIS TRANSITION JOYFULLY. *Amen.*

My call to God

"Call upon Me in the day of trouble; I will deliver you, and you shall glorify Me."
Psalm 50:15 (NKJV)

The day of trouble came for our family on June 18, 1999. Six months after arriving in Mexico as missionaries, my husband, my oldest daughter and two young summer missionaries drowned in the waters off one of the beaches of Playa Linda (PLY-ah LEAN-dah).

As I contemplated the body of my 10-year-old daughter, I felt my strength leave me. With my hands raised up and my body bent over by the pain, I cried, "Father, I am not worthy to have You listen to me, and I don't deserve to receive anything from You, but please help us!" As my hands came down, my body received the strength needed to handle my "day of trouble."

"But how did God deliver you?" you might ask. We think of the word "deliver" as what a holy superhero would do to carry us away from trouble, danger or pain. The Hebrew word used in this verse means not only to rescue, but to equip, to prepare and to arm as you would a soldier. That is just what my Lord did for me.

As God made His presence real on that beach that day, not only I, but also my children, the surviving summer missionaries and the crowd that witnessed our tragedy saw Him, too. My children and I now have returned to Mexico as missionaries. One of the summer missionaries now works with our agency, and the other one is preparing to become a missionary. Many from the crowd that day are now Christians.

I continue to attempt to keep my part of Psalm 50:15: to glorify Him!

—GLORIA, MIDDLE AMERICA AND THE CARIBBEAN

Father, THANK YOU THAT YOU HEAR ME IN TIMES OF TROUBLE. LET MUCH BE ACCOMPLISHED FOR YOUR KINGDOM AS A RESULT OF THESE DEATHS. CONTINUE TO GIVE GRACE TO THIS FAMILY AND USE THEM MIGHTILY IN MISSIONARY SERVICE. *Amen.*

Tie my heart here

"I have given them your word and the world has hated them, for they are not of the world any more than I am of the world. My prayer is not that you take them out of the world but that you protect them from the evil one. They are not of the world, even as I am not of it." John 17:14–16 (NIV)

He sat across the table from us, calm, joyful and fully committed to giving his life to reaching the unreached people at the ends of the earth. I asked this godly man, "How long did it take you and your wife to feel at home on the field?" and waited for his deep, spiritual reply.

"It never happens," he said. How could he say that? He shared with us that the peace and calm does not come from ever feeling at home; however, it comes from becoming tied to the people God wants you to reach and knowing the Father's heart.

Tie my heart here,
Let it beat with the pulse of the people.
Let it love and be loved.
And when it no longer beats
Let my soul rise to Thee.
Bind my heart to You,
Let it beat as one with Yours.
Let it pump compassion through my veins
And let it always be my heart's desire
To come to Thee!

I penned this poem after this conversation as my prayer to the Father. After serving more than 20 years on the field, my friend recently went on to be with our Lord. He finally made it home!

—"CANDY," CENTRAL ASIA

Dear Lord, PLEASE CONFIRM YOUR CALL TO YOUR SERVANTS IN CENTRAL ASIA TODAY, A REGION WHERE CHRISTIANS ARE BEING PERSECUTED. GIVE THEM A SENSE OF YOUR PRESENCE SO THAT THEY WILL KNOW THAT YOU ARE THEIR DWELLING PLACE. GIVE ME A BURDEN TO PRAY FOR WORKERS IN THIS VAST REGION WHO MAY FEEL LONELY. *Amen.*

Giving joy for sorrow

"For I will turn their mourning into joy and will comfort them and give them joy for their sorrow." Jeremiah 31:13b (NASB)

The new chapel under construction was progressing so quickly that it was attracting onlookers. I had noticed the same man watching for several days and decided to engage him in conversation.

"Are you a believer?" I asked. "I used to believe in God, but I don't anymore," he said flatly. "How did you come to *not* believe in God?" I persisted.

He looked at me sadly, recounting painful years of infertility that he and his wife suffered before they conceived a little boy. Yet shortly before the due date, a complication arose and the baby was stillborn. "I locked myself in my room and fasted and prayed for two days and nights, begging God to tell me why He let this happen. He never answered," he said.

I remembered the painful losses of my own babies due to miscarriages, a daughter who was stillborn and two babies who died within hours of birth. I realized why I was there face to face with this man.

"When you were in your room praying, God did hear you," I said. After sharing my story and how God watched His own Son die on the cross, I said that God loved him and wanted to have a relationship with him. While we spoke during the next few minutes, the Holy Spirit's presence was strong. My joy was overwhelming as he prayed to receive Christ, and I sensed Jesus assuring me that the pain I had experienced ultimately allowed me to lead this man to Him. From death, life sprang up.

—KATHY, SOUTH AMERICA

Thank You, Father, THAT YOU CAN USE HEART-WRENCHING TRIALS TO GIVE AN OPPORTUNITY TO IDENTIFY WITH OTHERS WHO STRUGGLE AND NEED HELP. USE THE PAST IN MY LIFE AND THOSE OF MISSIONARIES TO CAUSE PEOPLE TO SEE THAT THERE IS A GOD, A GOD WHO LOVES THE WORLD. *Amen.*

Seeing things in light of eternity

"While we look not at the things which are seen, but at the things which are not seen; for the things which are seen are temporal, but the things which are not seen are eternal." 2 Corinthians 4:18 (NASB)

Everything was going wrong. Our house was being invaded by rats from the nearby garbage dump; the water tank had leaked overnight, dumping gallons of water into our neighbor's yard; and our washing machine broke down, leaving me with piles of laundry to be done by hand. And then the unthinkable happened. I went outside to find that the clothesline had snapped, and all the clothes I had scrubbed were now lying in the dirt.

As I stood there, I remembered a national pastor's wife who had worked tirelessly to feed volunteers from the States. After the volunteers left, she spent a day hand-washing her family's clothes. The next day while helping with a church plant, a storm hit during the time we were gone. Every item of the clothes she had washed was soaking in the mud. We took in the scene before us, and then this godly woman said, "Well, it's nothing to be sad about."

Her response that day gave me an eternal perspective as I rewashed my own muddy clothes. None of the problems I faced was worth causing sadness. I thought of the estimated 30,000 people who had died just a few days earlier in an earthquake, knowing that more than likely very few of them were prepared for eternity. That was something to be sad about.

My desire is that each difficulty I face will be seen in light of eternity.

—K.J., CENTRAL ASIA

Gracious Father, FORGIVE ME WHEN I WORRY OR COMPLAIN ABOUT INSIGNIFICANT THINGS. I KNOW THAT I CAN TRUST YOU TO TAKE CARE OF MY BURDENS, SO I CAST THEM UPON YOU. I PRAY THAT CHRISTIAN WORKERS WILL LOOK TO YOU DURING TRIALS AND THAT YOU WILL ENCOURAGE THEM WITH YOUR WORD. GIVE AN OPPORTUNITY FOR THE LOST OF CENTRAL ASIA TO HEAR THE TRUTH ABOUT YOUR SON, JESUS. *Amen.*

It's just eggs!

"You have not yet resisted to bloodshed, striving against sin."
Hebrews 12:4 (NKJV)

Which requires more resistance: occasional gunfire at night on the street where you live, or a constant cycle of questions—Is the water on or off? Is today our day to have electricity or not? Does the phone work? Does the gas station have fuel today? Are there eggs in the market?

I was reminded of such striving again this week. I went to buy eggs. All the vendors agreed, no eggs. A town of 30,000 people, and there were no eggs in the market.

When appointed as missionaries, we knew that we would be striving against sin. We didn't realize the many small frustrations in our daily lives that would be a part of that struggle. All the small frustrations lumped together made it challenging. If only the water was off—okay; if only electricity was off—okay; if only the phone was off—okay. But if all three were off at the same time, our family would say, "Let's go home." But then, we'd look around and laughingly continue, "But we *are* home."

Our circumstances were not perfect, but we made a choice that day not to look at them. We had to look at Jesus and remember Hebrews 12:3: *"For consider Him who endured such hostility from sinners against Himself, lest you become weary and discouraged in your souls"* (NKJV). When considering Jesus, our daily frustrations became smaller.

Okay, so there are no eggs in the market this week. But when I look at Jesus, it seems a small thing to do without.

—DAVID, CENTRAL, EASTERN AND SOUTHERN AFRICA

Heavenly Father, FORGIVE ME WHEN I ALLOW FRUSTRATION TO CAUSE ME TO SIN. MAY I LOOK TO THE EXAMPLE OF YOUR SON, WHO SUFFERED, KNOWING THAT MY SUFFERING IS NOTHING IN COMPARISON. GIVE MISSIONARIES IN UGANDA GRACE TO FACE TRIALS TODAY. *Amen.*

Hurting for the lost

"But you will receive power when the Holy Spirit comes on you; and you will be my witnesses in Jerusalem, and in all Judea and Samaria, and to the ends of the earth." Acts 1:8 (NIV)

The lostness was great, the darkness black and the oppression overwhelming in this Muslim country. I couldn't wait to leave.

I went about covered head to toe in local dress, with only my eyes showing. There were hardly any women on the streets. People stared at me. I certainly didn't have any words for them. In my head, I prayed for them—for peace, for His grace and mercy to be upon them. I kept repeating Jesus' name inside my head. He is my only strength.

I wish I could say I was strong, bold and courageous. I wasn't. I was overwhelmed with grief. The oppression was tangible. Can I believe He is at work in a place where I am sure He is not? Am I willing to go where I think, *Surely He wouldn't ask me to go there?* I have no answers. I do know the One who does, though. This is my only hope. And He is big enough. Does He know what He's doing, sending me here?

How can I not be changed forever by this experience? I long to be comfortable again, yet my world has been forever altered, a gnawing realization that there are those without freedom. Who will speak for them? Who will live among them and give them the message of hope? How can I say thank You to Him who freed me and then turn my back on those He's revealed to me?

—D.B., CENTRAL ASIA

Father, IT MUST BE OVERWHELMING FOR WORKERS IN COUNTRIES WHERE IT SEEMS THERE IS NO HOPE OF ANY CONVERSIONS. I PRAY THAT YOU WILL STRENGTHEN THEM FOR THE TASK. ENCOURAGE THEM THAT YOU ARE INDEED WORKING IN CENTRAL ASIA. ALLOW THEM TO SEE FRUIT, EVEN IF IT IS SMALL. *Amen.*

A mother's ministry

"So whether you eat or drink or whatever you do, do it all for the glory of God."
1 Corinthians 10:31 (NIV)

While putting away my daughter's cloth diapers, I thought about how much my ministry had changed. When we first came to Niger, I interacted with Fulani (foo-LAHN-nee) women almost on a daily basis. I spent many nights in a grass hut, cooked meals over an open fire and sat with the women as they pounded grain and gossiped. I felt like God was really using me to reach what was precious in His eyes.

That was all before we adopted our sweet daughter. She brings joy and blessing to our lives; but as I folded diapers, I realized just how much of my time is spent at our house in the capital city.

I envied other missionary women who have close contact with Fulani women. I even started missing that smelly grass hut and sleeping on an uncomfortable stick bed. Sure, our family still visits the villages, but not as often as before.

I dearly love my daughter, but I started to wonder how I was fulfilling my ministry. I used to feel fulfilled when I went out to the villages. As my thoughts drifted to the past, I was immediately reminded of 1 Corinthians 10:31: *"Whatever you do, do it all for the glory of God."*

Being a mother to my daughter *is* a major part of my ministry! Whether I'm at home folding cloth diapers or out visiting with Fulani women, it should be done with the right motives and a grateful spirit. We should do everything "for the glory of God."

—SHELLEY, WEST AFRICA

Father, YOU ARE THE SOVEREIGN KING OF THE UNIVERSE, WHO KNOWS EVEN ME. YOU GAVE ME THE FAMILY THAT I'M A PART OF FOR A REASON. HELP ME TO MINISTER TO MY FAMILY FOR YOUR GLORY. GIVE MISSIONARY MOTHERS OF YOUNG CHILDREN A SENSE OF PEACE THAT THEIR FAMILIES ARE THEIR MINISTRIES AT THIS TIME IN LIFE. *Amen.*

Melting icy hearts

"You have made my lot secure. The boundary lines have fallen for me in pleasant places." Psalm 16:5b–6a (NIV)

The moment we stepped from the plane, I felt at home. After six years of ministry in a major city in Far East Russia, God had laid on our hearts an isolated peninsula, two time zones farther east. Gazing upon the magnificence of God's creation, my breath was taken away. Two large volcanoes stood as sentinels, guarding the town. The Kamchatka (kom-CHAT-kah) peninsula truly was a "pleasant place."

The next morning, things didn't feel so pleasant. We spent our night sleeping in hats and coats, as our apartment had little heat. Bundling up, we prepared to attend our first worship service at a small Russian Baptist church. The temperature was 25 degrees below zero, and after riding 40 minutes in an unheated bus, I was convinced my toes were frostbitten. My husband, daughter and I flew off the bus, anxious to warm up at church. Entering the auditorium, my eyes fell on a welcome sight—two heating pipes running around the inside of the auditorium. I ran to the pipes, but no heat. My heart sent up a complaint, "Lord, what happened to the 'pleasant places' You promised me?"

I turned to greet 20 people gathered for worship. We worshiped for more than two hours in that frozen auditorium. Tears streamed down several faces as hearts were poured out in thanksgiving to God. My icy heart began to thaw. God reminded me that my "pleasant places" would be found among the warm hearts of Russian believers living in the glacial Kamchatka wilderness. God's warmth had made this a pleasant place.

—ROBIN, CENTRAL AND EASTERN EUROPE

Heavenly Father, IN COLD PLACES SUCH AS FOUND IN CENTRAL AND EASTERN EUROPE, GIVE MISSIONARIES GRACE TO BRAVE THE WEATHER AND THE WORD OF GOD TO MELT UNBELIEVING HEARTS OF THOSE THEY ENCOUNTER. BRING MUCH FRUIT IN THE FAR EAST OF RUSSIA FOR YOUR GLORY. *Amen.*

What saying yes means

"He who goes out weeping, carrying seed to sow, will return with songs of joy, carrying sheaves with him." Psalm 126:6 (NIV)

I read this verse when I was going through the interview process to come overseas for a two-year journeyman term. This verse was specifically for me, because I wept more over the decision than any other decision in my life. You see, adventure does not appeal to me in the least. In fact, the opposite characterizes me. I like to be comfortable, for my life to be consistent and to sit on the couch with my family. Yet God, in His amazing wisdom, decided to call *me* to go.

The uncertainty of leaving my family and their security made me cry a lot. This struggle was not with going to the ends of the earth, but simply with leaving my family.

Then, as I had been doing all that year, I turned to read in the Psalms; and God, once again in His amazing wisdom, gave me this verse. God promised even though there would be weeping, there would also be rejoicing.

Since the beginning of my journey, God and His Word have been so faithful. I still miss my family and weep often. But every time, God reminds me that the seed I have to sow is worth it. He reminds me that there will be songs of joy. I look forward to the day when we'll all rejoice around the throne. In the meantime, I've got some sowing to do. Many people still need to hear the story.

No matter the cost, we together need to share Christ with lost people around us.

—JESSICA, CENTRAL ASIA

Heavenly Father, BE ESPECIALLY CLOSE TO THOSE YOUNG WOMEN WHO HAVE LEFT FAMILIES IN ORDER TO MINISTER IN INTERNATIONAL LANDS. KEEP THEM CONTENT IN THE KNOWLEDGE THAT YOU ARE WITH THEM AND WON'T LEAVE THEM. HELP ME TODAY TO BE A WITNESS TO OTHERS, NO MATTER THE COST. *Amen.*

The outcome of a pothole

"I can do all things through Christ who strengthens me."
Philippians 4:13 (NKJV)

The remote villages in our region are accessed by sand and gravel roads. On one trip, my translator, J., and I came upon an enormous pothole. As we tried to bypass the edge, the truck slid into the hole, came out airborne into the opposing lane and finally landed on the side of the road, where I regained control.

Thinking of all the things that could have possibly gone wrong, Philippians 4:13 came to mind. I kept on driving, saying this verse and praying. Shortly, we encountered road graders smoothing the remaining road to our destination!

Traveling home, I told J. that if I saw a farmhouse, I would stop and talk to the occupants. No sooner had I said this than a path appeared to a house where an elderly man and his wife were sitting under a tree. J. and I shared the gospel with them.

After a long silence from the man, I quoted Revelation 3:20, to which the man replied, "I get up in the morning and pray for rain, for my cattle and for my family, but nothing happens. I don't understand why I pray. For a long time, I and the people that believe in the holy fire [ancestor worship] have been separated from Christians because of our belief, but now must be the time for me to believe in Jesus because today God came looking for me." They both accepted Christ.

If the road had not given us problems, two people might not have responded to the gospel. Praise Him!

—MARVING, CENTRAL, EASTERN AND SOUTHERN AFRICA

Lord, HELP ME TO PRAISE YOU ABOUT CIRCUMSTANCES RATHER THAN COMPLAIN. HELP ME NOT TO MISS OPPORTUNITIES TO SHARE YOU WITH OTHERS. I ALSO PRAY FOR THE PEOPLE OF NAMIBIA, THAT YOU WILL BRING MESSENGERS OF THE GOSPEL TO REACH THEM IN THIS VAST DESERT. *Amen.*

A godly servant

"Rejoice in the Lord always. Again I will say, rejoice!"
Philippians 4:4 (NASB)

If you passed her on the street, it is doubtful you would even take notice. Her bent body is petite, she wears plain dark clothing, and she walks with a slight limp. We met her for the first time on a cold Sunday at a little church. As the service concluded, she rushed to us, anxious to meet the visitors. As she approached, she searched deep into a large purse and produced a beautiful pair of hand-knitted wool slippers and gave them to my wife. Then with a big bear hug of love, she nearly squeezed the breath right out of me.

Her first name is Jeka (YEH-kah), but everyone calls her Baka (BAH-kah) Jeka. *Baka* means "Granny." She spends hours knitting slippers just to give away. One of her great joys is knitting white slippers for those being baptized. As she knits, she prays.

Further inquiry revealed a woman of strong, unwavering faith. She has been witness to two terrible wars, withstood nearly 50 years of communism, lived on the edge of poverty and suffered the pain and abuse of an alcoholic husband.

During their marriage, her husband would often come home drunk and physically assault her and the children. After her husband's legs were amputated due to diabetes, he continued his abuse, but she never ceased her loving care for him until his death.

God has noticed her contentment in all circumstances. On a glorious day in heaven, it will not surprise us to hear Jesus say, "Baka Jeka, come and sit close to Me."

—B.W.H., CENTRAL AND EASTERN EUROPE

Thank You, Father, FOR SERVANTS LIKE BAKA JEKA. MAY I BE A PERSON OF UNWAVERING FAITH IN THE MIDST OF DIFFICULT SITUATIONS. MAY I BE A LOVING PRESENCE TO THOSE WHO MAKE LIFE UNPLEASANT FOR ME. BE WITH MISSIONARIES IN CENTRAL AND EASTERN EUROPE TODAY, AND GIVE THEM ENCOURAGEMENT THAT WHAT THEY ARE DOING IS MAKING A DIFFERENCE. *Amen.*

Keeping a good sense of humor

"A merry heart doeth good like a medicine." Proverbs 17:22a (KJV)

Life is often filled with embarrassing moments, moments when you want to crawl into a hole. Living overseas regularly provides us with humbling experiences. In those situations, it becomes crucial to learn to laugh at yourself.

The most hilarious situation took place when we went to visit some friends who live in a rural setting. I came from the wide-open spaces of Texas but have been living in a Central Asian city of more than 3 million people. One day, one of our city friends took us out to the countryside where his brother lives.

All afternoon I commented to our hostess how much their place reminded me of Texas. She had a yard with grass and trees, a garden, fresh air, space and chickens. After drinking many cups of tea, I reluctantly asked my hostess to direct me to the outhouse. She took me to a little barnlike shack out in the chicken yard. It was definitely not an outhouse, but I wasn't going to complain. While I entered the dark barn, she turned her back to the doorway to keep watch. As my eyes slowly adjusted, I looked around for "the place." Not finding one, I went to the entrance and asked my hostess, "Where?" With broad sweeping gestures, she replied, "Anywhere you like!"

As we were walking back to her house arm-in-arm, she looked at me and asked, "So, is it like *that* in Texas?"

Having a good sense of humor and seeing the bright side of situations will make life more fun and bring pleasure to God.

—"CANDY," CENTRAL ASIA

Thank You, Lord, THAT LIFE JUST ISN'T AS SERIOUS AS I SOMETIMES MAKE IT OUT TO BE. THANK YOU FOR HUMOR AND THE ABILITY TO LAUGH. HELP ME TO SEE THE FUNNY SIDE OF THINGS DURING STRESSFUL SITUATIONS. GIVE WORKERS IN CENTRAL ASIA THAT ABILITY AS WELL. *Amen.*

W.I.T.T.Y.

"When Peter saw him, he asked, 'Lord, what about him?' Jesus answered, 'If I want him to remain alive until I return, what is that to you? You must follow me.'" John 21:21–22 (NIV)

While spending a summer in Tucson, Arizona, as a summer missionary, a friend of mine showed me these verses. She told me to write the acronym "W.I.T.T.Y." ("What is that to you?") in the margin.

Three years later and now in a different country, I have come to truly treasure those words of Jesus found in the Gospel of John. How easy it is to compare myself to other people. Like Peter, we often look at others and ask, "Lord, what about him or her?" instead of following the role He has for us.

God says, *Follow Me.* But instead of looking to the Lord, I sometimes look to the situations and qualities of others. I use the excuses, "Lord, they speak the language better … Lord, they are more outgoing than I am … Lord, they have more friends than I do … Lord, they are having an easier term than I am." Taking my eyes off God's purpose for me and placing my eyes on someone else's life shows a lack of contentment.

You must follow Me. He does not say if I want to or if it is easy; He says I *must* follow Him. God made me the way He did for a purpose. I am the only one who can follow God the way *I* can. You are the only one who can follow God the way *you* can. We must follow Him, and we must be content with our role while doing it.

—K.K., WESTERN EUROPE

Gracious God, HELP ME TO NEVER COMPARE MYSELF TO OTHERS BUT TO BE CONTENT IN WHO I AM IN YOU. MAY MISSIONARIES ALSO FOLLOW YOU AND BE CONTENT IN FOLLOWING. *Amen.*

Those bittersweet tears

"Those who sow in tears will reap with songs of joy. He who goes out weeping, carrying seed to sow, will return with songs of joy, carrying sheaves with him."
Psalm 126:56 (NIV)

I was ironing my dress for church. Such an ordinary thing, but at that very moment it brought back a flood of memories of home that brought homesickness and loneliness. I had been in Benin (beh-NIN) for some time, and you would have thought that I had gotten through this stage; but the weight of what I had left behind felt like it was crushing all of the air from my lungs.

The dress forgotten, I fell on my knees crying out to God to take away the pain of loneliness. I felt utterly alone, and I couldn't take it any longer. Was it worth it? Why was I even here? Could I make it for another year and three-quarters? All of these questions attacked my mind.

But then God sent me a reminder of His purpose. A song on a CD I was listening to spoke to me. "It's all about You, Jesus, and all this is for You, for Your glory and Your fame. It's not about me, as if You should do things my way ... "[1]

My tears turned to tears of joy. Not because the pain was gone, but because I knew God was using me to reach His world. It's not about me, but about Him.

When you weep, whether from personal pain or disappointments, let God turn your tears of sorrow into tears of joy, hope, love and expectation for those around you. Let Him take your eyes off yourself. You may still cry tears, but they will be sweet tears—bittersweet tears.

—DEBBY, WEST AFRICA

Father, BE NEAR TO LONELY MISSIONARIES. LET THEM FEEL YOUR PRESENCE AND PLEASURE. HELP ME TAKE MY EYES OFF MYSELF SO THAT I CAN TURN MY EYES TO THE LOVELY FACE OF JESUS. *Amen.*

1. Paul Oakley, *It's All About You*, Kingsway's Thankyou Music, 1995.

Go on!

"If you have raced with men on foot and they have worn you out, how can you compete with horses? If you stumble in safe country, how will you manage in the thickets by the Jordan?" Jeremiah 12:5 (NIV)

Ever feel like quitting? After a defeating day at work, after enduring hours in a traffic jam, and after hearing the kids cry all the way home, do you ever want to run away? Surprisingly enough, missionaries also have days like this. Oh, our traffic may be a little different overseas and the challenges might be more illogical. But our feelings are all the same!

In preparing to return to the States for furlough, we scoured local markets for the right trinkets to take to our friends and family. In one shop, we saw a new item—a lovely, blue, silk-screened banner in the characteristic local script. The verse, however, was Jeremiah 12:5. This not being a very familiar portion of Scripture, we skipped the purchase until we could pull out a Bible and make certain the passage was encouraging.

The days before heading back to the States were exhausting. We found ourselves weary and definitely not soaring like eagles (Isa. 40:31). When I finally settled down to look up the verse on the banner, I discovered just what I needed. The spiritual medicine was not one I really expected. Reading the verse was one of those Job moments—when you understand God's awesomeness and your own lack of understanding. It was an unexplainable shot in the arm, urging us, "Get up! Go on! Run the race! You can do it!"

We returned to the shop and promptly bought the silk banner to display for those future times when we feel we can't quite keep up with the horses.

—A WORKER IN THE PACIFIC RIM

I rely on Your strength, Father, EVERY DAY. HELP ME NOT TO GROW WEARY IN DOING GOOD. ENCOURAGE CHRISTIAN WORKERS TODAY TO FIGHT THE GOOD FIGHT. *Amen.*

SEPTEMBER V

God Before Me

Perhaps nothing is more challenging to the believer than pursuing the crucified life. I'm referring to the calling Christ described as denying ourselves, taking up our crosses daily and following Him (Luke 9:23). Paul described this same life another way in Galatians 2:20: "*I have been crucified with Christ and I no longer live, but Christ lives in me. The life I live in the body, I live by faith in the Son of God, who loved me and gave himself for me*" (NIV).

The challenge is tucked into Romans 12:1 as we're urged to "*offer [our] bodies as living sacrifices, holy and pleasing to God—this is [our] spiritual act of worship*" (NIV). *Living* sacrifices. That's the problem. *Dead* sacrifices have it a whole lot easier, in my opinion. Theoretically, we could offer ourselves in a flash of pain, be dead and be done with it. Nope. That's not Christ's way. Instead He called us to be sacrifices that are still kicking and squirming on the altar, making the decision daily as to whether we're going to stay on ... or hop off.

Followers of Christ are called to live and love sacrificially. We can take the theme of sacrifice from the Christian life about as successfully and biblically as we can take the cross from the life of Christ. You can't cut the heart out of a man and then expect him to survive. Nor will the Great Commission survive without sacrifice.

Keith and I consider the retreats we've shared with international missionaries to be among the greatest privileges of our serving life. The biggest shock for Keith was how normal the missionaries were. I think he expected them to have some kind of superspirit that made them able to follow God to the ends of the earth. Instead, they are regular people just like we are, and they'd be the first to tell you they don't have it all together.

Keith and I noted a common denominator, however, across the board: international missionaries are sacrificial. Every one of them was willing to make sacrifices. Some of them *huge*. Yes, there really are still many missionaries who live out in the bush without electricity, indoor plumbing, or, brace yourself, cell phones. Even those who have all of the above still make sacrifices like the close proximity of extended family, basic sanitation and church services in their own languages.

I'll never forget standing in the lobby of the hotel where our missionary refresher in Manila was being held. Most of the women didn't know me, so I got to observe them from a distance as they checked in. Over and over, many exclaimed with childlike glee, "Air conditioning!" A Houstonian has perhaps no greater respect for a soul than one who can live in oppressive heat and humidity with no air conditioning. Talk about squirming off an altar toward the nearest window unit!

You and I who aren't on the international field are also called to sacrificial living and loving. I have just as much respect for those of you who have had to place difficult things on the altar of God, foregoing your overwhelming desire for possession. Placing unforgiveness and the right to bitterness or a grudge on the altar can be among the most difficult sacrifices of all. Some sacrifice all sorts of physical comforts but take their anger to the grave. I've also watched plenty of people sacrifice the momentary comforts of untold addictions in order to pursue the radical and difficult path to liberty. Others have sacrificed the right to the pursuit of happiness with someone else by remaining married and faithful to a very difficult spouse.

Sacrificial living is made bearable and even wonderful two ways: The first one is the absolute marrow-deep conviction that anything we lose for the sake of Christ will turn to gain. We lay down our lives with the utmost confidence that the One we will find is the One who makes life worth more than a hill of beans. Living sacrificially is not only best for the kingdom, but it is best for us. No one is more miserable than a globe-head who thinks the universe revolves around him. God alone is Mr. Universe.

The second way sacrificial living is made bearable and wonderful is worship. Romans 12:1 tells us that living sacrifices offer spiritual worship to God. No worship is more expensive, more lavish than that which flows straight from the ache of sacrifice. Does it hurt? Worship

God with the pain! God reminded me of this when we kissed Amanda and her husband, Curt, goodbye and blessed their call to northern England for many months. I missed them so much. Every time I felt the loss, God seemed to whisper, *Worship Me with it, Beth. Bring that ache to My altar, and I will esteem it as a lavish offering.* He esteems yours just as highly.

Trust Him. Worship Him. And count your loss but gain.

—*Beth Moore*

Greasy fried eggs

"I pray also that the eyes of your heart may be enlightened in order that you may know ... his incomparably great power for us who believe. That power is like the working of his mighty strength, which he exerted in Christ when he raised him from the dead." Ephesians 1:18–20 (NIV)

Two fried eggs, drowning in a bowl of cotton oil. It was the sixth morning in a row, and it was the last straw. "I can't eat another bite of this greasy food," I whined to my husband, glaring at the offensive bowl. We had been living with a local family for almost five months, and the strain of cultural differences, greasy food, filthy toilets and lack of privacy was beginning to wear on me.

I felt ashamed of my weakness. Wasn't I low-maintenance? Hadn't I always been able to persevere in the most difficult of circumstances? Was I really cut out for this sort of work after all? A good Christian wouldn't cry over greasy eggs.

What concerned me most was failing in an area that I had always considered to be a personal strength. As I prayed that morning, God began to reveal to me my own pride. I did trust in His power to help me with my weaknesses, but I often relied on myself in areas I considered to be my strengths.

God used greasy food to teach me that victoriously serving Him does not hinge on my willpower or even on talents He has given me. Instead, God calls me to rely completely on His power in all circumstances. This power that He gives to every believer is the same power that He used to raise Christ from the dead. While I still haven't developed a taste for greasy eggs, I'm learning to rely more on God's great power than on my own personal fortitude.

—Joy, Central Asia

Father, forgive me for relying on my own personal strengths. I want to trust You in every area of my life. I confess my pride concerning _____. Thank You for Your forgiveness. *Amen.*

The treasured rug

"I have been crucified with Christ; and it is no longer I who live, but Christ lives in me; and the life which I now live in the flesh I live by faith in the Son of God, who loved me and gave Himself up for me." Galatians 2:20 (NASB)

Identifying with Christ and giving up oneself is a constant process. A few years ago, one of my assignments in seminary was to write a biography about a missionary. I wrote about Isobel Kuhn, who worked with unreached people groups in Asia from 1928 until her death in 1957.

Isobel had a beautiful rug that she carried with her to the mission field. When she lovingly set up her first home with her husband in a small town, she laid the treasured rug. Not long afterward, her neighbors stopped by unannounced. When the visitors were seated, one woman blew her nose into her hand and wiped her hand on the rug. Isobel was horrified, but she learned a lesson about dying to her selfish desires that day.

I had a good laugh reading the story and never thought that something similar would ever happen to me in East Asia. Imagine my horror when national believers, fresh from village work, entered my apartment with mud-covered footwear. One of them, his flip-flops and toes caked with mud, headed straight into my living room and made a beeline for my own beautiful rug, which had taken me weeks to find.

God is humorous and patient. He knew that giving up my selfish desires wouldn't be a quick, painless process. That day after these friends visited my apartment, Jesus reminded me of Isobel's generations-old story. Again, I bowed before Him and nailed on His cross my desires to live life my way. "It is no longer I who live, but Christ lives in me."

—A WORKER IN EAST ASIA

Father, YOU ARE SO PATIENT WITH MY SELFISH WAYS. TODAY I SAY THAT "IT IS NO LONGER I WHO LIVE, BUT CHRIST LIVES IN ME." I PRAY FOR MISSIONARIES TO ALSO DAILY SURRENDER THEIR TREASURES AND THEIR WILLS TO YOU. *Amen.*

Smelly or fragrant?

"But thanks be to God, who always leads us in triumph in Christ, and manifests through us the sweet aroma of the knowledge of Him in every place. For we are a fragrance of Christ to God among those who are being saved and among those who are perishing." 2 Corinthians 2:14–15 (NASB)

As a teenager, I worked at a variety store. Every Friday, employees from an onion-packing plant would come in to cash their paychecks. Their odor gave away their employment. They didn't try to smell like an onion; the aroma was a natural outcome of where they spent their lives, day-in, day-out.

With this picture in mind, God began teaching me about being an aroma of Christ. A lot of people think that a ministry is the same as an aroma—an expression of devotion to Him. Being an aroma is about essence, not about actions. Even though I believe firmly in what God has shown me through these verses, my biggest struggle is still in "doing" for the Lord instead of just "being" totally consumed by Him.

The word *missionary* implies "doing." Even in the newsletters that I send from Romania, I focus on what we've done, and I certainly don't report how I smell! I've learned that I try to live up to expectations of others. It's a real struggle.

In 1 Corinthians 4:4, Paul says, *"It is the Lord who judges me"* (NIV). Paul understood that we must not gauge our success by human standards. God doesn't measure success as we do. He wants to see a heart that has been conformed to the image of Christ. We are not to abide in Christ so that we get results in our work. We are to abide in Christ so that we are transformed into His image; we begin to look, sound and, yes, even smell like Him.

—KAREN, CENTRAL AND EASTERN EUROPE

Father, MAKE ME A SWEET-SMELLING AROMA TO YOU TODAY AS I OBEY YOU, AS I REST IN YOU AND AS I PRAY. MAY I NOT FOCUS ON MY CHRISTIAN WORKS, BUT MAY I FOCUS ON YOU ONLY. MAY MISSIONARIES FOCUS ON THEIR RELATIONSHIP WITH YOU RATHER THAN DEPENDING ON MINISTRY FOR FULFILLMENT. *Amen.*

Priorities

"'My thoughts,' says the LORD, 'are not like yours, and my ways are different from yours. As high as the heavens are above the earth, so high are my ways and thoughts above yours.'" Isaiah 55:8–9 (GNB)

"What is the will of God for your life?"

Had you asked me this question a year prior to our appointment as missionaries, my answer would have been completely different. My life was happy and blessed by God, with a wonderful husband and two beautiful, healthy girls. At first I couldn't understand why God wanted to change something that seemed so good.

As we became obedient to His call, I was able to see more clearly the abundance of His grace and love for me.

As a pediatrician by training, part of my ministry in Honduras is co-ordinating and serving in medical brigades. One afternoon while working in a clinic by the Pacific Ocean, I went outside for a few moments. Long lines of people were waiting to be seen by the doctors. I felt the wonderful feeling of loving what I was doing! I could share Jesus at the same time I was providing free medical care. I didn't think I would get to a point where I enjoyed this kind of medical practice more than my former way of practicing.

What is His will for my life? That I bring honor and glory to His name in whatever I do. In return, He has given me many of the desires of my heart: more time with Him and more time with my daughters and husband. He has taught me that His plan for my life is perfect. Sometimes His ways are not like we dreamed, but His will is trustworthy.

—NANCY, MIDDLE AMERICA AND THE CARIBBEAN

Heavenly Father, THANK YOU THAT YOUR WAYS ARE BETTER THAN MY WAYS. THANK YOU THAT YOU CALL DOCTORS TO LEAVE PROFITABLE PRACTICES IN AMERICA TO SERVE YOU OVERSEAS IN COMPASSIONATE MINISTRY. USE THEM TO SHARE JESUS AS THEY ALSO ARE USED TO BRING HEALTH TO THE POOR. *Amen.*

A choice to surrender my will

"You shall have no other gods before Me." Exodus 20:3 (NIV)

Waiting in line to pay my electricity bill gave me plenty of time to observe worshipers at a Hindu temple across the street. At this ornate structure dedicated to the monkey god, Hanuman (HA-new-MAHN), men and women walked around various idols, chanted mantras and stopped to kiss honored temple walls. My thoughts ranged from horror at the blatant idolatry, to sorrow for the evident bondage, to anger as I wanted to ask the Lord to destroy the temple and its idols right then as a sign of His singular right to be worshiped.

Eventually I began to fidget in the long line, and my spiritual eyes began to lose focus. Satan immediately attacked, and the thought went through my mind that perhaps it was easier to observe mindless religious rituals than to be an obedient child of God. Submission to God's will and walking in the Spirit require a conscious choice, and sometimes I just don't want to yield. Maybe performing prescribed rites instead of working on my relationship with Him would be simpler.

At that point, the truth stepped in like a bolt of lightning. I realized that I wouldn't give up my relationship with Him for anything! Relationships, even one with God, do require time, effort and sacrifice; but a relationship with Him is what makes life worthwhile.

With my spiritual eyes back in focus, my prayers turned to the worshipers who needed to know about how to have this relationship with the living God, and I began to pray in earnest for opportunities to share about Him.

—CARLA, SOUTH ASIA

FATHER, THE ONE, TRUE GOD, THANK YOU THAT YOU DESIRE A RELATIONSHIP WITH YOUR FOLLOWERS. GIVE CHRISTIAN WORKERS AN EARNEST PASSION TO BRING TRUTH TO THE PEOPLE OF SOUTH ASIA. LORD, I MAKE A CONSCIOUS EFFORT TODAY TO SURRENDER MY WILL FOR YOUR WILL. *Amen.*

Releasing: an act of worship

"I know, O LORD, that a man's way is not in himself, nor is it in a man who walks to direct his steps." Jeremiah 10:23 (NASB)

I awakened in the middle of the night, wondering why I had to leave the country where I had built deep relationships. The decision was made for me without my input. Only God could hear and understand the sense of anger and heartbreak that I had.

It all started with a telephone call from a credible source, which revealed a plan that I would be kidnapped or killed on a particular day. My team decided that I should take this threat seriously, and they made the decision for me to evacuate immediately.

A few months later, at a women's retreat in Cyprus, the speaker asked, "What is God teaching you about all of life being an act of worship? Is God leading you to believe in something you have never seen or dreamed of before? Is there something God is asking you to release as an act of worship?" These questions caused me to think.

For me, I needed to release my area of service and the people group as an act of worship. He required me to lay them, and what I have gained from knowing them, at His feet.

One year after my evacuation, I awakened in the middle of the night feeling that my joy was back. I knew the Lord had charge over my life, and He gave me wonderful relationships in another place. God's plans far exceed our own. Even though He doesn't always explain His reasons for moving us, we can count on Him, for He will always see us through any change encountered.

—P.A.F., NORTHERN AFRICA AND THE MIDDLE EAST

Heavenly Father, MY LIFE IS IN YOUR HANDS. DO WITH IT AS YOU DESIRE. YOU KNOW THE LARGER PICTURE AND KNOW WHAT'S BEST FOR ME. THANK YOU THAT YOU ARE PATIENT WITH ME WHEN I THINK THAT A MISTAKE HAS BEEN MADE. *Amen.*

The offering

"For they all out of their surplus put into the offering; but she out of her poverty put in all that she had." Luke 21:4 (NASB)

The woman sat on the wooden floor, hands folded in her lap. "I don't have any money, but I will sing as my offering," she said as she was led to the center of the circle. Her face turned upward and radiated joy and thanksgiving as her sweet voice filled the church with song. Although her eyes had been veiled with blindness, they were not veiled to the love of Christ of which she sang.

The "church" floated on bamboo pontoons among a houseboat village on the river. It was four unpainted wooden walls with a tin roof. Inside, there were no chairs or keyboard. Yet, in spite of this simplicity, I sensed the powerful presence of God as I sat cross-legged on the floor among the other believers.

Captivated by the beautiful voice of a blind woman singing a praise offering to her Lord, I felt compelled to give generously. As a purple felt bag was reverently passed around, I placed my offering in it.

Although I did not understand the words of her song, I understood the words of her heart. God used that moment to reveal to me what true giving is all about. Tears welled up in my eyes as I realized that in God's eyes giving is not about how much you have to give, but rather about what you don't have after you've given. Somehow my generous offering didn't seem significant anymore. I, out of my surplus, gave an offering; but she, out of her poverty, put in all that she had.

—L., PACIFIC RIM

Father, MAY I NOT WITHHOLD ANYTHING FROM YOU. MAY MISSIONARIES ALSO GIVE FREELY THEIR LIVES TO SPREAD THE GOOD NEWS THROUGHOUT THE WORLD. *Amen.*

Not forgetting the offering

"A poor widow came and put in two small copper coins. ... He said to them, 'Truly I say to you, this poor widow put in more than all the contributors to the treasury; for they all put in out of their surplus, but she, out of her poverty, put in all she owned, all she had to live on.'" Mark 12:42–44 (NASB)

As my truck pulled up to the tiny church in a remote village, women began to gather. We soon filled the mud structure where it was dark inside. Logs lay in rows to provide seating on the dirt floor. Most all the women had babies tied to their backs and had already hauled water and wood, cooked a meal and walked several kilometers to the church. I stood by the one window cut into the mud wall to be able to read the Scriptures.

Three different languages were spoken, so I waited for my two interpreters as I thought through what to say next. As I gazed out the window, I could see ladies preparing our noon meal in a big black cooking pot. I finished my teaching and had just asked someone to ask God's blessing on the meal when a voice piped up: "We haven't given our offering!"

I stood there in tumult, trying to explain to God just how little these women had, as if He wasn't already aware. As each woman danced up to give her money, my heart broke. Then a woman poured coins, amounting to 20 cents, into my hand and asked me to make sure this money got to the right place.

God began to work in my heart, saying, *I own the cattle on a thousand hills. I don't need their money. Their willingness to obey My commandments and joyfully share what little they have is the gift I seek. Do not rob them or me of this joy.*

—GAYE, WEST AFRICA

Lord, MAY I JOYFULLY GIVE WHAT I HAVE TO YOU. BLESS THESE WOMEN IN WEST AFRICA WHO GIVE SACRIFICIALLY. STRENGTHEN THE MISSIONARIES WHO SERVE THERE SO THAT THEY CAN GIVE THEMSELVES TO OTHERS WHO NEED YOU. *Amen.*

Straddling the fence

"For God has not given us a spirit of timidity, but of power and love and discipline." 2 Timothy 1:7 (NASB)

One morning after my devotion, I felt the Lord directing me to enter an apartment building in France where hundreds of West African Muslims lived. Armed with a video of the *JESUS* film in an African language, I went from floor to floor asking strangers if they wanted to see a film in their tribal language. Time after time, each man turned me down. I thought to myself after the fourth floor, *Lord, I thought You called me here today.*

Finally, four men from the largest nomadic group in Africa warmly greeted me. They refused to believe that I had a video with people speaking their African language. However, when the tape started, they laughed aloud like schoolboys. They called out to their friends who were passing by their doorway. They said to their friends, "Come hear Jesus speaking our language. We can understand His message."

Since then, Djibril (gee-BRILL), one of the men most deeply touched by the gospel message, has testified often, "When I heard the words of Christ, something in my heart moved. I could not stop watching the video. I knew that I was hearing the truth."

These four men are hesitant to embrace Christianity. They and other Muslims want the assurance of salvation and the sense of belonging they discover in Christ; however, they hesitate if it means losing their sense of belonging in their old community.

Do you hesitate in giving Jesus your whole life? He wants it all and calls us to follow Him.

—TONY, WESTERN EUROPE

Father, MAY I NOT HOLD BACK ANYTHING FROM YOU. MY DESIRE IS THAT YOU ARE THE LORD OF MY LIFE. HELP PEOPLE GROUPS WHO HAVE IMMIGRATED TO EUROPE TO FOLLOW JESUS WHEN THEY HEAR THE GOSPEL MESSAGE. *Amen.*

Take my life

"I will not die but live, and will proclaim what the Lord has done."
Psalm 118:17 (NIV)

After I arrived in Lesotho (leh-SUE-too), I began volunteering at an orphanage. One child, B., instantly captured my heart. Her mother, who was HIV positive, suffered from tuberculosis (TB) during and after B.'s birth. Therefore, the child was exposed to TB and HIV at birth. After her mother's death, she came to the orphanage.

One day, I walked in the playroom to find B. crying. I picked her up and playfully raised her above my head. Suddenly, mucus fell from her nose and into my eye. Fear swept over me, as I knew I had just been exposed to HIV. The chances of transmission were slim, but I was still terrified.

The following days were filled with blood tests and the start of anti-retroviral medications. I called on my Savior for peace of mind. At first, I only wanted answers from God. "Do I have HIV?" "How will my parents react?" "Why is this happening?" I had watched many people suffer from AIDS, and I wasn't sure if I could do it.

After days in prayer, my attitude transitioned to a desire to see God glorified. Once again, I surrendered my life to His will for me.

Weeks later, B.'s test results returned. She was HIV negative! I rejoiced with her, grateful to the Lord of hosts—not only for knowing that B. was HIV negative, but that I was also.

It took this experience to help me understand what most Africans go through emotionally and spiritually. "Take my life and let it be consecrated, Lord, to Thee."

—AMY, CENTRAL, EASTERN AND SOUTHERN AFRICA

Lord, "TAKE MY LIFE AND LET IT BE CONSECRATED, LORD, TO THEE. TAKE MY MOMENTS AND MY DAYS. LET THEM FLOW IN CEASELESS PRAISE." THANK YOU THAT YOU PROTECTED THIS YOUNG MISSIONARY FROM AIDS. PROTECT OTHER MISSIONARIES IN AFRICA WHO WORK WITH THE HIV-POSITIVE. *Amen.*

In God's hands

"If we live, we live to the Lord; and if we die, we die to the Lord. So, whether we live or die, we belong to the Lord." Romans 14:8 (NIV)

My wife and I spent a week during a conference with our colleague, Dr. Janette Shackles, prior to her untimely death in a car accident. She kept all of us laughing as she shared her adventures since coming to Africa.

Two stories I will not forget. One was about a young man who was not expected to live. While performing surgery, she prayed, "God, if You'll spare his life, I'll make sure he hears the gospel." He did survive, and Janette shared the gospel with him.

Janette also told about her recent plane trip. Her flight stopped in Lomé (low-MAY), Togo, on the way to Abidjan (AB-ee-jhan), Ivory Coast. When the plane started down the runway to take off from Lomé, an alarm went off and the takeoff was aborted. After returning the passengers to the airport, the pilot made a test run and returned for the passengers. As they attempted to take off again, the alarm went off, but the pilot successfully took off. Although concerned, Janette said, "I must put my life in the hands of the pilot, just like so many people have put their lives in my hands during surgery." Immediately, she realized that even more importantly, her life was in God's hands. When I heard the tragic news about Janette's death, I thought about this story.

At a memorial service held in Ghana, Janette was remembered as a doctor who cared deeply for her patients and their eternal destination. Following God cost Janette her life. How willing are we to follow Him no matter the cost?

—ROGER, WEST AFRICA

Oh, that I may follow You, Lord, NO MATTER THE COST. THANK YOU FOR THE LIFE OF THIS DOCTOR WHO FOLLOWED YOU IN LIFE AND DEATH. MAY HER LIFE BE REMEMBERED AS A TESTIMONY OF YOUR FAITHFULNESS. *Amen.*

God teaches His children

*"The Lord said to him, 'Who gave man his mouth?... Is it not I, the LORD?
Now go; I will help you speak and will teach you what to say.'" Exodus 4:11–12
(NIV)*

In studying a difficult, tonal language, I realized that language school was "God's school of humility" for missionaries. Over and over, I felt like a failure and had to humble myself like a child.

My frustration often brought me to tears, but not in public. One day, I broke. The teacher handed the class a book of stories and asked which one we should start with. With my best attitude I said, "Number eight looks interesting!" For two hours we struggled to read that story. I felt as though the whole class was furious with me for choosing such a hard story!

When the teacher left the room at break, I put my head down on the desk and sobbed like a child. With a master's degree in education and 30 years of teaching experience, it was easy to fall into the trap of trusting my knowledge, my diligent studying and even my motivation instead of trusting God's provision for me. Moses had to learn this, too; and God quickly set him straight with the admonishment, "Go! I will teach you what to say."

Can we trust God's teaching? Yes. The God who gave the languages at Babel gives us the words to talk to our neighbors, the street vendor and the university teacher. He does this for His glory. We cannot boast in anything but what He is teaching, and so we must trust how He teaches us. Sometimes His methods are humorous, sometimes frustrating and sometimes we cry like the children He wants us to be.

—W.S., PACIFIC RIM

Heavenly Father, LEARNING LANGUAGES MUST BE EXTREMELY DIFFICULT FOR MISSIONARIES IN A NEW COUNTRY. HELP THEM, LORD, TO LEARN QUICKLY. LET THEM FULLY TRUST YOU IN LEARNING A LANGUAGE. GIVE ME THE WORDS TO SPEAK TO THOSE I ENCOUNTER TODAY. *Amen.*

Do I think too highly of myself?

"For since the creation of the world God's invisible qualities—his eternal power and divine nature—have been clearly seen, being understood from what has been made, so that men are without excuse." Romans 1:20 (NIV)

As a new missionary in Guatemala, experiencing and learning about the Mayan culture has been exciting, fascinating, time consuming and troubling. It is exciting to learn firsthand about a culture that I would have otherwise only known through books. It is fascinating because of interesting facts and mysteries. It is time consuming and can't be learned in one day. It is troubling in that natural beauty is all around, but many do not know the Creator.

I once knew a North American who felt it was her mission to do something good for God by working in Guatemala. Her actions repeatedly demonstrated disdain for the Guatemalan culture and that anyone who did not live up to her standards could not possibly be saved. God used this situation to teach me important lessons. I am not here to change any life; only the Holy Spirit can. I am not here to judge or condemn, for that is the work of God. I am not here to save anyone, because only Jesus can save.

God placed me here to present Jesus to the people of Guatemala. My prayer is that God will use this culture to help me see His truth more clearly. I pray that I will never have prejudice in my heart toward people who are not like me. I pray that bridges may be built in order to present the truth of God in a way that will draw people to Him rather than push them further away.

—JaDonna, Middle America and the Caribbean

Creator of all people, FORGIVE ME WHEN I JUDGE OTHERS WHO ARE NOT LIKE ME. FORGIVE ME WHEN I REGARD MYSELF TOO HIGHLY. FATHER, YOU CAME TO SAVE ALL PEOPLE, PEOPLE WHO HAVE DIFFERENT CULTURES AND VARIED APPEARANCES. MAY I NEVER PUT MYSELF ABOVE OTHERS. *Amen.*

Shrinking in the King's hand

"But he said to me, 'My grace is sufficient for you, for my power is made perfect in weakness.' Therefore I will boast all the more gladly about my weaknesses, so that Christ's power may rest on me." 2 Corinthians 12:9 (NIV)

I, the newcomer, have been staying in a village where it has been hard to sleep without a hut and difficult to eat new foods. Getting a pair of earplugs was a big help, and now I've found out that the villagers want to build for me my own hut.

The most significant thing to come from this stay in the village was that two men, who are believers, approached me. They are both new Christians and know very little, but they seem sincere and eager to grow. I started reading the Bible with them, since both are barely literate. Others have listened in on our discussions. I have been greatly encouraged by having these new friends.

The work here is difficult, and things never seem to work the way I think or expect, but it is an unspeakable comfort to see the Spirit at work, completely outside of my efforts. I knew before I came that I couldn't live in this village without God's help. Now I have experienced that profound inadequacy. I really can't do it by myself. It is such a strange joy to feel myself getting smaller, weaker and more insignificant, and then suddenly realize that it is the weak that the Father almost always uses to conquer the darkness and spread His glory.

Who would have known that God would have provided two new brothers in Christ so that I would not be alone!

May I be so blessed as to shrink in the hand of our King!

—DUSTIN, WEST AFRICA

Father, MAY MISSIONARIES HAVE THE WISDOM AND SENSITIVITY TO WORK ACCORDING TO YOUR PLAN RATHER THAN TRYING TO DO IT THEMSELVES. MAY THEY BE FILLED WITH THE SPIRIT TO STAND AGAINST THE FORCES OF DARKNESS. MAY I ALSO DEPEND ON YOU ALWAYS IN EVERYTHING THAT I DO. *Amen.*

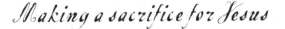

Making a sacrifice for Jesus

"I urge you therefore, brethren, by the mercies of God, to present your bodies a living and holy sacrifice, acceptable to God, which is your spiritual service of worship." Romans 12:1 (NASB)

Opening the Bible that lay in my lap, I began to tell the biblical story of the "widow woman" to this small group of Guajibo (gwah-HEE-boh) people. With all eyes upon me, I told how her unconditional faith expressed itself through the sacrificial giving of all she possessed that day at the temple. Jesus took notice of this woman when she, out of her poverty, put in all that she had to live (Mark 12:41–44). She became a perfect example of the living sacrifice about which the apostle Paul wrote about in Romans 12.

The old woman who owned the house where I told these stories had complete understanding, and she seized her opportunity to put her own faith into action. Undeterred by the fixed stares from those about her, she quickly walked to me and boldly pressed her live sacrifice—a plump laying hen—into my hands. I stared at the gift and thought my heart would burst as this woman reminded me of the widow with the two copper coins. I knew that I had a glimpse of what emotions surged within Jesus as He watched the widow in the temple.

The travelers who wander from one hillside to another don't carry a Bible under their arm or packed away in some protective pouch. They don't concern themselves over an articulate three-point sermon. Yet during any given evening in front of an open fire, they can be heard retelling the Bible stories they've heard as they, too, gather in prayer and fellowship.

—CAROL, SOUTH AMERICA

Father of mercy and justice, HELP ME TO TELL YOUR STORY LIKE THE GUAJIBO BELIEVERS WHOSE LIVES TRULY ARE LIVING SACRIFICES, ACCEPTABLE TO YOU. *Amen.*

"If there is anything left, we will eat"

"For I testify that they gave as much as they were able, and even beyond their ability. Entirely on their own, they urgently pleaded with us for the privilege of sharing in this service to the saints." 2 Corinthians 8:3–4 (NIV)

Fourteen women stood in a circle as we prayed for the young Costa Rican woman who was about to leave as a missionary to a Muslim country. All of them were committed to pray for our church's first international missionary. But what brought tears to my eyes that afternoon was not their commitment to pray.

In many evangelical churches across Latin America, God's Spirit is raising up a missionary movement from areas that have traditionally been *our* mission fields. From our small church in San José (san ho-SAY), Costa Rica, He called out "Farisa" to go to one of the darkest corners of Central Asia.

When Margarita's turn came to pray that afternoon, she prayed, "Lord, You know our family's commitment to the faith promise offering so that Farisa can go to another land. As I've told my children, 'First, we will give the offering, and then if there is anything left, we will eat.'"

She continued her prayer, but I didn't hear the rest. Tears flowed as I realized that this woman, whose husband was dying of cancer, was truly committed to the high cost of reaching the world for Christ. She was teaching her children where a Christian's priorities should lie.

In the United States, the vast majority of those who support missions do so out of relative wealth. But the missionary movement from the Two-Thirds World (outside the U.S., Canada, England and Europe) is being supported in most cases out of dire sacrifice.

—WILMA, MIDDLE AMERICA AND THE CARIBBEAN

Oh Lord, I AM HUMBLED BY THE PURITY OF HEART, THE INDESCRIBABLE LOVE AND THE SACRIFICIAL COMMITMENT OF LATIN AMERICAN WOMEN WHO GIVE OUT OF THEIR NEED AND COUNT IT ALL JOY. FATHER, I PRAY THAT MY HEART WOULD BREAK TO THE POINT OF GIVING TO MISSIONS WITH EXUBERANCE, NOT ONLY BECAUSE OF THE VAST LOSTNESS AND DEPRAVITY OF THE PEOPLES OF THE WORLD, BUT BECAUSE THE SUPREME SACRIFICE OF REDEMPTION HAS ALREADY BEEN MADE FOR THEIR SALVATION, IF ONLY THEY HEAR. *Amen.*

A chance to die

"Truly, truly, I say to you, unless a grain of wheat falls into the earth and dies, it remains alone; but if it dies, it bears much fruit. He who loves his life loses it, and he who hates his life in this world will keep it to life eternal."
John 12:24–25 (NASB)

One summer morning, I woke up with a real sense that I had no purpose for that day. *It's Saturday*, I thought. *This is a day for going out to eat, working around the house, sports on TV, visiting family and friends.* None of that was going to happen since the familiar events of a Saturday were thrown out the window in a new country. I was depressed, and the heat was sweltering.

My Bible was open and I was praying, yet I couldn't change the way I felt. I continued in my Scripture readings where I had left off. I came to a familiar verse, but this time it packed a punch: *"... unless a grain of wheat falls into the earth and dies, it remains alone; but if it dies, it bears much fruit."* I realized by the Spirit that, yes, my life is over. It's over because my life and serving Christ are at odds with each other. I can't have my life and the life of Christ at the same time.

The Spirit brought to mind the title of a book I've read about Amy Carmichael, *A Chance to Die*, by Elisabeth Elliot. That Saturday morning, I had a chance to die to personal desires. Each day, the Spirit says gently to my heart, *Here before you is a chance to die and live for Christ.* I have a chance to die to myself during temptation or during a trial.

Putting our selfish desires to death is painful, but it is glorious to live as Christ lives!

—JASON, CENTRAL ASIA

Oh Father, WHAT PATH AM I WALKING DOWN WITH YOU? IT DOES SEEM SO NARROW. PLEASE GIVE ME GRACE TO LIVE FOR YOU AND TO DIE TO MY OWN SELFISH DESIRES. ENCOURAGE CHRISTIAN WORKERS IN CENTRAL ASIA TODAY TO LIVE FOR YOU AND TO FORGET WHAT IS BEHIND THEM. *Amen.*

Packing light

"Let us strip off every weight that slows us down, especially the sin that so easily hinders our progress." Hebrews 12:1b (NLT)

Forget Atkins! I found that two years of traversing rugged southwest China as an itinerant village researcher has a way of helping you lose weight more effectively than any diet plan. Having spent much time living out of a backpack and trunks, I quickly learned the art of minimizing to make life less cumbersome.

My childhood years as a pack rat behind me, I soon found my new Spartan mind-set spilling over into my daily life as I became obsessed with getting rid of nonessentials. Living as simply and lightly as possible was of utmost importance.

However, I soon found myself wearing an inexplicable burden even when I wasn't hiking. *My child,* He said, *in all your striving, you've forgotten to narrow your interests, your energies, your entire life down to Me and only Me. This is the simple life.*

I sank in shame beneath the weight of the realization that I'd neglected ridding my heart of excess baggage, all its tendencies toward rebellion and unfaithfulness. Paul's exhortation to live weightlessly and unfettered rang in my ears, reminding me of the necessity of doing away with every superfluous part of my life that does not glorify the Father.

Why would I not cast aside those things I was never meant to carry? I don't whittle down toothbrushes before every trek into the mountains, but now I am determined to shed habits, weaknesses, misguided affections and distractions that deter me from reaching my true home in a manner worthy of Him who calls me there.

—A WORKER IN CHINA

Father, I PRAY THAT I WILL NOT CARRY THOSE THINGS THAT DETER ME FROM BEING CONFORMED TO THE IMAGE OF YOUR SON. REVEAL THOSE THINGS TO ME EVEN NOW. *Amen.*

Control freak solution

"The LORD had said to Abram, 'Leave your country, your people and your father's household and go to the land I will show you.'" Genesis 12:1 (NIV)

I am a control freak. When I am on a trip, I want to hold the map or drive the car. On road trips, my friends usually tolerate this without too much complaint. In the grand scheme of life, however, this tends to get me in trouble. Recently, God has taught me about "letting go of the map." I made Him my Navigator years ago, but I keep trying to peek over His shoulder to find out where we are going.

For many years, I felt God leading me toward the international mission field. After getting rid of some selfishness in my own heart, I said, "Okay, I'll go. But where are we going?" I felt much like Abraham when God said, "Leave your country, your people and your father's household and go to the land I will show you."

The time came to take a huge step of commitment, including quitting my job and selling my car. The day before I had to select my specific job location, I was still clueless. I continued to wait on God.

In His timing, the Lord showed me my next step and whispered, *This is the way; walk in it* (Isa. 30:21, NIV). Taiwan wasn't where I thought I would be, and the timetable wasn't as I expected, but it was perfect, as His will always is. In each of our lives, He gives a similar call. And, just like Abraham, He simply asks us to trust Him, even when we can't see the final destination.

—S.B., EAST ASIA

Father, I CONFESS THAT I OFTEN TRY TO BE IN CONTROL OF MY LIFE RATHER THAN ALLOWING YOU TO LEAD ME. TAKE MY LIFE AND LET IT BE WHOLLY YOURS TODAY. I PRAY FOR WORKERS IN EAST ASIA TO TRUST YOU FOR EVERY STEP RATHER THAN DEPENDING ON THEIR OWN STRENGTH. *Amen.*

He is everything

"The life I live in the body, I live by faith in the Son of God, who loved me and gave himself for me." Galatians 2:20 (NIV)

I watched my dreams slip away: dreams for our work with an unreached people group in China, dreams for us, dreams for our children. I had been diagnosed with a rare condition for which there is no cure. The pain was so severe that I wanted to escape this life. Then the body of Christ interceded for me. Many were struck with migraine headaches after praying, while I was granted rest and sometimes sleep.

The Lord led me to Matthew 8:17: "*He took up our infirmities and carried our diseases*" (NIV). It seemed He was bearing on His body my sickness. But my condition was getting worse. The saints had prayed the door open for my freedom, but I wasn't small enough yet to fit through it (John 3:30).

"I didn't know my life would turn out this way," I complained to the Lord, as I thought of my children growing up with a bedridden mother, insane with pain and unable to care for them.

Whose life? He reminded me gently. So in the darkness of my prison, I laid down every gift He had given me. I laid down my ministry, dreams and hopes. I died to myself, and He healed me.

Now I am nothing; He is everything. It is not my ministry; it is His. I don't teach; He does. I am merely a warm body in the room watching Him perform miracles I can't explain.

I wouldn't wish what I went through on anyone, but I wouldn't trade what I have become in Him for anything.

—A WORKER IN CHINA

Father, THANK YOU FOR THE LESSONS YOU HAVE TAUGHT ME THROUGH TRIALS. YOU ARE EVERYTHING. ANY MINISTRY THAT I HAVE IS YOURS. I PRAY THAT MISSIONARIES WILL NOT BE SELF-ABSORBED BUT BE TOTALLY ABSORBED BY YOU. *Amen.*

Is it worth it?

"For the eyes of the LORD range throughout the earth to strengthen those whose hearts are fully committed to him." 2 Chronicles 16:9a (NIV)

My first year in Senegal was full of trials. I moved eight times within three months. My house burned down. I lived in remote conditions with undependable transportation, poor food and an unreliable telephone. I made my own toilet out of a plastic bucket. I had illnesses I've never heard of. I had power outages and a zillion mosquito bites. I was lost too many times to even count, not to mention the language barriers I faced every day. I was mocked, laughed at, ridiculed and persecuted.

Would I do it again? Yes! I was protected, provided for and blessed. I was never alone. I was loved, held, watched and kept by my Lord.

The Lord blessed me with new friends, and Sereer (suh-RARE) families adopted me as one of their own. Opportunities to show His love and to distribute the Word to thousands have been the results of these friendships. Experiencing rough times myself allows me to help others through periods of grief, such as wrapping my arms around a woman who lost her newborn.

My Lord continues to show me why I am here. I am blessed to see the Lord's hand at work, knowing that even what may seem bad at the time serves a far greater purpose to get me where *He* wants me to be. My being in Senegal is worth what I have endured.

Does God want you to get out of your comfort zone? Maybe. Are you willing? I hope so. You will be blessed.

—BECKY, WEST AFRICA

Father God, IT IS WORTH IT TO FOLLOW YOU! CAUSE ME TO REFLECT ON THIS QUESTION THROUGHOUT THE DAY: AM I WILLING TO GET OUT OF MY COMFORT ZONE? I PRAY THAT THE WORK FOR CHRIST IN SENEGAL WILL BE FRUITFUL. *Amen.*

Available to do God's work

"The sacrifices of God are a broken spirit; a broken and a contrite heart, O God, You will not despise." Psalm 51:17 (NASB)

"Call" is a word often reserved for great and lofty aspirations. The words describing the experience of God's call are not easily found. The word "missionary" can bring about the same thoughts as "call." Christians sometimes see missionaries as superhumans who are so perfect in their spiritual walks that God pulls them out of the mundane to do extraordinary things.

In my case, that's not true. The mission call in my life has been the most humbling experience I have ever had. Why? Because I've come face to face with expectations and have fallen short. God knows full well who I am, but sometimes I still wonder if He knows how vulnerable and frail my faith is.

I'm a new missionary, green and wet behind the ears. I haven't seen a whole village accept Christ or thousands baptized in a row. I don't even know the language yet! And I'm a little scared, because I don't want to fail God. I don't want to fail my spouse, my kids, or all those wonderful saints who are praying for my family. I especially don't want to fail the people I've come to help.

It's hard to remember that it's not me who has to do the work, but that I am just supposed to be available to God so He can do His work. I'm realizing that I don't have to be superhuman to do God's will, but I do need a heart that trusts Him where He leads me.

—NICOLE, CENTRAL, EASTERN AND SOUTHERN AFRICA

Dear Lord, STRENGTHEN THE CALL OF MISSIONARIES AROUND THE WORLD TODAY. LET THEM SEE YOU AT WORK AMONG THE PEOPLE THEY ARE SERVING. GIVE THEM PURE HEARTS THAT TRUST YOU. SHOW ME TODAY HOW I CAN TRUST YOU MORE. *Amen.*

Leaving the past behind

"Let me hear Your lovingkindness in the morning; for I trust in You; teach me the way in which I should walk; for to You I lift up my soul."
Psalms 143:8 (NASB)

My family had been ministering among the Ngäbe (in-GAH-beh) people in the western jungles of Panama for eight years. We had grown to love them and their simple lifestyle. Through God-arranged circumstances, we transferred that work into the hands of others. We moved into a different job to train Christian nationals to reach their own people using chronological Bible storying.

Over time, I missed my friends in the village, I worried over the people we had left behind that still did not know God, and I even missed life in the jungle! One morning, I read these words in *Keep a Quiet Heart* by Elisabeth Elliot: "I thought I would be a jungle missionary for the rest of my life." I knew exactly how she felt. I felt like God was saying, *That's exactly right. You wanted something, but that's not My plan for your life. Now you have a choice to make. Will you continue to grieve over what has been left behind, or will you follow My plan?*

I decided that morning that wherever God leads, I will go, even though it might not be what I would choose for myself. On furlough, I often meet people who say to me, "You know, I thought God might call me to be a missionary one day, but He never did." After my experience, I wonder how many of those people really wanted something different for their lives and simply did not respond to God's call.

—MELODIE, MIDDLE AMERICA AND THE CARIBBEAN

Father God, MAY THE CHOICES I MAKE BE THE ONES FOLLOWING YOUR WILL FOR MY LIFE. AS YOU DIRECT ACCORDING TO YOUR WORD AND CHARACTER, AND AS I FOLLOW, MAY I NOT LOOK BACK AND GRIEVE OVER WHAT I LEFT BEHIND. MAY THOSE WHO FEEL CALLED TO MISSIONS LISTEN TO YOUR VOICE AND OBEY. *Amen.*

Passing the baton

> *"The things which you have heard from me in the presence of many witnesses, entrust these to faithful men who will be able to teach others also."*
> 2 Timothy 2:2 (NASB)

After spending time in the jungle looking at the bottom of a dried-up well, I am convinced that if the woman at the well had had running water, she would not have been as receptive to the living Water offered by Jesus.

But she didn't have running water. She had to walk to the well, haul water out of the well and walk back home—only to do it all again the next day. Because she didn't have running water, she was ready for living Water. She was ready to accept that change.

After leaving my jungle home, I am convinced that if we had been allowed to choose when our team would leave, we would not have left when we did. We would have spent more time with the Guarayos (gwa-RIE-ose) people. We would have done more to improve their quality of life. We would have learned more of their language.

But we didn't get to choose. We had to stop working on our long-term projects and throw ourselves into equipping the believers to be able to lead the ministry after we left.

Because we didn't get to choose when we left, real leadership came forth in the church. Because we didn't get to choose, 42 stories from the Bible have been translated into Guarayu (gwa-RIE-oo), the language that God gave the Guarayos. Because we didn't get to choose, we found ourselves in the midst of an amazing lesson on trusting God.

What is keeping you from trusting Him?

—KRISTEE, SOUTH AMERICA

Father, HELP ME TO HAND OVER MINISTRY AT THE APPROPRIATE TIME SO THAT OTHERS CAN GROW IN THEIR FAITH. GIVE MISSIONARIES THE GRACE TO TURN OVER MINISTRY WHEN TRAINING IS COMPLETE SO THAT THEY CAN MOVE TO OTHER AREAS TO MAKE NEW DISCIPLES. *Amen.*

Surrendering life goals

"Now to Him who is able to do far more abundantly beyond all that we ask or think." Ephesians 3:20a (NASB)

At the airport, there is a gypsy woman who uses the lobby to target the people waiting for passengers. She offers visions of the future for a donation. Sometimes she teases the people who are passing by to gain attention of potential clients. I was at the airport saying goodbye to friends recently, and she took note that I was standing near. Very loudly, she shouted that she had a vision for me. Everyone turned attention toward us. Quickly, I dashed far away from her.

So many people I meet want to know their future. In view of their suffering, frustrations, losses and grief, they want something to believe in. I am learning to surrender my future to God.

As a single missionary, I know something about the death of a vision. My dreams for the future were good and godly, but they were mine. Had I not surrendered them, they could have kept me from responding to God's invitation to international missions.

As I experience God at work around me, no longer do I want a life based on possibilities and visions of chance, a life spent trying to make dreams come true. I want a God-planned and purpose-filled life. And I want others to experience the same. I want others to know that our loving God has something more for us than our own personal wants. He offers the reality of a living relationship with Himself and an abundant life filled with possibilities that we cannot begin to imagine.

—BOBBI, CENTRAL AND EASTERN EUROPE

Father, FORGIVE ME WHEN I HAVE MY OWN AGENDA RATHER THAN FOLLOWING YOUR PLAN FOR MY LIFE. THANK YOU THAT THOSE WHO FOLLOW YOU TO THE INTERNATIONAL FIELD GAVE UP PERSONAL GOALS TO SHARE CHRIST WITH A LOST WORLD. GIVE ME A PASSION TO SUPPORT THEIR WORK WITH MY PRAYERS AND RESOURCES, NO MATTER THE COST TO MY TIME OR WALLET. *Amen.*

Walking for Jesus

"It shall be that you will drink of the brook, and I have commanded the ravens to provide for you there." 1 Kings 17:4 (NASB)

Brand-new Christians were to meet in the village of Ouanobe (WAH-no-bay) for discipleship, fellowship and discussion on how to share the gospel with Marense (muh-RON-say) and other Muslims around them. Four women from my village and I were going to walk the 35 miles to the meeting. At 3 a.m., we woke and took off through the bush. It was two hours before I saw the sunrise. With my heart full of joy, we shared songs, scriptures and encouragement.

We stopped along the way to rest under a mango tree. Opening my Bible, I read the story from 1 Kings 17 about when God told Elijah to go to the brook. It was there that the ravens brought him food. I shared with the women how God would provide for us.

The last two miles of the trip were by moonlight, and I was really struggling. Then the women began to minister to me, reminding me that God would provide. We arrived in Ouanobe at 10:30 p.m.

The meeting in Ouanobe was like a spiritual retreat. Other missionaries and I watched as the Marense led the meeting. Many of the Marense caught the vision of taking the gospel to those around them. On the last day of the meeting, the women from my village stood up and said, "If we can walk here in God's strength, He will enable us to go to villages closer than this one to share His gift of salvation!"

—TIFFANY, WEST AFRICA

Heavenly Father, YOU ENABLE US TO DO FAR MORE THAN WE CAN IMAGINE. THANK YOU FOR THESE AFRICAN WOMEN AND YOUNG MISSIONARIES WHO ARE WILLING TO DO WHATEVER IT TAKES TO SPREAD THE GOSPEL. CONTINUE TO USE THEM TO REACH MUSLIMS IN WEST AFRICA FOR CHRIST. *Amen.*

Whatever it takes to spread the gospel

"But the Lord said to Ananias, 'Go! This man is my chosen instrument to carry my name before the Gentiles and their kings and before the people of Israel. I will show him how much he must suffer for my name.'" Acts 9:15–16 (NIV)

Several Miskito (mees-KEE-toh) pastors visited the small village of Tasbapain (TAHS-bah-PINE). As a result, a small group of believers was established. These new believers asked if a pastor could be sent to help them start a church in their village.

A young man named Joram (hor-AHM), who had been assisting one of the established pastors, was willing to go. He, his wife and their two children left their extended family and fields, carrying everything they owned in three sacks. They traveled in the back of a pickup truck for three hours over difficult dirt roads and then walked for three hours into the village of Tasbapain.

Three months later, Joram came into town to see me since I am a nurse. Joram's wife was sick. Both children were thin with bloated bellies. I gave him parasite medication and vitamins. He excitedly told me about the new Christians and growth of the church in Tasbapain.

I still wasn't sure how to treat Joram's wife and children until another pastor told me that Joram and his family had nothing to eat. Since the group of believers in Tasbapain was small, they were not able to help much. Joram and his family were eating nothing but wild bananas and yucca root, which have little nutritional value. Joram, his wife and children were literally starving.

They were willing to take on hardship to spread the gospel. I was humbled by the passion that Joram had to spread the good news.

—VIOLA, MIDDLE AMERICA AND THE CARIBBEAN

Lord, HELP ME TO BE WILLING TO SERVE WHEREVER YOU CALL ME, WHATEVER THE COST. PLEASE PROVIDE THE NEEDS AND ENCOURAGE THE MISKITO PASTORS OF HONDURAS AND NICARAGUA AS THEY STRUGGLE PHYSICALLY. MAY THEY BE A LIGHT IN THE DARKNESS. *Amen.*

How much will it cost?

"He said to me: 'It is done. I am the Alpha and the Omega, the Beginning and the End. To him who is thirsty I will give to drink without cost from the spring of the water of life.'" Revelation 21:6 (NIV)

The street was lined with people waiting to see medical volunteers from America.

"Do you want to see the dentist, nurse, physical therapist or eye team?"

"How much will it cost?"

"Do you want someone to pray with you?"

"How much will it cost?"

They all seemed incredulous that the services were free. One elderly gentleman asked that our team pray for his disabled wife. The team prayed and asked the husband if they could go and pray with her.

"How much will it cost?"

They followed the man and entered his apartment. His 80-year-old wife was sitting on the couch, eyes closed. The husband lovingly raised the worn face of his bride of many years. She opened her eyes and became aware of the visitors for the first time.

"Dear, these men are here to pray for you."

Her only spoken words: "How much will it cost?"

Yes, there was a cost. It cost Jesus Christ everything. It cost the Americans who traveled so far at their own expense to work long hours in less than comfortable conditions. It cost our Russian-speaking Christians. They came face to face with the question, what will it cost for us to continue working here?

We pay the cost so that others may receive the gift of salvation. What cost are you willing to pay to see others come to Christ?

—CATHY, CENTRAL AND EASTERN EUROPE

Father, YOU GAVE YOUR ONLY SON THAT WE MIGHT HAVE LIFE. MAY I MAKE SACRIFICES IN MY LIFE IN ORDER TO SEE OTHERS COME TO CHRIST. SEND MANY VOLUNTEERS TO EASTERN EUROPE FOR THE CAUSE OF CHRIST. *Amen.*

Yes, teach me!

"Though I am free and belong to no man, I make myself a slave to everyone, to win as many as possible. ... To the weak, I became weak, I have become all things to all men, so that by all possible means I might save some. I do all this for the sake of the gospel, that I may share in its blessings."
1 Corinthians 9:19, 22–23 (NIV)

My "paper assignment" said I was to train pastors' wives. I studied an African language and read books about Northern Africa. I was ready, or so I thought.

At my first meeting with village women, I introduced myself and mentioned why I came to their country. Their first question was, "What can you, a youth, never married, teach us? You do not know us or the hardships of our lives." Truth hurts—it cuts a person down, but usually to the right size.

They were right. I had never married, and that made me a youth in Africa. Plus, I did not know what it was like to be an African woman. I knew the freedom of America and the relative ease of our modern society. What did I have to teach them?

Finally, I asked the women if they would teach me. If, during their training of me, they found something worthy in my life, maybe then I could teach them God's Word. Laughter erupted because it was the first time a missionary had ever asked to work with them in the fields. However, the apostle Paul said, "I have become all things to all men."

My "training" went well. I learned from the women, and they saw His light in me. They asked me to teach His Word. We sat together under the mango tree and studied the Scriptures.

Sometimes, the best way to witness is by getting a new perspective. Are you willing to be vulnerable so God's Word can be received?

—D.S., NORTHERN AFRICA AND THE MIDDLE EAST

Father, MAKE ME VULNERABLE TO UNDERSTAND OTHERS. HELP ME TO SEE LIFE FROM THEIR PERSPECTIVES. MAY YOU OPEN DOORS THAT WILL LEAD TO MINISTERING TO OTHERS. TAKE AWAY MY STUBBORN PRIDE! TEACH ME TO BE YOUR HUMBLE SERVANT. *Amen.*

Molded by the Potter

"The word which came to Jeremiah from the LORD saying, 'Arise and go down to the potter's house and there I will announce My words to you.'"
Jeremiah 18:1–2 (NASB)

I had everything that I really wanted. I was a mother of two lively pre-schoolers and a wife to a wonderful man. We owned a little house, had great friends and ministered through our local church. I was content.

My husband began to talk seriously with me about serving God overseas. I didn't even want to pray about this at first. Yet not communicating with God left me even more anxious. I struggled to open my spirit to God's communication, but my ears were muffled and my vision clouded by my ideas of what my life would be like in a foreign land.

At some point, God led me to these verses in Jeremiah. Jeremiah watches the village potter molding a pot on the wheel. Then the potter chooses a different shape and use for the vessel. He begins again, shaping the pot for its new purpose. God tells Jeremiah that it's His choice what to do with Israel. I knew what God was saying to me. He had the right to change my plans, to shape me so that I could be involved in an eternal plan. I grieved over the loss of my plan and the dreams that would never be fulfilled. But my Father was patient, and He continued to change my focus through many scriptures, songs and sermons.

Trusting Him with my life and the lives of the people I love has freed me to be part of His plan and make His purpose my own.

—CANDICE, NORTHERN AFRICA AND THE MIDDLE EAST

Loving Father, YOUR PLANS ARE NEVER FOR DESTRUCTION, BUT FOR GOOD. CALL MANY PEOPLE TO SERVE AS MISSIONARIES IN NORTHERN AFRICA AND THE MIDDLE EAST, A LAND THIRSTY FOR TRUTH. MAY I NEVER BE SO COMFORTABLE WITH MY LIFE THAT I IGNORE YOUR PLANS! MOLD ME INTO THE PERSON YOU DESIRE. *Amen.*

OCTOBER V

Spiritual Warfare

The devil is mean. To doubt that is a serious mistake. He plays hardball. He plays curveball. He plays anything but fair. And, most of all, he hopes to play you. The kind of Christian who actually tries to do this thing well is the very one he wants the most.

Satan is into numbers, not names. He wants to kill as many birds with one stone as possible. That's why he wants people of influence more than anyone. He'll also do anything he can to shut down those who show the potential for influence. Take Peter, for instance. At the time of Christ's earthly ministry, Simon Peter fumbled the ball as often as he carried it. Satan, however, watched him closely and knew he had the potential and the passion to be dangerous to the kingdom of darkness. So he came for him.

If you read the 22nd chapter of Luke carefully, you'll note that Christ obviously allowed Satan to "*sift [Peter] like wheat*" (v. 31, NASB). Christ had the authority to forbid the enemy that right. Why didn't He? Because Peter apparently had some things that needed sifting. We can take this truth to the spiritual bank: Christ never allows Satan a sieve unless the object could use a sift. In effect, we might imagine Christ putting it something like this: "You can either let Me prune you [John 15], or I can use the devil to scare it out of you." Trust one who knows: You want the former, not the latter.

I may not know a ton about biblical contentment, dear brother or sister, but I know a heap about spiritual warfare. I've learned a few things the hard way. The devil is very real, and he's trying to get to Christ by getting to us. We are not imagining that the heat of spiritual battle is wildly intensifying. Satan's fury is escalating just as Revelation 12:12 promises: "*He is filled with fury, because he knows that his time is short*" (NIV).

In the final movie based on J. R. R. Tolkien's trilogy, *The Return of the King*, Gandalf senses the intensification of evil and makes a statement that sends chills up my spine: "The board is set. The pieces are moving." As we prepare for the return of the real King, the board is set and the pieces are indeed moving.

Satan is sly. His motto? "Whatever works." He doesn't come in a red suit carrying a pitchfork. He fools spiritual people most easily when dressed as an angel of light. He comes as a friend. A Judas. Something that comforts our dysfunctional souls, pats our fleshy heads and sympathizes with our strongholds. *I understand you,* demon-Judas claims. He tries to gain our trust and assure us of things like this: *No one could blame you. You deserve this. No one will ever know. God will forgive you anyway. You can't help it. Go ahead. Don't resist it. It's not that bad. Everybody's like this. No one's really free. Indulge. No harm done.* Then one day Judas kisses you on the cheek and betrays you, and you see him for who he is. The result isn't pretty.

The devil is after all of us. Revelation 12:11 tells us we overcome him by the blood of the Lamb and the word of our testimony. Once we've been covered by the blood of the Lamb, Satan can't uncover us. So what's an accuser to do? Go for our testimony. The more powerful the testimony, the more powerfully he'll try to take it. The devil wants no one more than a wholehearted, sincerely devoted lover of Christ. He knows, however, that they don't often bite obvious bait. They must be seduced (2 Cor. 11:2–3). And that's his specialty.

I want to say a word in behalf of devoted servants of God who have been "had" by the devil. Folks out there who don't follow Christ closely enough to threaten the devil have no idea the level of warfare servants who are a threat are fighting. I'm not making excuses. Sin still stinks, and allowing ourselves to be seduced is evidence of severe foolishness. I'm simply saying that those fighting the daily battles on the front lines need a tremendous amount of prayer and accountability. It is hot out there, and many of us have been burned. This I will also say: Many of us got burned because we refused along the way to let God deal with our stuff. We allowed some areas of our lives to remain unsanctified and therefore uncovered, and the enemy knew just where to hit us. If he's anything at all, he's an experienced archer. He doesn't bother shooting fiery darts at well-covered places.

Let's all wise up. Some of us aren't fighting the fire; we're playing with fire. Flirting with the devil. Stop it! Stop it now before all hell literally breaks loose.

"Test everything. Hold on to the good. Avoid every kind of evil. May God himself, the God of peace, sanctify you through and through. May your whole spirit, soul and body be kept blameless at the coming of our Lord Jesus Christ. The one who calls you is faithful and he will do it" (I Thess. 5:21–24, NIV).

—*Beth Moore*

Wading through evil

"The eyes of the LORD are on the righteous and his ears are attentive to their cry."
Psalm 34:15 (NIV)

A dense Amazon jungle lined each side of the river, but the dugout canoe glided smoothly through the water. The ride was peaceful, yet we knew what awaited us just around the next bend.

The indigenous people were secure in their daily routines, but they didn't know joy, love and peace that only God can provide. This was replaced by the fear of the witch doctors and the belief that their village had been turned over to evil spirits.

That night, the drumbeats of the witch doctors mingled with the sounds of the jungle, interrupting the rest that we so desperately needed. Fighting the only way we knew how, our prayers and songs of praise were lifted from our hammocks to our Father above. Surrounding ourselves with His presence was our only hope of wading through the evil and reaching these people with God's love.

Daily the spiritual battle raged around us. Dedicated, unceasing prayer was our weapon. And in the midst of the darkness, God paved the way. Finally, after years of attempting to break down the walls, a crack appeared in the spiritual fortress, and God's Word has been openly shared among some of the people in the village.

The few present opened their hearts and minds. Their faces lit up with eagerness as the Bible stories were shared for the first time. As they continue to seek answers, Jesus Christ will be made known. This is just the beginning. May God's glory continue to shine through the darkness!

—MARGIE, MIDDLE AMERICA AND THE CARIBBEAN

Almighty God, YOU ARE BREAKING DOWN THE WALLS AND FORTRESSES IN PLACES WHERE DARKNESS FORMERLY CONTROLLED. THANK YOU FOR THE WEAPON OF PRAYER. CONTINUE TO SHINE YOUR LIGHT IN THE CARIBBEAN BASIN FOR YOUR GLORY. *Amen.*

Worthless blessings

"I will bless them. ... I will send down showers in season, there will be showers of blessing. ... They will know that I am the Lord, when I break the bars of their yoke and rescue them from the hands of those who enslaved them." Ezekiel 34:26–27 (NIV)

Life in Ethiopia is often experienced on the roads by greeting people and enjoying the kinship of others. People are everywhere, whether in the villages or the cities.

My 6-month-old son loves to accompany me on daily walks around our community. I will strap him on my back as we go to the market, the post office or our neighbors' homes. An afternoon walk allows us the opportunity to intersect peoples' lives, build relationships and share the joy Christ gives us with others.

Quite often, the "foreign baby" is the main attraction of the day. Ethiopians are incredibly gracious, overwhelming us with affection and warm greetings. "How are you? Did you spend the night well? How is your health?" they ask politely. They will spend time shaking our hands and giving my son kisses. Ethiopian women, however, typically give more than kisses.

It isn't unusual for my son to be spit on by elderly Ethiopian women ... as a blessing! Ethiopians fear that evil spirits will enter a beautiful baby. To safeguard the baby, they will spit on the baby, hoping the spirits will think the baby is not beautiful. When we return home, my son gets a good bath!

Spiritual darkness is repulsive, just as spittle is in the face. It is my prayer that these superstitions and fears will be replaced with the truth. I look forward to the day when Ethiopian women will shower blessings from the Father over their children.

—J.L., NORTHERN AFRICA AND THE MIDDLE EAST

Heavenly Father, MAY YOUR SPIRIT DRAW ETHIOPIANS TO TRUTH THROUGH YOUR WORD. MAY THEY HAVE THEIR EYES OPENED TO SEE THAT YOU ARE THE ONE WHO BLESSES, AND YOU ARE THE ANSWER TO FREE THEM FROM THE BONDAGE OF DARKNESS AND FEAR. *Amen.*

Bound in the belief of reincarnation

"The god of this world has blinded the minds of the unbelieving, that they might not see the light of the gospel of the glory of Christ, who is the image of God."
2 Corinthians 4:4 (NASB)

After walking down steps, I climb into a rickety boat on the Ganges (gan-GEES) River. This "holy" river is milky white from the pollution. Two boys rowing are silently straining to move the boat against the current. As I look at the city just before sunset, I see temples lined up as far as the eye can see—temples to more gods than I can count. Small fires are everywhere—burning bodies of the dead. Families pilgrimage to this place with the bodies of their dead in order to cremate and throw the ashes into the Ganges. They believe that this act will usher them into a higher state in their next life.

My attention is diverted to a man carrying a pelvis bone. According to their traditions, certain bones should not be allowed to burn completely, so they throw them in the river.

Sacrifices of dance, incense and fire are offered by Brahmin priests in order to receive special blessings and good karma. Heard are loud drums, bells and a man singing Hindu worship songs.

The hour spent on the river reveals the heart of Hinduism. It portrays the belief that rituals and good deeds will give a better life the next go-round. Until they achieve perfection, they believe they will continue in the cycle of reincarnation.

I ask the Most High to use me to bring a message of hope and freedom to these people. They need to know the God that holds mercy in His hands.

—C., SOUTH ASIA

Father, OPEN THE HINDUS' EYES TO LOVE, YOUR VERY ESSENCE. USE CHRISTIAN WORKERS TO COMMUNICATE THE LOVE OF CHRIST TO THOSE AROUND THEM. HELP ME TO BE A TESTIMONY TO HINDU PEOPLE IN MY OWN COMMUNITY. *Amen.*

Light versus darkness

"I have come as Light into the world, so that everyone who believes in Me will not remain in darkness." John 12:46 (NASB)

Every year, the Hindu community in our country celebrates a festival called Thaipusam (tie-POOH-sahm). During this festival, devotees to the Hindu lord Murugan (MOO-roo-gun) journey on a walk of faith, piercing their bodies with skewers and hooks and walking for miles as proof of their devotion.

One Sunday we realized the Thaipusam walk for our city was being held that night, and the temple right next to the church was the center of the festival! The church lot was literally engulfed in a sea of Hindus.

As we sang praise choruses inside the church, we were bombarded by the incredibly loud Hindu music and beating drums coming from the throngs of people outside. The sense of spiritual oppression was real. Then the power went out for a minute or so and came back on. Several minutes later, the power went out again. Then again. Each time the power went off, the music from the temple seemed even louder. It was as if we were witnessing physical effects of an unseen spiritual battle.

As Christians, we are assured of victory through Jesus Christ. Our God is the only true God. He proved His faithfulness on that night as well. You see, the main event of that Sunday's service was the baptism of 11 migrant factory workers from the Hindu kingdom of Nepal! I watched the light and joy on the faces of these former Hindus as they celebrated their new life in Jesus Christ, even as those still trapped in darkness raged around us.

—C.W., PACIFIC RIM

Heavenly Father, YOU ARE THE TRUE GOD. PENETRATE THE DARKNESS WITH YOUR LIGHT. STRENGTHEN CHRISTIANS IN AREAS WHERE HINDUISM DECEIVES THE MASSES. *Amen.*

Dispelling the Darkness

"I am sending you to them to open their eyes and turn them from darkness to light, and from the power of Satan to God, so that they may receive forgiveness of sins and a place among those who are sanctified by faith in me."
Acts 26:17–18 (NIV)

Spiritual warfare is intense on the upper Suriname (sir-AH-nahm) River. A group recently came to minister to the Saramaccans (sair-ah-MAH-cans) in Jesus' name. On the second night of the trip, they witnessed the salvation of many in the village where they were staying.

In the middle of the same night, loud shouts woke them. Two of the Saramaccan pastors were having nightmares. The two explained their dreams to the team. Oddly enough, they both dreamed the *exact* same thing—darkness was coming up over the river just above the village. The men identified the darkness as the power of Satan. Everyone stayed up for a while, praying for the two pastors.

The next morning, the team heard drums and shouting, this time down by the riverside. There they discovered a group from the village who was swaying to the beat of drums. When one would fall down, five or six others would pick the person up over their heads and throw the person into the water. This continued all day long.

One of the Saramaccans explained that in the middle of the night, three anacondas had become trapped in some fishing nets. They believe that a powerful spirit lives in the anaconda. Thus, they conducted the ceremony so as to appease the spirits.

The battle continues to rage today in this village, but there is a vibrant and growing church bringing the Saramaccans from darkness to light, from the power of Satan to God.

—TIM AND JUDY, MIDDLE AMERICA AND THE CARIBBEAN

Father, YOU HAVE ABSOLUTE AUTHORITY OVER THE DOMINION OF SATAN. I PRAY THE POWER SATAN HAS OVER THE SARAMACCAN PEOPLE WILL BE BROKEN, AND THE LIGHT OF JESUS WILL DISPERSE THE DARKNESS. IN THE NAME OF JESUS, I ALSO PRAY THAT I WILL BE MORE THAN A CONQUEROR TODAY OVER THE DEVIL'S SCHEMES AGAINST ME. *Amen.*

Are you having a bad day?

"For He rescued us from the domain of darkness, and transferred us to the king-dom of His beloved Son, in whom we have redemption, the forgiveness of sins."
Colossians 1:13–14 (NASB)

I had heard sermons on spiritual warfare and had a deep appreciation for what we were taught on the subject while at the training center. I knew that the Lord would never forsake me, but it was not until I was in a city dominated by spiritual darkness that I experienced spiritual warfare. It was not dramatic, but rather the enemy looking for every little way that he could tempt me to be unfaithful to the Lord of my life.

His process was something like this:

Step 1: Plan the attack to be while her husband is out of town.

Step 2: Weaken her physically through fatigue from the intense heat, or better yet, make sure she winds up in the hospital.

Step 3: Destroy the structure needed in the home for homeschool-ing and temporary single parenting by taking her house helper from her.

Step 4: Make sure she loses Internet service so that she can't e-mail her husband.

Not all these things happened when my husband traveled, but at least two of them did each time. Jokingly, I tell my husband that he can't travel anymore. Of course that would hinder ministry greatly.

The Lord is showing me how He demonstrates His strength through my weakness. Recently, I was able to allow God to do just this. Even my child remarked, "Mom, you are handling this very well." I was able to share with him that I had prayed for wisdom and that the Holy Spirit was giving me love, joy and peace.

—S.S., SOUTH ASIA

Father, I RECOGNIZE THAT EACH DIFFICULT SITUATION IN MY LIFE IS AN OPPORTUNITY TO EXPERIENCE YOUR OVERCOMING GRACE. PLEASE ENCOURAGE WIVES WHO SERVE YOU, ES-PECIALLY WHEN THEIR HUSBANDS TRAVEL. WHEN WE'RE CAUGHT OFF GUARD BY SATAN'S ATTACKS, HELP US TO QUICKLY COMMIT OURSELVES TO YOU AND TO RESIST THE ENEMY'S TACTICS. *Amen.*

What if?

"Be strong and of good courage; do not be afraid, nor be dismayed, for the LORD your God is with you wherever you go." Joshua 1:9 (NKJV)

As I came to our gate, a truck pulled in front of me and some men jumped out. They forced their way into my vehicle, bound me and threw me in the backseat across the floorboard.

As I lay on the floor, I heard God speaking to me *loud* and *clear*. He told me to sit back and enjoy the ride. Prayer helped me stay calm as the bandits drove the truck across potholes, ditches and washboard surfaces. I had no idea where we were or where we were going. Despite this, I felt at total peace. God kept telling me that He was in control. I began praying and singing praises. After an hour and a half, the joyride was over. The bandits finally threw me out on the side of the road. I was fine!

After returning home, my mind started playing tricks with me. Replaying the scene, my thoughts twirled with "what ifs." It was hard to sleep. Praise God that scriptures came to mind and settled me down. So I began praying for Satan to be far removed from me. Each time a "what if" surfaced, I prayed or sang. God's love enveloped me. The "what ifs" didn't happen, so why be anxious?

Without the Lord, my ride with the bandits could have been life threatening, but His grace is sufficient. Giving every thought to the Lord during and after the situation is what brought total peace instead of fear.

—LINDY, CENTRAL, EASTERN AND SOUTHERN AFRICA

Precious Father, YOU ARE WORTHY OF MY TRUST. I KNOW THAT YOU WILL NOT LEAVE ME OR FORSAKE ME. PROTECT ME FROM THE EVIL ONE. PROTECT MISSIONARIES IN DANGEROUS SITUATIONS TODAY. PRESERVE THEIR VERY LIVES. *Amen.*

Twelve spies

"So watch your step, friends. Make sure there's no evil unbelief lying around that will trip you up and throw you off course, diverting you from the living God." Hebrews 3:12 (MSG)

Remember the 12 spies sent to check on the Promised Land? The majority told the bare facts about the land. Conquering the inhabitants would be difficult. The people were huge. It brought everyone to tears and discouragement.

I have often thought that I would never be like the 10 pessimistic spies, but I have lost hope in seeing salvation for the people around me. I have been discouraged to tears. Ten spies—that's me!

But in the story, God said to Moses, *"How long will these people treat me like dirt? How long refuse to trust me?"* (Num. 14:11, MSG). Have I been treating God like dirt by my musings and worries? I want to enter the Promised Land with my people just as much as Moses did. Like Moses, I didn't volunteer for the journey. I was enlisted. But I'm part of the army and will not retreat.

Those who did enter the Promised Land—what were their hearts like? I listen to Joshua's and Caleb's voices. Is there any of their spirit in me? *"The land we walked through and scouted out is a very good land—very good indeed. If GOD is pleased with us, he will lead us into that land. ... And he'll give it to us. Just don't rebel against GOD! And don't be afraid of those people. ... They have no protection and GOD is on our side. Don't be afraid of them!"* (Num. 14:7–9, MSG).

Oh Lord, give me the heart of Joshua and Caleb!

—A WORKER IN THE PACIFIC RIM

Father God, GIVE HOPE TO MISSIONARIES WHO ARE NOT SEEING RESULTS FROM THEIR EFFORTS TO EVANGELIZE. ENCOURAGE THEM THAT ONE DAY YOU WILL BRING GROWTH TO THE SEEDS THAT THEY PLANTED. MAY YOUR SPIRIT COVER THIS AREA IN THE PACIFIC RIM SO THAT MANY WILL TRULY COME TO CHRIST IN REPENTANCE. *Amen.*

When trials elevate self-pity

"Though he slay me, yet will I hope in him." Job 13:15a (NIV)

One difficult situation after another made its way into our lives. I didn't have time to get over one thing until another invaded. I began to feel discouraged. Discouragement led to spiritual and emotional fatigue, and I didn't feel like praying or seeking the Lord in His Word. Then I began to feel guilty and undeserving of anything God could give, so I avoided Him. Avoiding the Lord leads you straight into the arms of hopelessness and deception.

God has to be so mad at me. He's just waiting to drop the hammer and give me what I deserve, I thought. "What if?" became a constant refrain as many lies and worries attacked my mind every day. I made the mistake of mulling over them instead of counterattacking with the truth of God's Word. Finally, I came out of my spiritual coma by asking God's forgiveness, accepting it with thanksgiving and reading His Word. I didn't do it because I felt like it. I did it in order to return to my first love for God and to leave the misery behind.

"Come to me, all you who are weary and burdened, and I will give you rest" (Matt. 11:28, NIV). Jesus said to me, *Trust Me. Live and breathe in My love.*

Do life's stresses and heartaches have you disturbed and defeated? Don't get lost in the feelings. Hang on to the truth in God's Word. Trust Him with whatever comes, because remember—He's working it all together for your good!

—ANITA, SOUTH AMERICA

Father, GETTING SIDETRACKED BY TRIALS IS A STRUGGLE FOR ME. WHATEVER HAPPENS, LORD, I PRAY THAT I WILL BE TRUE TO YOU. THANK YOU THAT YOU ARE FORGIVING AND FAITHFUL WHEN I AM FAITHLESS. HELP ME TO KEEP TO THE STRAIGHT PATH. HELP MISSIONARIES AS WELL STAY FOCUSED ON THEIR RELATIONSHIP WITH YOU. *Amen.*

Needing new life

"For we did not follow cleverly devised tales when we made known to you the power and the coming of our Lord Jesus Christ, but we were eyewitnesses of His majesty." 2 Peter 1:16 (NASB)

Joy is a typical Ewe (YOU) young lady. She is not ambitious for money or position. She is a gentle-spirited girl whose greatest hopes are to fall in love, have a family and be freed from tormenting nightmares and fears that have plagued her for years. An evil spirit visits Joy on a nightly basis. Women of Joy's culture call this spirit "the dark oppressor."

According to Joy, the spirit climbs onto her chest and presses upon her as if to crush the life out. The only remedies Joy knows for warding off this spirit are to sleep with a knife under her pillow and to carry with her verses of the Koran written on small sheets of paper.

Joy has other problems in the physical realm as well. She has long since been of marrying age, and her parents are forcing her to get married. As she reflects on the torments of her nights and her days, Joy says, "I want a new life." Joy has heard some about Jesus, but she has not been convinced that she should believe in Him and follow Him.

Joy needs prayer, the power of the Lord in her life and truth to be preached so that she may find faith to confess Jesus as Lord and to experience redemption from the kingdom of darkness. Thank God He has sent His laborers to walk, pray and share with her consistently as she makes her journey toward His kingdom!

—"ELIZABETH CARMICHAEL," CENTRAL ASIA

Holy Father, I PRAY THAT YOU WILL WORK IN THE LIVES OF THOSE BOUND IN THEIR TRADITIONAL BELIEFS BY SPIRITS OF DECEPTION. REVEAL YOURSELF THROUGH YOUR WORD AND TESTIMONIES OF CHRISTIANS TO THE EWE PEOPLE, WHO NEED THE FREEDOM OFFERED BY THE PRINCE OF PEACE. HELP ME TO TAKE AUTHORITY IN THE NAME OF JESUS OVER OPPRESSIVE THOUGHTS AND ATTITUDES THAT THREATEN TO CONSUME MY MIND. *Amen.*

River spirits

"How long will you waver between two opinions? If the Lord is God, follow him; but if Baal is God, follow him." 1 Kings 18:21 (NIV)

As we neared the Kaabong (kah-BONG) River, we encountered a group of 20 women. I was mostly ignoring them until my national friend asked me to play the first song for them from a cassette tape. The cassette was of a Lokolia (low-koh-LEE-ah) group singing songs from a week before.

Almost everyone stayed for the entire song, but you could tell that they were less than enthusiastic and even a bit antagonistic. When the song finished, our companion told the Bible story of the fall of Lucifer. Afterward, I said, "The river spirit that you sacrifice to is one of the fallen angels that God cast out of heaven. God made them and is stronger than them. Why would you pray to them instead of to God? Be careful that you are not deceived by them as Lucifer deceived them."

As we left, a middle-aged woman grabbed our companion and said, "We know who you are now. If you steal our river spirit and it does not rain this year, we will come after you."

Perhaps our "showdown at Mount Carmel" is in the making. I remembered what Ahab said to Elijah in 1 Kings 18 when he saw him after some years of drought: *"Is that you, you troubler of Israel?"* Elijah responded, *"I have not made trouble for Israel. But you and your father's family have. You have abandoned the Lord's commands and have followed the Baals"* (vv. 17–18, NIV).

May we never put anything before the one, true God!

—JOHN, CENTRAL, EASTERN AND SOUTHERN AFRICA

Holy Father, YOU REQUIRE THAT WE NOT PUT OTHER GODS BEFORE YOU. YOU ARE THE ONE, TRUE GOD! I EXALT YOU AS THE KING OF KINGS AND LORD OF LORDS! BRING LIGHT AND TRUTH TO THE PEOPLE OF UGANDA WHO WORSHIP THE SPIRITS RATHER THAN YOU. *Amen.*

Mothers seeking protection

*"Therefore this is what the sovereign LORD says: I am against your magic charms
with which you ensnare people like birds and I will tear them from your arms;
I will set free the people that you ensnare like birds. ... Then, you will know that
I am the LORD." Ezekiel 13:20, 21b (NIV)*

I visited an organization that works with unwed women. These women
decided to keep their children, despite cultural pressures. Most of these
women were disowned by their families. Some of these women were
raped. Some became pregnant through incest. Some were pregnant because of their own choices.

As I talked with the girls, one wanted me to meet her baby. I quietly
prayed for the child's salvation one day.

As the girl continued to introduce me to the other 11 babies, I
noticed that one was unhappy. They claimed the baby was sick, but as
I knelt to touch the child, I noticed that there were strings of beads
wound between the child's center finger and wrist. On the bracelet was
a charm of the hand of Fatima (FAH-tee-mah)—an item within folk
Islam for warding off evil. I asked if I could hold the child, and as I did,
I noticed a strange aroma surrounding the child. This young baby girl
was covered in incense!

As I held the child, I prayed for her protection from these evil
amulets and methods. I prayed for the mother who put these upon her
child in hopes of protecting this frail life. As I prayed, I realized how
every mother seeks to protect and comfort her children. I try to do
the same with my own children. The best way to comfort and protect
children is to give them over to God. He is stronger than any charm
this young mother could ever buy.

—L., NORTHERN AFRICA AND THE MIDDLE EAST

Heavenly Father, MY CHILDREN (PRESENT AND FUTURE) BELONG TO YOU. RIGHT NOW I PRAY
FOR _____. GUIDE THEM AS THEY MAKE CHOICES IN LIFE. *Amen.*

Go away!

"Begone, Satan!" Matthew 4:10 (ESV)

What is your worst animal fear? Spiders, snakes or maybe rats? My worst fear is encountering snakes. Sure enough, just a few months after living in South Asia, I came face to face with my worst fear.

One day when I came out of the store, I noticed some young men who were colorfully dressed in religious garb. I kept my eyes down and hoped they would not approach me. To my dismay, they came within the circle of my downward vision. I looked up and came face to face with a snake—a big snake. It was around the neck of the fellow who blocked my way.

The young man picked up the head of the snake and brought it close to my face. I instinctively backed up a step and said, *"Jao!"* (JOW-oh), which means, "Go away!" I tried to step around him, and he came to my vehicle. I got in quickly and locked the door. To my dismay, I realized I had left the window of the car down. I started rolling my window up, and he pressed his face and hands against the window. He stared at me and started to say things that I could not understand. I sensed a real presence of evil.

A response welled up in me to look him in the eyes and say, "In Jesus' name, go away!" He immediately removed his hands from my window and turned and left. The threat was gone because there is power in the name of Jesus.

—S.S., SOUTH ASIA

Father, GIVE CHRISTIAN WORKERS POWER IN THE NAME OF JESUS TO SEND SATAN RUNNING! THANK YOU THAT I AM A CONQUEROR OVER EVIL BECAUSE OF JESUS. *Amen.*

The powerful name of Jesus

"It was for freedom that Christ set us free; therefore keep standing firm and do not be subject again to a yoke of slavery." Galatians 5:1 (NASB)

We sat under the stars with more than 350 of our Zambian sisters at a women's meeting. My mind could not stay focused on the message. I could not block out the pitiful cries coming from a small building in the distance.

I knew the minute we adjourned that I had to go there to pray for those sick babies. So my friends and I trekked our way through the darkness with the aid of one small flashlight.

When we got to the door, we saw the silhouettes of the sick and hurting. Ivey, our translator, announced that we wanted to pray for those who were ill. Immediately, a mass of people came forward or called out to us.

We placed our hands on babies and mothers and prayed loudly over all of the noise. As we called on the Healer, Jehovah-Rapha, women fell to the floor—manifesting demons. The powerful name of Jesus, the One who came to set the captives free, brought them to their knees. Once we finished praying there, we moved our prayer session to a more private place.

Some women chose freedom that weekend. They rebuked their former masters, burned their charms, confessed their sins and began a new life in Christ. It was an amazing show of God's power.

There is nothing present in our lives or past that He cannot free us from; we only have to be willing to call on the name of Jesus. John 8:36 says, *"So if the Son sets you free, you will be free indeed"* (NIV).

—CINDY, CENTRAL, EASTERN AND SOUTHERN AFRICA

Your Name is Almighty God! YOU ARE THE MOST HIGH! ALL THINGS BOW TO YOU, FOR YOU ARE THE ONE, TRUE GOD! THANK YOU THAT I HAVE POWER OVER THE EVIL ONE IN THE NAME OF JESUS. *Amen.*

Let them dine with Jesus

"Behold, I stand at the door and knock; if anyone hears My voice and opens the door, I will come into him and will dine with him, and he with Me."
Revelation 3:20 (NASB)

We have walked to many villages and usually have been welcomed warmly. Most Muslims serve us a meal out of respect, although they do not eat with us due to a religious prohibition against eating with Christians. Eating together implies a close relationship.

One of our visits was to a man considered by villagers to be sinless and spiritually powerful. There is a belief among the Fulbe (FULL-bay) that God cannot refuse the prayer of such a man. He had heard about us before our arrival and knew who we were. About 25 of his students of the Koran stayed close-by so as not to miss the approaching conflict. We all sat down under a mango tree. Part of me yearned to tell him, tell them all, about Jesus; and the other part, I admit, was fear. This man was not sinless, and I knew that I could not allow this mistaken belief to intimidate me.

The leader avoided religious discussions and preferred to ask us about our homeland. At one point he criticized America, but we quietly reminded ourselves that we were here to tell people of Christ instead of getting involved in political debates. He served us a meal but did not eat with us. Toward the end of our visit, we presented him with Scripture, which he reluctantly accepted.

I have thought often of this greatly respected and feared man. He leads many astray, yet God wants all men to know Him. We desire to see Muslims dine with Jesus and to be free from false doctrine.

—ROBERT AND RHONDA, WEST AFRICA

Father, THANK YOU FOR WELCOMING ME TO YOUR BANQUETING TABLE. I PRAY THAT MUSLIMS IN WEST AFRICA AND ACROSS THE WORLD WOULD CHOOSE TO SIT AT YOUR TABLE AS WELL. Amen.

Looking toward the Promised Land

"Commit your way to the Lord, trust also in Him, and He shall bring it to pass."
Psalm 37:5 (NIV)

Old Pedro is a diviner in the village of Morrocoy (moe-rroh-COY). His family is animist, like most of the Guajibo (gwa-HEE-boh) people group. On a back wall of their house is a shelf. The sight of the shelf with its herbs, potions and paraphernalia is a powerful reminder that behind the apparent friendliness of the Guajibo awaits the prince of darkness with his legion of spirits.

Pedro rose to greet me, leading me to the trunk of a mango tree near the back of his hut. Something was about to take place. News had spread throughout the village that another diviner from this community was trying to prevent my move into the village. Old Pedro's only rational hope for this diviner's outrage was the cure in the bottle that fit snug in his pants' back pocket. Pedro pulled out the small bottle and pressed it toward me.

With his fist still tightly grasped around the bottle, I quickly thanked Old Pedro for his care of me without taking the bottle. Then I began to tell the story of Joshua and the obstacles he and the Israelites faced as they prepared to enter the Promised Land. Only by obeying God's instructions could Israel have victory over Jericho. Joshua needed to believe God's Word to be true and to faithfully act upon it.

Just as His timing came for Israel through Joshua to enter the Promised Land, God's timing will come for me to enter the Guajibo villages. Through prayer, faith and obedience, that day will come.

—CAROL, SOUTH AMERICA

Eternal Father, I REST IN THE KNOWLEDGE THAT IN YOUR PERFECT, PRECISE TIMING, WALLS OF RESISTANCE COME TUMBLING DOWN AND NO EARTHLY POWER CAN STAND AGAINST YOUR PURPOSES. I PRAY THAT YOU WILL OPEN DOORS FOR THE GOSPEL THAT NO MAN CAN SHUT AND THAT THE GUAJIBO AND OTHER UNREACHED PEOPLE GROUPS WILL TURN TO YOU AS LORD OVER ALL. *Amen.*

Power over the enemy

"'Lord, even the demons submit to us in your name.' He replied, 'I saw Satan fall like lightning from heaven. I have given you authority to trample on snakes and scorpions and to overcome all the power of the enemy; nothing will harm you. However, do not rejoice that the spirits submit to you, but rejoice that your names are written in heaven.'" Luke 10:17–20 (NIV)

Roger works with university students in the Democratic Republic of the Congo. He came to know Christ a few years ago, but his family still practices traditional African religions, consults witch doctors and worships their ancestors. When his sister came to live in Kinshasa, Roger prayed that she would become a Christian.

Soon after arriving in the capital city, Roger's sister became very ill with tuberculosis. Roger grabbed some students from his Bible study and rushed to the hospital to pray. His sister was barely conscious as the group prayed for her.

Suddenly, the sick woman started screaming at the top of her lungs. The voice that came out was not her own, but the voice of a demonic spirit. The voice screamed in agony anytime the group prayed.

Roger addressed the spirit, "In the name of Jesus Christ, come out." The sister fell into a deep sleep as the group prayed over her.

When the sister woke up, Roger shared about the sacrifice Jesus Christ made for her, and she asked Jesus into her life. Even though she died three days later, Roger rejoiced that she would be in heaven.

The Bible came to life right before the students' eyes. "I understand the Bible even more than before. This experience was just like when Jesus cast out spirits," Roger said. "That day, Acts came alive for me and my students. When you see God work like this, you can't keep quiet."

—DEBBIE, CENTRAL, EASTERN AND SOUTHERN AFRICA

Holy Father, THERE IS NO ONE LIKE YOU. YOU ARE KING OF KINGS AND LORD OF LORDS! THANK YOU FOR THE AUTHORITY I HAVE OVER SATAN IN THE NAME OF JESUS. AS LUTHER'S HYMN SHOUTS, "ONE LITTLE WORD WILL FELL HIM!" *In Jesus' name, amen.*

Point of decision

"The weapons we fight with are not the weapons of the world. On the contrary, they have divine power to demolish strongholds." 2 Corinthians 10:4 (NASB)

Chronological Bible storying is a method used for those who can best benefit from hearing and sharing Bible stories orally. We began storying with the Subba (SUE-bah) family when we heard that the father was ill. We offered to pray for him, and God gave us an opportunity to share the truth with him and his family.

We got to see God at work in amazing ways. Money was provided through the generosity of another for the father to have medical tests. The doctor found that he had an ulcer and was able to treat him. He was healed within weeks, and he and his family knew it was the Lord answering our prayers. Because of his healing, the Subbas, who are Hindus, no longer worship any of their gods. Although they have not yet accepted God's free gift of salvation, they believe that everything that we have shared with them from the Word is true. They had never heard any of the Bible stories, and it is pure joy for us to see their faces as they hear these truths for the first time.

They have reached a point of decision. The enemy is notorious for fiercely attacking those who seek to leave the dominion of darkness.

Do you know someone who is close to coming to Christ? Do not give up in your ministry to him or her, and keep praying fervently that this person, just like Mr. Subba, will have the boldness and desire to follow the one, true God.

—A WORKER IN SOUTH ASIA

Heavenly Father, I PRAY IN THE NAME OF JESUS THAT THE STRONGHOLDS PREVENTING THIS FAMILY AND OTHERS IN SOUTH ASIA AND _____ WILL BE ABOLISHED. I PRAY THAT THEY WILL HAVE THE BOLDNESS, STRENGTH AND DESIRE TO FOLLOW YOU. GIVE ME STRENGTH, FATHER, TO CONTINUE TO LOVE, PRAY FOR AND MINISTER TO THESE. *Amen.*

In spirit and truth

"God is Spirit and those who worship must worship Him in spirit and truth."
John 4:24 (NIV)

After spending several days in my little village house with no running water or electricity, I headed into town. I could only spend a few days there, and I had a lot to get accomplished. As I reached the outskirts of the village, my attention turned from my list of things to do to intercessory prayer.

I met a procession of voodoo priestesses returning from a ceremony. Voodoo is a religion in southern Benin (beh-NIN) that worships spirits and ancestors. At first, I thought I would just step aside, but then I decided against this. Greetings are such a big part of the culture, and the women might have been offended had I not greeted them. So I did. Almost all of them greeted me in response, many of them shaking my hand.

But the thing that was so strange was that every single one of them greeted me in the language of her vodun (the spirit that would possess during the ceremony). Never had anything like this happened to me.

It could have been creepy or even a little scary; but as I walked away from them, I wept because they do not know the one, true God who is greater than all the spirits they worship. I wept because they do not know they are living in bondage and fear of vindictive spirits instead of serving God.

God set me free from the kingdom of darkness to which I, too, once belonged. He loves the people of Benin and longs to give them freedom from fear.

—DEBBY, WEST AFRICA

Heavenly Father, REVEAL TRUTH TO BENIN SO THAT VOODOO CAN BE SEEN FOR THE LIE THAT IT IS. SPIRITUALLY ARM THE MISSIONARIES WITH THE ARMOR OF GOD SO THAT THEY CAN STAND AGAINST SATAN AND HIS DECEPTION. FREE THESE PRIESTESSES FROM THE CHAINS OF SATAN. *Amen.*

Miracles and protection

"Your ways, oh God, are holy. What god is so great as our God? You are the God who performs miracles; you display your power among the peoples."
Psalm 77:13–14 (NIV)

In South Asia, Jesus is still in the miracle business. John 10:38 says to believe the miracles, so that you will be convinced that Jesus is the Son of God. Many people have believed in Jesus Christ because of amazing miracles they have witnessed.

Sherpa is a young man who grew up in a Hindu family. His father was a Hindu high priest who conducted religious ceremonies and *pujas* (POOH-jahs). (*Pujas* involve idol worship and rituals to placate gods and demons or to pray for protection.) His mother was mentally ill and tormented by demons for many years because of her husband's activities in the spirit world.

One day a Christian woman shared the gospel of Christ. Sherpa's mother believed and was immediately freed from the tormenting demons. Her mind became sane. As a result, Sherpa and his whole family believed—even his father.

After they became Christians, Sherpa and his sister used to run away from their Buddhist government school and hide whenever monks or lamas would come to conduct *pujas*. While they were hiding in the fields, he and his sister would pray fervently that they would not be found and forced to worship idols or participate in the *pujas*. When the monks would leave, Sherpa and his sister would return to school. No one ever saw them leaving or returning, and they were never missed.

Whenever I hear stories in which the power of God is demonstrated against the evil one, I am reminded that no one is as great as our God.

—J.D., SOUTH ASIA

O Lord, WHERE AMONG THE HEATHEN GODS IS THERE A GOD LIKE YOU? WHERE ARE THEIR MIRACLES? ALL THE NATIONS WILL COME AND BOW BEFORE YOU, LORD. FOR YOU ARE GREAT AND YOU ALONE ARE GOD. BRING FREEDOM THROUGH CHRIST TO PEOPLE GROUPS IN SOUTH ASIA WHO HAVE BEEN TRADITIONALLY CLOSED TO THE GOSPEL. *Amen.*

Like Mary Magdalene

"After this, Jesus traveled about from one town and village to another, proclaiming the good news of the kingdom of God. The Twelve were with him, and also some women who had been cured of evil spirits and diseases: Mary (called Magdalene) from whom seven demons had come out. ..." Luke 8:1–2 (NIV)

The village medium sat with almost 200 other Saramaccans (sair-ah-MAH-cans) watching the *JESUS* film. For the first time in her life, she heard the story of God's love through the sacrifice of His Son. When the invitation was given to follow Christ, she committed her life to Him together with all of her children and 170 others.

The event was not only the beginning of a spiritual awakening among this remote tribal group, but also the beginning of an incredible transformation for this woman. She later described how seven evil spirits inhabiting her house had tormented her. These spirits would take possession of her, and she would begin to speak for them. Her neighbors believed every word she said, and the village would offer sacrifices at the village totem poles to appease the spirits.

After her conversion, she discovered her freedom in Christ and locked up her house, turning her back on her former way of life. The other villagers became angry about the radical changes made by the former medium, her children and several other women.

During the following months, the woman helped to start the first church in her village. When she heard the story of Mary Magdalene, she wept and said, "That was my life." When she was baptized, she asked the church to change her name to Maria Magdala, the Saramaccan way of saying Mary Magdalene. Today, Maria has taught herself to read so that she can study the Bible and share it with others.

—TIM AND JUDY, MIDDLE AMERICA AND THE CARIBBEAN

Lord of lords, I WORSHIP AND PRAISE YOU FOR WHO YOU ARE, ONE WHO DEMOLISHES SATANIC STRONGHOLDS, SETS CAPTIVES FREE, AND RADICALLY TRANSFORMS AND EMPOWERS THOSE WHO TURN TO YOU. I PRAY THAT, LIKE MARY MAGDALENE, NEW CONVERTS IN SARAMACCAN VILLAGES WILL CONTINUE TO PROCLAIM, "I HAVE SEEN THE LORD!" *Amen.*

"Jesus has greater power than the spirits I serve"

"You are from God, little children, and have overcome them; because greater is He who is in you than he who is in the world." 1 John 4:4 (NASB)

The witch once caused fear in the people of her village in the Sudan. Because of her power, the people did whatever they could to appease her. Every time she would perform her magic, a crowd formed.

One day, two believers came to visit the village and saw a crowd. They joined to see what was going on and, immediately, the witch was unable to perform her magic. The two believers prayed that the Lord would enter this place. When the witch realized that her magic wasn't working, she stopped and said, "There are people among us who do not belong here." She looked around the crowd and pointed to the two believers. She demanded that they leave.

"Why should we leave?" they asked.

"The spirits are angry with you," she replied.

"We come by the Spirit of God in the name of Jesus," the believers said. "We have come to free you from these spirits in the name of Jesus."

The witch became scared and demanded again that the believers leave. So they stepped just outside the place where she was practicing her magic and continued to pray. The witch resumed her practice, but her magic still failed. She went out to the men and told them that Jesus had greater power than the spirits she served. She then accepted Christ as her Savior. When the crowd saw what she had done, they accepted Christ as well. About 150 people accepted Christ during the following days.

There is no one like Jesus! Nothing is impossible with Him.

—A WORKER IN NORTHERN AFRICA AND THE MIDDLE EAST

Lord, I PRAY THAT CHRISTIAN WORKERS AND BELIEVERS, ESPECIALLY IN THE SUDAN, BUT ALSO ACROSS THE WORLD, WILL BE BOLD TODAY TO SPEAK AGAINST THE POWERS OF DARKNESS. I PRAY THAT I, TOO, WILL BE BOLD AND REALIZE THAT THE ENEMY HAS NO AUTHORITY OVER ME. *Amen.*

A place to belong

"I go to prepare a place for you ... I will come again, and receive you unto myself."
John 14:2–3 (KJV)

Daouda (DOW-duh) was from one of the fanatical families in Sokode (SEW-koh-day). He had been living with Summer Institute of Linguistics translators as their live-in guard. Many Christians witnessed to Daouda, but he remained firmly entrenched in Islam. His wife was also a Muslim.

Christians prayed for Daouda and his wife, Assana (ah-SAH-nah), to be saved. When Assana began to hear about Jesus, she was confused and prayed to God to reveal the true way. One night in a dream, Jesus said, "I am the true Way. Follow Me." She accepted Christ and began praying for her husband. Months later, Daouda became a Christian, but his family totally rejected him.

We had lived peaceably with the Kotokolis (KOH-toh-KOH-lee) until the unexpected and sudden death of Daouda. His death was a challenge for church leaders who had to talk with the extended family about having a Christian funeral. The family finally agreed.

Days after the burial, we visited Daouda's wife. She told us that ordinarily Daouda's family couldn't sleep at night after a death because of the cries of the departed soul. (The Kotokolis believe that the person's soul hovers until the third day, when the *imam* prays that God would forgive the departed's sins, thus allowing the soul to find a resting place.) "But," she said, "when my husband died, everybody in the house slept normally. They were all astonished that they heard no crying. I told the family that it was because my husband was a Christian and had immediately found his resting place."

—PATSY, WEST AFRICA

Father God, HOW CHALLENGING IT IS TO HEAR OF THE UNWAVERING FAITH OF THOSE WHO FACE REJECTION, RIDICULE AND TREMENDOUS PERSONAL LOSS, YET REMAIN TRUE TO YOU. MY PRAYER IS THAT KOTOKOLIS WILL REMEMBER THE TESTIMONY OF HIS PEACEFUL DEATH AND OPEN THEIR HEARTS TO JESUS, THE PEACE GIVER. *Amen.*

Fear of death

"I am the resurrection and the life. He who believes in me will live, even though he dies; and whoever lives and believes in me will never die."
John 11:25–26 (NIV)

Most of the time, we walk to our villages. One particular week, I saw something strange. Each home and village has three paths entering and exiting. I noticed that these paths had ash spread across them in the form of a cross. I asked Arterio what it meant.

Arterio said, "The Jur believe there is a demon that rides around on a lion. At night, he comes into the village and sucks the blood from a person. In the morning when the family wakes up, that person is dead. This demon has been sighted, and word has spread. Now everyone is afraid. So they are putting the ash on their paths to prevent the demon from killing their family members."

Hebrews 2:14–15 refers to Jesus: "*He himself likewise partook of the same nature, that through death he might destroy him who has the power of death, that is, the devil, and deliver all those who through fear of death were subject to lifelong bondage*" (RSV).

You may find Arterio's explanation hard to imagine, but it confirms what Scripture says about the fear of death. It also highlights the reason missionaries move to difficult places like the Sudan. They learn a language and culture in order that they might tell a people group how to be free from the fear of death through faith in Jesus Christ.

Maybe you know someone who is also afraid to die. Share the good news that God offers eternal life to all who put their confidence in Jesus.

—JOHN, CENTRAL, EASTERN AND SOUTHERN AFRICA

Father, I KNOW THAT WHEN BELIEVERS DIE, THEY ARE IMMEDIATELY IN THE PRESENCE OF THE LORD. THANK YOU FOR THAT ASSURANCE. SPEAK THROUGH CHRISTIAN WORKERS IN THE SUDAN SO THAT MANY WILL BE RELEASED FROM THE BONDAGE OF FEAR. *Amen.*

The Difference Christ makes

"I will ransom them from the power of the grave; I will redeem them from death. Where, O death, are your plagues? Where, O grave, is your destruction?"
Hosea 13:14 (NIV)

My friend, Sizakele (see-zuh-KAY-lay), asked if I would pray for her sister-in-law, who was in the hospital. Mrs. Ndlovu (in-DLO-voo) had been sick for several months with AIDS, transmitted to her by her husband.

When I arrived at the hospital, the room was full with her family. As I walked to her bedside, it was apparent that she was near death. I learned that Mrs. Ndlovu was a Christian. I bent over her, stroked her head and read Psalm 23. I told her that God was with her as she walked through the valley of death. She could barely open her eyes, but the tears streamed down her face. I prayed for her, kissed her on the forehead and said my goodbyes. A few hours later, she died quietly. She was at peace with Jesus.

It was only a week later that Sizakele also lost her sister to AIDS. Before her death, the father insisted that his daughter did not have the dreaded disease but a spell had been cast on her. He insisted that a sangoma (san-GO-mah), a spiritual medium, could heal her. He carried his daughter to a *sangoma*, where she died without knowing Jesus. He had put his faith in tradition and ancestor worship to save his daughter, instead of Jesus.

Sizakele saw the difference Christ made between her sister-in-law and sister. Putting faith in tradition rather than the person of Jesus is a barrier that must be broken in order to find true life.

—CINDY, CENTRAL, EASTERN AND SOUTHERN AFRICA

Lord, MY HEART SHARES YOUR GRIEF THAT THE MAJORITY OF PEOPLE WHO FACE DEATH TODAY DO SO WITHOUT PERSONALLY KNOWING YOU AS LORD AND SAVIOR. FATHER, I ASK THAT THE MASSES WHO ARE INFECTED WITH HIV WILL HAVE THE OPPORTUNITY TO HEAR AND RESPOND TO THE GOSPEL. BREAK THE CHAINS OF THE ENEMY IN SOUTHERN AFRICA AND BRING RESTORATION AS ONLY JESUS CAN GIVE. *Amen.*

Rejection of the infidel

"He who listens to you listens to me; he who rejects you rejects me; but he who rejects me rejects him who sent me." Luke 10:16 (NIV)

Athletic and passionate about soccer, Eddie sprained his ankle. It developed into a bone infection that spread throughout his body. Antibiotics were needed, but the family had no money.

Wracked with pain and fever, Eddie lay weakly on a mat. Missionaries offered to carry Eddie to a hospital. The infection was so severe that he would almost certainly lose his leg, but there was still time to save his life. In this culture, the offer could only be accepted by the head of the extended family.

A quick meeting was called. Eddie's family had never known Christians but could not forget what they had learned since childhood. They had heard that Christians are immoral people; they deceitfully draw Muslims away from the prophet Muhammad and the Koran, forcing them to embrace Christianity. Such apostasy would bring shame to their family and evoke the wrath of an angry Allah upon them for dishonoring Islam.

Eddie was their beloved son, but the risk was too great. It would be better, it was decided, for Eddie to die than to receive help from "infidel Christians."

The missionary sat silently, trying to absorb such an inconceivable reality. How could they actually choose death for their son when they could have chosen *life*?

Fear roots itself into the heart and soul of this people group. Somehow, God can reach them. But on this day, the missionary couldn't imagine how. This day, he could only mourn for a boy who wanted to live but lost his life to a culture of fear.

—R.B., PACIFIC RIM

Father, THE BONDS OF FEAR HAVE ENSLAVED MANY WHO DON'T KNOW YOU. I ASK THAT YOU WOULD BREAK THE CHAINS THAT IMPRISON THOSE IN THESE VILLAGES OF THE PACIFIC RIM. ALLOW MISSIONARIES TO GAIN THE TRUST OF THOSE WHO SO DESPERATELY NEED CHRIST. *Amen.*

Freedom from the ancestors

"Can a woman forget her nursing child, and have no compassion on the son of her womb? Even these may forget, but I will not forget you. Behold, I have inscribed you on the palms of My hands." Isaiah 49:15–16 (NASB)

She was plodding down the path amid corn stalks, chickens and playing children. One small girl held her hand as the woman saw a group meeting under a mopani (moe-PAH-nee) tree. Ladies sewing and listening to an American was enough to get anyone's attention. Cautiously, Snodia and her daughter sat down close enough to hear Bible stories.

On Saturdays, Snodia continued to come to hear the stories. I learned that her newborn had died just a few weeks prior.

In Zimbabwe, there is a cultural tradition among non-Christians to hold a ceremony at the grave of a relative who has been dead a year. A witch doctor is hired to "summon" the spirit of this ancestor so that he can ask it where it wants to reside for eternity. Then the witch doctor assigns this spirit, according to their beliefs, to live in something like a tree, person, rock or animal.

Snodia's baby was born the same day as her dead grandmother's "coming back" ceremony. Thus, the witch doctor said that Snodia's baby would receive the ancestral spirit, and Snodia couldn't feed the baby for two weeks to see if the ancestral spirit was pleased with the assignment. Her baby died.

And so did the heart of Snodia until she heard that God loved her. After hearing God's Word for several weeks, she gave her heart to Jesus. She died from AIDS within two years, but she is in the presence of her Creator!

What bondage is it that keeps one from following Christ? Jesus can conquer anything.

—KIM, CENTRAL, EASTERN AND SOUTHERN AFRICA

Dear Lord, THANK YOU FOR YOUR GREAT LOVE FOR EVEN ME! SHOW YOUR LOVE AMONG THE PEOPLES OF THE EARTH SO THEY WILL KNOW THAT YOU WIPE THEIR SINS AWAY. PRAISE YOU, FATHER, FOR YOUR EVERLASTING LOVE. *Amen.*

Cracking the egg

"This sin will become for you like a high wall, cracked and bulging, that collapses suddenly, in an instant. It will break in pieces like pottery."
Isaiah 30:13—14a (NIV)

Throughout the Bible, names of people and places held great meaning and significance. Who would imagine that same concept would be found in Mali (MAL-ee) with the Dunn people. The name *Dunn* translates as "egg." If my name meant "egg," I'm not sure I would be thrilled, but these people are happy about their name. For many months, this love for being called "egg" was a mystery to me.

From the moment I entered the village, the people were friendly yet cautious. Being the first American in the village, they were just as curious about me as I was of them. They did, however, allow me to work in the fields with them, although they thought my hands were too soft.

Finally, after months of working and talking together, one of them trusted me enough to reveal the significance of their name. One can tell an egg is an egg from the outside, but he has no idea what is inside until he cracks it. No one really knows what is hiding inside the shell. This definition has proved true in my experience. The people seem friendly, but I still don't know what is in their hearts and minds.

The exciting part of this journey is that the egg is beginning to crack! May the shell continue to crack by the love of Jesus.

God showed me to ask, what is the egg in my life? What am I trying to hide from the world or from God? Eggs were created to be cracked and used.

—LORI, WEST AFRICA

Father, THANK YOU THAT YOU ARE BRINGING THE GOSPEL TO THE DUNN PEOPLE GROUP OF MALI, WEST AFRICA. CONTINUE TO "CRACK THE SHELL" SO THAT YOUR WORD CAN PENETRATE INSIDE THEIR HEARTS. MAY I EXAMINE MYSELF TODAY TO SEE WHAT I AM TRYING TO HIDE FROM YOU OR OTHERS. *Amen.*

Breaking the bonds of a slave

"Jesus replied, 'I tell you the truth, everyone who sins is a slave to sin.' Now a slave has no permanent place in the family, but a son belongs to it forever. So, if the Son sets you free, you will be free indeed." John 8:34–36 (NIV)

A missionary had been teaching a Bible study for several weeks in a Dominican home. The husband in the home was actively serving in the new church, but he and his wife were having marital problems. The Holy Spirit was convicting the wife and teaching her the truth about Jesus and His salvation through the Bible studies. That night, the missionary asked the wife if she would like to ask Jesus into her heart.

The wife replied, "Yes, I would; but I can't." She then began to explain the problems in her life that she felt kept her away from Jesus. She kept repeating, "I want to, but I can't." Knowing the hold that Satan had on this lady, the missionary told her to just begin to pray to Jesus. One could sense the struggle of darkness against the light of Jesus as the lady began asking Jesus to help her with her problems. There was a long pause, and then the missionary softly said, "Jesus wants to help you, but He first must enter your heart." The lady responded through tears, "Jesus, I open the door of my heart to You." Then the sobs began as she let Jesus release the slavery of sin that had such a hold on her.

The lady was extremely shy, but on Sunday at the church she announced, "I accepted Jesus as my Savior and Lord on Monday, February 2, 2004." Now her face literally glows with the peace and freedom of God, and she has now told her sister about Jesus.

—SHARON, MIDDLE AMERICA AND THE CARIBBEAN

Father, BREAK THE STRONGHOLDS IN THE LIVES OF THOSE WHO COME INTO CONTACT WITH MISSIONARIES TODAY, ESPECIALLY IN MIDDLE AMERICA AND THE CARIBBEAN BASIN. BREAK THE STRONGHOLDS IN MY FRIEND, _____, SO THAT HE/SHE WILL OPEN TO THE GOSPEL. *Amen.*

The biggest snake

*"Pray at all times and on every occasion in the power of the Holy Spirit. Stay
alert and be persistent in your prayers for all Christians everywhere."*
Ephesians 6:18 (NLT)

On a trip to Thailand, my husband had a vivid dream. An angel repeated, "You must pray for your house; it is not protected." God had my
husband's attention. He spent the next two days, from time to time, in-
terceding for our house and family, asking God's protection. He stayed
longer in Thailand while the kids and I went back to our country.

The day before my husband returned, construction workers found
a six-foot cobra two houses down. When it reared its ugly head, everyone screamed and ran for their lives. Our helper slew the monster, and
its body was paraded around the neighborhood.

I then found out that when we were in Thailand, our helper had
killed three baby cobras living in our front yard, where our children
played! Our helper was apparently afraid to tell me with my husband
gone.

My husband told his English-as-a-Second-Language class this story,
and one of his students said, "You know that we believe evil celestial
spirits possess the cobras. It is amazing that your family was not hurt. I
don't think the evil spirits like you."

With intercessors praying for the deliverance of our country and
protection of our family, we must present a threat. These events have
not deterred us, but only strengthened our resolve to see our country
freed from the "biggest snake" and his minions.

You may wonder, *Do my prayers really make a difference half a world away?*
If you could be here for just a week, you would know they most certainly do.

—A WORKER IN THE PACIFIC RIM

Father God, YOU ARE THE MOST HIGH. BECAUSE OF YOU, I AM MORE THAN A CONQUEROR
OVER SATAN AND HIS SCHEMES. PROTECT MISSIONARIES IN THE PACIFIC RIM, WHO FACE
SPIRITUAL WARFARE DAILY. MAY YOUR LIGHT SHINE THROUGH THEM IN THE MIDST OF THE
SPIRITUAL DARKNESS. *Amen.*

Fighting, not retreating

"You have seen with your own eyes all that the LORD your God has done to these two kings. The LORD will do the same to all the kingdoms over there where you are going. Do not be afraid of them; the LORD your God himself will fight for you." Deuteronomy 3:21–22 (NIV)

We ignored the jackhammers for weeks, sure that the home across the alley in our Hakka (HAH-kah) Chinese town was being remodeled for new owners. However, we discovered that the townhouse ten yards from our front door would become a Taoist (DOW-ist) temple. I was shocked. Didn't the enemy even consider us a threat?

There are days when I shut my doors, retreating into a safe world of housekeeping, Christian music, husband and kids. I don't want what is out there coming in here. I am aware of how weak I really am.

Reading in Deuteronomy, God spoke to me through Moses' words, *"You have seen with your own eyes all that the LORD your God has done to these two kings. The LORD will do the same to all the kingdoms over there where you are going. Do not be afraid of them; the LORD your God himself will fight for you."* I worshiped.

Today, the doors of my home are open. God's Spirit is so powerful that this house cannot contain Him. Those passing by on the streets can't help but be knocked back by the glory of the Lord. I'm ready to tell Taoist priests about Jesus. For I have seen what the Lord my God has done to dispel the power of darkness. He will do the same to all dark kingdoms where Satan still reigns. I'm not afraid; God will fight for me.

After the intercession of many believers, the temple never material-ized. God fought for me. No kingdom stands against Him!

—D.T., East Asia

Father, give me the courage to actively combat the spiritual forces of dark-ness that invade my country. Do not let me hide from the evil that is going on around me. Help us as believers to take back what the enemy has taken in our country that was founded on Christian principles. I also pray that workers will fight the present darkness in East Asia. *Amen.*

NOVEMBER V

Compassion

Our theme for the month of November is compassion. First Peter 3:8 tells us to *"be sympathetic, love as brothers, be compassionate and humble"* (NIV). I'm not sure any outreach has the cavern-deep impact of compassion. People are still deeply moved—even shocked—when someone with no obvious invested interest demonstrates lavish concern in their trial. That we care is still the loudest Christian creed the world around us will ever hear.

Christ issued a troubling prophecy in Matthew 24:12. He warned that toward the end of this age, *"the love of most will grow cold"* (NIV). I'm convinced one reason will be the desensitization of our emotions through uncensored media news coverage and entertainment. Our human natures protect themselves. Over the long haul, the more violence and suffering we see, the less moved we naturally will be. Left to our natural defenses, we will ultimately succumb to hardening of the heart.

This is a plea that we continue to risk the pain of caring. Of seeing and hearing things that break our hearts so that compassion can bleed through the cracks. My friend and worship leader Travis Cottrell said something recently I can't get off my mind: "It hurts so bad to love so much." Yes, it does. And one way we'll know if we're continuing to take the risk of loving is if we're sharing the burden of hurting.

I embarrassed myself half to death on an airplane not long ago because I read some letters from various sisters in Christ tucked in my folder by my correspondence assistant. I cried so hard that the flight attendant fretted madly, handing me every small square cocktail napkin she could get her hands on. I've learned from experience that airplane napkins (the kind with the name of the airline on them) are useless for sobbing and nose blowing. There are days only a roll of toilet paper will do. This was one of those days ... only no roll. In the midst of making a fool of myself, the only thing good that came out of it was a sense that God was saying, *When you quit caring, you need to quit.*

But there are times my heart just gets tired. You, too? That's when we're tempted to clog our own valves and shut off our hearts. There's a better answer, however.

As the world grows colder and colder and we're tempted to get harder and harder, we've got to be willing to draw from our Source. Psalm 116:5 tells us *our God is full of compassion* (NIV). Lamentations 3:22–23 tells us His *compassions never fail. They are new every morning* (NIV). God's compassion is always full, never fails and is ever new. The sun rises every morning on all the manna of mercy we'll need that day to make it. Even the manna we'll need to help someone *else* make it. Sometimes we just sit and listen. Other times we weep while they weep. Still other times they demand a word from us. These are times we need God's help not to say something stupid.

Isaiah 50:4 says, *"The Sovereign* LORD *has given me an instructed tongue, to know the word that sustains the weary. He wakens me morning by morning, wakens my ear to listen like one being taught"* (NIV). As John 12:49 says, God will teach us *"what to say and how to say it"* (NIV). Love is one thing we're told never fails. Our rule must be to speak the language of love. We must keep lending God our empty hearts like bone-dry canteens and ask Him to pour forth into them His very own love (Rom. 5:5). Loving words will then spring from the overflow (Luke 6:45).

In the midst of feeling like we can do so little, we can also open our mouths to pray with the gush of fresh compassion. I've been in many prayer meetings where I felt the Holy Spirit pour His mercy and power upon us, but an unplanned one jumps into my mind most readily. Keith and I were serving at the East Africa missionary conference in Nairobi. We'd already been in session for several days, so our Bible study and worship times had intensified pretty dramatically. From the beginning of the conference, all of us were made aware of a young missionary mom who was unable to attend because her 2-year-old daughter was sick. During the next 48 hours, this precious child was hospitalized so chronically ill that the unthinkable seemed imminent. She desperately needed medical care that was unavailable where she was.

I was in the middle of teaching a session when I saw a woman slip in the back, whisper something in the ears of the leadership team and slip out into the hall with them. I then heard muffled cries. I was scared to death the child had died. We soon stopped what we were doing and learned that tiny Rachel was at death's door. We all hit the floor with either our knees or our faces, and the most spontaneous prayer meeting I've ever attended broke out. I have never in my life heard such compassion flow freely in the form of prayer. I felt like I could hear the very groans of the Holy Spirit described in Romans 8:26. The other missionary moms could enter into the pain in a way that we on the visiting team could not. Though we were overcome with emotion, they seemed overcome with the very empathy of Christ. We cried out and cried out for God's mercy.

Stories don't always end the way this one did and yet, strangely, God is just as faithful. We were told the next day that Rachel's fever broke around the same time the spontaneous prayer meeting erupted. She was able to board a plane with her courageous young mom very shortly and get the extra medical care she needed in the States.

God didn't need us. He invited us to enter into the depths of His compassion and feel with Him there.

Read 1 Peter 3:8 again. What in the world does being humble have to do with being compassionate? True compassion comes from the open admission that we, too, have known pain and weakness.

—*Beth Moore*

Comforting those who grieve

"Weep with those who weep." Romans 12:15b (NASB)

I walked up the dimly lit staircase, taking time to avoid the debris. Rolled-up mattresses and tattered baby strollers were scattered throughout the stairwell. I could hear people on the other side of the thin walls speaking unfamiliar African languages. "Lord, I am relying on You," I repeated.

Normally my husband accompanied me into the lower-income apartments of France, but he had another engagement. Nevertheless, an African Muslim immigrant in Paris needed me.

Days before, she had suffered a miscarriage. After being released from the hospital, she needed friends to surround her as she worked through the grief. I had been invited to spend the day with her and her lifelong friends from her village back in Africa.

Together, we attended to the woman's needs. We sat together. We took turns leading the conversation. We ate lunch together in an African manner. A colorful tablecloth was laid on the floor, and we sat encircled around the common platter in the center. With our hands and large spoons, we shared from the dish, just as we were sharing my new friend's sorrow.

Throughout the afternoon, I prayed with my friend. I reminded her of God's compassion in time of trouble. I offered her promises from the Bible that would build upon what she already had learned through our previous Bible studies. Yet I can't help but think the most important thing I did that day was that I simply took the time to be by her side and to share her grief.

—JAMIE, WESTERN EUROPE

Father, MAY I NEVER BE TOO BUSY TO SHARE THE SORROW OF THOSE AROUND ME. WHETHER IT'S BRINGING A MEAL, MAKING A VISIT, OR HOLDING A HAND, HELP ME TO MINISTER TO OTHERS WHO ARE GRIEVING. I PRAY THAT MISSIONARIES ACROSS THE WORLD WILL BE ABLE TO DO THE SAME TODAY. *Amen.*

Seeing the masses

"Jesus said, 'When he saw the crowds, he had compassion on them, because they were harassed and helpless, like sheep without a shepherd.'"
Matthew 9:36 (NIV)

After language class, my husband and I returned to our small campus apartment to review our lesson and to prepare for our next class. Before we knew it, evening had descended and we'd studied nonstop for many hours. We decided to take a break and ride our bikes downtown.

As we got in the bike lane, I tried to stay close behind my husband's bike while still keeping up with the rest of the bikers. Rush-hour traffic was all around us. Buses overflowing with workers careened from one lane to the other, pulling over to let off their passengers at various stops. Taxis whizzed past us at an alarming rate, darting in and out of the bus lanes and crowding the bikers onto the sides. With difficulty, we made it to our destination without mishap.

We stopped on a bridge overlooking the downtown streets, stretching our tired legs after the strenuous ride. We looked at each other and thought, *What are we doing here?* After four months of language study, were we any closer to speaking coherent sentences? We didn't think so.

And, then, as we looked again at the masses of people down below, God gave us a glimpse through His eyes of those living and dying without knowing His Son, Jesus. Together we thought, *God, thank You for sending us here!* Many have never heard the gospel. How could we not be here, sharing His love, His light and His Son, Jesus? God puts us in a place for a specific purpose.

—A WORKER IN CHINA

Father, GIVE ME YOUR EYES TO SEE OTHERS AROUND ME, TO SEE THEIR NEEDS AND THEIR HURTS. FILL MY HEART WITH YOUR COMPASSION FOR MY LOST NEIGHBORS, COLLEAGUES AND FAMILY MEMBERS. AND LORD, MAY MY LOCATION ALWAYS BE IN THE CENTER OF YOUR WILL. *Amen.*

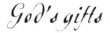

God's gifts

"Every good gift and every perfect present comes from heaven."
James 1:17 (GNB)

The rainy season in Uganda has begun, and with it comes the relief that crops can be planted and life will be sustained. We awaken each morning to the *thud, thud, thud* of many hoes breaking the ground as men and women plant their seeds of hope for a satisfying yield.

As clouds gather in the dark sky, the workers shade their eyes and read the weather above them. With the first drops from heaven, the people pause from their work, find solace under a tree and enjoy rest as they watch God do His part in keeping them fed. I observe from my front porch as the world around turns fuzzy gray through sheets of rain.

Then the shower quickly stops. It's as if God lifts His watering can and says, *That's enough. Now just have faith.* The birds begin to sing again in the mango trees, and the children come bursting out of their dark mud homes into the warmth and joy of the sun. God is so good to send the rains and to then perfect it with His creation enjoying His life-giving light.

Every breath we draw, every word we speak and every new day we are blessed by the gifts from the Father above who knows our needs before we ever voice them. What a joy to serve a God who enjoys His children! I imagine His great delight as He waters the Ugandan soil and then watches His precious people pause to thank Him for providing their daily bread.

—A WORKER IN CENTRAL, EASTERN AND SOUTHERN AFRICA

Dear God, MAY I NEVER TAKE YOUR COUNTLESS BLESSINGS FOR GRANTED! MAY YOU MAKE THE GROUND FERTILE FOR SPIRITUAL HARVEST IN UGANDA AND IN MY OWN NEIGHBORHOOD. *Amen.*

Unconditional kindness pays off

"Make sure that nobody pays back wrong for wrong, but always try to be kind to each other and to everyone else." 1 Thessalonians 5:15 (NIV)

An IMB missionary led a team of volunteers from Texas into remote Muslim villages in South Asia. In one village, the team shared the gospel. The local *imam* (EE-mahm) (Muslim pastor) became irate and forced the Christians to leave his village.

A Muslim background believer (MBB) working with the missionary visited the same village six months later. The village was totally underwater. This is the only flood that the village had ever seen in its history. The missionary worked out a plan with the MBB to distribute food in the village.

During the relief effort, six Muslim men approached the MBB. These men had heard the gospel presented by the Americans the year before and witnessed the team being escorted out of the village. They asked who supplied the food. The MBB told them that it was from the same Americans who had been thrown out of the village. One man said, "Why are these Christians giving us food when our people treated them badly?"

That day, and on several subsequent trips to the village, the national believer shared that God could also change their hearts. Within nine months of the Americans' visit, 28 Muslims from the village were baptized and a church was started.

When Jesus preached the Sermon on the Mount to the multitudes, a nugget of truth tucked within was the golden rule: *"However you want people to treat you, so treat them"* (Matt. 7:12). As a result of the kindness of a group of volunteers, even when persecuted, Muslims have come into the kingdom.

—A WORKER IN SOUTH ASIA

Thank You, Father, FOR THE DEDICATION OF VOLUNTEERS WHO ASSIST CHRISTIAN WORKERS AND SOUTH ASIAN CHRISTIANS IN SPREADING THE GOSPEL. MAY YOU SEND MANY VOLUNTEERS THIS YEAR THROUGHOUT THE WORLD. SHOW ME IF I AM TO TAKE MY VACATION TIME TO BE A VOLUNTEER OVERSEAS. *Amen.*

Generosity in the extreme

"Out of the most severe trial, their overflowing joy and their extreme poverty welled up in rich generosity." 2 Corinthians 8:2 (NIV)

Lalo (LAH-low) is the pastor of the Miskito (mees-KEY-toh) church in Waspam (wahs-PAHM) on the Coco River of Nicaragua. He and his wife have eight children and two grandchildren living with them. Lalo makes a living by planting beans and rice, but he rarely has enough money to support his family.

One day a man floated down the river with his family on a small raft. His wife was pregnant and having problems. The doctor in Waspam said that the only way to save her life was to take her to the regional hospital eight hours away. The ambulance would take the parents, but not the preschool boys. So the man left the two poorly clothed boys at the house at the Baptist church and told one of Lalo's older children that he would be back in a few weeks.

Lalo cared for the boys as if they were his own. When no one returned for the children after several weeks, I asked Lalo what he would do. He replied, "I will raise them as my own. How can I do anything less when God has entrusted me with these children?"

Eventually, the parents with the new baby did return. The pastor's family was sad to see the children go, and Lalo asked why they had brought the children to the Baptist church. The father replied, "I heard you were good people and could be trusted." Before they left, Lalo shared Christ with him.

Are we willing to sacrifice for others in need?

—VIOLA, MIDDLE AMERICA AND THE CARIBBEAN

Lord, TAKE AWAY MY DESIRE FOR UNIMPORTANT THINGS IN THIS LIFE. HELP ME TO BE GENEROUS IN ALL THAT YOU HAVE GIVEN ME. THANK YOU, LORD, FOR PEOPLE LIKE LALO WHO MINISTER TO THE MISKITO PEOPLE. GIVE HIM AND OTHER NATIONAL PASTORS IN THIS REGION MANY OPPORTUNITIES TO SHARE YOUR LOVE. *Amen.*

Dignity

> *"For I was hungry, and you gave Me something to eat; I was thirsty, and you*
> *gave Me drink; I was a stranger, and you invited Me in.'"*
> Matthew 25:35 (NASB)

The fear in her eyes is evident as she hesitantly enters the iron gate. Ahead, she sees a young woman who invited her to eat breakfast. She follows the welcoming woman to a table.

Now that she is seated, bread is placed on a plate before her and stew is poured over it. She tries to eat with some pride, but the hunger is too overwhelming. She attacks her food with both hands. Her head stays down, focused on getting every morsel of food into her mouth.

As she finishes, her head raises to observe the surroundings. Cautiously, she watches as others are served a meal. Some are missing fingers and have to use the palms of their hands to eat. Others have dirty clothing. Each one is seated with kindness. Slowly she stands and puts the piece of fruit by her plate into her tattered bag. More than likely it will be her next meal.

The next day, the gates are wide open, and this time she is able to return the welcoming smiles. The hunger is not so bad, and she eats with one hand. There is peace in this place that they call church.

Now she comes every day for breakfast. She walks with dignity as she passes through the gates. She takes her place at the table and nods a greeting to the other ladies already seated. The foreigner sets the water near her plate. They make eye contact, and the foreigner whispers a prayer of blessing in the name of Jesus.

—SARAH, SOUTH ASIA

Dear Jesus, I REALIZE THAT LOVE IS SPOKEN IN MY ACTIONS, NOT IN MY WORDS ALONE. USE ME TO MINISTER TO THE HUNGRY AND NEEDY. I PRAY FOR HUMANITARIAN PROJECTS SUCH AS THIS ONE IN SOUTH ASIA. ALLOW CHRISTIAN WORKERS TO BE A PICTURE OF CHRIST IN THEIR ACTS OF KINDNESS AS THEY MEET PHYSICAL AND SPIRITUAL NEEDS. *Amen.*

A job for the church

"Grow in the grace and knowledge of our Lord and Savior Jesus Christ. To Him be the glory both now and forever." 2 Peter 3:18 (NKJV)

One morning, while working as a nurse among Colombia's displaced population, I examined a 3-day-old baby who had not eaten since birth. The mother informed me that the physician had written an order stating she couldn't breastfeed because of the medication she took for severe epilepsy. Instead she was to use a supplement for the baby that was outrageously expensive. She had no means to buy the formula, so she had given the infant occasional teaspoons of water. It was a miracle that this child was still alive! The child would die within the next day or two if he didn't obtain proper nutrition. I couldn't do anything except click my pen on my prescription pad, stare at the frail baby in front of me and strain my brain for a solution.

But God has a way of working out everything. We had been trying to teach new churches to work together, ask God for the answers and not rely on the international missionaries to solve all their problems. It didn't matter how small or poor the church was, God could work through them to help care for one another and provide physical, emotional and spiritual needs.

God was able to use a baby to demonstrate this aspect of church growth. Four other nursing women in the church volunteered to take on the responsibility. It was amazing to see how God not only provided for the child, but in a manner that took the emphasis off the foreigners and focused it on Him.

—MELISSA, SOUTH AMERICA

Father, YOU ARE GRACIOUS TO DESIGN THE CHURCH AS A FUNCTIONING BODY TO LOOK AFTER EACH OTHER. STRENGTHEN MY CHURCH TO BE ONE THAT SHOWS COMPASSION TOWARD ITS MEMBERS AND THE COMMUNITY. I PRAY FOR MY PASTOR TODAY TO BE A MAN OF GOD AND SHEPHERD OF YOUR CONGREGATION. *Amen.*

A special meal

"So if the Son liberates you (makes you free men), then you are really and unquestionably free." John 8:36 (AMP)

"Mother, it's almost four o'clock."

My eyes popped open hearing my son's soft voice at my bedroom door. Grabbing my alarm clock, I saw 3:45 a.m.—the prison banquet! We had promised to take our African co-workers, along with all the food, to the prison at 4 a.m. so they could begin cooking. The banquet was scheduled for 10 a.m. Within 20 minutes, we were bouncing over the dirt roads of Togo (TOH-go), spilling kerosene from the lamps in the back of my truck. After a few more trips, we had most of the food cooking on primitive mud stoves, preparing a meal for 450 men.

The idea had originated with my son, Peter, since I did health care and Bible studies at the prison, and we had been planning and looking forward to it for months. Peter had come from the States to speak at the banquet.

Later, the men stood shoulder to shoulder for Peter's message. When they learned that they were getting a special meal, they cheered as if they were being released! We shook the hands of each of the men in their cells and gave them each a New Testament and T-shirt that had John 8:36 printed on it in French, the language of the country.

But the most exciting part of the day was seeing the hundreds of men who decided to give their lives to the Lord Jesus as Peter told them about the greatest gift of all, God's dear Son.

—LINDA, WEST AFRICA

Thank You, Lord, THAT YOU CONTINUE TO OPEN PRISON DOORS SO THE MESSAGE OF SALVATION CAN BE GIVEN SO THAT PRISONERS CAN BE LIBERATED FROM SIN AND BECOME CAPTIVATED BY YOUR GRACE. I PRAY THAT THE NEW BELIEVERS IN TOGO WILL BE GROUNDED IN YOUR WORD AND BECOME RADIANT MESSENGERS OF THE GOSPEL TO FELLOW INMATES AND FAMILY MEMBERS. *Amen.*

Hope in a hopeless situation

"And the God of all grace, who called you to his eternal glory in Christ, after you have suffered a little while, will himself restore you and make you strong, firm and steadfast." 1 Peter 5:10 (NIV)

A team member and I were given a tour of Bauleni (bah-OO-lay-nee) compound by the organizer of the caregivers to AIDS patients. She took us through the rubbish-strewn footpaths, past the most primitive living conditions anyone can imagine. Very few have electricity, and none have running water. They live in small two-room blockhouses with many people living in these cramped conditions. Cooking is done outside, so the smell of food cooking is mixed with the smells of the sewage and rotting trash.

One patient we visited was a young woman in her last stages of the disease; she was lying on a mat. The smell of decay hit me. She did not have the strength to brush off the flies that were covering her body. Around her were her four children, the eldest being 9 years old. Her single complaint was of a sore neck from lying in the same position. I could only give her some pain pills and some cool water. We prayed for her, and she said she did know Jesus as her Lord. A beautiful smile lit her face.

This was one of the most painful but wonderful days in my life. The needs are overwhelming. I know that I can't help everyone; it is humanly impossible. With the Lord as my guide, I hope to provide much more than physical comfort to these people so close to death. The AIDS pandemic appears hopeless to the world, but it can still be an opportunity of hope through eternal life with Jesus.

—HELEN, CENTRAL, EASTERN AND SOUTHERN AFRICA

Father of all grace and comfort, HOW UNSPEAKABLY PRECIOUS IS THE PRICELESS TREASURE OF YOUR ETERNAL PRESENCE INDWELLING FRAIL, TEMPORAL VESSELS OF CLAY. GRANT A SPECIAL GRACE THIS DAY TO THOSE WHO SUFFER INCREDIBLE PAIN AND POVERTY AROUND OUR WORLD, AND STRENGTHEN MISSIONARIES WHO MINISTER TO THEM. *Amen.*

A suitcase of shoes

"If you believe, you will receive whatever you ask for in prayer."
Matthew 21:22 (NIV)

In the Amazon rain forest of Brazil, there is a town called Manaus (mah-NAH-us), which is in the middle of the jungle. We have a church in an area called Puraquequara (poo-day-kay-QUA-dah). We call it the "end of the road."

After seeing so many children naked or with ragged clothes, we felt led by the Lord to start a clothing ministry. We asked volunteers coming to this area to bring used children's clothing with them. We had asked for clothing, but one team brought in a suitcase of shoes. Since it never gets cold here, shoes have not been a high priority.

We carried the shoes with us when we went to Puraquequara to tell the stories of the Bible. One of the newly believing families with seven children passed by the church. After greeting us, the children sat on the steps of the church and were trying on shoes.

A man walking by saw this shoe exchange and became excited. He spied a pair of shoes resembling boots that he wanted for his son. We would not give them to him, as it is our policy to see the child first. He left in a hurry and returned later with the boy. We tried the shoes on, and they fit perfectly. He later told the pastor they had been praying for a pair of shoes for the child but didn't have money. A few weeks later we saw the man, and he was still praising the Lord and giving thanks for the shoes.

—TOMMY AND TUBBY, SOUTH AMERICA

Compassionate Father, I PRAISE YOU THAT NOTHING IS TOO GREAT OR TOO SMALL TO BE ASKED OF YOU. I PRAY THAT THE CHILDREN WHO RECEIVED THE GIFT OF SHOES GIVEN IN YOUR NAME WILL BECOME THE ONES WHO TAKE THE GOSPEL OF CHRIST THROUGHOUT THE AMAZON RAIN FOREST OF BRAZIL. *Amen.*

A selfish heart changed

"He who is kind to the poor lends to the LORD, and he will reward him for what he has done." Proverbs 19:17 (NIV)

She was the fifth stranger who had come that day in need. "I have a problem," they each said. Why did they all expect *me* to clothe and feed their families?

I forced a smile in greeting, wondering if a few coins or a piece of bread would get rid of her quickly. She was thin, making her near-term pregnancy obvious. "My baby is coming sooner than I thought. I have no towel to wrap him in," she pleaded. Compassion filled me as my earlier irritations melted away. Why was I so selfish?

I folded a towel and gave it to her, along with a few pieces of fruit and a bar of soap. Her face lit up as she clapped thank you. I lay in bed that night praying for her.

Two days later, a note arrived saying she had delivered a baby boy. She wanted me to come and name her son. Humbly, I named him David, a man after God's own heart. She seemed pleased with his name.

Later I found out that she had tested HIV positive before delivery. Her husband rejected her and his unborn child. Because she was tested, she was able to receive medications to reduce the chance of her baby contracting the disease.

Six months passed, and I received a photo of chubby little David. "Look how our David is growing!" a note said.

The next time my day is interrupted with a person's need, I hope I will see it as God's invitation for a blessing.

—BECKY, CENTRAL, EASTERN AND SOUTHERN AFRICA

Father, YOU SEE INTO MY HEART. SOMETIMES IT'S UGLY. FORGIVE ME FOR MY SELFISHNESS AND CHANGE MY HEART AS YOU DID FOR THIS MISSIONARY. PROVIDE FOOD FOR YOUR CHILDREN IN ZIMBABWE WHO ARE DESPERATELY HUNGRY AT PRESENT. GIVE MISSIONARIES COMPASSION AS THEY MINISTER TO THE NEEDY. *Amen.*

Set free

"You have freed me from my chains." Psalm 116:16b (NIV)

As I entered the house, my eyes went to 7-year-old Joshua on the couch. I touched his face and felt sharp, protruding bone. His arms and legs were sticks, his belly swollen. He struggled to breathe.

His father said, "We know it's only a matter of time." Joshua wanted to be placed on a mat. Joshua settled down, and I prayed. I asked God to walk with my friend and to embrace him with love and peace. Within minutes, the child took his last breath. Just before he died, Joshua's eyes focused on something in the distance, he uttered some words, and he left. I believe he saw Jesus reaching down to carry him home.

My friend shook the child, calling his name, hoping beyond hope that he would breathe again. Then he carried the body into his bedroom, sat on the bed and gently rocked him—sobbing and crying to Jesus.

That evening I returned for the burial. The coffin was placed on two chairs for viewing. Two men hammered down the lid, sealing the coffin. As I heard the pounding, I thought of Jesus' death, imagining how afflicted and grieved God was at the death of His only Son.

After the burial, I addressed the father who had lost his only son. I told him that I could not know his pain, but God did. God also grieved and cried when His only Son died on the cross for us. Therefore, He and He alone could give true consolation and comfort to his heart.

—A WORKER IN WEST AFRICA

Father, IS THERE NO END TO THE TERRIBLE PANDEMIC OF AIDS? BRING HOPE TO AFRICA. LET PEOPLE HEAR ABOUT YOUR PLAN FOR STAYING FREE OF THIS DISEASE. BY YOUR WORD AND THE POWER OF YOUR HOLY SPIRIT ENABLE THEM TO LIVE PURE AND HOLY LIVES. LORD, SHOW ME THE PART I'M TO HAVE IN THE AIDS CRISIS. *Amen.*

What shall we do?

"The King will answer and say to them, 'Truly I say to you, to the extent that you did it to one of these brothers of Mine, even the least of them, you did it to Me.'" Matthew 25:40 (NASB)

Her name is Pauline. She is 3 years old but looks 18 months. She has orange hair, stick legs and arms and an extended stomach with constant bowel trouble.

Down the road from her house is a clinic where she could go to have a blood analysis to determine what might be afflicting her under-developed body. The cost would be 200 kwanzas, about $2.50. In three years, she has been to the doctor once.

Her mother died at age 22 with malaria, as did an older sibling. Her father has abandoned her, so she lives with her grandmother, who is pregnant with her ninth child; three of the other eight have already died. The family of a dozen lives in a small two-room house, and none of them have any meaningful employment.

Without help, Pauline will die at an early age. With help, her family will learn to pass the responsibility for her on to someone else, namely us. It is the constant dilemma we face in a place like Angola. How to help in a positive and responsible manner is a decision we have to make day by day. What shall we do? We can't ignore her, because she lives 50 feet from our house. What would our Lord do?

After weighing the options, we will take Pauline to the local clinic and take it one step at a time. It may result in a host of sick children arriving at our doorstep, but how can we do less than this?

—SCOT, CENTRAL, EASTERN AND SOUTHERN AFRICA

Father God, YOU LOOKED OUT INTO THE MULTITUDE AND FELT COMPASSION. HELP ME TO HAVE A COMPASSIONATE HEART TO MEET NEEDS THAT YOU CALL ME TO MEET. GIVE MISSIONARIES WISDOM TO DISCERN WHICH ONES YOU DESIRE TO MEET THROUGH THEM. *Amen.*

Demonstrating love

"But God demonstrates his own love for us ..." Romans 5:8 (NIV)

Nestled on the high Andes (AN-dees) Mountains, our church members meet in Quito (KEE-toh), Ecuador. Teaching children's Sunday School, I hope they can understand a story about Jesus with my limited language skills. Our Sunday School room is normally housing for sheep when they are not out to pasture, so the fresh air and beauty outside were more inviting near the end of our lesson. We climbed the mountainside to the playground.

On the way back to the church, a girl carried her 4-year-old sister down the steep mountain slope. However, when she tripped and fell, the younger one tumbled down the mountainside. As I realized what had happened, I ran sideways down toward her as fast as I could.

The small girl was bleeding badly from her mouth and nose, with other scrapes and bruises. I swept her up in my arms, continuing to run for water and something to stop the bleeding. Her mother was at the market selling her wares while the father was in the church.

I held this child for a long time, wiping her blood and tears, applying pressure to her wounds and looking into her beautiful brown eyes. I held her close, comforting her as if she were my own. The bonding with the children of my people group took place as I demonstrated care.

God showed that He wanted me to display my love for them. The message of love was well received. It doesn't take much to make a lasting positive impact on a child.

—KYLEEN, SOUTH AMERICA

Heavenly Father, SHOW ME HOW I CAN BE A POSITIVE INFLUENCE ON A CHILD. USE MISSIONARIES IN SOUTH AMERICA TO BE LOVING EXAMPLES, A VERY PICTURE OF OUR LOVING FATHER. *Amen.*

People are watching

"Praise be to the God and Father of our Lord Jesus Christ, the Father of compassion and the God of all comfort, who comforts us in all our troubles, so that we can comfort those in any trouble with the comfort we ourselves have received from God." 2 Corinthians 1:3–4 (NASB)

Our work in South Asia has been slow going and, quite frankly, sometimes discouraging. One morning, however, God gave me a small encouragement and helped me realize how blessed we are to be here.

One of our workers cut his foot deeply and was not able to work. Ray asked him to come to our home daily by rickshaw so that we could clean his foot and bandage the cut. The injured man did not have the materials to keep it clean otherwise, and he wanted his foot to have every opportunity to heal quickly. Each day that he came, our Hindu house helper observed. Later he commented that Ray was a kindhearted man. He further stated that service to friends was Ray's service to God, although he doesn't know the true God that we know yet. He told me that I was lucky to have Ray as my husband. This small act of compassion touched this man who had been cut, the Hindu worker who observed and me in my discouragement.

Hindus worship many different gods, so our helper was probably not thinking of our God. However, God spoke to my heart and told me to remember that people are always watching how we live. A breakthrough was made.

When I am discouraged and thinking that I am not doing much here, I need to remember that people are watching. Am I showing people the love of Jesus as I go about my life, wherever I may be?

—PAM, SOUTH ASIA

Heavenly Father, THANK YOU THAT YOU HAVE GIVEN JESUS AS THE FLAWLESS EXAMPLE OF HOW TO LIVE. I PRAY THAT MY LIFE AND THE LIVES OF CHRISTIAN WORKERS WILL BE A REFLECTION OF CHRIST'S LOVE AND COMPASSION THROUGH OUR ACTIONS AND WORDS. *Amen.*

Raisins and prayers from a child

"Follow my example, as I follow the example of Christ."
1 Corinthians 11:1 (NIV)

In rural Haiti (HEY-tee), voodoo was declared an official religion (a religion of sorcery and magic) in 2003. My wife and I were working with volunteers from Alabama to help cap a water source for a community in a heavy voodoo area. Delores and another nurse saw patients with medical needs while the men worked on the water project. We asked God to break down the barriers that Satan had built in this area.

We took our adopted 4-year-old, TiNana (tee-NAH-nah), with us on the project. Before we adopted her, she was dying. The pediatrician at the hospital told us that we were wasting our money trying to save her. My wife prayed by the bedside, "This sick child has been abandoned, Lord, and if You don't love and care for her, nobody will. Help her to be strong and to be a blessing as she grows up, so that she can have a special place of service for You." God answered our prayers.

TiNana took raisins while we worked on the water and medical project. One day she was found to have her own "line of patients." She gave people raisins, saying in Creole, "This should make you feel better; but if you don't feel better, please come back."

Later that week, the physical water source was provided and the living Water was given to 40 people who found Jesus. That last day of the project, TiNana was seen calling people forward to bow their heads as she prayed for them.

—SAM, MIDDLE AMERICA AND THE CARIBBEAN

Loving Lord, THANK YOU FOR REMINDING ME THAT YOU USE THE WEAK THINGS OF THE WORLD TO CONFOUND THE WISE AND THAT EVEN A CHILD CAN BE AN INSTRUMENT OF HEALING TO TROUBLED SOULS IN HAITI. HELP ME TO COME HUMBLY BEFORE YOU WITH CHILDLIKE FAITH, UNASHAMEDLY REACHING OUT TO OTHERS WITH SPONTANEOUS LOVE AND COMPLETE ABANDONMENT TO YOU. *Amen.*

Being a Good Samaritan

"By this all men will know that you are my disciples, if you love one another."
John 13:35 (NIV)

The cold baptismal waters streaming down their faces could not hide the joy of the Lord. Before their salvation, José (ho-SAY) and Maria with their infant son had been to the small church meetings a few times. Like most Quichua (KEE-chew-ah) young adults, they were more interested in the things of the world than a relationship with the Lord. However, this all changed after a crisis invaded their lives.

When I arrived on a Tuesday evening high on the Andean (AN-dee-an) mountainside in south Quito (KEE-toh), several people were not there. Maria was missing. During a robbery at her parents' home, she had been kidnapped. Maria's mother and others went out to try to find her. José had not come home from work yet.

In the middle of our church meeting, we learned that the two had not found Maria. Shortly after, Maria found her way home, but she had been drugged and robbed. The distraught mother invited the church members to come to her house to visit the young woman and her husband.

More than 20 of us crowded into the small room. Maria was shattered. José was broken. As we prayed for and ministered to them, their faces began to brighten, as this group loved them in their sorrow and need.

A few weeks later, the story of the Samaritan woman was shared at the church. At the close of the story, José and Maria responded with several others to accept Christ. Love had won the battle for their hearts.

—RUSS, SOUTH AMERICA

Loving Father, MAY I BE SELFLESS TODAY AS I MINISTER TO OTHERS IN NEED. HELP ME TO BE ESPECIALLY SENSITIVE TO MEMBERS OF THE CHURCH BODY WHERE I BELONG. I PRAY FOR YOUR POWER TO BE DISPLAYED IN SOUTH AMERICA SO THAT REMOTE GROUPS WILL KNOW THE GOD WHO IS ALMIGHTY. *Amen.*

Aching for the lost

"With all prayer and petition pray at all times in the Spirit, and with this in view, be on the alert with all perseverance and petition for all the saints."
Ephesians 6:18 (NASB)

Laughter drifted out the door of Lighthouse Baptist Church in Mdant-sane (m-dant-SAH-nay) township, South Africa. As the Baptist women's group shared what Jesus had done in their lives, their faces glowed with joy.

During the testimonies, Lydia came to me with her hands across her abdomen. She said, "My stomach is in pain." Lydia winced, grabbed her stomach again and continued speaking. "We are sitting here in our church having a great talk about Jesus," she said. "But in this neighborhood, many are in darkness without Jesus. The Holy Spirit is causing my stomach to ache for these people. We *must* go out there and share with them."

I was amazed to hear a simple confession of hurt for the lost. I had taught the women about prayerwalking, and now they wanted to go out into the streets and dirt paths to do it!

These women didn't just walk along the dusty road praying. They sang songs and witnessed loudly to anyone who was within hearing distance! God gave them an open door to give those in darkness the Light. When we returned, we prayed and wept over the lost souls within rock-throwing distance of our church and asked Jesus to save them.

This newfound compassion for the lost all started because a beautiful Xhosa (KOH-sah) woman listened to her stomach, alerting her to the Holy Spirit speaking. When the Lord shows up, He causes such a disturbance within us that we must go wherever the darkness is and give the glorious light.

—LINDA, CENTRAL, EASTERN AND SOUTHERN AFRICA

Father, CAUSE ME TO ACHE FOR THE LOST AROUND ME AND THOSE THROUGHOUT THE WORLD. GIVE ME THE SAME PASSION AS THIS AFRICAN WOMAN WHO IS WILLING TO GO OUT INTO THE STREETS AND DIRT PATHS TO SHARE JESUS. *Amen.*

Fulfilling God's Desires

"From everyone who has been given much, much will be required; and to whom they entrusted much, of him they will ask all the more." Luke 12:48b (NASB)

"Strong," the meaning of the boy's name, is my new friend. In his 16 short years, he has been through many difficulties. As an orphan, he owns nothing except the clothes on his back, but he is rich in his love for Jesus and the Word. It was through missionary workers of another organization that he heard about Jesus at his orphanage. Now he stays at a halfway house run by Christians.

One day, I gave Strong a lift to the train station. While in the car, we were having a discussion on spiritual things, and I asked him what he wanted to do the next year after he finished school. He said he was burdened that so many of his people group have yet to hear about Jesus. He desires to be a preacher of the good news throughout his country. His decision came after a challenge from Luke 12:48. Strong said that the Father had done much for him, and he now wanted to do much for the Father.

The Holy Spirit brought great conviction in my life through Strong that day. I had to ask myself if I was fulfilling God's desires for me. I knew that my list of blessings from the Father would likely far exceed those of Strong. The Bible states that God expects more from those who have been given more. He has blessed us in America with religious freedom, access to Bible study and growth, tremendous teaching and financial resources. What are we going to do with those blessings?

—D., CENTRAL ASIA

Father, THANK YOU FOR THIS YOUNG MAN WHO IS STRONG IN FAITH. WATCH OVER HIM AS HE BRINGS THE GOOD NEWS TO MUSLIMS. BLESS HIM AND OTHERS LIKE HIM MANY TIMES OVER FOR FAITHFULNESS TO YOU. I PRAY THAT I WILL FULFILL YOUR DESIRES FOR ME. *Amen.*

Taking time to minister

"Now to Him who, by ... the (action of His) power that is at work within us, is able to (carry out His purpose and) do superabundantly, far over and above all that we (dare) ask or think (infinitely beyond our highest prayers, desires, thoughts, hopes, or dreams)." Ephesians 3:20 (AMP)

"Please pray for Mrs. T. I think she's getting really close to making a decision." Our short-term missionary friend continued to meet with Mrs. T weekly.

One such trip had been especially harried. We were running late. As I tried to turn the van around on the crowded ice hill of a parking lot, my stress grew. "All this work for someone who's probably never going to believe anyway," I sighed to myself.

I had never been to Mrs. T's house before, so I decided to pop my head in and say, "Please be kind," a typical Japanese greeting, much like, "What's new?"

As we stomped the snow off of our boots, Mrs. T stood in the entryway, surprised that I had come that day. "Can you stay?" she asked me. I eagerly agreed.

She said, "I asked my husband last night if I could become a Christian. In answer to my prayer, he actually set down his newspaper and listened! He said that I could become a Christian today! I wanted to pray the sinner's prayer, but I wanted to pray in Japanese. That's why I can't believe you're here!"

That was the first time I had ever been to her house—it was God's timing to a T! A day that the enemy wanted to take for himself turned into angels rejoicing over Japan. And not only did the kingdom gain an incredibly vibrant Christian that day, but I gained a Japanese best friend.

—KATHY, PACIFIC RIM

Lord, I PRAY FOR A WILLING HEART TO MINISTER TODAY, EVEN IF IT IS NOT CONVENIENT. USE MISSIONARIES IN JAPAN TO SHARE CHRIST WITH THE LOST. THANK YOU, GOD, THAT YOUR PERFECT TIMING IS MADE KNOWN IN UNEXPECTED WAYS. *Amen.*

A simple act of love

"This is My commandment, that you love one another as I have loved you."
John 15:12 (NKJV)

Sheer exhaustion clouded her young face. With eyes downcast, she told me she was not sleeping. She shares a tiny room with six other Chinese students that have brick-hard beds and little heat or hot water. Immediately, I invited Ava to come home with me. Entering our apartment, joy spread across her face. We settled in for an evening of talking, dinner, movies and popcorn.

After dinner we suggested going to McDonald's for a sundae. My roommate and I put on our coats and shoes as Ava quietly watched us. "Don't you want to come with us?" I asked. She ran to me and hugged me, saying her parents left her alone as a child, not wanting to do things with her! Walking together in the cold night air, I asked, "Are you feeling better?" "I am very happy," she replied.

She didn't have gloves or a scarf, so I wanted to purchase them for her. After much protesting, she accepted my gifts. I knew she had been raised in a loveless home with parents who despised each other. Love is what we as children of the King receive every moment. She is just learning about His love.

Before bed, Ava enjoyed a hot soak in a bubble bath. Rested the next morning, a breakfast of oatmeal and apple muffins ended her brief visit. I pray it brought her joy and comfort. It was a simple act of love for us to give this to her—the Father's love through us.

—A WORKER IN CHINA

Heavenly Father, THROUGH SIMPLE ACTS OF KINDNESS, HELP ME TO LOVE THOSE AROUND ME. MAY WORKERS IN CHINA REACH OUT IN LOVE TO THOSE WHO HAVE NOT EXPERIENCED SUCH LOVE SO THAT THE LOST CAN HAVE A PICTURE OF YOUR LOVE. *Amen.*

Loving those who are different

"I will also make you a light for the Gentiles, that you may bring my salvation to the ends of the earth." Isaiah 49:6b (NIV)

I noticed the man on my way to the grocery store. He always sat on a stool outside his front door.

One day, I introduced myself. "I see you sitting here when I walk to the store," I said. He asked me what I did. When I told him, he grew a little defensive and quickly retorted, "My name is Ricardo. I'm a communist ... and an Apostolic Roman Catholic."

"A communist *and* a Catholic?" I asked, grinning. "I didn't think those two went together." He saw the humor in what he had said and admitted that he and the local Communist Party didn't get along.

I asked him about his life, his family, his church and how he had lost the use of his right side. He spoke of his stroke six years earlier.

I began to visit Ricardo often. One day, I stopped by his house unexpectedly. Although surprised, he invited me in. "No religious leader has ever visited my house," he said with resignation. "They have never shown any interest in my welfare. I've only known you for a few weeks and here you are, sitting in my house, visiting me."

I smiled and prayed silently, *Lord, help me be a friend to Ricardo. Don't let me see him as a "soul to be won." Let me offer my friendship. Let Jesus be Jesus in me.*

The Great Commission impels us to reach out to those with whom we have nothing in common—to go to the overlooked and the lonely, to those who believe differently than we do.

—P.J., MIDDLE AMERICA AND THE CARIBBEAN

Father, IMPEL ME TO REACH OUT TO THOSE WITH WHOM I HAVE NOTHING IN COMMON. LET OTHERS SEE JESUS IN ME. DRAW THEM TO YOURSELF THROUGH ME. GIVE MISSIONARIES THIS SAME DESIRE DAILY. *Amen.*

"God bless you!"

"What a wretched man I am! Who will rescue me from this body of death?"
Romans 7:24 (NIV)

The scourge of the people of the former Soviet Union is alcoholism, although they call it a tradition. Alcohol is a part of every holiday celebration, social gathering and business meeting. For some, it's part of the daily commute home. For many, it is a bottomless pit they have fallen into with no way out.

As I was caught in crawling traffic, this societal plague was close enough to touch. An old woman was standing near a busy intersection in the city of Kiev (kee-EV), Ukraine (YOU-crane). Her clothes were dirty, and her skin was weather-beaten. As cars stopped at the light, she walked up to each one with her hand extended. Realizing that my turn was approaching, I found a few coins and rolled down my window. I was already putting them into her hand when I smelled the alcohol. I was surprised, but the glazed look in her eyes was unmistakable.

I wanted to take the coins back, knowing that I had just given her vodka money! Instead, as she peered gratefully into the car, I said, "God bless you." These words made her stop and take pause. They were not new to her, because it's a fairly common saying in Ukrainian. But, they were spoken to *her*. All at once her countenance changed. The light turned green, but it seemed as if she wanted me to linger there with her, basking in the hope, the grace and the power of those three little words.

—KATIE, CENTRAL AND EASTERN EUROPE

Father, I PRAY THAT MISSIONARIES IN THE FORMER SOVIET UNION WILL SEEK OUT THE DEPRESSED, HOPELESS ALCOHOLICS WHO NEED JESUS IN THEIR LIVES. LET THEM KNOW THROUGH YOUR SERVANTS THAT YOU LOVE THEM AND WANT TO REDEEM THEM. I PRAY THAT YOU WILL GIVE ME PATIENCE AND LOVE FOR THOSE THAT I KNOW WITH SUBSTANCE ABUSE PROBLEMS. I SPECIFICALLY PRAY FOR _____ RIGHT NOW. *Amen.*

He is enough

"My God shall supply all your needs according to His riches in glory in Christ Jesus." Philippians 4:19 (NASB)

For several months, my husband and I had been teaching health and nutrition in a small village. One out of five children in Bolivia die before the age of 2, mainly due to poor nutrition and hygiene. It seemed there was never enough time or resources to meet the needs around us.

During the last week of classes, we were told that another child had died of diarrhea. How many times had I shown the mothers how to prepare a simple rehydration solution? It costs pennies to make and could have saved the life of the child. Another family, we were told, had chosen to take their child to a *curandero* (coo-rahn-DARE-oh), or witch doctor, rather than consult the health promoter. That child had also died.

Traveling home that night, I cried out of disappointment and frustration. "I've had enough! I've seen enough poverty to last a lifetime. I've seen enough children die to last two lifetimes. I can't do this any longer. I want to go home!"

The next morning I awoke with the thought, *This week is Thanksgiving.* My next thought, which I truly feel came from God was, *Make Thanksgiving cards.* In my craft files, I came across a Thanksgiving poem. As I copied the poem for each card, the words began to sink in, first to my mind then to my heart: "Thank God there is enough. In God there is enough love to cover every mistake, enough light to brighten the darkest hour, enough power to meet every need."

—CYNTHIA, SOUTH AMERICA

You are enough, Father. THANK YOU FOR YOUR LOVE THAT IS ENOUGH. WHEN CIRCUMSTANCES OVERWHELM ME, WHEN SITUATIONS SEEM HOPELESS, I KNOW THAT YOU HAVE ENOUGH POWER TO MEET EVERY NEED. GIVE THIS REASSURANCE TO MISSIONARIES TODAY WHO LIVE AND WORK IN AREAS OF EXTREME POVERTY. *Amen.*

Seeing clearly

"The Lord has done this, and it is marvelous in our eyes." Psalm 118:23 (NIV)

The petite woman had patiently waited for her turn to have her eyes checked. The American volunteer was amazed when the woman could barely see the big *E* on the eye chart. She prayed there would be a pair of glasses with the right prescription and frame size for this woman. The optometrist and assistants also sensed the urgency and rejoiced when a pair was found among the thousands generously donated. The glasses not only improved her vision, they looked fabulous! Everyone cheered as she read through several lines of the chart.

As the woman began her walk home, she examined her hands. She pulled off a leaf and looked at it in wonder. Along the road, she observed nature, colors and people and marveled in the gift of sight she had just received.

Later, the woman returned with an orchid plant of delicate white and lavender blossoms. She handed it to the volunteer who had administered the screening test. Then she said, "I recognized my children getting off the school bus today, not by the color of their clothes, but by their faces. I saw my children's faces!"

We'll never know who donated those glasses, and the donor never saw the incredible joy those glasses brought the mother. As this woman and others continue attending craft classes and Bible study at the center where the volunteers held the clinic, we pray that they will have their spiritual eyes opened to clearly see Jesus as Savior.

—LORETTA, SOUTH AMERICA

Gracious God, HELP ME TO OBEY YOUR WORD AND THE PROMPTINGS OF YOUR SPIRIT TO GIVE JOYFULLY TO MISSIONS EVEN WHEN I MAY NOT SEE THE FRUIT OF MY GIFTS. LORD, THANK YOU FOR THE PHYSICAL AND ETERNAL BLESSINGS THAT PEOPLE HAVE RECEIVED BECAUSE VOLUNTEERS SACRIFICIALLY GAVE OF THEIR TIME, EXPERTISE AND GIFTS TO MINISTER TO NEEDS IN BRAZIL AND IN OTHER COUNTRIES. *Amen.*

A tsunami of grief

"Jesus wept." John 11:35 (NASB)

The devastating power of the Indian Ocean tsunami captured our attention on December 26, 2004. Television images brought the devastation into our homes, along with the knowledge that the earth momentarily wobbled on its axis. Talk about shaking up our world!

Southern Baptists were on the ground offering help within a few days of the disaster. They were quickly involved in providing medical care, feeding the hungry, clearing up the rubble, burying bodies, providing clean water and reconstruction.

One of the most helpful ministries was profoundly simple and personal. Showing compassion, offering help and simply listening were acts of love that deeply impacted victims who had lost loved ones. One female volunteer patiently listened to, cried with and hugged women who had lost their husbands and children. After being helped by a volunteer team, one man commented that many aid workers offered physical help, but "you people have joined us in our tears."

What else could the followers of Jesus do? While some groups around the world held dialogues to consider where God was in all this, believers working in the disaster zone sensed that "Jesus wept." These two words in John 11:35 tell us something incredibly important about our Master. He wept when He heard his friend had died and joined in the grief the sisters experienced.

What was Jesus doing during the tsunami? He was weeping over the tragic loss of life, just as He weeps every day to see thousands die without knowledge of His sacrifice for them.

—A WORKER IN THE PACIFIC RIM

Compassionate Father, THANK YOU FOR DEMONSTRATING YOUR LOVE THROUGH BELIEVERS AS A RESULT OF THE DEVASTATING TSUNAMI WHICH HIT SOUTHEAST ASIA AND OTHER AREAS. WE PRAY FOR THOSE PEOPLE WHO ARE STILL RECOVERING FROM THE LOSS OF LOVED ONES, PERSONAL PROPERTY, HOPES AND DREAMS. MAY MANY TURN TO JESUS, THE ONE WHO WEEPS FOR THEM. *Amen.*

Who is my neighbor?

"'So which of these three do you think was the neighbor to him who fell among the thieves?' And he said, 'He who showed mercy on him.' Then Jesus said to him, 'Go and do likewise.'" Luke 10:36–37 (NKJV)

My son, Paul, and I were returning a video to the rental store in our neighborhood in Seoul, Korea, when we saw someone in need of help. There was a little, hunchbacked Korean grandmother struggling with a huge load of cardboard and metal items on a small cart. The load had shifted, and she struggled to straighten it up without toppling.

I stopped the car on the side of the road. The woman was in the middle of the well-traveled road. With the grace of God, I told the grandmother that I was going to help. Paul and I started turning the small cart upright with its load and then straightened the things on it. I continued to talk to her as we worked, telling her that we would pull the cart to where she was going.

A young Korean couple who had come from the church nearby saw the three of us and decided to help also. We worked hard to get the cart ready to move again and finally managed to take it to where she was going. As I held on to one side and Paul the other, the grandmother pulled on my shirt and asked, "Are you a missionary?" Surprised at the question, I answered, "Yes," and told her why I was in Korea. By the time we arrived at the grandmother's destination, I had shared about Jesus and His love for her. As we left, the old woman continued to bow over and over again, thanking us.

—GRACE, PACIFIC RIM

Father in heaven, HELP ME TO NOTICE NEEDS AROUND ME TODAY. FOR MISSIONARIES TODAY, I PRAY THAT THEY WILL SEE INTERRUPTIONS AS OPPORTUNITIES TO SHARE THE GOSPEL. *Amen.*

Love even thy noisy neighbor

"If you really keep the royal law found in Scripture, 'Love your neighbor as yourself,' you are doing right." James 2:8 (NIV)

I was ready for a good night's rest, but the walls began to shake and the thump of a bass began. Then came the electric guitar and the voices of the neighbors and their guests. Drunken singing, sounds of breaking glass and flirtatious laughter obnoxiously interrupted my attempt to fall asleep.

I prayed and tried to sleep. At midnight, my oldest son cried out, thinking there was an intruder in the house. I put him back to bed and comforted him until he fell asleep. I, however, was wide-awake and even angrier. I wanted to call the police to complain, but my Spanish was not good enough. Instead, I asked God for one of the common outages of electricity, but the party continued and my anger intensified.

Then it happened. The festivities continued, but God spoke to me. In my heart I felt Him say, *You're praying for yourself, but you should be praying for them. Pray for them.* Reluctantly at first, I touched the shared wall between the apartments and began to pray. I prayed that these neighbors might one day understand God's love and accept the salvation that He offers.

It is impossible to be angry with people when you are praying for them. The Bible says, *"Love your enemies and pray for those who persecute you"* (Matt. 5:44, NIV). Jesus also tells us to "love your neighbor as yourself." That night, I began to understand the love I am to have for my noisy, unsaved neighbors, even in the early hours of the morning.

—TERRIE, MIDDLE AMERICA AND THE CARIBBEAN

Father, ROOT OUT ALL BITTERNESS AND ANGER THAT IS WITHIN ME TOWARD _____, OR ANY THAT HAS THE POTENTIAL TO DEVELOP. I PRAY FOR THIS PERSON TODAY. REMIND ME TO PRAY FOR THIS PERSON OFTEN, AND MAY YOU FILL ME WITH YOUR LOVE FOR THIS PERSON. MAY YOU CONVICT MISSIONARIES TODAY WHO HARBOR ANY BITTERNESS TOWARD THEIR NEIGHBORS. *Amen.*

Looking up to see those around you

"Behold, I say to you, lift up your eyes and look on the fields, that they are white for harvest." John 4:35 (NASB)

Throughout the Gospels are accounts of Jesus weeping and being moved to compassion as He saw the multitudes. He also encouraged His disciples to lift up their eyes and see. I know why now.

It was a hot summer afternoon at a Mexico beach and we were celebrating the 10th birthday of one of our daughters. We had been missionaries for only six months when the unthinkable happened. My husband, oldest daughter and two young summer missionaries were caught in a strong undertow and drowned.

As I knelt beside the bodies, my mind was filled with a thousand thoughts. How would I tell our families about our tragedy? What would become of our ministry in Mexico? How would I raise my other children without my husband? As my head was bowed, I was occupied with real concerns.

Then I lifted my eyes. Many people had gathered around us. I knew my loss was great, but I knew the loss of these around me was even greater. Mine was temporary; theirs was eternal.

I said, "This is my husband, daughter and friends. They are now in the presence of their Lord and Savior. What if you were the ones on the sand? Do you know where your soul would be?"

In the town of Playa Linda (PLY-ah LEAN-dah) there was not a church, but there is one now. It is filled with many who were on the beach that day. If we only take the time to lift up our eyes and see, the outcome of a trial could have miraculous results!

—GLORIA, MIDDLE AMERICA AND THE CARIBBEAN

Father, THANK YOU FOR ETERNAL LIFE. THANK YOU FOR PEACE THAT YOU GIVE IN THE MIDST OF DIFFICULTIES. MAY I NEVER TAKE MY EYES OFF YOU. HELP ME TO SEE THE NEEDS OF THE LOST TODAY. *Amen.*

Gifts from God

"For I testify that according to their ability, and beyond their ability, they gave of their own accord, begging us with much urging for the favor of participation in the support of the saints." 2 Corinthians 8:3–4 (NASB)

As I go out, I carry a large bag with me, anticipating whatever need may come up. I have a water bottle, French Bible, Bassar (bah-SAR) New Testament, sometimes a tape recording and medicine. I treat headaches and stomachaches, worm infestation, skin infections, colds and coughs and even hangnails.

After a bout with malaria myself, I missed the weekly Bible study. Early the next morning, several women came to my house. They said, "You help us when we are sick, so we have come to pray with you and help you if we can." Each one prayed for my healing. Then they pulled out 300 CFA (about 50 cents) and gave it to me to buy medicine. "You always share what you have with us and we had no pills to give you, so this will help you buy what you need." I realized then that I had taken it for granted that I had medicine whenever needed.

How could I take their money? I did not need it to buy medicine. They needed it so much more. Scripture says it is more blessed to give than to receive, but I found it harder for me to receive than to give. Then I began to see that sometimes I have the same attitude toward God's gifts to me. There are things I "have" that I think I've provided for myself. But ultimately, all gifts are from Him. To graciously receive the gifts God bestows on us, either by His own hand or through others, is a lifelong lesson.

—GAYE, WEST AFRICA

Father, HELP ME TO RECEIVE YOUR GIFTS GRACIOUSLY. FORGIVE ME OF PRIDE AND OF TRYING TO ACQUIRE MY NEEDS WITHOUT YOUR DIRECTION. THANK YOU FOR THESE AFRICAN WOMEN WHO TAUGHT ME A LESSON ON GIVING AND FOR THE MISSIONARY WHO TAUGHT ME ABOUT RECEIVING. *Amen.*

Christmas Around the World

I am filled with anticipation as we celebrate the birth of Christ thematically throughout the month of December. While not every entry focuses on the advent of Christ, many of them will usher you around the globe for the holidays. I pray that you will gain insight into the tenderness and complexities of celebrating Christmas as an American missionary on foreign soil.

I can't think of a better time of year for you and me, who do not share their vocation, to be especially prayerful. Think particularly of the numbers of missionaries from any Christian denomination who may find themselves in a different land and culture for the first time during the holidays. Some of them are surrounded by entire communities that take no thought at all of the birth of Christ. Surely some of these dear servants share the emotions of the children of Israel in a strange kingdom so far from home. "*How can we sing the songs of the Lord while in a foreign land?*" (Ps. 137:4, NIV).

Then imagine the delight of Christ as He inclines His ear to hear "The First Noel" rise like Christmas incense from that community. Surely the sound is sweeter than all the angels He has "heard on high, sweetly singing o'er the plains." After centuries of silent nights bearing no praises, the sound barrier is broken by one obedient couple who bend their knees and with tears of loneliness streaming, sing, "Joy to the World!" Yes, the whole world. Christ, the unrealized desire of all nations!

Such hope is what sends a believer so far from the place they call home. They dare hope against hope that next year another set of knees may bow. Then another. And yet another. Slowly, ah, but surely! Has God not promised that people from "*every nation, tribe, people and language*" will one day stand "*before the throne and in front of the Lamb*" (Rev. 7:9, NIV)?

"*How, then, can they call on the one they have not believed in? And how can they* believe in the one of whom they have not heard? And how can they hear without someone preaching to them? And how can they preach unless they are sent? As it is written, 'How beautiful are the feet of those who bring good news!'" (Rom. 10:14–15, NIV).

Why feet? Because they were willing to go. Nothing is more beautiful to God than feet callous from obedience.

A few thoughts to begin our Christmas theme: Galatians 4:4–5 reads, "But when the time had fully come, God sent his Son, born of a woman, born under law, to redeem those under law, that we might receive the full rights of sons" (NIV).

Give careful attention to the wording, "when the time had fully come." On the kingdom calendar of God, time does not *go*. It *comes*. Humans, in our egocentricity, perceive that time *came* when we were born and has been *going* ever since. Every now and then as I'm getting ready for my day, I glance in the mirror to brush the night out of my hair and nearly jump out of my skin with fright. "Who is that? How can I be this … this … *old*? Where did my drill team uniform go?" Ever feel like that? Okay, forget the drill team uniform, but do you ever wonder where time is going?

While for us, time seems fleeting; for God, time is arriving. From His desire for the fellowship of nations, God slipped this thing we call "time" out of eternity and the first *beginning* was born. "In the beginning God created the heavens and the earth" (Gen. 1:1, NIV). Then the time came for God to breathe a soul into Adam. And the time came for Eve. And the time came for Abraham and the time came for a covenant in which "all peoples on earth" would be blessed through one man. And the time came for Egypt. And the time came for Exodus. And the time came for conquest. And the time came for judges. And kings. And captives.

The time came for silence. Then the time came for the loudest "Word" God would ever shout as the living Logos, Jesus Christ, was made flesh to dwell among us. For God so loved the world He sent His only begotten Son (John 3:16). Time fully came. And time will fully come again. This time, every knee will bow—from every tongue, tribe and nation—and every tongue will confess, *"Jesus is Lord!"* (Phil. 2:11).

Beloved, time is coming in your life. Not going. Time is coming more quickly than you know to see Christ face to face. As time finds you in this very spot, in this very season, what has the time come for you to do? No, we're not all called to be missionaries, but we are indeed all called (Rom. 8:30). Time has come, not for someone else, dear one, but for you.

What is God telling you deep in your heart that it is time for you to do? Like the missionaries with whom we've sojourned here for a year, you neither have it all together nor feel particularly suited, but would you be willing to be like them in another way? Would you agree to simply be obedient and let God do the rest? Find your place in this world and fulfill your calling with everything you've got. Your part awaits you.

Do it.

—*Beth Moore*

Side by side

"He spoke and said to those who were standing before him, saying, 'Remove the filthy garments from him.' Again he said to him, 'See, I have taken your iniquity away from you and will clothe you with festal robes.'" Zechariah 3:4 (NASB)

Recently, I attended the ceremony of an installation of a chief at a local village in Togo (TOH-go). It was a grand event that does not happen often. Everyone attends, young and old, even if it means walking miles to the event. There are chiefs from other villages and government officials in attendance. Each person, whether important or ordinary, is in his best dress. Crowns even adorn the heads of dignitaries.

At this particular event, there was one lowly, uninvited guest. He was wearing dirty rags. To the bystanders, the poor man was considered the local "crazy man." As important officials made glorious speeches to the throngs of people, the "crazy man" walked in front, made his own speeches as he looked into the sky and shook his fist to his imaginary friends. He was so much a part of the village that the people ignored him and avoided contact with him. I could only feel pity and pray for the man.

But as I watched, there was one man who walked up to the "crazy man" and gently placed his arm around him. Then, side by side, he led the man outside of the crowd. I knew that there was a lesson God wanted to teach me.

Christmas this year will be sweeter. God didn't avoid me when I was in the filthy rags of sin, but He walked along beside me and brought me to salvation. Jesus walks along beside me even when I momentarily avoid Him. May I stay ever close to Him!

—KATHY, WEST AFRICA

Father, THANK YOU FOR SAVING ME. THANK YOU FOR TAKING AWAY MY FILTHY GARMENTS AND CLOTHING ME WITH RIGHTEOUSNESS BECAUSE OF YOUR SON, JESUS. MAY YOU DRAW THE UNLOVELY OF THE WORLD TO YOURSELF THROUGH YOUR SERVANTS. HELP ME TO MINISTER TO THE POOR, THE NEEDY AND EVEN THE HOMELESS THIS CHRISTMAS SEASON. *Amen.*

Ask and you shall receive

"Ask, and it will be given to you; seek, and you will find; knock, and it will be opened to you." Matthew 7:7 (NKJV)

The East Sea Team in Ulsan (ool-SAHN), South Korea, had begun to plan the program for their Christmas banquet. Students who attend the English Bible classes and their families were invited to the banquet. With the customs of Christmas as the theme, five customary items and their Christian meanings were chosen to present.

One of the items to present was the candy cane. A team member had e-mailed her Sunday School class in the United States to request a supply of candy canes. But since the request was made on Thanksgiving Day, only a week before the banquet, she wasn't sure the class would get the e-mail in time to send the candy canes immediately. Having candy canes would allow the telling of the story of Jesus using the candy as a symbol. The team prayed that the candy canes would arrive for the banquet.

Not long after the prayer, the doorbell rang. A delivery of two big boxes from the Sunday School class was placed before us. The first box was filled with supplies for a ministry to fishermen, along with other items. The second box, to the team's surprise, held candy canes! Four older adults jumped up and down, giving praise to God! This was the first time for all the team members to experience asking for something, the doorbell literally ringing, and the need being met right then and there.

Even in the little things, God is faithful when we ask Him anything according to His will.

—A WORKER IN THE PACIFIC RIM

Thank You, Father, FOR YOUR PROVISION IN THE LITTLE THINGS AND FOR KNOWING WHAT I NEED EVEN BEFORE I ASK. I PRAY THAT I WILL TRUST YOU TO MEET ALL MY NEEDS. GIVE MISSIONARIES MANY OPPORTUNITIES TO USE THE CHRISTMAS MESSAGE TO SHARE CHRIST. *Amen.*

Rely on My protection

"Or let him rely on My protection, let him make peace with me."
Isaiah 27:5 (NASB)

My family and I were experiencing fear firsthand. Not from the government, but from one of our students. Even now we can't explain what the root of the problem was, but he had become very angry and had attacked one of our teachers. Regardless, he demanded to remain in school. His roommates were also angry and declared they would settle things "with fists."

Tension was high at the school, and my kids were worried about their dad going to teach that night. I was sitting in the living room, preparing for my quiet time with the Father but truly paralyzed by the event.

I told the Father I was scared. "I know that You have not given us a spirit of fear, but one of love, power and self-discipline, but Lord, I am still afraid," I cried. The Father quietly reminded me that I needed to stay on schedule with my quiet time. So, somewhat reluctantly, I turned to the next passage in Isaiah.

Chapter 27 was about the deliverance of Israel, and as I read verse five, the words jumped off the page: *"Let him rely on My protection"* (NASB). The Father was saying to me, "You, too, need to rely on My protection. I am sovereign." As I received these words, His peace flooded my soul.

Throughout the next month, tension at the school eased. Then, on Christmas Day, one of the student's roommates said, "Okay, I want to know about this Jesus." On New Year's Day, we had a new brother. God is amazing.

—A WORKER IN EAST ASIA

Thank You, Father, THAT I CAN CAST MY CARES UPON YOU. THANK YOU THAT YOU HAVE NOT GIVEN ME A SPIRIT OF FEAR, BUT OF LOVE, POWER AND SELF-DISCIPLINE. I RELY UPON YOUR GRACE AND POWER WHEN THE EVIL ONE COMES AGAINST ME. *Amen.*

Found by translation

"The law of the LORD is perfect, reviving the soul. The statutes of the LORD are trustworthy, making wise the simple." Psalm 19:7 (NIV)

Nancy is a neighbor who is a teacher of English. In her short life, she has experienced many difficulties. As we became closer friends, I would try to turn the conversation to spiritual matters. She considered herself a Muslim but did not observe any Muslim religious practices.

When Nancy called or came over and asked what I was doing, I would answer, "Reading the Bible." I made frequent references to how God helps us when we have problems in our lives. I left my open Bible on the table. I displayed a Nativity set at Christmas. She remained frustratingly oblivious.

The week before Christmas, I had been asked to give a testimony at our Christian gathering. When I got a cancellation from my regular translator, I found myself looking for a last-minute substitute for the next morning. Then I thought—*Nancy!* When I asked her to translate a spiritual lesson, she said, "Great!"

The next day, Nancy stumbled over many of the words I used, such as "Savior" and "sin," because they weren't in her vocabulary. Our small group was patient with my fractured testimony, because they, too, had been praying for her salvation. By the end of the meeting, Nancy gave her life to Jesus! It happened so fast, I wondered if she truly understood. But since then, she has remained steadfast to her newfound faith, despite family persecution. She says, "I will never leave my Jesus." Now we laugh about what it took to get her attention—translating God's Word.

—JANET, CENTRAL ASIA

Father God, THANK YOU FOR THE POWER OF YOUR WORD. I PRAY FOR TRANSLATORS FOR CHRISTIAN WORKERS TODAY. SPEAK TO THEM THROUGH THE MESSAGES AND THE WORD THAT THEY TRANSLATE FOR SERVANTS OF GOD AROUND THE WORLD. *Amen.*

All I need

"I said to the LORD, 'You are my LORD; apart from you I have no good thing.'"
Psalm 16:2 (NIV)

Every year I ask the Lord to reveal something new to me about the Christmas story. This Christmas, I've been shown what seems to be a simple, fundamental truth that is easy to miss during the busy season.

In February 2002, my family was called to serve as missionaries in the Caribbean region. Except for clothing and some sentimental items, we sold most everything that belonged to us. This included the majority of our Christmas decorations, some of which we'd had most of my life. When our first Christmas on the field came, it was more difficult to be in the "Christmas spirit" because the familiar Christmas decorations were not displayed. The weather wasn't cold, and we definitely don't get snow. On top of that, we had no special friends or family to share the joy of the season.

As I sought the Lord, I expected to hear something new about the circumstances surrounding the Christmas story. Instead, what I was shown was the actual heart of Christmas, which in turn changed my own heart. It occurred to me that while all these things symbolize Christmas, all of these things are not Christmas. I learned that Jesus is enough. Jesus is Christmas. When all the stuff—the lights, gifts, trees, food and even friends—was taken away, it came down to Jesus. He is the only reason to be celebrating. I learned that everything I need for Christmas, and for my life, is found in Jesus. Apart from Him, "I have no good thing."

—SARAH, MIDDLE AMERICA AND THE CARIBBEAN

Father, MAY YOU BE THE FOCUS OF MISSIONARIES WHO ARE AWAY FROM FAMILY DURING DECEMBER. MINISTER TO THEM, AND SHOW EACH ONE, AS WELL AS MISSIONARY CHILDREN, THAT YOU ARE ALL THEY NEED. *Amen.*

A time to celebrate Jesus

"She will bear a Son; and you shall call His name Jesus, for He will save His people from their sins." Matthew 1:21 (NASB)

My first Christmas in a Muslim country was a new experience. Incredibly, I had seen a few festive decorations around town, but these were put up only to celebrate the coming new year.

Deciding to share about Christmas, I invited my language tutor to my home. She was curious about this holiday that Americans celebrate, so it was a perfect opportunity to share Christ in a relaxed way. We made Christmas cookies together, talked about the meaning of Christmas, decorated my mini tree and watched a dramatized portion of Matthew on video portraying the birth of Jesus. My friend had thought that Christmas was simply a New Year's celebration, as most people in this Muslim country believe, rather than a day with religious meaning for Christians.

As we viewed the video, she followed along in a New Testament of her own language. Afterward, I asked her if she would like to keep the book. She said that she would. This is the first copy of Scripture she has ever had.

I was just thinking how interesting it is to live in a country where Christmas isn't commercialized or even recognized. I found myself even forgetting that it was Christmas without all the decorations and present buying I am used to in America. However, one of the great joys for me has been that I'm not distracted by all the things Christmas really is *not*. It's easier to be more focused on the Son in order to share with friends and those I meet.

—ABBY, CENTRAL ASIA

Father, I CELEBRATE YOUR SON AT THIS SEASON OF THE YEAR! THANK YOU THAT YOU LOVED ME ENOUGH TO SEND JESUS TO THIS EARTH TO DIE FOR MY SINS AND TO RISE AGAIN SO THAT I MIGHT HAVE NEW LIFE. I PRAY THAT YOU WILL GIVE MISSIONARIES ACROSS THE WORLD MANY OPPORTUNITIES TO SHARE ABOUT THE MEANING OF CHRISTMAS. OPEN MY EYES TO THE OPPORTUNITIES THAT YOU ALSO GIVE ME TO SHARE JESUS WITH OTHERS. *Amen.*

Crossing borders

"But Peter and John replied, 'Do you think God wants us to obey you rather than him? We cannot stop telling about the wonderful things we have seen and heard.'" Acts 4:19–20 (NLT)

Crossing the border with two large bags of Bibles, I prayed for safety. The Bibles were for people in the mountains. The police usually never searched my car—why should this time be different?

As I pulled up to passport control, the police motioned me to pull over. They rustled through my belongings and found all 250 loaves of the "living bread." As they took me into their office, I prayed for courage.

Through a whole battery of questions, God gave me peace. God gave me questions to ask *them* about their knowledge of the Bible. I asked, "Why is it wrong to offer people something that can give them hope?" The only answer they had was one they were taught to say.

The police chief came in and motioned me to come with him to another room. He wrote out my charges. Then the chief and I had a great conversation. He indicated that he was not a practicing Muslim. At that moment, God gave me such a love for this man and the ability to let him know, that since it was Christmas, he could have the Bibles as a gift. (I knew that I wouldn't be getting them back.) After three hours, we smiled, shook hands and he let me go.

I rejoice that those whom I often fear were given a chance to hear the gospel.

With whom is God telling you to share the gospel? He overcomes our fears and barriers so that all may hear.

—J.C., NORTHERN AFRICA AND THE MIDDLE EAST

Father, MAY I BE WILLING TO RISK STATUS AND COMFORT TO SHARE CHRIST WITH THE LOST. MAY I BE WILLING TO CROSS THE BORDER INTO NEW OPPORTUNITIES TO MINISTER TO OTHERS. USE THESE DEAR SERVANTS OVERSEAS TO BRING YOUR WORD ACROSS COUNTRY BORDERS. *Amen.*

Missing the meaning

"But whenever anyone turns to the Lord, the veil is taken away."
2 Corinthians 3:16 (NIV)

As a missionary working with Muslim women, I was surprised to find out that many Muslims living in Paris celebrate the secular aspects of Christmas such as Santa Claus, Christmas trees and jingle bells. They totally reject the true reason for the holiday, the birth of Jesus Christ.

One of my Muslim friends had a Christmas tree in her home, under which she placed all the gifts she had bought for her family. She also threw a large party on Christmas Eve for her friends and neighbors, all of whom were Muslims. One afternoon before Christmas, my roommate, Mae, and I had the opportunity to explain to our friend the real meaning of Christmas. She just could not fathom that Christmas was a religious holiday. She emphatically stated that Christmas was just for children; it was only about Santa Claus and presents. We left her apartment brokenhearted, because she could not understand. As a Christmas gift, we gave her daughter a book telling the true story of Christmas and prayed that she would read it with her daughter.

During our last visits with our friend before leaving Paris, we gave her a Bible and a video of the *JESUS* film. Her first response was that she could now read about the birth of Jesus and learn more about Christmas. She admitted that she had read the book we had given her daughter. We celebrate that she can accept that Christmas relates to Jesus Christ now and pray that soon she will accept the sacrifice of Christ on the cross.

—A.E., NORTHERN AFRICA AND THE MIDDLE EAST

Heavenly Father, MAY THOSE WHO CELEBRATE THE HOLIDAY RATHER THAN THE SON BE MADE AWARE OF THE TRUE MEANING OF CHRISTMAS. USE WORKERS IN NORTHERN AFRICA AND THE MIDDLE EAST AND IN SECULAR AREAS SUCH AS FRANCE TO EXPLAIN THE BIRTH, LIFE, DEATH AND RESURRECTION OF JESUS. *Amen.*

The Christmas circle

"But the angel said to them, 'Do not be afraid, for behold, I bring you good news of great joy which will be for all the people.'" Luke 2:10 (NASB)

When my husband and I responded to God's call to come to Southeast Asia, packing was a challenge. There simply wasn't room for the holiday decorations I had accumulated during the years. All that remained for our new home was a Nativity set that I had bought in a neighboring country.

With great care, I placed the ceramic pieces on my table. An angel was in the back; Mary, Joseph and the baby were in front; wise men were on the right; and the shepherds and cattle were placed on the left. The standard American setup.

The next day while I was at language school, my house helper looked at the Nativity. When I came back later that day, my carefully arranged pieces were now in a circle, all mixed up, with the baby in the middle. Thinking she had dusted and didn't know how to arrange them correctly, I moved them back in the proper order. The following day, the Nativity scene was once again in a circle. This went on for more days until I finally asked her why she kept moving the pieces—after all, everyone knows shepherds and wise men have definite stations in life, and her arrangement just wouldn't happen.

She pointed to the scene and said, "Jesus should be the center of everything." Pointing to her heart, she continued, "Just like in here." Pointing to the wise men, then to a shepherd and then to herself, she continued to teach me, saying, "He loves us all the same."

—BRENDA, PACIFIC RIM

Dear Lord, TODAY I MAKE JESUS THE CENTER OF MY LIFE IN EVERYTHING THAT I DO. I WILL TREAT OTHERS AS I WANT TO BE TREATED. HELP ME TO LIVE BEFORE OTHERS WITH THE EVIDENCE THAT YOU CONTROL MY LIFE. *Amen.*

Eating humble pie

"Your attitude should be the same as that of Christ Jesus. ... And being found in appearance as a man, he humbled himself and became obedient to death—even death on a cross!" Philippians 2:5, 8 (NIV)

After arriving in Latvia (LAT-vee-ah), our family began the arduous process of learning Russian. Many missionaries refer to the Russian language as the language of heaven because it takes an eternity to learn it! Day after day, month after month we spoke on the level of a 1-year-old. My husband often said it was like being a message in a bottle.

At the home of a national family, we eagerly wanted to communicate, but it was impossible. So we drank tea, ate pastries and smiled a lot.

We were so needy. We couldn't open a bank account, obtain a post office box or even order a meal without a national there to speak for us. We must have seemed like children to them as they taught us how to dress, how to eat their foods, how to ride a city bus and how to live in an arctic climate.

During my quiet time one day, I began to reflect upon Jesus. He knew all about the heavenly Father, yet He came as a tiny infant. Being the Word Himself, He had no words with which to communicate. He was utterly helpless, dependent upon Joseph and Mary for His needs. The ones He came to serve had to serve Him as He waited day after day, year after year in order to tell us about the Father.

We could identify with Jesus. The ones we came to serve ended up having to serve us, but in the process we learned dependence upon them and upon God for all our needs.

—CATHY, CENTRAL AND EASTERN EUROPE

Lord Jesus, YOU UNDERSTAND WHAT IT'S LIKE NOT TO BE ABLE TO COMMUNICATE WITH OTHERS ABOUT THE FATHER. MAY I LEARN FROM YOUR HUMILITY AND ASK THAT YOU MAKE A WAY FOR ME TO CLEARLY SHARE THE GOSPEL WITH _____. FATHER, GIVE MISSIONARIES WHO ARE LEARNING A NEW LANGUAGE A MIRACULOUS ABILITY TO GRASP THE GRAMMAR AND PRONUNCIATION WHILE ALSO GAINING UNDERSTANDING. *Amen.*

"Where's baby Jesus?"

"For unto you is born this day in the city of David a Saviour, who is Christ the Lord." Luke 2:11 (KJV)

The lines of the script had been memorized, the costumes were ready and the participants of the small village congregation of Bom Jardim (bohn jar-JEEN) were excited but nervous about their first Christmas play. After the cast members took their places, the pastor began to narrate the Christmas story. Things went along relatively smoothly until the time came for Mary to give birth to baby Jesus.

The director of the play scanned the crowd in search of the infant who had played the role of baby Jesus in the previous rehearsals. To her dismay, he was nowhere to be found. In despair she cried out, "Where's baby Jesus?" The painful response came from somewhere in the back of the crowded church building, "He didn't come today."

With that, the director began to frantically search for another child who would be suitable for the part. Her eyes fell on a mother who was nursing her baby. The director politely grabbed the baby and passed it to Mary. The play came to an end, and the final hymn was sung.

Suddenly, one of the cast members yelled out, "We forgot about Simeon and Anna!" As soon as they walked in and Simeon declared, "Now dismiss your servant in peace, for my eyes have seen your salvation," the final hymn was sung again and the play ended with applause.

"Where's baby Jesus?" still rings in my heart as I think of the many lost people who do not have an answer to that question.

—KATHY, SOUTH AMERICA

Precious Jesus, I DON'T HAVE TO WONDER WHERE YOU ARE, BECAUSE YOU ARE WITH ME. HELP ME TO SHARE THIS TRUTH WITH OTHERS AS THEIR HEARTS ARE TENDER. *Amen.*

A wonderful day

"For God so loved the world that He gave His one and only Son, that whoever believes in him shall not perish but have eternal life." John 3:16 (NIV)

In Uruguay (oo-roo-GWI), Christmas is called "Family Day," a day for families to be together. The scents of the traditional Christmas Eve barbecue of lamb, sausages and steak are evident all over town. At midnight, families go outside to set off fireworks. Some neighborhood children knock on house doors, asking for money to stuff the traditional Judas doll that they'll set on fire at the stroke of midnight.

Juan comes from these traditions. We first met Juan as he was experiencing many difficulties. He was in the hospital suffering from a stroke. His son had committed suicide, and his wife had left him. He had no hope. Juan was a firm atheist.

Concerned family members asked for a pastoral visit when they thought he was near death. Juan did accept Christ, was baptized and is now a faithful church member.

As we were taking him home one hot Sunday afternoon a week before Christmas, he began to talk about the past. As I listened to him, I saw a glimpse of the new life in Christ that Juan has received.

I'll never forget his words: "I am so excited about Christmas. I always loved Christmas because it was 'Family Day,' and we were all together. Now it is even more special. It is the day we remember the birth of Jesus. I never knew that Christmas was Jesus' birthday. What a wonderful day Christmas is!"

Indeed, what a wonderful day Christmas is! Embrace the message of Christmas rather than the traditions of the season.

—DEBORAH, SOUTH AMERICA

Make this Christmas, Father, ONE THAT IS FOCUSED ON JESUS AND NOT ON THE TRADITIONS OF THE SEASON. USE THIS TIME AS AN OPPORTUNITY FOR MISSIONARIES AND ME TO TELL PEOPLE WHAT CHRISTMAS TRULY CELEBRATES. *Amen.*

Following skeptically or wholeheartedly

"Immediately Jesus stretched out His hand and took hold of him, and said to him, 'You of little faith, why did you doubt?'" Matthew 14:31 (NASB)

Peter took the step of faith. He leaped out of the boat when Jesus called. His feet skimmed across the water. Nevertheless, his strong start fizzled out. He was sinking and afraid for his life. Then Jesus reached out, lifted him up and put him safely in the boat with the loving rebuke, "Why did you doubt?"

So many times, we're tested like this. My supervisor suggested that our team and about 25 other friends should travel to a remote town in western China for Christmas. We planned to share the good news of Christ's birth with our ethnic-minority target group by helping organize a program at the local high school. I was ready to go.

Then the doubts came. I agonized about various scenarios. The trip would require four days there and four days back on hard roads. We would be crossing 12,000-foot passes in December with children and infants. Was this wise? Could the vehicles handle the terrible road conditions, with or without snow? I was taking my focus off Jesus and shifting it to worst-case possibilities.

The trip finally came and went. We made it safely there and back with no snow. More importantly, we got to share God's story through drama and song with 500 lost people in the school. We even performed "Shout to the Lord" on Christmas night at the town square in front of 2,000 people.

I realized that there's no reason to doubt when we're following the voice of the One named Faithful and True (Rev. 19:11, NIV).

—A WORKER IN CHINA

Heavenly Father, WHEN YOUR DIRECTION IS OBVIOUS, HELP ME NOT TO DOUBT. YOU ARE WORTHY OF MY TRUST. I PRAY THAT CHRISTIAN WORKERS WILL TRUST YOU ALSO IN SEEMINGLY LARGE AND IMPOSSIBLE PROJECTS. *Amen.*

Cutting up with a turkey

"Delight yourself in the Lord and he will give you the desires of your heart."
Psalm 37:4 (NIV)

When we first arrived in Colombia just before Christmas, one of our colleagues wanted our children to have a holiday to remember. At the time there were no frozen turkeys in the store, so Rosemary bought a live one and had it prepared for the meal. On Christmas Day, however, Rosemary discovered that her new helper had cut this turkey up for frying. The traditional turkey meal was ruined.

Two clever heads got together, and this problem was solved. My husband, Robert, was a surgeon, as was another missionary, so they proceeded to suture that turkey back to its original form! We baked our "very special turkey" as planned. It has been 30 years since that memorable event, and my children have never forgotten that first Christmas in Colombia.

This is a funny incident in the beginning of our missionary career, but it holds a spiritual truth that helped us through many discouraging and difficult times. A sense of humor, creativity and dependence on Him, especially when things did not turn out the way we planned, helped things work out for good. Sometimes we missed our family, comfortable lifestyle and friends in the States; but when we were in America, it didn't take us long to miss Colombia, the place God called us to minister.

As we are where God wants us to be, doing what He wants us to do, we can be happy knowing that we are in His will. He enjoys giving gifts to His children, even a very special turkey with a great story to remember forever.

—DOLORES, SOUTH AMERICA

Father, WHAT A DELIGHTFUL REMINDER OF YOUR GOODNESS TO US AND YOUR BLESSING WHEN WE FOLLOW YOUR WILL. HELP ME TO KEEP A SENSE OF HUMOR TODAY WHEN THINGS DON'T GO MY WAY. COMFORT MISSIONARIES THIS CHRISTMAS SEASON AS THEY ARE AWAY FROM FAMILY AND FRIENDS. *Amen.*

An unexpected gift

"'I tell you the truth,' Jesus replied, 'no one who has left home or brothers or sisters or mother or father or children or fields for me and the gospel will fail to receive a hundred times as much in this present age (homes, brothers, sisters, mothers, children and fields—and with them, persecutions) and in the age to come, eternal life.'" Mark 10:29–30 (NIV)

I dreaded my time with my loud, bullheaded language tutor, Sherrie. Nearing Christmas, my homesickness swelled. As the tears began to flow, I seriously considered calling to say that I was sick. I truly felt sick. From deep within, however, came the strength to make it through another lesson. I hoped that somehow through this relationship, Sherrie would come to know Christ, and I would grow to love her and her country. Little did I know that God had a lesson for me. He didn't just want to love *her* through me; He wanted to love *me* through her.

After two grueling hours of language study, I somehow shared about my homesickness in my limited vocabulary. The next day, Sherrie asked my co-worker what things she did with her daughter during the holidays. Upon learning of their Christmas shopping tradition, Sherrie immediately wanted to take me shopping. She had no idea that I was afraid of public transportation and feared getting lost in a city of more than 3 million. By subway and bus, we traveled to the bazaars and hunted for Christmas presents for my children. How God loved me through an unexpected person!

After one of our language lessons, Sherrie had seen the gingerbread houses our kids had made and learned of our tradition. On Christmas Day, she showed up at our team Christmas party with a beautiful gingerbread village—her gift to us. I wept. That day I truly understood the verses in Mark 10.

—"CANDY," CENTRAL ASIA

Dear Lord, PLEASE GIVE ABUNDANT BLESSING TODAY TO THOSE WHO HAVE LEFT LOVED ONES IN ORDER TO SHARE THE GOSPEL OF CHRIST ABROAD. DURING THIS CHRISTMAS SEASON, GIVE THEM A FAMILY OF BELIEVERS TO CELEBRATE YOUR SON'S BIRTH. *Amen.*

The baby from the feeding trough

"He came to His own, and those who were His own did not receive Him."
John 1:11 (NASB)

No room at the inn? Hogwash! After traveling through the snowy Himalayan foothills, it felt great to reach a smoky one-room inn. My horse was taken to a communal stable, and I was glad not to spend the night with that sweaty beast. Another random thought also slapped me: *Family is important in all cultures.*

Jumping from these thoughts to the Bible, what was happening to Jesus on the night of his birth? Joseph had arrived in his hometown. Why wouldn't his relatives provide a room for one of their own? Could *you* turn down a mother in labor and a relative from your door?

We have heard stories of how kind the inn owner was to provide Mary with a stable because the inn was too crowded. Nonsense! What kind of person compels a pregnant woman to have her firstborn child in a stable? For that matter, is any stable clean enough for the birth of a child? What about a baby in a feeding trough? Atrocious!

You cannot get more destitute than how Jesus started out, regardless of how bad your situation is. Jesus chose to live in the most deplorable conditions of human history. Your life cannot be rougher than His was. From the very beginning, He was rejected by those who should have loved Him most.

If they treated the Master this way, can you expect to fare better? But take heart—the One who was born in lowliness has been raised to heights beyond our imagination. He is the King of kings and Lord of lords!

—DANIEL, CENTRAL ASIA

Oh Jesus, YOU CHOSE TO LOWER YOURSELF IN ORDER TO EXPERIENCE WHAT EVEN THE MOST DESTITUTE PERSON COULD EXPERIENCE. YOU UNDERSTAND ALL OF US, INCLUDING ME. YOU HAVE BEEN TEMPTED IN ALL THINGS, BUT DID NOT SIN. THANK YOU THAT I CAN RELATE TO YOU, EVEN THOUGH I AM NOTHING BEFORE YOU, THE GREAT AND HOLY SON OF GOD. THANK YOU FOR LOVING ME. *Amen.*

Humble beginnings

"Your attitude should be the same that Christ Jesus had. Though he was God, he did not demand and cling to his rights as God." Philippians 2:5–6 (NLT)

Another language blunder, but I never imagined it would be so meaningful. It was our fourth Christmas in China, and we had recently moved from a large capital to a remote town.

Each Christmas, we made a manger out of bamboo and filled it with hay, then we wrapped a doll in a blanket and placed it in the manger in our living room. A floodlight shining on the doll's face helped remind us of the wonder of Christmas.

I explained to a Chinese guest that when Jesus was born, He was placed in a feed trough. Instead of saying the Chinese word for "manger," I accidentally used the word for "toilet." My wife quickly corrected me, and we laughed at my mistake.

Reflecting later, it wasn't stretching it to say that Jesus was born and then placed in a toilet. The trough most likely didn't smell much better, and compared to the glory He had enjoyed in heaven, a feed trough surrounded by smelly animals probably did seem comparatively like a toilet.

I realized that the sacrifices made to live in this remote town were pathetically small when compared to those that Jesus made in leaving heaven to come to earth. I was encouraged, though, to think that moving to this town was in line with the Christmas message.

Jesus left a place of comfort to seek the lost in an uncomfortable and remote place called earth. It took a language blunder to be reminded that our relocation was merely our humble attempt to follow His example.

—A WORKER IN CHINA

Father, IT IS HARD TO GRASP THAT YOUR SON EMPTIED HIMSELF TO BE MADE INTO THE LIKENESS OF MAN. MAY I NEVER FORGET THE PRICE HE PAID FOR ME. MAY I ALWAYS REALIZE THAT MY SACRIFICES ARE NOTHING COMPARED TO HIS. *Amen.*

The language of Christmas

"When they heard this sound, a crowd came together in bewilderment, because each one heard them speaking in his own language." Acts 2:6 (NIV)

Our Christmas celebration began with the showing of the *JESUS* film at the request of a new Jula (JEW-lah) believer named Ike. The showing was a lesson in how powerful it is to hear the Word of God in one's own language.

We showed the film in the new believer's courtyard with 100 people watching. In the part where Jesus heals a demon-possessed man, several people laughed. A friend of ours—who is not a believer—told everyone, "That really happened." After that, most became thoughtful and interested. One man said he previously had seen the film in French, but that this was the first time he understood what was being said since it was in his native language, Bambara (BAHM-buh-ruh).

After the film, we read Scripture verses leading to the birth of Jesus. At this point, people were hungry, children started playing and distractions were evident. I felt discouraged because people weren't listening.

Then Ike began to read the Christmas story while noise and distraction continued. God revealed a miracle before me. Here was a man who had never read in his heart language before he started studying the Bible. Here was a man who was sharing his new faith in his own courtyard. Here was a man who was celebrating his first Christmas!

Many prayers were answered for this event to happen. We don't know the results of this night, but God promised that His Word does not return void—and I know that His Word impacts greatly when spoken in one's own language.

—D., WEST AFRICA

Father, YOUR WORD IS SWEET AS HONEY IN MY MOUTH. MAY MISSIONARIES AND I SPEAK THE SWEET WORDS OF THE SCRIPTURES TODAY. THANK YOU FOR THE *JESUS* FILM, WHICH HAS LED SO MANY TO BELIEVE IN JESUS. CONTINUE TO BLESS IT AS IT CONTINUES TO BE TRANSLATED IN EVEN MORE LANGUAGES. *Amen.*

The world in my living room

"But the angel said to them, 'Do not be afraid. I bring you good news of great joy that will be for all people. Today in the town of David, a Savior has been born to you; He is Christ the Lord.'" Luke 2:10–11 (NIV)

Serving the Lord through international missions is fantastic. I would be miserable doing anything else. However, there is one time of year that seems difficult—Christmas. I am thousands of miles away from my extended family and friends and from "normal" holiday activities. Many missionaries serve in countries where Christmas isn't celebrated or it's celebrated differently. So we make new holiday traditions.

One Christmas, I was feeling particularly homesick. Since I work with refugees seeking asylum, many of my friends were experiencing similar emotions. We decided to have a Christmas celebration at our house, and people from nations all over the world were gathered around our Christmas tree. Some were believers, but most were not. We had Bibles in several languages, and we read the story of the coming Messiah from each one.

As I listened, I realized that Christ is the *great news* for *all* people. I couldn't help but praise God for showing me a glimpse of what heaven will be like. People from every nation and tongue will bow before His throne in worship and praise. Christmas made this possible. The gift of Jesus and His incredible salvation is to be shared with the world, and I had the privilege of having part of the world in my living room.

Since that Christmas, we open up our home to the world. It's the best tradition ever! Even you can invite people from other countries to your home at Christmas and give them love and comfort during the holidays.

—JODY, WESTERN EUROPE

Father, MAKE IT POSSIBLE FOR ME TO INVITE PEOPLE OF OTHER NATIONALITIES INTO MY HOME OR TO MY CHURCH FOR CHRISTMAS. MAKE MANY OPPORTUNITIES FOR MISSIONARIES TO DO THE SAME AS A WAY TO INTRODUCE JESUS TO OTHERS. *Amen.*

Look on the bright side

"For as he thinks within himself, so he is." Proverbs 23:7a (NASB)

Christmas was coming, but none of my children and grandchildren could visit our new country of service. I was depressed. The city was gray, cold, muddy and wet. Since the weather was miserable, I did not want to leave the house to buy a big pot to cook dinner for a few guests that night.

My last-minute shopping for the pot made me impulsively purchase a ridiculous-looking hat to keep me warm. As I trudged toward home, the gypsy "flower ladies" descended on me. I finally gave in and picked out two bunches of holiday-looking greenery with red berries.

As I stopped in at my neighborhood market to pick up a few items, I caught a glimpse of myself in the dirty store window. I looked awful in that funky little hat. Hurrying down one of the aisles, I happened to see another lady wearing a hat very similar to mine. "If only I looked as nice in my hat as she does," I fretted to myself. And you will never believe this! That same lady had red berries in her cart. "But hers are fresher and nicer than mine," I whispered under my breath.

As I headed for the checkout, the Holy Spirit got a real laugh at me. The far wall of the market was mirrored, and I was the "other" shopper! He also convicted me. So many days I focus on the negative. It's sadly comical how we rant and rave over things that don't really matter.

—L.G.G., CENTRAL ASIA

Heavenly Father, YOU HAVE BLESSED ME SO MUCH, AND SOMETIMES I LOOK AT THE NEGATIVE THINGS AROUND ME INSTEAD OF THE POSITIVE. HELP ME TO HAVE A POSITIVE ATTITUDE, TO TRUST YOU AND TO CONFESS A COMPLAINING SPIRIT. TODAY, I PRAY THAT WORKERS IN CENTRAL ASIA WILL BE CONTENT WHERE GOD HAS PLACED THEM. *Amen.*

Branded, but exonerated

"The Lord has heard my cry for mercy; the Lord accepts my prayer. All my enemies will be ashamed and dismayed; they will turn back in sudden disgrace."
Psalm 6:9—10 (NIV)

"Your posters have been torn down or marked with a large X with the words, 'Dangerous—this is a sect' scribbled across them." This was the anxious message from Irina, a Far East Russian home missionary.

After traveling 10 hours in subzero temperatures, we arrived with a busload of Russian students. We wondered who would have defaced the posters advertising our Christmas concert. After prayer, we continued as planned.

The scenery, costumes and instruments were unloaded and assembled on the stage. A slow trickle of people, mostly children, began entering the auditorium. A quick glance revealed a figure dressed in a long, black robe. It was the local Orthodox priest, encouraging people to leave the concert and handing out propaganda about cults and Protestants. We watched in dismay as people left.

"Please, sir, we invite you to attend our Christmas presentation. It is based on the Bible, and we assure you there will be nothing that you would find offensive" we said to the religious leader. Refusing to listen, he resumed his position at the entrance.

Even though the crowd was sparse, the concert went on as planned. Afterward, we watched a woman approach the priest. "This Christmas concert was wonderful. I am ashamed for our church. You should be ashamed of your un-Christian behavior in defacing their posters and turning people away from the concert," she said.

The priest bowed his head, turned and trudged down the road. God had sent a member of the priest's own church to fight the battle.

—ROBIN, CENTRAL AND EASTERN EUROPE

Father, CHRISTIANS EVERYWHERE ARE MISUNDERSTOOD, JUST AS JESUS WAS. ENCOURAGE CHRISTIAN MISSIONARIES WHO ARE FALSELY ACCUSED OF BEING PROPAGATORS OF A CULT, AND LET THEM KNOW THEIR WORK IS NOT IN VAIN. *Amen.*

Got the holiday blues?

"She will bear a Son; and you shall call His name Jesus, for He will save His people from their sins." Matthew 1:21 (NASB)

As I stepped out of a cold shower, I found myself giving in to self-pity. It was Christmas Eve and the second day this week that our electricity had been turned off. More than likely, we would be without power on Christmas Day as well.

As I pondered the thought of what Christmas would be like without the use of any modern-day conveniences, I found myself becoming increasingly saddened at the outlook. Cold showers in a dark bathroom ... no hair dryer to fashion picture-worthy hairdos ... no scents of a special breakfast ... no twinkling lights on the Christmas tree ... and no heaters to make our home feel warm and cozy. But as I quickly dressed in the dark, cool air, wallowing in my preholiday blues, the Lord reminded me of a few important things.

That first Christmas, Mary and Joseph were also far from home and, of course, living without electricity. I'm doubtful that there were any special foods to snack on as the shepherds and Mary and Joseph gathered in the stable. Mary probably didn't look her best to entertain strangers and angels in her humble delivery room. But none of that mattered. Shepherds were in awe, angels rejoiced, and Mary and Joseph marveled because they were witnesses to the birth of God's own Son.

With or without electricity, we want to marvel at a God who became like us in order to show men the path back to Him.

—A WORKER IN EAST ASIA

Father, FOCUS MY HEART TODAY ON JESUS, THE TRUE MEANING OF CHRISTMAS, SO THAT I WILL NOT BE DISTRACTED BY INCONVENIENCES OR BUSYNESS. *Amen.*

Luanda: a portrait of Bethlehem

"And she gave birth to her firstborn son; and she wrapped Him in cloths, and laid Him in a manger, because there was no room for them in the inn."
Luke 2:7 (NASB)

It must be Christmas time in Luanda (lou-AHN-dah).

The road is flooded as the rains come, and a river of dirt washes under our gate. Young people are blocking off the street asking for contributions. The police are stopping cars and asking for money. The lines for petrol are over one hour long. The temperature is 95 degrees Fahrenheit, and the humidity is about the same. And the all-night parties in the street really do go on all night long.

Not exactly your Christmas-card picture of the season, but similar to what it must have been like in Bethlehem 2,000 years ago. The daily life of women carrying water, men lying in the fields, children playing in the streets of dirt and animals wandering untended would have been the same for Jesus as it is for our Angolan neighbors. In the same way that many people in Bethlehem were unaware of the miracle in the stable, so many in the streets here are unaware of the miracle of Christmas.

That, however, is changing. The churches are active in promoting the message of Christmas. National radio is reading the Bible on the air and playing meaningful Christmas songs. A few years ago church attendance was actively discouraged, and Christmas was celebrated as "Family Day."

There are still challenges to face. AIDS continues to grow more menacing. While 25% of children die before the age of 5, people are still living under the fear of a bad harvest.

Yet this is the best Christmas season in a long time.

—SCOT, CENTRAL, EASTERN AND SOUTHERN AFRICA

Hallelujah, what a Savior! THANK YOU, FATHER, THAT YOU SENT JESUS TO SAVE THE WORLD! THANK YOU THAT ANGOLANS ARE HEARING ABOUT JESUS. TAKE YOUR MESSAGE INTO THE INTERIOR OF THIS COUNTRY THAT HAS BEEN RAVAGED BY WAR FOR SO LONG. *Amen.*

A shepherd's choice

"And there were shepherds living out in the fields nearby, keeping watch over their flocks at night. ... the angel said to them, 'Do not be afraid. I bring you good news of great joy that will be for all the people.'" Luke 2:8, 10 (NIV)

A common sight in the Andes (AN-dees) of Ecuador is shepherds caring for their flocks along the highways and on the sides of the mountains. Even on the edges of the city of Quito (KEE-toh), the Quichua (KEE-chew-ah) people are frequently seen moving their sheep, goats and cattle from place to place where they might find grass along the sides of the roads. The women and children are usually the ones caring for the sheep and cattle. Seldom do we see a man caring for these animals, because it is one of the lowliest jobs here.

How exciting it must have been when the angels brought the good news to those shepherds on the Bethlehem hillsides! How exciting it is now to bring the good news to the Quichua people and see them respond! They are being freed from the bondage of the traditions of their past, but not from the threats of their neighbors, because they have dared to leave those traditions behind.

It is never easy to leave cultural tradition that is in opposition to the ways of God. Can you imagine how the lives of the shepherds in Bethlehem changed? Although they may have continued to herd sheep, they had met the Shepherd, who would one day die and rise again for them. Friends and family probably thought that these Jewish shepherds had been out in those fields too long and were going crazy!

Understanding these Quichua shepherds helped me to gain a little more insight to the Christmas story.

—RUBY, SOUTH AMERICA

Thank You, Father, FOR THE FREEDOM I HAVE TO WORSHIP THE RISEN LORD. I PRAY FOR THE QUICHUA PEOPLE OF ECUADOR WHO SUFFER PERSECUTION FROM FAMILIES, NEIGHBORS AND COMMUNITY LEADERS BECAUSE THEY HAVE CHOSEN THE BETTER WAY. MAY I NEVER TAKE FOR GRANTED THE FREEDOM WHICH I HAVE. *Amen.*

Little Christmas angels proclaim good news

"Shout joyfully to the Lord, all the earth." Psalm 100:1 (NASB)

Groggily, I glanced over at the clock—4 a.m. What was that noise outside? I dragged myself out of bed to find more than 100 Indian children waiting for me, their faces illuminated by small candles and exploding sparklers. It was Christmas Day, and their faces were radiant.

An older boy from this South Asian children's home motioned everyone to follow behind his rusty bike. The boys spent most of the previous day rigging a battery-powered speaker system to it. We walked out the gate and headed for a village.

Interrupting the crisp morning air, a loud, scratchy, speaker voice screamed, "Happy, Happy Christmas!" Children shouted joyfully, "Merry, Merry Christmas!" This happy procession continued shouting and singing through one village after another. Villagers stepped out of their homes to see the commotion.

I asked if anyone got mad at the children for waking them up at 4 a.m. "But sister," came the reply, "if we didn't do this, no one would know that it's Jesus' birthday." He pointed to the older boys walking along the edge of the group. "They are telling the Christmas story to everyone we meet."

In this 99.9 percent Hindu area of South Asia, these children proclaimed Jesus' light in a vast darkness riddled with false gods.

When the microphone finally made it into my hands, I screamed in my best Telagu (tay-LAH-goo) accent, "Happy, Happy Christmas!" The children responded with shouts followed by exploding fireworks in the sky. It's the day of our Savior's birth, and everyone should know!

—SUE, OVERSEAS CORRESPONDENT

Father, EVERY DAY IN MY LIFE, I HAVE SOMETHING TO CELEBRATE! YOUR COMING TO EARTH TO BRING ETERNAL LIFE TO ALL PEOPLES BRINGS JOY AND PASSION TO SHARE THE GOOD NEWS THAT WILL CHANGE THE WORLD! THANK YOU, GOD, FOR THE GIFT OF JESUS! *Amen.*

True celebration

"For there is born to you this day in the city of David a Savior, who is Christ the Lord." Luke 2:11 (NKJV)

This was our 10th Christmas outside the United States. As always, we missed family, trips to the mall, cold weather and Christmas programs at church. We were excited, however, to have a group from Kentucky with us during a week in December. They helped us decorate the tree, and then we headed out to the small village of Tagabati (TAH-guh-BAH-tee).

There are only two believers in the village, so most people had never heard the gospel. The team shared the Christmas story as they stood under an awning next to the mosque. There were animals in the street, children running and yelling, various smells surrounding us and a group of Muslim men listening to the story of Christ's birth.

As I listened, it was as if God said, *This is the true celebration of Christmas. Just as it was the first time in the lowly cow stall, in a dusty, dirty, smelly village, the story of your Savior is being proclaimed to the needy and the lost. Christmas is not the gifts, the snow, the music or the food. It is not the things that make you comfortable. Christmas is the telling of the good news. It is the chance for the sinner to rejoice.*

With tears, I could almost hear the angels singing, "Glory to God in the highest, peace on earth, good will to all men."

Never forget what Christmas really is: the good news of salvation told to those who are afraid, hungry and in need of a Savior.

—BRAD, WEST AFRICA

Father God, NEVER LET ME FORGET THE TRUE MEANING OF CHRISTMAS. LET THIS TIME OF YEAR BE AN OPPORTUNITY TO SPREAD THE GOOD NEWS THAT JESUS CAME, DIED, WAS BURIED AND ROSE AGAIN FOR ALL PEOPLE GROUPS, INCLUDING THE SONGHAI OF WEST AFRICA. *Amen.*

Refreshed

"Come to Me, all who are weary and heavy-laden, and I will give you rest. Take My yoke upon you, and learn from Me, for I am gentle and humble in heart; and you shall find rest for your souls. For My yoke is easy, and My burden is light." Matthew 11:28–30 (NASB)

I went for a walk, and everything was gray. The volcano Tungurahua (toon-go-RAH-wah) produced its constant cloud of ash, which had fallen over Riobamba (ree-oh-BOMB-bah). The sidewalks, windows, walls and streets were gray. The air was hazy, and I could feel the grit on my face and even on my teeth. I returned home, tired and frustrated.

Later that week, our family drove up snowcapped Mount Chimborazo (cheem-boh-RAH-soh), which towers two miles above Riobamba. Within half an hour, we had left the grayness behind and were driving through snow-covered hills. We stopped at a place to let the children play. As far as we could see, everything was covered with untouched snow. Our family threw snowballs, made snow angels and enjoyed ourselves. The air was crisp and clear. We returned to the city refreshed.

In the same way that my family and I needed a break from the ever-present volcanic grit, I personally need time away from the constant pressures of daily life. I must deliberately set my mind on the things of God, not the things of the world.

I don't have to go up a mountain to do so. Daily, I have to withdraw from the stresses of my world and spend time in the comforting, refreshing presence of my Father. It is there, in prayer and in His Word, where I can rest and prepare myself for the tasks of my day.

Are you tired and frustrated with the pressures of life? Daily spend time in the presence of your Father.

—DONNA, SOUTH AMERICA

Father, I DESIRE TO SPEND TIME WITH YOU AND YOUR WORD. REFRESH ME TODAY AND EVERY DAY DURING THIS SPECIAL TIME. MAY MISSIONARIES AND I NOT BECOME SO BUSY THAT WE IGNORE THIS QUIET TIME NEEDED DAILY. *Amen.*

A hedge of protection

"All the days ordained for me were written in your book before one of them came to be." Psalm 139:16b (NIV)

"May you relish everything there ... Soak it all in, don't forget anything ... These are going to be some of your sweetest memories ... What a privilege we have to serve Him." These are words I read in an e-mail from a friend the day before New Year's Eve, 2003. I didn't realize how God would use her encouragement and wisdom.

Just before my first anniversary in Southern Africa, a friend and I decided to ring in 2004 by attending a worship service. As we headed into town for the late event, it was dark, raining and windy. I suddenly noticed a tree down in our lane, so I called out my friend's name quickly. When she saw it, she swerved to miss it and then swerved back into our lane. The back tires began to slide and the car rolled down an embankment. The car stopped between two trees.

After climbing out of the car, we waited on the side of the road for the ambulance. I thought about how close we came to death and about my friend's words in the e-mail. It is only by the grace of God that we survived.

Why did I have to experience that? God allowed the accident to show me that He is active in my life every second of the day! He will do whatever it takes to protect His children so that His perfect plan can unfold. Seeing God at work that night was the ultimate way to begin a new year of serving Him!

—LAURA, CENTRAL, EASTERN AND SOUTHERN AFRICA

Father, YOU ARE MY SHIELD, MY ROCK AND MY FORTRESS. I AM NOT AFRAID WITH YOU AS MY CHAMPION. PROTECT MISSIONARIES IN DANGEROUS PLACES, AS THEY TRAVEL AND AS THEY ENCOUNTER THOSE WHO REJECT THEM. *Amen.*

Focused on our own patch of dirt

"Do not conform any longer to the pattern of this world, but be transformed ..."
Romans 12:2 (NIV)

I often drive past an intersection that has a huge tree in the middle of it. A group of street beggars have made their home on the tiny patch of dry dirt around the tree. Usually there are a few women and several children living under the tree. They wear the only clothes they own, tattered and dingy gray from constant use. Sometimes they are begging from the cars stopped at the traffic light. Other times they are scouring for food scraps, picking lice from one another's hair or sleeping. This is their life, their world. And they are totally oblivious to the noise around them—blaring horns, cars passing rickshaws, bicycle riders jingling bells, three-wheelers zooming, pedestrians crossing the busy intersection and animals wandering in and out of traffic.

One day I noticed that two of the beggar boys had made a swing in the branches of the tree. Their malnourished arms and legs resembled knobby broomsticks. They had no chance for education and no future ahead of them. But they were happily swinging, uncaring of the chaos swirling around them.

As I watched, I wondered how closely our own lives mirrored theirs. Our lives revolve around our own little "turf," oblivious and uncaring of the chaotic lost world. Like the beggar boys on the swing, have we become so conformed to the world around us that we no longer hear the cries for help or see those in distress? Are we only focused on our little patch of dirt?

This new year, may we focus on others.

—JENNA, SOUTH ASIA

Lord, HELP ME KEEP MY EYES AND EARS OPEN SO I CAN KNOW YOUR HEART FOR THIS WORLD! KEEP MY HEART TENDER SO THAT I DON'T MISS ANY OPPORTUNITY TO GLORIFY YOU IN AND THROUGH MY LIFE. *Amen.*

Seeing beyond the garbage

"What is more, I consider everything a loss compared to the surpassing greatness of knowing Christ Jesus my Lord, for whose sake I have lost all things. I consider them rubbish, that I may gain Christ and be found in him."
Philippians 3:8–9 (NIV)

At a New Year's retreat in Bangladesh, I found an idyllic spot for my quiet time—a secluded bench atop a cliff overlooking rice fields and waterways. The sun was warm, the distant sound of villagers echoed, my Bible lay in my lap, and I had a whole hour ahead of me—pretty close to perfect!

Then a man with a basket on his shoulder strolled up to the cliff edge and dumped garbage over the side, right in front of me! Not such a perfect spot now. I looked over the side, and there was a mound of trash piled at the bottom. He must have wondered, *Why is that foreigner sitting there in front of the garbage dump?*

That knowledge didn't chase me off. The prospect of a quiet hour with the Creator of the beauty that I could see blinded me to the ugliness of the garbage that I couldn't see. It was another lesson from God about learning to look at the world through spiritual eyes.

Sometimes the places where international missionaries serve aren't much prettier than garbage dumps. Maybe even the place where you live is not optimum. Yet the Father wants us to look beyond the physical world and see Him with our spiritual eyes. When we desire to know Him above all things, we can do this. In my quiet time that morning above the dump, God led me to Philippians 3:8–9. Those words became my New Year's resolution—to know Him more! Knowing Him allows me to continue when life seems more like a garbage dump.

—T.D.F., SOUTH ASIA

Oh God, MAY I BE WILLING TO LOOK PAST THE "GARBAGE" THAT DISTRACTS ME FROM KEEPING MY EYES FOCUSED ON YOU. MAY I KNOW YOU MORE THIS NEW YEAR, AND MAY I HEAR YOUR VOICE THROUGH YOUR WORD AS I FACE EACH DAY. I PRAY FOR CHRISTIAN WORKERS ALL OVER THE WORLD TO DEDICATE THEMSELVES AGAIN TO SEEK ONLY YOUR WILL AND TO GIVE YOU ALL THE GLORY. *Amen.*

The grand adventure

"Who am I, O Lord God, and what is my house that You have brought me this far?" 2 Samuel 7:18 (NASB)

I found myself in the middle of a 16-mile hike in Hungary, surrounded by people I had just met but only able to communicate with one other person. It was a surreal moment. The culmination of months of planning and years of prayer were realized as I looked up and saw nothing but the vastness of the sky. At a time when I could have felt utterly alone, I did not. I instead smiled, as I knew my Lord was by my side. He promised me new adventures, so I continued to climb.

With my face toward the sky, I was struck with the absurdity of the situation. A recent college graduate leaving her family and everything she's ever known to move across an ocean would be considered unusual by most. But, then again, there is nothing usual about following Christ.

However, saying yes to Him is the best decision we can make. With Christ, we can look at the sky from whatever country we currently call home and know that He painted it for us.

I ask myself the same question that King David did in 2 Samuel, and after a few months of living in a foreign land, I have found my answer. I do not possess a wealth of talent, I am not an educated theologian, and I do not even have the experience of most. I simply trust Christ and follow Him. He is the One who fulfills dreams and gives hope for a new year of serving Him.

—STACY, CENTRAL AND EASTERN EUROPE

Heavenly Father, THANK YOU FOR CALLING YOUNG COLLEGE GRADUATES TO FOLLOW YOU OVERSEAS FOR TWO-YEAR TERMS AS JOURNEYMEN. MAY YOU GIVE THEM WONDERFUL ADVENTURES AND AN OVERWHELMING FEELING OF YOUR PRESENCE. MAY I ALSO FOLLOW WHEREVER YOU LEAD ME. *Amen.*

ABOUT BETH MOORE AND
LIVING PROOF MINISTRIES

God captured Beth Moore's heart at a very young age. Her first love was a man with long, dark hair, tan and weathered skin, and loving eyes. When she saw a picture of His face tacked onto the wall in Sunday School, she knew Jesus would be the love of her life. Like many children brought up in church, she learned about the Bible, His love letter to her. Beth's love for Jesus Christ grew over the years, and at the age of 18, she committed her entire life to God.

The Lord is now using Beth Moore to encourage women through her Bible studies and conferences not only to stand on the Word of God, but to know what it says. Beth began speaking at local women's luncheons and retreats more than 20 years ago. As her ministry grew, Beth began writing full-time and speaking all over the United States. In 1995, the Lord led her to establish Living Proof Ministries to guide women to love and live on God's Word.

Living Proof is committed to fanning the flame in others for God and His Word. Every message, program, tape, book or product offered through this ministry is diligently directed toward this goal. Living Proof Ministries was founded upon Hebrews 4:12 (NASB): *"For the word of God is living and active and sharper than any two-edged sword."*

Beth and her husband, Keith, not only have a passion for the Word, but for missions as well. They have ministered to missionaries in many parts of the world, twice in Africa. While in Africa, the idea for this book was born. Their daughters, Melissa and Amanda, and son-in-law, Curt Jones, also are involved in ministry.

FOR MORE INFORMATION ABOUT BETH MOORE AND
LIVING PROOF MINISTRIES, SEE WWW.LPROOF.ORG.

FINDING YOUR VOICE

After reading stories of courage, faith, miracles, prayer and personal reflection of ordinary people who just happen to be missionaries, perhaps you might be asking yourself, *What is my response? How can I have a voice that is faithful to see the peoples of the world come to Christ?*

This book is a collection of what God is doing around the world, yet it uniquely allows the reader to apply spiritual lessons, broaden the view of the world and pray meaningfully for God's work. God wants you to faithfully be involved in His plan for the world. Yet He first wants you to know that He loves you so much that He gave you His Son as your Savior and that once you accept His Son, He has a plan for your life—a plan that will give you the voice of the faithful.

The following pages will help you find your voice. Information and Web sites will assist you in how to become a Christian, how to pray even deeper for international missionaries, how your church can become more involved in world missions, and how you can go on a short-term mission trip or become a career missionary. Although the International Mission Board is a denominational organization, their desire is that all Christians will be encouraged to expand their worldview through reading this book. Whether being involved in missions through other evangelical organizations or the IMB, God is using many to bring the gospel to all people groups.

According to Isaiah 66:18, *"The time is coming to gather all nations and tongues. And they shall come and see My glory"* (NASB). What is your response?

HAVE YOU HEARD GOD'S VOICE?

God loves you and wants you to experience peace and life. But it's just not any life He has in mind for you; it's life that's abundant and eternal.

But there's a problem. Because of our nature, we humans disobey God and go our own ways; we are separated from God. The good news is that the problem has an answer: Jesus Christ. He died on the cross for our sins and rose from the grave. In this way, Jesus bridges the gap between God and people. When we trust Jesus Christ and receive Him into our hearts by our personal invitation, we begin experiencing God's peace and the abundant, eternal life He planned for us.

HOW TO RECEIVE JESUS CHRIST
1. Admit your need for forgiveness and peace.
2. Commit to turn from your sins, believing that Jesus Christ died for you on the cross and rose from the grave.
3. Through prayer, invite Jesus Christ to forgive your sins and accept Him as Savior and the Lord of your life.

Once you've trusted Christ as Savior—or if you are still struggling with that decision—please quickly get involved with a Bible-teaching church. Building relationships with other Christians and hearing God's Word taught will provide invaluable encouragement and accountability.

A Message from the International Mission Board

Every day I read missionary reports and newsletters confirming the power of the gospel that dispels the spiritual darkness pervading the world. As I visit missionaries overseas, I see how their obedience to God's voice is bringing hope out of despair and bringing salvation from the bondage of sin. I also see spiritual warfare evident in religious opposition, governmental restrictions, loneliness, discouragement, conflict and illness. It is not without risk or danger that missionaries serve overseas. But the passion in their hearts to see a lost world come to saving faith in Jesus Christ compels them.

Our most effective strategy for fulfilling the Great Commission is sending and supporting God-called missionaries to live throughout the world. The International Mission Board is part of the Southern Baptist Convention, the nation's largest evangelical denomination, claiming more than 40,000 churches with nearly 16 million members. In 2004, 5,000-plus IMB missionaries and their Baptist partners overseas reported more than 600,000 baptisms—each representing a life changed by the good news of Jesus. I'm reminded of the words of Jesus in Matthew 24:14: *"This gospel of the kingdom shall be preached in the whole world as a testimony to all the nations, and then the end will come"* (NASB).

We don't know when that end will come, nor do we fully understand God's criteria for completing the Great Commission; however, it is evident that those words of Jesus are being fulfilled. Our mission task remains focused on the vision of John in Revelation 7:9 (NIV) and that day when there will be *"a great multitude that no one could count, from every nation, tribe, people and language"* gathered around the throne, worshiping the Lamb of God!

—Jerry Rankin, President
International Mission Board, SBC

LIFT UP YOUR VOICE

The International Mission Board invites you to join 1 million believers in a yearlong emphasis on intercessory prayer for missions and the lost worldwide.

To find out how your church can participate in the Lift Up Your Voice call to prayer and learn about the small group discussion guide and promotional resources, call the International Mission Board at (800) 999-3113 or visit http://voicesofthefaithful.com.

"Ask of Me, and I will surely give the nations as Your inheritance, and the very ends of the earth as Your possession." Psalm 2:8 (NASB)

To learn more about the International Mission Board, visit http://www.vof.imb.org

How to Pray for International Missionaries and People Groups

Throughout this book you've come heart to heart with international missionaries—and probably realized they're not much different from you. They need your prayers. By daily voicing prayers for specific missionaries, you'll become a key instrument in God's design for strengthening His workers throughout the world. If you don't know any missionaries by name, start by choosing missionaries who have written these devotionals. Though you don't know the missionaries' full names, God does.

These ideas will get you started in praying for missionaries as the Holy Spirit guides you:

1. Pray that missionaries will love God with all their hearts, souls, and minds and will love all others as themselves.
2. Pray for protection from the evil one and for good health.
3. Pray for wisdom and attentive spirits to God's direction and leadership.
4. Pray that missionaries will deny themselves and follow Jesus anywhere.
5. Pray for moral purity in thought, sight, word and action.
6. Pray that missionaries will have courage, boldness and strength in the Lord. Pray they will have favor with local governments.
7. Pray that family relationships will be filled with love, respect and honor. Pray that single missionaries will find strong relationships to strengthen their walk with the Lord.
8. Pray that the gospel will spread rapidly throughout the people group the missionaries are working to reach.
9. Pray that relationships with missionary colleagues and local believers will reflect Christ.

10. Pray for daily needs to be met: safe drinking water, nutritious food, housing and transportation.
11. Pray for the building of strong prayer networks among local and stateside partners. Pray for good connections to stateside churches.

Pray the following for the people groups of the world:
1. Pray that the light of Christ will replace the darkness in the lives of the lost.
2. Pray for the breaking down of religious barriers, for freedom from spiritual bondage, and for people to experience dreams and visions pointing them to the truth of Jesus Christ.
3. Pray that the gospel will penetrate the hearts of the people via every means possible, such as radio, television, tapes, videos, e-mail, the internet, drama and medical clinics.
4. Pray for the translation of Scripture—both written and oral stories—for each people group, asking for protection and accuracy for translation teams. Intercede for the careful and strategic distribution of Christian literature so that people will be drawn to the Word.
5. Pray for the development of training materials as well as praying that biblical, theological and leadership training be accessible for emerging church leaders.
6. Pray that as people come to Christ, they will catch the vision of the Great Commission and boldly share their faith, leading to a church-planting movement among the people.

FIND INTERNATIONAL MISSION BOARD PRAYER
RESOURCES AND REQUESTS AT HTTP://WWW.VOF.IMB.ORG

Your Church's Role in Missions

Has God touched your heart through missionary stories in this book? Are you wondering what to do next? Think about leading your church to a deeper missions commitment. God has made your church unique, with its own combination of people, talents and resources. And He has plans for using those gifts in the Great Commission. Use the suggestions below to start exploring God's missions plans for your church:

CATCH THE VISION. Start in God's Word. Lead your church through Scripture so the entire congregation will share God's heart for all nations to worship Him.

DEVELOP A STRATEGY. A comprehensive missions strategy follows Acts 1:8, encompassing local, state, national and international missions, and lets the whole church be involved. That strategy should include knowing, praying, giving and going.

KNOW. Educate church members on how they can be involved in missions. Invite missionaries to speak in worship times, small groups or even a missions conference. Establish a missions center with literature, videos and other tools to use in multiple settings—from small groups to churchwide worship. Southern Baptists may order many free resources at *http://www.vof.imb.org*, and products for sale are available for anyone.

READ. *Lives Given, Not Taken: 21st Century Southern Baptist Martyrs* is an intimate portrayal of ordinary people who followed God's voice. Written by Erich Bridges and Jerry Rankin, it is a book about danger, spiritual warfare, surrender and sacrifice. But it also is about call, compassion,

an enduring witness and God's glory. Order at *http://www.
vof.imb.org*

Empowering Kingdom Growth: To the Ends of the Earth is about
God's desire for all peoples and nations to worship Him.
Fulfilling God's desire takes prayer, alignment with His purpose, change of priority, strategic witness and committed
partners. Read along as Jerry Rankin shares his perspectives
on global evangelization and how churches can fulfill the
Great Commission. Order at *http://www.vof.imb.org*

PRAY. Design a prayer strategy that will allow the entire
church body to participate. Ask missionaries who have visited in your church to send you regular prayer requests. Find
other missions prayer resources at *http://www.vof.imb.org*

GIVE. As you teach biblical stewardship, keep the missions
challenge before your congregation and provide opportunities to give to local and global evangelization. Let your
church know how their giving makes a difference in reaching the lost for Christ.

GO. Consider serving alongside missionaries on a volunteer trip. Train with your team before you go, and make sure
your church gives you time to report and celebrate God's
work when you return. Learn about Southern Baptist volunteer opportunities through the International Mission
Board at *http://www.vof.imb.org*

If your Southern Baptist church would like coaching on how to become
more involved in international missions, call the church services team
of the International Mission Board at (800) 999-3113. Or find more
missions information at *http://www.vof.imb.org*

 439

Who, Me? A Missionary?

When Beth Moore's husband, Keith, first went to a missionary retreat, he realized missionaries have no common denominator—except a willingness to go in response to God's call. Is God calling you to be a missionary? Are you willing to go?

Many missions agencies provide means for Christians of all denominations to serve as missionaries. Check with your church leadership to learn what options are best for you. If you're an active member in a Southern Baptist church, the International Mission Board may be the right choice. The IMB needs workers from all walks of life—teachers, pastors, lawyers, agriculturists, homemakers, carpenters and so many others—to help with the task of sharing the gospel.

You can serve from two years to your entire career. Southern Baptists planning to work as long-term missionaries begin their service as missionary apprentices who serve three- to four-year terms. Apprentices may move toward one of two longer-term categories: career missionaries or missionary associates. Short-term Southern Baptist missionaries live and serve overseas for two to three years through the journeyman and masters programs and the international service corps.

To learn more about going as a long-term or short-term Southern Baptist missionary, go to http://www.vof.imb.org, or call (888) 422-6461.

Not sure if God's calling you to be a missionary? God often uses volunteer missions projects to help discern that call. Options are available for Southern Baptists from students to retirees through the IMB. You can join an existing volunteer team or form your own team.

Explore IMB volunteer missions opportunities at http://www.vof.imb.org, or call (800) 999-3113.

INDEX

March

April

May

June

JULY

OCTOBER

November

December

A Brand-New Year's Worth of Inspiring Stories from the Front Lines of Faith

Hike mountain paths, jolt down rutted desert roads, and pick your way through teeming markets and crowded urban slums. Meet boisterous children, worried parents, anxious teens, and curious seniors—all hungry, whether they know it or not, for the Good News.

Witness moments of looming danger and crushing heartache, moments of shining hope and pure miracle. Be inspired anew by those who dare to obey God's call to take His story to the ends of the earth.

ISBN: 978-0-8499-2071-4

Now available in trade paper: ISBN 978-0-8499-4623-3

THOMAS NELSON
Since 1798

WHEREVER BOOKS ARE SOLD
OR AT VOICESOFTHEFAITHFUL.COM